𝑓**P**

ALSO BY AMITAI ETZIONI:

Social Problems
Genetic Fix: The Next Technological Revolution
The Active Society: A Theory of Societal and Political Processes
Political Unification: A Comparative Study of Leaders and Forces
Modern Organizations
Winning Without War
A Comparative Analysis of Complex Organizations
An Immodest Agenda: Rebuilding America Before the Twenty-First Century
Capital Corruption: The New Attack on American Democracy

THE MORAL DIMENSION

Toward a New Economics

AMITAI ETZIONI

THE FREE PRESS
New York London Toronto Sydney Singapore

THE FREE PRESS
A Division of Simon & Schuster Inc.
1230 Avenue of the Americas
New York, NY 10020

First Free Press Paperback Edition 1990

THE FREE PRESS and colophon are trademarks
of Simon & Schuster Inc.

Manufactured in the United States of America

10 9 8 7 6 5

Library of Congress Cataloging-in-Publication Data

Etzioni, Amitai.
    The moral dimension.

    1. Economics—Sociological aspects.   2. Economics—Moral and ethical aspects.
3. Social choice.   4. Paradigms (Social sciences)
I. Title. HM35.E89   1988   174'.4   88-368
ISBN 0–02–909901–3

This book is dedicated to the memory of Minerva Etzioni, who died on December 20, 1985. Her commitment to transcendental causes, caring for her family and fellow persons, and her joy of life are reflected in these pages.

Contents

Preface

Are men and women akin to single-minded, "cold" calculators, each out to "maximize" his or her own well-being? Are humans able to figure out rationally the most efficient way to realize their goals? Is society mainly a marketplace, in which self-serving individuals compete with one another—at work, in politics, and in courtship—enhancing the general welfare in the process? Or do we typically seek to do both what is right *and* what is pleasurable, and find ourselves frequently in conflict when moral values and happiness are incompatible? Are we, first of all, "normative-affective" beings, whose deliberations and decisions are deeply affected by our values and emotions? And to the extent that we rely on evidence and reason to choose our course, what techniques have been developed to help us proceed in view of our limited ability to know? What problems does the reliance on these techniques introduce, to add to our innate difficulties? Assuming human beings see themselves both as members of a community and as self-seeking individuals, how are the lines drawn between the commitments to the commons and to one's self? At issue is the paradigm we use in trying to make sense out of the social world that surrounds us, and of which we are an integral part; the paradigm we apply in the quest to understand and improve ourselves, those dear to us, and those not so dear.

We are now in the middle of a paradigmatic struggle. Challenged is the entrenched utilitarian, rationalistic-individualistic, neoclassical paradigm which is applied not merely to the economy but also, increasingly, to the full array of social relations, from crime to family. One main challenger is a social-conservative paradigm that sees individuals as morally deficient and often irrational, hence requiring a strong authority to control their impulses, direct their endeavors, and maintain order. Out of the dialogue between these two paradigms, a third position arises, which is advanced in this volume. It sees individuals as able to act rationally and on their own, advancing their self or "*I*," but their ability to do so is deeply affected by how well they are anchored within a sound community and sustained by a firm moral and emotive personal underpinning—a community they perceive as theirs, as a "*We*," rather than as an imposed, restraining "they." Explicating this new synthesizing paradigm, that of the I&We, and the deontological ethics that are involved, is the subject of this volume. It examines, too, the new paradigm's implications for individual decision-making and for the market, and its place within society. We ask, under what conditions can persons act effectively and rationally, are markets efficient, and communities viable?

At first it might seem that at issue are merely the foundations of the social sciences. The neoclassical paradigm is dominant these days not merely in economics but it also plays a major role in all other social sciences. But even those who are little interested in the social sciences must concern themselves with the struggle of the paradigms because, either via the social sciences or directly, these paradigms deeply affect our intellectual and ethical views and judgments.

In this discourse special attention is paid to the study of economic behavior because neoclassical economics is the flagship of the neoclassical paradigm. Also, this work draws on a kind of Guttman-scale point: If one can show the merits of assuming a key role for moral values, and affect, and social bonds in the study of economic behavior, there should be little doubt that such assumptions are of merit for the understanding of other elements of personal behavior and the social world.

The laying out of our I&We paradigm, based on a moderate version of deontological ethic, proceeds by dealing with three over-arching questions: What are the sources of human valuations, or goals? (Part I: beyond pleasure, a judging person). How are the means to advance our goals chosen? (Part II: beyond rationality, the normative/affective person). And, who are the key actors? (Part III: beyond individuality, the commons).

At first we ask: What are our goals? What are we after? The neoclassical paradigm assumes that people seek to "maximize" one utility. In early (and quite a few contemporary) writings by economists this utility is identified as the individual's pleasure or interests. (In some latter-day work the pleasure of others is also encompassed by the term "utility," or else utility is treated as merely a formal attribute.) This view of the goals of women and men is a form of utilitarian ethics.

We draw instead on a different ethic, on a deontological position that assumes that human beings pass moral judgment over their urges. Thus, moral commitments are a *cause*, as Fried (1964) put it, that in part explains behavior. For example, people save not merely to consume in their older age but also because they believe it is indecent to become dependent on the government or on their children. And people pay taxes not merely because they fear the penalties, but also because they consider their government to be a legitimate institution.

To put it differently, neoclassical economics seeks to determine the mechanisms (mainly, price) that will make for the most efficient allocation of resources, the allocation most able to satisfy people's wants. However, it tends to see these wants as centered on self-happiness, and to be clearly ordered and expressed in one over-arching utility. The finding that people have several wants, including the commitment to live up to their moral values, and that these wants cannot be neatly ordered or regulated by prices, provides a starting point that is fundamentally different from that of the neoclassical premises. From this different starting point we can launch a fresh study to understand individual behavior, economic and otherwise, to study society, and the economy within it. The far-reaching implications of this shift in premises are addressed in Part I.

Second, the notion that people rationally seek the most efficient means to their goals is replaced with a new-decision making model that assumes that people typically choose means largely on the basis of emotions and value judgments, and only secondarily on the basis of logical-empirical considerations. Even when they are making decisions within the rather limited zone in which they wish to draw only on logical/empirical considerations, their decisions are still *sub*-rational due to their rather limited intellectual capabilities. In short, *people typically do not render rational decisions.* They brush their teeth but do not fasten their seat belts; they continue to smoke twenty years after the Surgeon General's report; they purchase costly, unsuitable life insurance and pay stock brokers for useless advice, and so on. However, *sometimes they do act relatively more rationally* and we are able to identify the conditions and forces that promote such higher levels of rationality. In addition, we find that drawing on emotions and on value judgments is often an effective, not a distorted, way of making choices and rendering effective decisions (Part II).

Thirdly, who are the "actors," the "units" that make most choices? The neoclassical paradigm sees free-standing individuals, rendering decisions on their own. This notion is replaced here with a concept of persons as members of social collectivities—collectivities that, to a significant extent, shape individual decisions. Free individuals, able to render relatively rational decision-making, are found only within communities, because only in such communities do people find the psychic and social support that, we shall see, is required to sustain decisions free of pressures from the authorities, demagogues, or the mass media. Individuality does exist, but only within these social contexts. (Part III, Chapter 11).

What provides for social organization, for the coordination of millions of activities that make up society and the body economy? Neoclassicists tend to see exchanges as the prime basis of social organization and to view the market as a system unto itself. Here both exchanges and markets are viewed as subsystems, set within the context of society, culture, and polity. These contexts determine to a large extent whether or not the market is given sufficient freedom to be efficient, or granted too much liberty, undermining the essential societal context. (Part III, Chapter 12).

From the viewpoint of the particular deontological paradigm evolved here, the I&We, individuals are not free-floating atoms within the society and the economy, nor do they relate to one another mainly on the basis of their personal attributes; their relations are shaped to a significant extent by their place in various social structures, which are forms their collectivities acquired. (Individuals may change these over time, but at any one point in time are largely subject to them.) These structures, in part, reflect shared values, and in part, power.

Followers of the neoclassical paradigm assume that firms and other economic actors have no power over the market; they must follow its dictates. In contrast, the deontological approach advanced here recognizes the centrality of power. It assumes that *no exchange occurs among equals* but that one or more parties have a power advantage reflected in the "exchange" ratios (the amount of resources one actor has to invest to gain a comparable unit from another). For example, Mexicans need to work four times as much at the same pace using the same capital as Americans if they are to buy a U.S.-built car, while Americans will have to work only a fourth as much to buy a comparable car from Mexico. Moreover, far from being limited to economic power, economic actors frequently use political power (their leverage over the government) to advance their economic goals. Thus, economic processes are often deeply affected by a few powerful firms, labor unions, and other "special interests," rather than being free to follow their own dynamics (Part III, Chapter 13).

The issues explored here range way beyond the technical, conceptual matters of what constitutes a workable theory of decision-making in economic and other matters.* At issue is human nature: How wise are we, and what is the role of morality, emotions, and social bonds in our personal and collective behavior? Also at issue is the extent to which free-standing individuals are the foundation of our society; or does the foundation consist of persons integrated into small groups and communities? Who is best able to maintain the mental equilibrium required to make free choices and to render effective decision-making, to combine an efficient and innovative economy with a viable and free society?

Following the publication of several articles that preceded this volume, and discussions of its contents with colleagues, the author encountered strong reactions of the kind previously faced only when he dealt with issues such as the United States involvement in the war in Vietnam, multilateral nuclear disarmament, and the future of the family. Hence, it seems necessary to note that the author does not expect that the prevailing neoclassical paradigm will be abandoned; indeed, much of what it has contributed might well be integrated into a more encompassing paradigm. At the same time, it seems only prudent that some fraction of the effort dedicated to constructing theories, to guiding research and improving understanding of the personal and societal realm, especially

*For an overview and propositional inventory, see pp. 253–57.

of choice and economic behavior, should be invested in attempting to advance new paradigms, paradigms that might synthesize the work of neoclassicists and other social scientists, and that once in a while such paradigms should be granted a fair hearing.

A. E.

Cambridge, Massachusetts, 1988

Acknowledgments

Minerva Etzioni encouraged me in conceptualizing and launching this book in 1983–84. Her loss left the book on the shelf for nearly a year, causing discontinuities that I tried to bridge. Many friends stirred me back to life and work; I cannot list them all or thank them adequately. Special gratitude, though, is due to my sons—Benjamin, Dari, Michael, Oren and Ethan—who, while deeply hurt themselves, helped me find my way back to this project.

Joy Brookbank put the volume through endless alterations on her word processor, providing the author with first-hand responses and suggestions. Most important, from co-worker she turned into a supportive friend during very trying times.

Several chapters are the outgrowth of articles previously published in referred journals. I am most grateful to the suggestions of anonymous readers, and to the editors of *Economics and Philosophy* (Michael McPherson and Daniel Hausman); *Journal of Psychology and Economics* (W. Fred van Raaij); *Journal of Post-Keynesian Economics* (Paul Davidson); *Journal of Behavioral Economics* (Richard Hattwick); *Kyklos* (Rene L. Frey); *Journal of Public Policy* (Richard Rose); *Journal of Policy Analysis and Management* (Raymond Vernon); and *Social Science Quarterly* (Robin Williams), containing also the Frank (1987) response essay.

In developing my ideas on socio-economics I greatly benefitted from numerous discussions with economist colleagues, none to be held responsible for my misunderstandings. These include Van Adams, Brian Boulier, Jessica Einhorn, Bob Goldfarb, John Kwoka, Joe Pechman, Paul Streeten, Tony Yezer, and, above all, Joe Cordes. Colleagues in other social sciences I am most grateful to include Tom Burns, Matt Greenwald, Robert Mitchell, Paul E. Peterson, Paul Stern, Steve Tuch, Ruth Wallace, and above all, Dennis Wrong. I am also indebted to discussions with Peter Caws, James Childress, William Griffith and, above all, Douglas MacLean. Following the suggestion of Rod French, we created a faculty seminar on socio-economics, in which many of the above participated. Rod also was the one to call my attention to the deontological literature.

Oren Etzioni and Ethan Etzioni patiently argued out many points of this volume, from its ethics to its possible expression in mathematical terms.

The final version of the book was prepared during my year as Thomas Henry Carroll Ford Foundation Professor at the Harvard Business School (1987–88). Here a large number of colleagues made numerous very stimulating and thoughtful suggestions that led to many revisions in the volume. These, far from being confined to just economics, or "business," ranged from matters of philosophy to psychology, from sociology to political science. The staff was most dedicated in their assistance.

My exposure to neoclassical economics started with my training by Don Patenkin at the Hebrew University in Jerusalem; it grew when I served as a research assistant at the Institute of Industrial Relations, at the University of California at Berkeley; it benefitted from a year as a guest scholar at the Brookings Institution, and from work on reindustrialization in the White House, 1979–80.

Research assistants who helped this volume are first and foremost Tim Miller and Mark Brian Smith. I was also assisted by Kathy Wilson, Gita Bhatt, Lucy Ferguson, and Ken Cobb.

The volume is a product of the Socio-Economic Project, supported by The George Washington University and the Center for Policy Research. The work was completed at the Harvard Business School.

1

The New Paradigm: Underlying Themes

TOWARD A NEW SYNTHESIS

Both social scientists and intellectuals draw on overarching sets of assumptions—or paradigms—to organize their efforts to understand our world, the goals we pursue, the ways we choose means to advance our goals, and the ways we relate to one another as we proceed as individuals or in unison. When these paradigms are used to formulate theories and policies that are limited in their empirical and ethical scope, the study of our world suffers, and so do efforts to administer to its ills. This book argues that the neoclassical paradigm—that of a utilitarian-based version of radical individualism—needs to be integrated into one that is more encompassing. After outlining the differences in the core assumption between the prevailing neoclassical paradigm (most noted, in the groundwork for neoclassical economics) and an emerging deontological paradigm (that of the I&We charted here), the differences between the two paradigms are explored from social philosophic, ethical, epistological, historical, and methodological viewpoints. Finally, ways to synthesize the two paradigms are indicated.

The neoclassical paradigm is a utilitarian, rationalist, and individualist paradigm. It sees individuals as seeking to maximize *their* utility, rationally choosing the best means to serve their goals. They are the decision-making units; that is, they render their own decisions. The coming together of these individuals in the competitive marketplace, far from resulting in all-out conflict, is said to generate maximum efficiency and well-being. The notion of a community, to the extent that it is included in this paradigm, is often seen as the result of the aggregation of individual rational decisions.

These utilitarian assumptions are found at the roots of neoclassical economics (for additional discussion, see p. 46). However, they play a key role in major theories in all contemporary social sciences. Since

1

there is much more to neoclassical economic *theory* than these assumptions, and since the assumptions serve to form social science theories
other than neoclassical economics, it seems useful to refer to them as a
neoclassical *paradigm*. This paradigm plays a key role in contemporary
political science (e.g., in the Public Choice school); in psychology (e.g., in
the balance theory, which sees group members as continuously calculating the merit of membership rather than that of being "involved" or
"committed"); in sociology (e.g., exchange theory); and even in anthropology (in works that argue that preliterate tribes conform to the laws of
neoclassical economics, e.g., Schneider, 1974), history (e.g., North, 1981),
and law (e.g., Posner, 1977). Moreover, the neoclassical paradigm plays a
major role in our public policy, dialogues, intellectual life, and the social
and political philosophies that the public embraces. While outside the
social sciences, the terms used in public discourse to refer to the neoclassical paradigm have changed over the decades, currently the terms *laissez-
faire* conservative and libertarian are most often used to refer to it.

The neoclassical paradigm, and the theories formulated by drawing
on its assumptions and core concepts, have been criticized as unrealistic,
unproductive, and amoral (Malinowski, 1922; Parsons, 1937; Thurow,
1983; Allvine and Tarpley, 1977; Wilber and Jameson, 1983). However,
the defenders of the neoclassical paradigm and theories can offer a
strong response to these criticisms: They can challenge their critics to
point to theories of behavior that are more productive than the prevailing one. "You cannot beat a theory with nothing," is more than a clever
rejoinder—it is a somewhat overstated but far from unfair comment on
the state-of-the-art.

Where do we go from here? The question concerns the way scientific
and intellectual progress is attained. In this area we build on Thomas
Kuhn's insight on the role and dynamics of paradigms. They provide an
orderly way of organizing our thinking about a disorderly world. Developing a paradigm involves large investments that encompass many hundreds of thousands of human work-years, the expenditure of billions of
dollars on data collection and analysis and elaboration of models, and
the considerable effort entailed in reaching consensus, among those who
share a given paradigm, about what one should assume the world is like.
The magnitude of these investments provides a reason for holding on to
vested paradigms. In addition, there are matters of ego-involvement and
prestige pecking order that need not concern us here, and matters of
ideological commitments to which we turn below.

As long as there is no other productive paradigm, it is difficult to object to efforts to maintain the neoclassical paradigm, even if it encounters
some so-called "stubborn facts" (facts incompatible with the theory), or
other limited challenges (for instance, discovery of some internal incon-
sistencies). In fact, it is proper to attempt to shore up, augment, or modify the paradigm, and the theories that build on it, to absorb challenges,

in the hope of avoiding a paradigm shift; it is also proper to preserve the mainframe of the prevailing paradigm—as long as there is no successful alternative, even if these efforts cannot be successfully completed (or can only be completed by introducing far-fetched assumptions, or at the price of rendering tautological parts of the theory). So far, no such alternative seems to have arisen. As Ulen wrote (1983, p. 576): ". . . many of the most recent presidential addresses to the American Economic Association have been highly critical of received micro- and macro-economic theory. However, there has not yet been an offering of a new paradigm." If by a new paradigm he means one that is successful, able to provide a context to a wide array of evidence, and gain consensus, he is surely right. He goes on to recognize "the profession's quite natural attempt to plaster over the current paradigm's cracks with such ingenious fillers as transaction costs and rational expectations." (Ulen, 1983, p. 576.) While more than cracks have appeared in the facade, the procedure, to reiterate, is not merely "natural" but legitimate.

Indeed, Ulen's own work further illustrates the point. After referring to a review of the literature by Nelson and Winter (1983, p. 577) that shows "the limited abilities of organizations and individuals to optimize," Ulen wonders if this is sufficient reason to replace orthodox theory rather than "merely patching it." Another student of the same challenge (Rubin, 1983, p. 719) wonders if this means that the neoclassical paradigm must be "scrapped," or that the new approach (in this case, evolutionary economics) can be absorbed into neoclassical economics, a procedure which he strongly prefers. Others try to evolve new paradigms.

If and when such efforts are successful, it does not mean that the neoclassical paradigm will crumble. There have been several sciences in which two paradigms co-existed simultaneously in open competition for long periods of time. Marxism, after all, is a paradigm that does seek, among other things, to explain economic behavior. It long co-existed with the neoclassical paradigm, neither driving it out, nor being driven out by it.

The thesis developed in this volume suggests a different interparadigmatic pattern: The self-oriented, rational behavior "modeled" by neoclassicists is assumed to occur within the context of personality structure and society. These, in turn, are perceived not merely as reflections of the aggregation of individual acts but as being formed to a significant extent by forces and dynamics that are fundamentally different, in ways to be specified, from those assumed by the neoclassical paradigm. That is, rather than abandon neoclassical concepts and findings, they are viewed here as dealing with subsystems within society (markets) and personality (in which rational decision-making is circumscribed, substituted *and,* on occasion, supported by emotions and values). In other words, the approach followed here is one of *codetermination:* It encompasses factors that form society and personality, as well as neoclassical factors that form markets and rational decision-making. Moreover, we can go beyond suggesting that both approaches need to be synthesized; we can specify to some extent how they are related to one another: The paradigm advanced here seeks to characterize the *context* within which the forces that the neoclassical approach focuses on are played out, a context that sets limits and provides direction to those forces. (For additional discussion *re* personalities, see Part II, especially Chapter 6; for society, see Part III, especially Chapter 12.)

CORE ASSUMPTIONS

A major virtue of the prevailing neoclassical paradigm is that it states its core assumptions very clearly. This work progresses by changing these core assumptions and by exploring the consequences of such a change. Three basic changes are made concerning what people are after, how they choose their ways, and who is doing the choosing.

Where the neoclassical assumption is that people seek to maximize one utility (whether it is pleasure, happiness, consumption, or merely a formal notion of a unitary goal), we assume that people pursue at least two irreducible "utilities," and have two sources of valuation: pleasure and morality (the subject of Part I).

The neoclassical assumption that people render decisions rationally (by a definition to be clarified) is replaced by the assumption that people typically select means, not just goals, first and foremost on the basis of their values and emotions. Far from always "intruding on" or "twisting" rational deliberations, values and emotions render some decision-making more effective. This holds not just for social behavior, such as courtship, but also for economic behavior, say relationships with one's employees or superiors. The circumstances under which people do act the way neoclassicists assume they generally behave—rationally (to one extent or another)—are accounted for in the paradigm evolved here (the subject of Part II).

The neoclassical assumption that the individual is the decision-making unit, is changed here to assume that social collectivities (such as ethnic and racial groups, peer groups at work, and neighborhood groups) are the prime decision-making units. Individual decision-making often reflects, to a significant extent, collective attributes and processes. Individual decisions do occur, but largely within the context set by various collectivities.

The same point holds for the relationship between society and the market as a *sub*system. The neoclassical assumption that the market economy can be treated as a separate system, a system that is basically self-containing, and whose distinct attributes can be studied by the use of a perfect competition model, is replaced here with the assumption that the economy is a subsystem of a more encompassing society, polity, and culture. It is therefore assumed that the dynamics of the economy, including the extent to which it is competitive, cannot be studied without integrating social, political, and cultural factors into one's paradigm. Moreover, social collectivities are to be viewed, not as aggregates of individuals, but as having structures of their own, structures that place individuals (and other subunits) not according to their individual attributes, but which deeply affect their dealings with one another. (See Chapter 11.)

The significance of structure is highlighted in this volume by the study of one major structural attribute, the political power of select economic actors. Instead of assuming that the economy is basically competitive, and hence that economic actors (mainly firms) are basically subject to "the market," possessing no power over it (monopolies are regarded as exceptions and aberrations), the deontological I&We paradigm evolved here assumes that power differences among the actors are congenital, are built into the structure, and deeply affect their relationships. We shall see that power differentials are gained both by applying economic power (the power that some actors have over others, directly, within the economy) and by exercising political power (the power that some actors have over others, indirectly, by guiding the government to intervene on their behalf within the economy). (See Chapter 12.)

These fundamentally different assumptions make up what is referred to here as the I&We paradigm (one of a larger possible set of deontological paradigms). The term highlights the assumption that individuals act within a social context, that this context is not reducible to individual acts, and, most significantly, that the social context is not necessarily or wholly imposed. Instead, the social context is, to a significant extent, perceived as a legitimate and integral part of one's existence, a We, a whole of which the individuals are constituent elements.

The internalization of the social context, the *partial* overlap between the I's and the commons, is an essential difference between the neoclassical and the deontological paradigm evolved here. The neoclassical paradigm either does not recognize collectivities at all, or sees them as aggregates of individuals, without causal properties of their own, and as external to the person. The individual is viewed as standing detached from the community and from shared values, calculating whether or not to be a member, whether or not to heed the values' dictates. The deontological paradigm evolved here assumes that people have at least *some* significant involvement in the community (neoclassicists would say "surrender of sovereignty"), a sense of *shared* identity, and commitment to values, a sense that "We are members of one another." (Baldwin, 1902, p. 3.) Hence, adhering to shared values is often a matter not of expedient conformity but of internalization of moral values, at least in part (Wrong, 1961, p. 186).

In the same way that neoclassical economics is the flagship of the neo-classical paradigm, a theory referred to from here on as socio-economics is an attempt to provide a theory of economic behavior within our deontological, I&We, paradigm.

SOCIAL PHILOSOPHICAL FOUNDATIONS: THE I&WE

Tories and Whigs, Over- and Under-Socialization

The dialogue between the prevailing and the challenging paradigms builds on basic differences in social philosophy: the two positions contain divergent views of human nature (are people basically knaves or nobles?) and of social order (are individuals naturally harmonious—or is man wolf to man?).

While not every neoclassicist who works on wage differentials or saving rates subscribes to the social philosophy of Adam Smith's invisible hand and to its *laissez faire* implications, these concepts obviously lie at the base of the prevailing neoclassical paradigm. Sociologists refer to the implied view of the person as "undersocialized" because individuals are assumed to be the effective actors, able to act independently and to be psychologically complete unto themselves. It is a view of the social order as resting on the marketplace, as basically composed of individual trans-actions (even if those are of households and small firms), and as basically self-regulating. The state has a minimal and negative role. If this view recognizes the role of the community at all, it plays no role in the main frame of the paradigm. "The community is a fictitious body, composed of . . . individual persons". (Bentham, 1960 Chapter 1, paragraph 2.) Here lies the deeper root of the view of economics not as a science that deals with goods and services but with the logic of choice (Barry, 1978, p. 5). Whose choice? Neoclassicists answer: That of unfettered individuals (Granovetter, 1985).

The historical roots of this social philosophy of radical individualism explain much about its slant. It was promulgated and advanced by an intellectual and political movement referred to as Whigs (in those days, "liberals"), in opposition to an authoritarian monarchy and a tightly woven society that imposed its moral code via the established religion (Guttridge, 1942). While Whigs embraced many other ideas, the essence of their position continues to have influence in contemporary social sciences, in intellectual circles, and in the public-at-large, long after the historical circumstances against which the original Whigs railed had vanished. Leading contemporary Whigs include Friedrick Von Hayek, Milton Friedman, and Robert Nozick.

Historically, the main challenge to the Whig's worldview, that underlies the neoclassical paradigm, has been not the recent liberal notion of a significant and positive role of the state, but the social-conservative, Tory, view that considers community and authority as social foundations. Here the nation, the fatherland, the church, or society take priority over the individual. While *laissez faire* Whigs perceive the state to be created by individuals, for individuals, Tory conservatives view the community as a body into which individual cells are incorporated. Individuals are assumed to be born with unsavory predispositions and not at all inclined to live harmoniously with one another. They must be inoculated with values to develop their moral character, and authority is needed to keep on the lid of social order. The danger of mob anarchy is seen as greater than that of authoritarianism.

Sociologists refer to this collectivist "Tory" view as the "over-socialized" view of human nature (Wrong, 1961). Historically it preceded the Whigs; it was the medieval social philosophy of the church and the monarchy, that, at the onset of modernity, argued against claims for individual rights and those of new, rising classes. It is at the root of Emile Durkheim's main works, Talcott Parsons' sociology, some branches of political science (especially that of Leo Strauss), and a good part of anthropology.

Durkheim argued that morality is a system of rules and values provided by society, imbedded in its culture, and that individual children acquire these as part of the general transmission of culture. Non-rational processes, such as identification with parents, play a key role. (Durkheim developed this position in direct response and opposition to the utilitarian view that moral values were the product of individual adults, and their intelligent judgment of other adults' actions. Kohlberg, 1968, p. 486.)

For Parsons, the core concept is functionalism: the acts of individuals are, in effect, evaluated in terms of their contribution to the social order, which in turn is introduced into the individuals via socialization, and reinforced by social control. These concepts do not exactly parallel but reflect the notions of a strong community (focused around one set of ultimate values, drawing on tightly knit social relations) and a potent state (to reinforce the values of the community). Typically, authority in this context is viewed as legitimate power. A wit suggested that while economics shows us how to make choices, sociology shows us that we have none. That is not quite a correct rendition of the two disciplines, but it does apply to the ideal type of Whig and Tory positions.

The centuries-old tug-of-war between these Whig and Tory worldviews, and their effects on social science paradigms, are far from defunct. See, for example, the treatment of trust. Trust would seem at first to be one of those typical Tory social-scientist concepts that Whigish economists may assume exist but need not bother to explain (Luhmann, 1979). Trust, of course, is pivotal to the economy, and not merely to social relations, as, without it, currency will not be used, saving makes no sense, and transactions costs rise precipitously; in short, it is hard to conceive a modern economy without a strong element of trust running through it. But when one asks what accounts for the extent to which individuals do trust one another, and for the level of trust in society, the differences between the two worldviews come into sharp relief.

Tory social scientists have a simple answer: Trust is a value with which youngsters are inoculated by their "socialization agents" (parents, educators, peers). Those who violate the value are either re-educated to embrace it, or punished until they abide by it, and others are deterred from transgressing. Whigish economists see trust as arising out of previous transactions, based on rational calculations and efficient "rules of thumb." For example, if A is your customer, and you verified his credit worthiness for the last N transactions, it is rational to skip checking it the $N+1$ time (assuming the transactions are relatively small and the costs of checking are relatively high). Thus, to Whigs a high level of trust reflects not successful socialization but either numerous prior reiterations, small stakes, or high verification costs. The differences in perspective, illustrated by their perspectives on trust, hold for a myriad of other such concepts encompassed by the two paradigms.

I&We, The Responsive Community

This volume seeks to advance a third position. Its social philosophical foundation may be characterized as the responsive community, or, in deference to my master-teacher, Martin Buber, the "I&We" view. At the core is the assumption of creative tension and perpetual search for balance between two primary forces—those of individuals, and those of the community, of which they are members. If one views the community as merely an aggregation of individuals temporarily joined for their convenience, one leaves out the need for commitment to serve shared needs and for involvement in the community that attends to these needs. If one sees the community as the source of authority and legitimacy, and seeks, in the name of duty, to impose behavioral standards on individuals—and on oneself—this leaves an insufficient basis for individual freedom and other individual rights. It also prevents the community from being creative and responsive to a changing world, by constricting the evolution of differing positions, which could in time replace the community's dominant values, thereby benefitting it.

The term *responsive community* is used to accord full status both to individuals and to their shared union. A responsive community is much more integrated than an aggregate of self-maximizing individuals; however, it is much less hierarchical and much less structured and "socializing", than an authoritarian community. We need to reject the Hobbesian notion that individuals must subordinate their basic rights as a prerequisite for security. Threats to security are not so high as to require that we all yield to the Leviathan to shield us. Nor can we build on the Lockeian notion that all rights are vested in individuals, who may or may not wish to delegate some of these rights, on the basis of their deliberations, to a community. *Individuals and community are both completely essential, and hence have the same fundamental standing.*

From this synthesis there results an unavoidable, indeed a deeply productive tension between the two basic elements of the responsive community. Individuals may pull to diminish the community; the community may pull excessively to incorporate individuals. But if neither element gains ascendancy, and if the excesses of one are corrected by shoring up the other, a balanced, responsive community may be sustained.* Schopenhauer is credited with the aphorism that people are like porcupines in the cold: They freeze if they get too far apart, but stick each other if they get too close.

As a first approximation, the discussion so far has used the traditional reference to individuals and to the community as two clearly distinct entities. In this terminology it makes sense to refer to assemblages of individuals deciding to form a polity, and to discuss aggregates of individuals without community, for example in exploring the notion of "the greatest happiness of the greatest number." However, a basic insight of sociology and psychology is that this concept of an individual is an optical illusion. *The individual and the community make each other and require each other.* The society is not a "constraint," not even an "opportunity," *it is us.* (Radicals may say that "the" society is not of the people, but imposed on them. If enough people share this view, they may change the society to be more "theirs." Hence, while any particular societal structure may be viewed by some as imposed, society in principle is ours and part of us.)

While it is possible to think abstractly about individuals apart from a community, if individuals were actually without community they would have very few of the attributes commonly associated with the notion of an individual person. Such individuals typically are mentally unstable, impulsive, prone to suicide, and otherwise mentally and psychosomatically ill (Srole, 1975). Certainly such isolated individuals have little in common with the level-headed maximizers assumed by the Whigish neoclassical paradigm. The I's need a We to be.

Misplaced Liberty

The significance of viewing individuals as members of social collectivities (such as ethnic groups and local communities) rather than as freestanding beings, is highlighted by the different treatment accorded to liberty in the neoclassical and the I&We paradigms.

*Much more needs to be said on this subject and volumes have been written. For major contributions see Walzer (1983); Bellah, Adsen, Sullivan, Swidler, Tipton (1985); essays by Jencks and by Featherstone in Gans, Glazer, Gusfield, and Jencks (1979).

At the core of the neoclassical paradigm is the assumption that free-standing individuals are the decision-making unit, the actors. This is much more than a working hypothesis; it is an article of faith grounded in a deep commitment to the value of liberty. Neoclassicists argue that if one assumes that the preferences of individuals can be manipulated or changed by social forces, one undermines the foundations of liberty—the notion that each individual is able to render decisions on his own. This is the reason neoclassicists assume that preferences are given, why they ignore the effects of education, of persuasion (including persuasive advertising), and the role of leadership, as if economic man was a biological-psychological miracle, born fully formed, say in his mid-twenties (Maital and Maital, 1984, p. 65) with his preferences "immaculately conceived" (as Kenneth Boulding put it to a 1985 George Washington University Seminar on socio-economics).

The same commitment to liberty is at the root of the assumption of consumer sovereignty and the tendency of neoclassical economists to disregard the role of class, power, and societal structures. Typical neoclassicists argue that people know best what is best for them, and hence should not be interfered with by the government. However, to recognize that people preferences are in part socially shaped is not to argue for a government to make decisions for them, but to acknowledge the need to deal in one's theory with significant historical, cultural, and societal forces. Only when these are allowed into one's paradigm can a systematic search begin for the conditions under which liberty may be protected from—or enhanced by—these forces.

The insights and findings of psychologists and sociologists indicate that individuals who are typically cut-off and isolated, the actors of the neoclassical world, are unable to act freely, while they find that individuals who are bonded into comprehensive and stable relationships, and into cohesive groups and communities, *are* much more able to make sensible choices, to render judgment, and be free. Indeed, the greatest danger for liberty arises when the social moorings of individuals are cut. The atomization of the individuals, the reduction of communities into mobs, which resulted in the individuals' loss of competence, of their capacity to reason, and their self-identity (Kornhauser, 1959; Fromm, 1941) is the societal condition that has preceded the rise of totalitarian movements and governments. The best protection against totalitarianism is a pluralistic society laced with communities and voluntary associations, as observed so keenly by Alexis de Tocqueville. The I&We paradigm is as much concerned with individual liberties as is the neoclassical. However, it assumes that liberty requires a viable—albeit not overbearing—community, and seeks to study the conditions under which such a community evolves and is sustained.

As we see it, *individuals are neither simply depositories of their society's values nor free agents*. They struggle to form their individual course, both building on and fending off the values their societies set, never free of them, yet never mere subjects. Similarly, on the macro or societal level, competition is beneficial as long as it is properly embedded in a supportive societal context, which ensures that the prerequisites of competition are met while limiting its scope. That is, social order is not the result of imposition by authority, or an aggregation of individual pursuits, but a community setting within which people are free, and without which they are not, and within which they continuously vie over the borderline between freedom and order.

While some individuals may be over-socialized, say, to the point they loose their self-identity and self-control in the We of a charismatic social movement, while some others are undersocialized, often deviant, criminal or insane—society requires a balance, and builds on properly socialized individuals. These individuals balance shared and self needs, respond to internalized values but are also able to calculate consequences. To be properly socialized does not mean that one is unable to compete, act rationally, or to be self-oriented; there are areas in which such behavior is compatible with the community's values. However, in each such area there are moral limits beyond which such behavior may not be carried (for instance, those imbedded in the "rules of the game," in sports, politics, and in the economy). And, there are significant differences among sub-areas of behavior as to the appropriate mix of the two modes (e.g., within the family or among friends, vs. at work). Hence, it might be useful to think about competition/cooperation ratios, and ratio differences among areas of behavior, noting that proper socialization never favors all-out competition.

ON THE SIDE OF DEONTOLOGICAL ETHICS

The ethics that underlie the neoclassical paradigm are utilitarian. While not all utilitarian philosophies are hedonistic or self-centered, the neoclassical paradigm is both. (For documentation and qualifications, see Chapter 2). Typically, the paradigm assumes a *unitary self*, that the person is a bundle of unambiguous and stable preferences (March, 1978, pp. 595–96). Moreover, the person is seen as a *black box*, responding to changes in the environment (in inputs or in constraints) rather than to internal processes or structures. In contrast, the I&We paradigm assumes that individuals experience perpetual inner tension generated by conflicts among their various basic urges (or desires), among their various moral commitments, and between their urges and their moral commitments.

Critics argue that a conception of a multiple self makes theorizing "too easy" because, when desires win, it is said to be the work of the "lower" self (or *id*); and when values do, the "higher" self (or *superego*) is said to win, but nothing is actually explained. Fair enough. However, the paradigm advanced here begins with the multiple self as a primary concept, but goes on to seek specific theorems about the social and intrapsychic conditions under which one part of the self is more powerful than the other.

While the self is conflicted in many ways, this volume *focuses on one major type of conflict,* because (1) an explanation of one such conflict suffices to show the productive quality of the concept of a multiple self; because (2) the particular line of conflict studied here has been particularly neglected; and because (3) it is pivotal to the author's ethical position. The line of conflict this volume focuses on is between moral values and other sources of valuation, especially pleasure. (The two, we shall see, are not necessarily in opposition, but in effect often do pull in divergent directions). Both moral values and other valuations may reflect prior socialization and may contain cognitive elements (see Abelson on "hot" and "cold" cognitions, 1976). However, once formed, we see moral values that contain a prescribed element ("thou shall . . .") and an interpretive element or rationale ("because . . ."), as distinct from desires, urges, and other sources of preferences.

The neoclassical paradigm does not merely ignore the moral dimension but actively opposes its inclusion. Thus, it is stressed that various individuals may have *different* rankings of preferences over a field of choice, but none can be deemed to be *better.* Indeed, Crouch (cited by Winrich, 1984, p. 994) adds that "Unwillingness to accept this conclusion has been and still is a source of much mischief in the world." Winrich (1984, p. 994) responds: "And how lucky we are that such mischief abounds; complete relativism justifies all choices no matter how distorted, perverse or destructive." Other neoclassicists, we shall see, belittle the role of values, or see them as but one source of "tastes" among many others. We hold that moral commitments deeply affect all behavior, economic included.

The ethical position we build on is moderately deontological. Deontology is a major school of ethics, akin to utilitarianism in its scope, encompassing different sub-schools (e.g., acts vs. rule-deontology), and has its share of internal differences (Beauchamp, 1982, p. 109). To do justice to but one of its leaders, Immanuel Kant, would take us far afield. There are also several deontological positions the author does not share. Instead of engaging here in a major digression on ethics, the discussion focuses on that one element of deontology used here.

The essence of the deontological position is the notion that actions are *morally right when they conform to a relevant principle or duty.* (The term deontology is derived from the Greek *deon* which means binding duty.) Deontology stresses that the moral status of an act should not be judged by its consequences, the way utilitarians do, but by the "intention." For example, a person who sets out to defame another is acting immorally, whether or not the person succeeds in actually damaging the one he or she seeks to defame.

Deontology uses as the criterion for judging the morality of an act, not the ends it aspires to achieve, nor the consequences, but the moral duty it discharges or disregards. Deontologists point out that consequences, the hallmark of utilitarians, often cannot be predicted. Hence, treat others as you seek to be treated—as an end, and not as a means. It is a judgment one must make long before the consequences of one's act are known. Deontologists are also fond of pointing out that utilitarians would regard two acts that yield the same outcome as equivalent, even if one of them involved a transgression (say, deception), and the other did not. Clearly, we say, the act without deception is superior. Moderate deontologists, a position we build on here, do take consequences into account as a secondary consideration. This brings the position closer to moderate utilitarians, who do take intentions into account—but as a secondary criterion. To put it differently, a moderate deontological position provides the foundations for inclusion of neoclassical concepts and findings as a subset.

Important for the analysis to follow, is the deontological observation that a major source of the conflict in the self is commitment to discharge one's duties, and, more generally, to act morally. There is more to life than a quest to maximize one's satisfaction.

EPISTEMOLOGICAL POSITIONS: BEYOND RATIONALISM

There is a close link between the oversocialized (Tory), undersocialized (Whig), and properly socialized (I&We) view of the person, and the varying assumptions about the intellectual capacity of the human race, "the rationality of man." The undersocialized view is closely linked to the enlightenment notion, which is very sanguine about an individual's ability to reason. It assumes that people set their own goals, in neatly patterned ways, and the ways they pursue their goals are open to evidence and to inferences drawn logically—i.e., that people abide, in effect, by the same principles that scientists are expected to follow but often do not. An individual may err in his or her decisions, but when "exposed to valid norms for logical, scientific, and statistical thinking, he will bow down before them, acknowledge his errors, and seek to reform his practices." (Shweder, 1984, p. 23–28.) This assumption is at the core of the neoclassical paradigm.

The oversocialization school is linked to what has been called the "romantic" view, that holds that the foundation of knowledge is to be found in the particular culture to which a person belongs. The world is not out there to be discovered, to be known, but is created by "man" (as a collectivity). Not merely ideas and practices, but also the frameworks of thinking, what is considered factual, and logic itself, are "beyond the scope of deductive and intuitive reasons ... neither rational nor irrational but rather nonrational." (Shweder, 1984, p. 28.) What is logical to a member of one culture is not to a member of another. Anthropologists report that people of different cultures hold beliefs that seem bizarre to us (one must feed ancestral spirits daily; souls transmigrate), and draw conclusions by canons whose logic we fail to see. According to this viewpoint, *all* facts and logical conclusions are evident merely to those who share a paradigm. Not only is what is held to be true defined by the prevailing paradigms, but the criteria by which such statements are validated are strictly subjective or integral to one's paradigm. Marxists, psychologists, and neoclassical economists "make sense" only if you buy their core assumptions *and their* particular modes of validation.

The position advanced here represents a middle course that has been evolving between the two "ideal type" positions of enlightenment and romanticism, although it is closer to the romantic pole than to that of enlightenment. Accordingly, people are viewed as pursuing goals they acquire from their communities, and inner moral and emotive developments, referred to from here on as "normative-affective" factors.

The goals people pursue, such as happiness or wealth, are not universal, or stable over time, but are greatly varied and changing, and often cannot be arranged into a neat over-arching mono-utility—in part, because people are members of divergent social collectivities that conflict with one another; in part, because to some extent, individuals do develop their own goals that conflict with those of their collectivities. Hence, one cannot simply dismiss normative-affective factors as either reflected in "the utility" (or in preferences) or as captured by constraints, the way neoclassicists tend to do, but must seek to understand the dynamics of the forces that determine a person's socialization, as well as his or her deviation or rebellion against a socially prescribed set of goals. The social, philosophical, ethical, and empirical reasons in support of this position are presented in Part I.

Most important for the study of choice is the notion that means, selected to realize goals, are often chosen partially or even solely on normative-affective grounds, and not only on the bases of logical/empirical considerations. In some situations normative-affective factors prescribe the only acceptable means to the goal, and taboo all others. To tell a Jew that the New Testament is shorter than the Old Testament, and is hence a more economical means of salvation, is irrelevant, as only one Testament is acceptable. To tell an American that a flag with one star is more economical than one with fifty is completely beside the point. In other areas, normative-affective factors greatly limit means to a subset of those that objective observers recognize as relevant. And these factors affect the choice by "coloring" some of the options that are considered, with negative normative-affective valuations, while strongly favoring others—whatever their logical-empirical merits. Normative-affective factors also interrupt reasoning, distort cognitive frameworks, and cut short the search for the best means. At the same time, normative-affective factors also serve to render some decisions more effective. For example, in an emergency they guide one's response—run!—without search, analysis, and so on. And they ensure that other decisions will be not merely efficient but also caring, fair, and will otherwise serve goals that transcend self-interest. Thus, normative-affective factors are not inherently "bad," as they set aside, correct, or balance logical-empirical considerations.

Finally, there is a limited zone, within which normative-affective factors allow or even encourage choices based solely or chiefly on logical-empirical grounds. Hence, individuals are found to be much more limited in their ability to reason than is often suggested; typically, we shall see, they are sub-rational at best.

Some neoclassicists have argued that by using rules of thumb provided by the culture, evolution, or experience, individuals can conduct themselves rationally with little or no calculation or deliberation. This position is rejected here because the rules themselves are not rational, and are deeply infused with values and other social factors. Besides, individuals are quite unable to judge the logical-empirical merit of the rules. Decisions may be regarded as more or less rational, but rarely are they highly rational.

METHODOLOGICAL POSITIONS

Many of the specific theorems advanced below are constituted as building stones of a theory of socio-economics, formulated within the I&We paradigm. (Other theories, within this paradigm, might include socio-psychological, socio-educational, socio-political, and socio-cultural theories). "Political economy" might have been a more evocative term than socio-economics, but it is avoided because in recent years this term has been associated with the works of neo-Marxists and other economists of a similar political persuasion not shared by the author. Also, historically the term refers to a pre-specialization, pre-differentiation era, a stage that preceded the rise of various analytic disciplines, a period in which various factors that the disciplines now make their specialized domain were studied as one amalgam, as part of social philosophy or political economy. While socio-economics favors a measure of cross-disciplinary integration, it does not return to the womb of early political economy but attempts to link spheres that will remain distinct. It seeks to integrate elements of economics and of other social sciences into one theoretical system, but not to fuse them.

The author is painfully aware that cross-disciplinary efforts, of the kind launched here, exact a price. As one draws on several disciplines one inevitably sacrifices some detail and even precision in the quest for scope. In economics there are numerous elaborations of many models and theorems; no attempt is made here to discuss those when the basic theorem which they elaborate is challenged. In psychology there are hundreds, sometimes thousands, of iterations of a basic experimental format; no attempt is made here to review these nuances when the basic format is questioned. Hopefully the gain in scope and integration will compensate for these sacrifices.

Our approach is one of first approximation. A trap that ensnared previous efforts to provide for new paradigms was the desire to provide a full-blown substitute to the governing neoclassical paradigm. This may well be impossible in view of the hundreds of thousands of labor-years that have been invested in developing the neoclassical paradigm and the theories, especially neoclassical economics, formulated in this framework. The place to start, it seems, is with a very elementary new paradigm. If this proves to be productive, others may join to expand, revise, and elaborate it. Hence, this work is, at best, a first cut.

It might be worth noting briefly the wider intellectual and societal context of endeavors to reintegrate economics and other social science disciplines. In the intellectual realm the quest for overcoming excessive fragmentation has been reflected in a movement that sought a unified theory for all sciences, in the criticisms of the separation of the "two cultures," in expressions of concern about the relations between the two sides of the brain, and in the tension between normative and positive approaches to science. Socio-economics, as a deontologically based theory, is a building stone of endeavors to bridge these schisms.

Socio-economics seeks to construct a cross-disciplinary bridge between exchange and structure, bridging together the market, polity and society; in the study of choice, it combines the study of reason with values and emotions. And, as we shall see, socio-economics brings positive (logical-empirical) and normative (prescriptive) considerations closer together, without losing the distinction between factual and value judgments.

This book is in part meta-theoretical, as justifications are provided for the selection of assumptions and concepts; and in part it is a work of theory-building, as specific propositions are advanced that use concepts rather than mathematical terms. Just as the author did not start these trains in motion, this discourse is obviously not the last station. Further development, elaborations, specifications and testing of the propositions here outlined are, of course, the next steps.

The author draws on the same devices other social scientists use in such works: logical and substantive arguments, analogies, reference to commonly known and readily observed facts, as well as citations of previously published empirical studies. The purpose of the work is to suggest that the paradigm advanced here is a potentially productive one; empirical validation obviously must follow, but typically is not included in such works. There is a division of labor between those who develop theories and those who test them.

Claims that the theory advanced here is productive are based on the reality of its assumptions, the scope of its explanatory power, its potential predictive power, and its avoiding the sin of overdetermination without being simplistic. These claims deserve a brief explanation without going into the numerous subpoints and side issues raised in the generation-long debate about the F-twist and related issues.

Economists as a rule do not deny that their assumptions about human nature are highly unrealistic, but instead claim, following Friedman (1962, 1982), that the absence of realism does not diminish the value of their theory because it "works," in the sense that it generates valid predictions. Without going into the questions raised by the definition of reality involved (see Moe, 1979, pp. 216 ff.), this is surely not an argument against theories whose assumptions are both much more realistic and predict at least as well, a status sought for socio-economics.

Most important, philosophers of science have almost universally rejected Friedman's position (Boland, 1979). It is very widely agreed that the purpose of a theory *is* to explain. Otherwise, when predictions prove to be valid, we do not know why, and hence are unable to foretell under what conditions they will continue to hold or fail, or may need to be adapted.

Once one takes for granted that the role of theory is to explain, the next question is the scope of its explanatory power. There is little virtue in constructing theories that, even if they predict *and* explain, encompass a very small range of phenomena. This was the case, for example, when with very limited observations they sought to establish the proportion of people who stop at a stop sign, or come to church or work on time (Loether and McTavish, 1980, pp. 127, 167). Nor is there merit in a theory that explains small parts of the variance of several kinds of behavior (reflected in correlations), rather than a significant chunk of the variance (as indicated by variance measurements). Social scientists are too quick to be satisfied with correlations; a theory is to be evaluated by how much of its subject the theory explains, assuming that the subject itself is not trivial.

In developing such theories, parsimony (or simplicity) is a virtue, while overdetermination (including ever more variables to widen a theory's scope) is a danger. However, as others have already pointed out, particularly Hirschman (1984), simplicity can be overdone. Especially in the age of advanced computers and artificial intelligence, a theory that adds a few more variables but accounts for much more of the relevant variance, is to be preferred over simpler but much less encompassing theories. We draw on this point later when we argue in favor of moving from the highly simplistic concept of one utility to recognizing the significance of several, without opening the floodgates to numerous ones.

Finally, just because neoclassicists often argue that their theories predict, and that therefore it does not matter if they are oversimplified, unreal, or do not explain, it does not follow that one can accept this claim without critical examination. First of all, major neoclassical theorems are often formulated in such a way that they either cannot be falsified or are very difficult to refute, thereby constituting complete or near-tautologies. Sen (1977, p. 322), for instance, writes: "It is possible to define a person's interest in such a way that no matter what he does he can be seen to be furthering his own interests in every isolated act of choice." Arrow (1982, p. 1) refers to the basic rationality theorem as applied by most economists as "a weak hypothesis, not easily refuted and therefore not very useful as an explanation, though not literally a tautology." (He is only somewhat more sanguine about the later iterations.) Latis (1976, p. 11) argues that the theory of the firm is "inappropriate" for an important segment of market situations because it does not lead to testable models. The same has been shown for many other neoclassical theorems.

Another way the neoclassical theory is protected from evidence, and rendered immune to data, is to view challenging facts as signs of temporary and limited aberrations without specifying how long they must persist, or what scope they must reach, before their challenge to the theory is indicative of an inherent fault. For example, neoclassical theoreticians of the firm declare that any pursuit of goals other than profit is but a step on the way to profit in the longer run (Kahn, 1959, p. 671; same point used by monetarists, see Meltzer, 1980, p. 43). However, the time frame of the "longer run" is not specified. The same failures to specify are found in statements about "disequilibrium."

When neoclassicists turn to empirical testing, they very often engage in rather little testing and considerable manipulation of the data. Often, when neoclassicists compare specific expectations a theorem yields to sets of previously collected data (rather than collecting data *after* the theorem has been advanced)—the neoclassicists induce a "fit" by adding variables and assumptions on an ad-hoc basis (Machlup, 1952, p. 73). This is a legitimate procedure as long as one understands that these post hoc variables (and the relations posited among them, and other variables, members of the theory) must be "validated" using different sets of data than those used to develop the theorems at issue.

Thus, if one finds that people who live in areas likely to be flooded do not buy flood insurance, although the premiums are low and the information is at hand, one may suggest that the reason is that individuals are "anxious." This however adds nothing to prediction until one checks, for instance, if the same "anxious" people also neglect to purchase life insurance. After all, if they are anxious about their property . . .

Cross (1983, p. 3) made this point well:

> When we defend the maximization paradigm by pointing to the similarity between its predictions and observed behavior, we often overlook the fact that the empirical "success" of many economic models is princi-

pally derived from accommodating adjustments in complementary hypotheses. . . . Market data are used to make inferences about the nature of preferences, expectations, and production functions through the mediating assumption of maximizing behavior, and unless these inferences are independently validated, it is impossible to uncover violations of the intermediary hypothesis . . .

For additional discussion see Sims (1980) and Leamer (1983).

When all is said and done, and even some rather dubious regression analyses are thrown in, predictions are still rare and frequently invalid. Leontief (1985, pp. 29–30) reports that 50 percent of all the articles appearing in the *American Economic Review* during a large part of the 1970s were purely mathematical, without any data; 22 percent contained highly massaged data ("cooked up"); of the four or five articles that did contain direct observations, two concerned only pigeons or mice.

Herbert Simon (1986, p. 24) in an article entitled "The Failure of Arm Chair Economics" provides many examples, concluding: in economics "bad theory survives; it does not predict very much, and when it does, it *predicts incorrectly*." (Italics added.) For additional evidence see Eichner (1983).

In short, for a theory to go beyond the prevailing neoclassical theories it must be more predictive, and explain more. We accept the claim that a theory must not be excessively complex, but see equal danger in excessive simplification. And, we join those many who argued that tautologies ("near" and complete) tend to be unproductive theoretical devices.

Above all, we need more induction. Science requires a judicious balance, admittedly fraught with tension, between logical (deductive) and empirical (inductive) elements. Neoclassical work, as indicated by its increasing mathematical nature, has become unbalanced. Statements such as "it's wrong [empirically] but done very elegantly [mathematically]" ought not to be seen as compliments; they suggest that neoclassical theorems have become a-scientific, logical perhaps but not empirically true. Socio-economics is less deductive and aspires to be closer to the data. If its contribution were limited to rendering the study of economic behavior and decision-making in general more inductive than the recent neoclassical works, restoring a balance between deduction and induction, it would be well worth the effort.

PART I

Beyond Pleasure:
The Case for Deontological
Social Sciences

This part of the book presents arguments and evidence in support of the position that those who study behavior in general, economic behavior in particular, should give up the assumption of a mono-utility world, propelled by one over-arching motive, pleasure, and recognize in their paradigm at least two irreducible sources of valuation or "utility": pleasure and morality. Support for this position draws on the logic of science, substantive conceptual arguments, some empirical evidence, and deontological ethical arguments.

Logically, we shall see, the position advanced by many utilitarians that all acts are pleasure-oriented has the same merit as multiplying all the variables in an equation by one; it adds precious little to one's understanding or ability to deal with the problems at hand. The basic concept of a mono-utility world does not meet an essential criterion of productive conceptualization: it does not differentiate. A latter-day neoclassical version suggests that the concept of utility may be stripped from its philosophical origins and psychological assumptions, and used as a strictly formal concept, as the common denominator of all human preferences. Such an encompassing use of the concept, we shall see, either violates the logic of science or forces one to return to the original narrow concept of utility, that of pleasure.

Substantively, we shall argue, moral acts (such as authentic altruism) provide a fundamentally different source of valuation and explanation of the reasons why people behave the way they do, than that provided by consumption and other sources of pleasure. According to major schools of conceptual definition and differentiation that are drawn upon below, morality and pleasure constitute distinct universes-of-content. If one ignores the distinction, by arguing that both kinds of acts are merely sources of "satisfaction," merely "another source of preference," and hence not different in principle, one overlooks important substantive differences between acts that discharge moral commitments and acts that enhance satisfaction. Furthermore, we shall see that there are pragmatic, predictive, and interpretative merits in maintaining the phenomenological distinction between the two kinds of acts.

Evidence is introduced below to show that people's behavior is systematically and significantly affected by moral factors that cannot be reduced to considerations of personal gain: Many people forgo "free rides" out of a sense of public duty and commitment to fairness; refuse welfare because it violates their dignity; choose to cooperate as their solution to the Prisoner's Dilemma, and so on. In most areas of economic behavior the "utility" of acting morally is evident from labor relations (e.g. in implicit contracts), to decisions to save (affected by the moral standing of being in debt); from limiting tax evasion (affected by a sense of whether or not the tax is fair), to lowering the cost of transactions (the higher the level of morality, the lower they are).

All said and done, the difference between the mono-utilitarian paradigm and the one advanced here comes down to alternative assumptions about human nature. We shall see that despite a genuine concern with finding effective heuristics, despite interest in a powerful science (mathemization), and a commitment to a positive ("neutral") science—at the root of the concepts used, the hypotheses advanced, and at the foundation of the neoclassical paradigm is Adam Smith's *Wealth of Nations* view: that self-serving people in a competitive market provide for the most efficient mode of social organization, especially of economic activities. In contrast, the deontological multiple-utility model advanced here is closer to the other Adam Smith, the author of *The Theory of Moral Sentiments*, not to replace the first, but to add the concept of morality to that of the pleasure utility, and the concept of community to that of competition. The merits of the resulting codetermining theory, of socioeconomics, and its I&We paradigm, lie in its logical, interpretative, predictive, policy-generating and ethical powers.

2

Pleasure, Altruism, and the Great X

There is a tendency in conceptual discussion of the kind that follows to lose sight of the underlying issue. The debate over whether or not it is productive to assume one over-arching utility is a debate over what motivates behavior. Is it all explainable by one basic motive (or a "mono-utility"), pleasure or self-satisfaction, or are people torn between conflicting forces, especially their pleasures and their duties? Are we, basically, but another species in the animal kingdom, or have we a nobler self, in continuous struggle with our baser part?

A critic of the mono-utility concept, central to the neoclassical paradigm, is faced with the problem of shooting down a set of targets mounted on a rotisserie: No sooner has he knocked down one, than a rather similar looking one appears, and before he is quite done with this one, a third one jumps into sight—and, soon thereafter, the first one reappears. Neoclassicists use three main variations of the concept: The original narrow concept, that of the pleasure of self, coined by early utilitarian philosophers, especially Bentham, and loaded with their psychological assumptions. Second, a latter-day, much expanded version, increasingly (although not widely) used, which encompasses the satisfactions an actor gains from his or her own consumption as well as that of others; i.e., it includes satisfactions derived out of benevolent acts and discharging community-minded duties. This concept is sometimes referred to as the interdependent utility. Finally, still other neoclassicists use the term utility as a formal attribute, a common denominator, according to which all specific quests for satisfaction can be ranked, a step needed to allow mathematization (and to shore up the assumption of a mono-utility world) but with no substantive attributes, the great X. These variations are all wanting, we shall see, but for different reasons.

The discussion in this chapter seeks to establish logical grounds (concerning proper conceptualization), as well as some preliminary substantive ones, for distinguishing between the concept of utility, of *satisfaction* (doing what one likes, enjoys, finds pleasurable), and the sense of *affirmation* that accompanies discharging one's moral commitments, commitments that are often in themselves taxing rather than pleasurable. That is, we are seeking grounds for recognizing a moral "utility" above and beyond a P (pleasure), I (interdependent), or X (formal) utility. Utility theory does not recognize the distinct standing of morality as a major, significant, source of valuations, and hence as an explanation of behavior, an omission which leads to a variety of defects outlined below.

THE PLEASURE UTILITY: COUNTER-FACTUAL

The original concept of "utility," as developed late in the eighteenth century largely by Jeremy Bentham and widely used in neoclassical economics, was narrowly self-oriented and straightforwardly hedonistic. "All actions are directed toward the gain of pleasure or the avoidance of pain." (Dyke, 1981, p. 31.) "The members of a household will seek to maximize their total utility. This is just another way of saying that the members of households try to make themselves as well off as they possibly can in the circumstances in which they find themselves." (Lipsey and Steiner, 1975, p. 142.) "As a customer you will buy a good because you feel it gives you satisfaction or 'utility'." (Samuelson, 1980, p. 48.) "People consume goods and services because their wants, or preferences, are served by doing so: they derive satisfaction from consumption. . . . *Utility* is simply a subjective measure of the usefulness, or want satisfaction, that results from consumption." (Browning and Browning, 1983, p. 56.)*

To understand this concept of utility it must be recalled that its origin and base are in utilitarian philosophy. It assumes that all means find their justification in the ends they serve; the ends give "utility" to the means. While there are non-hedonistic utilitarian philosophies, that of Rawls for instance, in which the end that bestows value is not self's pleasure, it is the hedonistic version of utilitarianism that lies at the root of modern economics. Adam Smith wrote: "We are not ready to suspect any person of being defective in selfishness." ([1759] 1969, p. 446.) It is postulated (Crouch, 1979, p. 2) that "a human being is a *purposeful* animal and the purpose is to maximize enjoyment of life." Happiness, satisfaction, and pleasure are used as synonyms (Dyke, 1981, pp. 10–11; Walsh, 1970, pp. 21–26). It is a position several neoclassical psychological theories share with neoclassical economics (Wallach and Wallach, 1983).

Moreover, many utilitarians grant moral approval to pleasure: it is "good"; pain is evil. Bentham (1948, p. 1) stressed that pain and pleasure are not only empirically our masters but also our ethical guides: "It is for them *alone* to point out what we *ought* to do, as well as to determine what we shall do." (Italics added.) They, he added, set the standards of what

*Throughout the volume, unless otherwise indicted, italics are in the text cited.

is right and wrong. Kohlberg (1968, p. 486) observes: "The Utilitarians suggested that actions by the self or by others whose consequences to the self are harmful (painful) are naturally deemed bad and arouse anger or punitive tendencies, and actions whose consequences are beneficial (pleasurable) are naturally deemed good. . . ." Brandt (1982, p.169) explains that the utilitarian assumption that happiness, the sole utility to be maximized, is intrinsically good in the moral sense, because "God aims to maximize the happiness of his creatures." (See also Little, 1957, p. 9.) (While there are significant bodies of utilitarian philosophies that are neither hedonistic nor ego-centered, the founding fathers of utilitarianism were both [see Frankena, 1973], and their work is at the basis of the neoclassical paradigm.) Once this gross value-judgment about the moral goodness of pleasure is removed, and one takes into account the fact that numerous acts that are pleasurable are also immoral, (see below, pp. 52–63), the door is open to the recognition that there are at least two major distinct sources of value, and that these are recognized in deontological philosophies, in our culture, in common parlance, and are also "revealed" in behavior.

THE INTER-DEPENDENT UTILITY: TAUTOLOGICAL AND AMORAL

Faced with the challenge that the pleasure concept of utility is amoral, asocial, and counter to basic facts about human behavior, neoclassicists point to a concept of utility that is in effect radically different but goes under the same name: one which contains service to others and a commitment to moral values, beyond the pleasure of self. A simple conceptual device is used: the consumption by others is made into a source of the actor's pleasure. (Hence the reference to it as the "interdependent" utility). When a person acts altruistically, this is explained by the suggestion that the pleasure of the person who benefits from this act has become a source of doer's pleasure, part of his or her utility.

Take gifts, for example. They have troubled neoclassicists because gifts suggest a different basis for exchange than economic advantage or profit. Neoclassicists have dealt with gifts in two ways: first, they have "reduced" the motives of the givers, suggesting that they are not truly altruistic but driven by self-interest. For example, those who give gifts are said to seek reciprocal gifts, reputation, status, approval, or some other "goods" the doer desires. Second, to the extent that gift giving (and other altruistic acts) cannot be reduced in this way, neoclassicists have suggested that the giver enjoys the receiver's consumption. "All we have to suppose is that the perception of one party, A, of the welfare of the other, B, is a variable in A's utility function such that when A perceives that B is better off, A's utility rises." (Boulding, 1981, p. 6). Lipsey and Steiner (1975, pp. 142–

43), comment on the statement that individuals will seek to maximize their utility:

> This assumption is sometimes taken to mean that individuals are assumed to be narrowly selfish and devoid of any altruistic motives. This is not so. If, for example, the individual derives utility from giving his money away to others, this can be incorporated into the analysis, and the marginal utility that he gets from a dollar given away can be compared with the marginal utility that he gets from a dollar spent on himself.

Margolis (1982, p. 11), after observing that "in recent years efforts to incorporate altruistic preferences within the conventional framework have become fairly common," adds:

> We have no more need to distinguish between the bread Smith buys to give to the poor and that which he buys for his own consumption, than to distinguish his neighbor's demand for sugar to make cookies from his demand for sugar to make gin in the cellar.

One neoclassical economist, whose paper was published in the distinguished *Journal of Political Economy*, was troubled by the fact that religious activities cannot be explained by "the expected stream of 'benefits' which an individual plans to receive" during his lifetime (Azzi, 1975, p. 28). Laboring to explain people's activities by some consumable good, he introduced the factor of "afterlife consumption," and suggested "this variable being at least partially a function of the household's investment of members' time in religious activities during their lifetimes." (Ibid.)

From our viewpoint, the concept of an interdependent utility, even if limited only to this life, is ethically lacking and methodologically deficient. Ethically, the I-utility concept remains true to the hedonistic version of utilitarianism: altruistic acts are explained by *actor's* pleasure; authentic altruistic acts, acts of self-denial or sacrifice, are incompatible with this concept. What would motivate them? is the implied utilitarian question. Of course, if one assumes that only the quest for pleasure (and avoidance of pain) *can* motivate people, one must conclude that saints enjoy their sacrifices; they "must be" masochistic. However, once one breaks out of the straitjacket of the one-utility paradigm, once one allows for other factors to explain behavior, one sees that normal people do some things because they judge them to be their duty, to be right, whether or not they enjoy these acts. Indeed, over the centuries numerous theologians and philosophers saw the uniqueness of human beings, when compared to animals, as residing in people's ability to pass judgment over their urges instead of automatically yielding to them. True, not all such judgments are ethical; they may, for instance, be aesthetic. However, moral values clearly play a pivotal role in the formation of many such judgments.

Furthermore, if one includes the need to act in affirmation of moral values in the utility's unified bundle of preferences, as one "taste" among many, an important question is silenced, namely, what makes some people's behavior more moral than that of others? This bundling occurs both because neoclassicists do not study the formation of preferences (a major defect to which we shall return), and second, because the moral preferences are lost among a myriad of others, such as preferences for California wines over those from France, or Pepsi over Dr. Pepper.

From a methodological viewpoint, the all-inclusive expansion of the concept of utility violates the rules of sound conceptualization. Once a concept is defined so that it encompasses *all* the incidents that are members of a given category (in the case at hand, the motives for all human activities), it ceases to enhance one's ability to explain.

As long as ego's and alter's pleasures are treated as equal in their status for ego's utility, the concept ceases to differentiate. Thus, if given X new resources, I advance my utility when I use these resources to enhance my consumption, and I advance it just as much when I give them to charity, or when I share them with those I love, or even when I burn them—the way the Kwakiutl do (Benedict, 1934, p. 143), presumably I enjoy the fire—what does the concept add? It simply sprinkles all a person seeks with the term "utility." Masochism, sadism, a quest for a fair or unfair return, all have the same status. To the extent that this "theory" aims to shed light on motivation it is a conceptual failure, because the purpose of introducing concepts is to call attention to meaningful distinctions. The same problem arose in the psychology of instincts, when people who were hungry were said to respond to their instinct, and those who were after sex to their instinct, and so on. (Before that, the ancient Greeks populated the world with endless gods, "explaining" each event with the working of a god assigned to produce it.)

Indeed, neoclassical economists seeking to explain non-selfish behavior have fallen into the very same trap by explaining "excessive" saving by a "bequest motive" (Laitner, 1979, p. 403; Shorrocks, 1979, p. 415), and religious activity by a "salvation motive." (Azzi, 1975, p. 24.) (Others have used concepts such as "a taste of discrimination," [Becker, 1957, p. 6,] and "a taste for nationalism," [Johnson, 1965].) Altruism is described as resting in part on "a taste for the perception of the welfare of others" (Boulding, 1979, p. 1383.). If, in attempting to explain a phenomenon, all one does is add a label to the description, such as instinct, motive, or utility, one explains nothing. The author joins two economists, Kalt and Zupan (1984, p. 281), who have written: " ... individuals may derive satisfaction from 'having done the right thing.'" I do not see what is gained by calling this consumption motive.

Several economists have recognized the unproductive tautological nature of this concept of utility which assumes that whatever one does "reveals" one's pleasure. As Stigler (1966, p. 57) points out: "a reason, we would be saying, can always be found for whatever we observe man to do" which "turn[s] utility into a tautology". Bowie and Simon (1977, pp. 194–95) write: "In the classical view, each consumer is a satisfaction maximizer, i.e., he is a rational egoist . . . This assumption is so obviously contrary to fact that economists have turned it into a tautology. Any consumer behavior is by definition an attempt to maximize satisfaction." The authors go on to point out that as a result "we no longer have an empirical theory about consumer behavior" and the theory becomes "utterly trivial" (ibid.). If one commits suicide, it is implied that life must have been worse than death (Hamermesh and Soss, 1974). In other situations in which some of the pleasures can be measured but still do not explain the act (such as a tax deduction that does not explain making a gift because the value of such deductions as a rule is lower than that of the gift), it is assumed that some other, unmeasured factor—say reputation in this case—"must" make up the difference. (If true-blue neoclassicists were to be asked, "But what about anonymous gifts?" I can practically hear them answering: "There are no completely anonymous gifts; they 'must be' given to impress one's wife, mistress, or accountant.") From a sheer methodological viewpoint it is more productive to hypothesize that the difference is due to a moral commitment.

To characterize the concept of utility as tautological is not a matter of calling attention to some technical failing, a minor methodological demerit that distresses logical purists. It suggests that the explanatory power which the original concept of utility, the P-utility, commands is lost when the notion of I-utility is introduced. To argue that people are pleasure-driven is a powerful hypothesis; it surely explains a good part of human behavior. True, it is often excessively extended, trying to explain more of human behavior than it can, but nevertheless it is an important part of the explanation. But once the satisfaction of one's own needs, and self-sacrifice, as well as service to others and to the community—once *all* these become "satisfaction," the explanatory hypothesis of the concept is diluted to the point where it becomes quite meaningless. One empties the concept in trying to save it and the paradigm built around it.

Beyond undermining its explanatory power, the all-inclusive expansion of the concept of utility, entailed in the notion of an I-utility, undercuts a core theorem of neoclassical economics, its central thesis concerning the source of order. The origins of the theorem go back to Adam Smith, who emphasized that the market as a *system* relies on each actor's pursuing his *self*-interest.

> It is not from the benevolence of the butcher, the brewer or the baker that we expect our dinner, but from their regard to their own interest. We address ourselves not to their humanity but to their self-love, and never talk to them of our own necessities but of their advantages. (Smith, [1776] 1937, p. 14.)

If there is no fundamental differences between "self-love" and love for others,* Smith's whole thesis vanishes. Indeed, if people can derive pleasure directly from serving others and the community, there is no need for an invisible hand to guarantee that individualistic pursuits will lead to the satisfaction of the common good. Indeed, the distinction between profit and loss becomes unnecessary: after all, one man's loss is another man's gain. It thus seems, on grounds of sound conceptualization, that the quest for self-satisfactions, and seeking to serve others (the public included) out of a sense of moral obligation, are best kept apart.

UTILITY AS A FORMAL CONCEPT: EMPTY

In another major attempt to shore up the mono-utility paradigm, neoclassicists suggest that the concept of utility, whatever its philosophical origins or the psychological "bedtime stories" it used to entail, should be treated as an abstract entity, with neither pleasure nor consumption as its content. It is merely a common denominator, an X, into which all other values can be converted or by which rank-ordering can be achieved. (A similar conceptual device appears in theology. When various proofs as to the nature of God do not work too well, God is described as the great X. It has often been noted that consumption or pleasure play the role of God in major secular formulation of Western culture.)

> The term suggests there is something called utility—like mass, height, wealth, or happiness—that people maximize. And indeed during the early history of economic analysis, it was assumed that goods provided utility or usefulness in some measurable, psychological sense. Although that misleading psychological conception has been abandoned, the name "utility" has stuck. So it is now simply a name for the ranking of options in accord with any individual's preferences. (Alchian and Allen, 1977, p. 40.)

Hirshleifer put it succinctly: "What modern economists call 'utility' reflects nothing more than the *rank ordering of preference*." (1976, p. 85, italics provided.) And Little (1957, p. 20) states: "It [utility] need not refer to anything". The units of X that various commodities generated, as translated into the anonymous common denominator, are sometimes referred to as "utils." "One could thus legitimately say in this language that one got 2 utils from a shot of Jack Daniels and considerably more from an evening with Marina." (Walsh, 1970, p. 24.)

Samuelson (1983, p. 91) criticizes this concept of utility as an "empty

---

*A reviewer pointed out here that if one's altruism encompasses one's children, there is still a need for the invisible hand to order the relations *among* the households. This is quite true. However, to the extent that altruism or mutuality encompasses those with whom one transacts, it supplements or replaces self-interest as the ordering mechanism. For evidence, see below.

convention," and as "meaningless in any operational, empirical sense." Indeed, the concept of X utility, if it is taken as devoid of any content, and as merely a formal factor according to which the various preferences can be ranked, disregards a basic prerequisite of science: Unlike mathematics, science requries substantive concepts. In mathematical calculations it is possible to use formal, content-less, common denominators because the elements that are being converted are themselves abstracts. Thus, for example, if one seeks to establish that 3/8 is less than 2/3, one can use a common denominator, like 1/24, without asking what the n/24 stands for or "means." However, when one seeks to compare, say, three breads and two pork chops, one cannot properly state that one bread generates 3 utils while one pork chop generates 9 utils, nor that a pork chop ranks higher, because to determine how many utils various items generate, or where they rank, depends on the substantive definition of the common denominator. All objects have multiple attributes such as calories, vitamins, minerals, and moral standings. Hence, their value, or util, *depends on which dimension(s) are being assessed* (Little, 1957, pp. 19ff).

Neoclassical economists in their own writing about the X-utility frequently slip into discussion of consumption and pleasure, thus returning the concept to that of P- or I-utility. For example, Kamerschen and Valentine (1981, p. 69) first explain that for deliberate choices to be made all the goods "must" have "some" common characteristics and "this common property is usually called utility". Soon, though, goods are equated with commodities, and satisfaction with desire: "*utility is simply whatever makes the commodity desired.*" (Ibid.) The next step is to view everything as a commodity: "Bourbon, dope, Bibles and opera all possess utility in varying degrees." (Ibid., p. 82.)

To the extent that neoclassical economists do not ask people about their choices but observe their behavior (their rankings are said to be "revealed" in what they buy under various constraints, especially that of their income), the studies run into severe empirical difficulties. It is not sufficient to show that at a given income level a rise in the price of coffee will lead people to buy more tea; one must deal with all the simultaneous changes in all other prices and "compensate" for the loss in across-the-board buying power. Even when this is attempted, under the extremely simplified and controlled conditions of experiments with rats, which are free to choose between only *two* items, one encounters great difficulties in interpreting the findings (Kagel, et.al., 1975, p. 36). Several economists whom the author queried about this matter at first responded, true to the formal notion of utility, that one need not know what motives "lurk" behind the preferences for the theory to be "very useful," "enormously illuminating," and "it predicts quite well people's behavior." When reminded of the difficulties listed above, they agreed that actually the theory's predictive record "is quite weak." Indeed, they added, at best the theory predicts the direction—not the magnitude—of change of behavior resulting from changes in prices.

In short, the concept of X-utility either forces one to return to one of the other two concepts, or—as a contentless variable—it is rather unproductive, if it can be applied at all.

A Note on Causes

All concepts of utility are defective because they do not offer an explanation of the sources of preferences and the factors that cause them to change, nor do they explain how consumers allocate their income among alternative goods to begin with. Such explanations are necessary because people change their preferences as the constraints under which they "implement" them change. Hence, changes in behavior may be due to changes in constraints *or* in preferences, often to some combination of the two. Without a conception and measurement of preference formation and dynamics, in which moral values play a pivotal role, a satisfactory theory of behavior is hard to imagine. The assumption that people's preferences are "set" or "stable," which is central to the neoclassical paradigm because it allows it to disregard changes in intentions and in those values that affect preferences, simply ignores the most elementary observations of daily experience. In response to the argument that absurd assumptions do not matter as long as the theory predicts, one must note: not well at all, it seems.

The suggestion that moral values and other factors that shape preferences are not the economists' turf is but one more reason to favor a shift to codetermination theory, one that combines economics with elements of other social sciences, to develop socio-economics. This, in turn, requires a new paradigm that considers more than one fundamental source of valuations, more than one "utility." (For additional discussion, see pp. 67–76, and Etzioni, 1986a.)

MORALITY AND MULTI-FACETED CHOICES

The Facets of Preferences

Even if one would accept the gross simplification that preferences are set rather than constantly changing, morality enters into choices because of the important observation that *choices are not simple, one-dimensional, one-time* (or one "stage") *events but are in fact mutli-faceted.** Many basic neoclassical economic models assume that each item has a single price; all

*For an excellent overview of the neoclassical view of preferences (or tastes) and a powerful criticism see March (1978).

offers and bids are made simultaneously; all bargains are struck and prices are set simultaneously, and the market clears in a flash. Then, the whole process starts all over again (Thurow, 1983). However, everyday observations and experience, as well as scientific experiments discussed later, show that many purchases are accompanied by or followed by feel-ings of guilt, shame, regrets, euphoria, a desire to share, pride, and other such feelings which, we shall see, are not merely ephemeral states-of-mind but have significant behavioral consequences; i.e., preferences have multiple facets. The moral significance of acts is one such major facet.

Evidence in support of this approach is provided in Chapter 5. Here a simple example will serve to illustrate the point. It is taken from diet-ing, which is the activity—the worship of the body—on which millions of members of industrialized societies, especially those who are well off, focus their moral-like efforts. They feel guilty when they indulge, and virtuous when they abstain. One may observe a person who usually does not eat dessert, then has some for three days in a row and skips lunch on the fourth day. One may view this behavior as a response to three days in which the price of desserts declined, followed by a day when the cost of desserts skyrocketed (assuming no change in income and other prices). A better explanation connects the events, and traces the accumu-lation of an initially not visible guilt, which is then "worked-off" at the skipped lunch.

Guilt is of course not the only feeling that "accompanies" choice and which has subsequent observable effects. And other sequences have been observed (Chapter 5). The diet example seeks merely to highlight the fact that the one-dimensional ranking of preferences misses much of what there is in a choice, including the moral factors which play a role that may not be revealed in every single choice, especially if a choice is viewed as a unidimensional event and complete unto itself. A colleague com-mented here that economists seek to predict *aggregate* behavior; they do not care whether or not one person diets on a particular day; those who do, and those who do not, will "average out." If Joe will violate his diet on Monday, Jane will keep hers, and vice versa on the other days of the week. The deontologist response is that moral factors have an "aggrega-tive" consequence. For example, a more approving view of divorce, as symbolized in the introduction of "No Fault" divorce, was a factor in increasing divorce rates (Weitzman, 1985). And the explanatory vari-ables, we shall see, are not an accumulation of changes in individual choices but whatever macro collective changes occurred with the society, changes in moral values being an important factor. Contrast, for exam-ple, the effects of a Constitutional amendment to balance the budget (as an expression of enhanced public responsibility, however technically flawed it might be), to decisions by millions of individuals to spend less.

Externalities as a Precedent

Neoclassical economists recognize in one major way that, in their concept of social costs or "externalities," prices do not reflect all that is of value, although they "ought to." Pollution is an often-cited example. Since it often costs industrialists nothing to dump wastes into a public lake, they are free to ignore the social consequences of their behavior. Neoclassicists suggest various mechanisms to incorporate these social consequences in "the price" and thus allow the market to protect the commons. However, these mechanisms are rarely introduced, and attempts to use them raise major problems. For example, there seems to be no objective way to determine at what level to set the artificial price, and in practice the process is as subject to political manipulation and bureaucratic entanglements as are other government interventions, such as farm or energy subsidies (Etzioni, 1985d). Hence there continues to be a need to determine and cope with social consequences, aside from whatever "the price" (or "the market") "says" or can be made to say. The same holds for the moral standing of an object or act; it often is only poorly reflected in its price.

Concern with the longer-run future is a major case in point. Without moral dicta, such as "you *ought* to worry about the future, about your children, about not becoming dependent," and "you ought to save," which provide a force to counter current pleasure/consumption, individuals may well save less than they will later feel they require (aside from the question of whether they will save "enough" from a social welfare viewpoint). Future consumption cannot motivate present saving because it does not generate present pleasure, but does inflict the pain of self-denial. Similarly, without a moral commitment to saving, people may indeed "free ride"—decide to consume now and let the government, and their kin or associates, take care of them "in the future." It is a gross error to depict the "saving" choice as between consumption now as against more consumption later, as if more consumption later could somehow generate a motivational force in the present. Consuming later inevitably entails deferred gratification. Deferred gratification is a "pain," not a pleasure, and hence is basically a *dis*incentive. In the hedonistic psychology that the neoclassical paradigm encompasses, there is little to explain deferred gratification. It finds an explanation in moral commitments, and in other value commitments and in deontological psychology, which encompasses the concept of a multiple self. Saving behavior is thus to be viewed as a conflict between consuming now and abiding with commitments to moral values to which the actors are committed in the same time frame, now. (Cf. Collard, 1978, pp. 158–65.)

This line of analysis predicts that, given the same income level and age, those persons will save more who have a stronger moral commitment to take care of themselves, and to not be dependent on others. Differences in value systems among societies also are expected to correlate with saving rates, as is evident when one compares contemporary Japanese and American societies. The differences in moral valuation of being in debt are a major factor in accounting for differences in the amounts saved. Saving is, of course, but one example. The same "corrections" are expected when we counter tendencies toward tax evasion, violating implicit contracts, not playing by the rules of the game, and violating other moral commitments that help maintain behavior that is not inherently satisfying.

Second, the societal consequences that individuals are said to ignore because they are not "theirs," such as dumping waste into a lake, are of course no other than theirs, their children's, friends', neighbors', fellow citizens', who all make up the society. They all drink from the lake they pollute. Morality motivates them to worry about public goods, to forgo free rides. It is clearly an important way to shore up the commons, and one that keeps the need for government intervention low—including the need to generate inducements!

Morality is a major way externalities are "introduced" into one's deliberations and decision-making, albeit often in conflict with the pleasure utility. Indeed, morality is a much more widely used and less costly and less coercive mechanism for attending to the commons* than government inducements or public "incentives" provided via the market.

Finally, the way neoclassicists "model" externalities points the ability to recognize more than one source of valuation: the price set by the market may be "corrected" by a distinct, significant source or sources of other concerns. In effect, the concern with externalities, with public goods, is often itself a category of moral concerns.

IN CONCLUSION

P-utility has long standing philosophical and psychological foundations; it provides a major explanatory concept and generates testable hypotheses. That is, it constitutes a logical, proper, and productive theoretical concept. To the extent that it is used to suggest that all (or practically all) behavior is explainable by pleasure or narrow self-interest, it is clearly wrong; we shall see that often behavior is, to one extent or another, moral and self-denying. To the extent that it is hypothesized that the pursuit of P-utility is *a major* explanatory factor, the hypothesis is clearly valid, but it points to the need to recognize other utilities.

The introduction of the concept of an I-utility muddles the issue because it tries to explain pleasure, self-interest, and the opposite kind of behavior—caring for others, and for the community—by the same con-

---

*This is not to suggest that all or most immediate benefits are immoral, or all claims by the commons are moral. See below, on the criterion for determining moral claims.

cept. It thus ceases to differentiate, and turns tautological. The concept of I-utility thus either explains nothing or, we have seen, requires the back door reintroduction of the distinction it seeks to avoid.

X-utility is a formal concept which in its pure form is a-scientific logic because it has no substantive content and hence is un-empirical. In its diluted form, in which X equals "satisfaction," it returns us to the key question: are all valuations of one basic kind and are they all mutually compatible, or do they constitute a partially incompatible, irreducible, conflicted universe?

3

Substantive Differences:
Moral Not Equal Pleasure

WORLDS APART

The language and conceptual paradigm of some preliterate tribes is reported not to include the concept "green." Members of the tribe refer to all the colors we call green or blue by one term, "blue." (Berlin and Kay, 1969, pp. 1–14.) From a more differentiated perspective, the members of this particular tribe are partially color-blind. Similarly, the neoclassical paradigm is too simple: it does not include a pivotal distinction between the sense of pleasure—derived from consumption of goods and services, and from other sources—and the sense of affirmation attained when a person abides by his or her moral commitments. These moral commitments are the main source of deontological judgments people pass over their urges (whether natural or reflecting socialization).

This chapter seeks to establish that moral affirmations and acts of pleasure can be clearly differentiated, and that they constitute distinct dimensions, both in terms of inner psychic states and in terms of the attendant behavioral consequences. We review the various antecedents to the bi-utility, deontological paradigm evolved here, briefly visit the work of scholars who point to distinct phenomena, and define the differences between the two conceptions. This exposition is followed by a substantive exploration of morality. Operational and empirical differences, as well as reasons the distinction between moral and pleasurable behavior, is claimed to be productive for purposes of explanation (theory building), for policy making, and from an ethical viewpoint, are discussed in subsequent chapters.

MOVEMENTS TOWARD A BI-UTILITY CONCEPTION

The idea that individuals pursue two or more utilities is hardly a new one. A major contribution to such an approach is found in the writings of the grandfather of neoclassical economics, Adam Smith. In *The Theory of Moral Sentiments* he observes that people act out of a conscience and are related to one another not merely via a market—in exchange relations, trying to maximize their interest—but also as people whose psychic well-being is deeply dependent on the approval of others, which in turn is based on acting morally, not on enhancing wealth. "How selfish so ever man may be supposed, there are evidently some principles in his nature, which interest him in the fortune of others, and render their happiness necessary to him." (Smith, [1759] 1976, p. 9.)

The fact that the position Smith took in *Moral Sentiments* is not easily reconcilable with the one he took in *The Wealth of Nations* has generated a small industry of writings interpreting the differences and generating ways to solve what has become known as *Das Smith Problem.* Suffice it to say here that most neoclassicists (and contemporary Whigs) tend to ignore the first Adam Smith in favor of the later. Similarly, while they are familiar with the works of Sen, Hirschman, and others cited below, neoclassicists tend to ignore their implication for the mono-utility, neoclassical paradigm.

These earlier authors, in the tradition of *The Moral Sentiments,* on which the author builds, are basically of two kinds: Those who acknowledge the need to introduce another source of valuation or "utility," but try, by hook or by crook, to show that somehow it can be reconciled with the mono-utility assumption after all, and those who seem ready to shift to a multiple-utility paradigm. (Those familiar with the way authors struggle to preserve orthodoxies will quickly recognize in neoclassical writings the symptoms of scholars who recognize the need for a major adaptation, and the difference between those who struggle to achieve it from within the prevailing paradigm versus those who are willing to break away. For discussion of neoclassical economics as an orthodoxy, see Nelson and Winter, 1982, p. 5ff.)

A work that well represents the first kind, of those who seek revisions from the inside, is the "economic theory of self control" by Thaler and Shefrin (1981). The behavior that troubles Thaler and Shefrin, and before them troubled Schelling (1960) (see also Schelling, 1984a and b), is that some people pay clinics to help them stop smoking, pay so called "fat farms" not to feed them, and put their monies into Christmas club accounts that pay no interest but require monthly deposits. This and other such behavior revealing weakness of will seems irrational to neoclassicists. What is the preference, the utility? If you wish to stop smoking, you stop; it is not efficient to pay others to make you stop. And to do so shows you are subject, simultaneously, to *two* conflicting forces. To those who draw on other paradigms, who assume that people have conflicted selves and that they often act inconsistently, non-rationally or irrationally, or rely on institutions to shore up their "higher" self to deal with their "lower" self, these phenomena are expected rather than surprising.

Thaler and Shefrin, writing in *The Journal of Political Economy*, reassure their readers that they will remove the challenge posed by observations of internally conflicted behavior by "a simple extension of orthodox models, using orthodox tools, that permits such behavior to be viewed as rational" (1981, p. 393.) They start by citing the pivotal insight by McIntosh, that acts of self-control (as evident in the cited behavior) are paradoxical for those who hold to the mono-utility conception unless it is assumed that the psyche contains more than one energy system, and that these energy systems have some degree of independence from each other (Ibid., p. 393–94). This notion, Thaler and Shefrin correctly observe, suggests that people have "*two* sets of preferences that are in conflict at a single point in time," (ibid, p. 394; italics provided), which leads the authors to refer to "a two-self economic man." (Ibid.)

From here on, Thaler and Shefrin resort to a rather complicated argument that suggests that the two-layered self is after all one entity, and through this reasoning they try to save the day for the mono-utility neoclassical model. We cannot do full justice to their full argument, but in short they assume: A person is to be viewed as an organization that consists of a planner and a doer; the doer is completely selfish and myopic; and the planner is concerned with a lifetime utility—a concept that is not further explained.

The connection between lifetime utility and moral values, as this social scientist sees it, should be briefly indicated. As we saw in the discussion of saving, hedonists live for the moment; they let others or the government worry about the future, including *their* future. Moral values often serve to counter such behavior, and mandate concern for the future. Thus, Thaler and Shefrin's notion of a lifetime utility and planner self, in effect, introduces a moral "utility."

Thaler and Shefrin (ibid., p. 395) further assume that "the planner [self] does not actually consume but, rather, derives utility from the consumption of the doer [self]" and that the planner "has some psychic technology capable of affecting the doer's behavior." Armed with these assumptions the rest of the argument is relatively easy. To put it more crudely but also more parsimoniously, according to Thaler and Shefrin when people maximize their immediate urges, the doers prevail; when people do not, it is because the planners acted. As both reside within the same person, above all because they are united by one organizing principle (the doer/planner relation, which Thaler and Shefrin assume), people can be seen as maximizing one utility. (Similarly, Harsanyi, 1955, distinguishes between "subjective" and "ethical" preferences, but sees the ethical ones as rare.)

Lindenberg (1983) develops a similar within-the-fold adaptation, although it is dynamic rather than static. He observes a tension between economic expediency and moral obligations. He deals with it by suggesting that actors have two "baskets," one containing all forces that advance their "normal" utility, and other containing all those that urge the actor to deviate from the course of action the normal utility favors. The two baskets are linked by the assumption of rational repetitive choices. Lindenberg provides the following example. Assume an actor faces two levers. A right lever that yields $100 with a probability of 0.7, and a left one that yields the same amount but with a probability of 0.4. The "pure" (i.e. "normal," rational) strategy would lead one to press only the right lever but because the actor also has "a taste for variety" the actor will occasionally press the left lever, say 25 percent of the time. This would make no sense if observed as an isolated event, but is explicable within the context of a series of identical choices. (Other scholars who worked along these lines include Siegel et al., 1964; Ofshe and Ofshe, 1970; and Alhadeff, 1982.)

Margolis (1982) provides a third attempt to deal with two utilities within one. He develops a model of dual rational choice that assumes a divided value system within each person. People are assumed to split their resources between pursuits of self-interest (including activities that benefit others) and those that benefit some larger social entity of which they feel they are an integral part, independently of any gains or pleasure they derive out of the group's well-being ("participation altruism").

This would seem very much like a bi-utility world. (Indeed, one section of Margolis' book is entitled "The Dual-Utilities.") However, Margolis introduces a Darwinian argument to account for the rule that balances and aggregates the two utilities, the "fair" share. The rule determines the relationship between the value of a person places on the last dollar spent on group interest (G') as compared to the value the person places on the last dollar spent on self-interest (S'), so that Weight $= G'/S'$. The larger the weight (W), the more the individual is inclined to favor self-interest. The fair share rule, which in effect defines the share of G and binds the two utilities into one, is thus a matter of survival, i.e., of self-interest. The Darwinian point is that groups need people with a certain proportion of G in order to survive. Given this assumption, it's no wonder that the individual can harmonize his or her group-utility and personal-utility in what Margolis calls a set of "ultimate" preferences.

It should be noted that Margolis deals only with public choices, such as voting, because he sees that here the neoclassical model's mono-utility fails to account for the amount of resources people actually allocate to such choices and goals. He sees no trouble for mono-utility models in the private choices made by consumers and producers, and hence in most economic behavior; in this he joins many neoclassicists who do not deny that there are some truly altruistic elements—i.e., of another "utility"— in private choices, but feel that in this sphere they "are so empirically unimportant as to allow the use of Occam's Razor. . . ." (Kalt and Zupan, 1984, p. 279.) That is, they are so limited that they may be safely ignored to enhance the parsimony of the theory.

Both the recognition of the conceptual need for a moral "utility," and the reluctance of neoclassicists to incorporate it into their models, are captured in the following passage, which, it should be noted, concerns public goals, not private economic goals: "Stigler (1972) has noted the possibility of altruistic motives in political action. These might take the form of a sense of 'civic duty,' that is, a duty to serve the interests of the public. Pursuit of such a duty is a consumption activity that yields utility in the form of the warm glow of moral rectitude." (Kalt and Zupan, 1984, p. 280.) So far, so good, if we disregard the somewhat prejudicial name given to moral activities—"consumption"—and the question of whether its essence is well depicted as an activity that yields a "warm glow." But Stigler is not ready to add a distinct category. He contrasts civic duties, which he says are driven by the consumption motive, with activities aimed at embracing some self-interest, which he calls investment motive. He then states: "The investment motive is rich in empirical implications, and the consumption motive is less well-endowed, so we should see how far we can carry the former analysis before we add the latter." (Stigler, 1972, p. 104; cited by Kalt and Zupan, 1984, p. 280.)

Sen (1977, p. 326), in his writing on "commitments," comes close to making a break without making it. "Commitment," not formally defined, is contrasted with concern for others when it is based on one's own welfare. Sen gives the following example. If you see another person being tortured and it makes you sick, you act out of sympathy. But if you think such action is wrong, you act out of "commitment." "Commitment is, of course, closely connected with one's morals," Sen explains (ibid., p. 329). The significance of the concept of commitment, he elaborates, is that it points to a source of preference, or value, other than being "better off." Sen emphasizes that his concern is not with the terminology but with keeping the *two dimensions* of value apart.

Next, Sen—like Margolis and Stigler—limits his challenge to the neoclassical mono-utility position on public choices. "How relevant is all this to the kind of choices with which economists are concerned. . . . I think one should immediately agree that for many types of behavior, commitment is unlikely to be an important ingredient." (Ibid., p. 330.) Sen adds that in the private purchase of many consumer goods, the scope for the exercise of commitment may show up rather rarely in "such exotic acts as the boycotting of South African avocados or the eschewing of Spanish holidays." He goes on to suggest that the concept of commitment is important not only for choices involving public goods, but also for work motivation and in a "number of other economic contexts." (Ibid., p. 333.)

Hirschman (1984) goes quite a bit further. He starts by noting that the economic models are too parsimonious. He then calls attention to the distinct human faculty of stepping back, being able to reflect on one's action (and to personally redirect them), unlike "wantons" (animals and people who behave like animals) who are entirely in the grip of their whims and passions. (He credits the distinction to philosopher Harry Frankfurt, 1971.) Hirschman points out that people thus have preferences and meta-preferences, and their actions are under the influence of both. Meta-preferences are similar to what is often referred to as values, that provide criteria for choosing among preferences.

As we see it, while there are non-moral criteria, moral criteria are by far the most common meta-preferences or values. McPherson (1984, p. 241), who reviews the deontological positions by Hirschman and a few others, writes: "Neoclassical theory, if it recognizes these conflicts [between preferences and meta preferences] at all, could do so only to disapprove; such conflicts mark an imperfection, a *failure* of rationality. . . ." (p. 241.)* In contrast, he cites Hirschman, who sees these conflicts as *various* states of happiness, as a source of richness for the person. That is, while Hirschmann does not tie the concept of meta-preferences explicitly to a moral utility, he comes close to completing the transition from a mono-utility to a multi-utility deontological paradigm than any of the other scholars cited.

A visit with the various works that grappled with the concept of multiple utilities highlights two questions: can the various sources of valuations be reconciled, summed up in one supra-utility, or are they sources of irreducible, different valuations? Explanations for concluding that the sources are irreducible are provided in Chapter 4. Second, the authors seek the source of other, "utilities." We hold that a main source of valuation other than pleasure is morality, rather than, say, aesthetic values or a desire for novelty (e.g. Scitovsky, 1978). It is this step that ties the concept of multiple utility to deontological philosophy. To further elaborate on a deontological concept of multiple utility, one must first explore the substance of the moral source of valuation.

A FUNDAMENTALLY DIFFERENT SUBSTANCE

What Constitutes a Moral Act?

An examination of the relevant literature leads one to the not surprising conclusion that philosophers, after being at it for many hundreds of years, have yet to produce a fully satisfactory definition of what is moral. Without attempting here to review the immense literature on the subject, the different approaches, and the difficulties that each encounters, we suggest that for the purposes at hand it suffices to consider moral acts as those that meet four criteria: moral acts reflect an imperative, a generali-

---

*A fuller review of antecedents to the line evolved here would encompass the work of those who see a continued struggle between the id and the superego, never fully resolved even in a strong ego; McGregor's (1960) work on "two" human natures; Schelling's writings about "two" selves (1984b); and Elster (1979), and select essays in his ed. (1985a).

zation, and a symmetry when applied to others, and are motivated intrinsically. (Each criterion is necessary by itself but not sufficient; in conjunction that may serve to define a moral act.)

The *imperative* quality of moral acts is reflected in that persons who act morally sense that they "must" behave in the prescribed way, that they are in fact obligated, duty bound. We are familiar from personal experience or introspection with the sense that one ought to do something because it is right, as distinguishable from doing it because it is enjoyable.

The notion of an imperative is supported by the observation that people set aside certain realms as commanding a special, compelling status. Durkheim (1947) points to the fact that people treat certain acts and considerations as "sacred," which need not mean religious. Walzer (1983, p. 97) lists fourteen major areas of "blocked exchanges," including basic freedoms (one has a claim on them, without paying for them), marriage (licenses for polygamy are not sold), and divine grace.

One characteristic of these "sacred" moral principles, Goodin (1980) suggests, is that in the areas of behavior to which they apply, they repudiate the instrumental rationality which includes considerations of costs and benefits. A person feels obligated to save a life, or to make a donation, and so on, without engaging in such calculations (Simmons, Klein, and Simmons, 1977). Indeed, the "instantaneousness" of such decisions is used by several researchers as an indication that a non-deliberate commitment is made (Fellner and Marshall, 1968).

Only after these principles are violated do people enter into a second realm of decisions, in which moral considerations are weighted as against others, and calculations enter. This hierarchy of moral principles explains why the fact people sometimes calculate how much to give—or if they give X, what it will do for their reputation, and so on—should not be used to argue that they do not have other "sacred," non-negotiable moral commitments. Morality affects their choices in two different ways: by heeding an absolute command in some areas or periods of time; and by preferring certain means, the moral means, over others, but not at all costs. People thus have both an absolute *and* an expedient morality. Similarly, the fact that people are less likely to heed a moral commitment if the costs are high, does not indicate that there is no imperative; indeed, such commitments are what drives up the costs of unmoral behavior. If, however, moral commitments are not reflected in behavior but only in verbal expressions or "attitudes," then one can conclude that there is no moral imperative.

The need for additional criteria to characterize moral acts arises out of the fact that there can be non-moral imperatives, for example obsessions with a forlorn love or even with an object, such as controlled substances or a fetish. The addition of the second and third criteria helps here to separate moral imperatives from others (Childress, 1977).

Individuals who act morally are *able to generalize* their behavior—they are able to justify an act to others and to themselves by pointing to general rules, their deontological duties. Statements such as "because I want it" or "I need it badly" do not meet this criterion because no generalization is entailed. "Do unto others as you wish others to do unto you" is a prime example of a generalized rule.

Symmetry is required in that there must be a willingness to accord other comparable people, under comparable circumstances, the same standing or right. (Otherwise, the moral dictum is rendered arbitrary. Such an arbitrary rule would state, "this rule applies to Jane but not to Jim although there is no relevant difference between them.") Racist ideologies, although they otherwise have the appearance of moral systems, in that they are compelling (to their believers) and possibly generalizable, fail to qualify as moral by this test.

Finally, moral acts *affirm or express a commitment,* rather than involve the consumption of a good or a service. Therefore, they are intrinsically motivated and not subject to means-end analysis (Dyke, 1981, p. 11). (The fact that there are non-moral acts that are intrinsically motivated does not invalidate this criterion. It only shows that the universe of such acts is larger than that of moral acts, and hence, as was already indicated, this criterion is necessary but not sufficient in itself.) As to the argument that moral acts themselves are not impulsive acts but reflect deliberations and judgments (especially evident when one must sort out what course to follow when one is subject to conflicting moral claims), these deliberations are not of the same kind as a means-end considerations; they require judgments among ends.

In purely moral situations, the means-end scheme does not apply. Moral means and ends, to the extent they can be analytically separated, are often fused in people's minds and behavior. Typically there is no room for choice behavior or comparisons of means in terms of relative efficiency. Marital commitments in our culture are symbolized by a wedding band; other items of jewelry will not do, even if they constitute much better investments. The very notion of a comparison of means in these contexts is considered, by the actors involved, to be highly inappropriate, if not "unthinkable."

Moral acts often concern intentions and processes, not outcomes. (This is not to say that outcomes do not matter, but the moral standing of an act is derived from its being in line with moral criteria. See discussion of the deontological position on pp. 11–13.) Unlike pleasure, which is a matter of achieving the desired end-state, moral commitments can be expressed by taking the proper steps (choosing the morally sanctified course) even when the sought-after result is not attained. For example, one can live up to a moral commitment when one testifies in court on behalf of a wronged party even if the person loses the trial, or when one donates blood to a relative who nevertheless dies.

To the extent that moral acts are concerned with consequences, how the consequences were attained is significant. The use of immoral means casts a dark shadow on the consequences: a stolen candle is hardly worth lighting in church; liberation achieved through a blood bath is defiled. In contrast, the pleasure obtained from a stolen apple is commensurate with that from one bought at full price (if not higher). A stolen $1,000 will buy as much as the same amount earned the hard way. In short, pleasure is a matter of consequences; moral action, on the other hand, is a matter of predisposition (or intentions), of processes, and consequences.

Some neoclassicists argue that while moral commitments may affect behavior, together with many other factors, they need not be examined separately because they are reflected in the preferences, and hence ultimately in the price; one need not study what "lurks" behind the preferences. "In the usual neoclassical formulation, a person is simply a bundle of preferences, and his moral ideals, if they enter the analysis at all, enter simply as some among his preferences—his taste for honesty being on a par with his taste for peanut butter." (McPherson, 1984, p. 243.)

In Chapter 2 (pp. 24–27) we saw that such lumping of moral factors with others hinders the study of the factors that enhance morality. We add here: moral factors affect not only the preferences but also the constraints. Well then, respond the neoclassicists, they will affect the costs, and therefore will implicitly be taken into account. However, to the extent that moral factors sanctify one pathway over all others, or heavily favor one, they must be explicitly included in one's paradigm because they make the choice in full or to a large extent, instead of merely limiting the choice; in the process they rule out options that are "preferable" from a P-utility maximization viewpoint. A case in point is the refusal of longshoremen to load ships that carried cargoes to Poland; they protested against the Polish regime's suppression of Solidarity, even though their action meant a loss of pay. This behavior might be said to be an esoteric exception which, even if not explicable by some hidden pleasure or expediency, does not matter much (Sen's avocados). However, studies of labor relations are replete with evidence of the loyalty of employees to the job, to management, and to the place of employment—and of commitments by higher-ranking personnel to those below them. Economists have frequently observed that labor "markets" do not "clear," that they do not behave as expected (Thurow, 1983, Chapter 7). Differences in the way commodities and human beings are viewed as legitimate objects of trade are a major factor accounting for this "difficulty." In short, choice-behavior in which significant subcategories of means are ruled out because they are considered immoral is common not only in families and communities but also in significant areas of economic behavior.

Much more could be added at this point about what constitutes a moral act. However, the preceding discussion may suffice to provide a suficient characterization of what these acts are for the purpose at hand.

The Relations Between Moral Commitments and Pleasure

When one contemplates the substance of the term "moral behavior," the kinds of acts the term encompasses, one finds another reason to maintain its distinctiveness: Moral acts are a source of value other than pleasure. *Indeed, many are explicitly based on the denial of pleasure in the name of the principle(s) evoked.* Doing penance, abstention from premarital sex, and Ramadan fasting are not what most people consider sources of pleasure. Indeed, moral behavior often entails some restraint of impulses, delay of gratification, or considerable effort; many pleasures are either morally neutral or prohibited under some circumstances. Thus, the typical format of many moral tenets is "Thou shalt not . . . ," the way most of the ten Commandments and numerous other religious and moral codes are formulated. And those that require affirmative acts, such as caring for senile parents or retarded children, require an effort people might well not undertake unless these acts are morally prescribed.

True, acting in line with one's moral values produces a kind of satisfaction, a sense of moral worth, but it is more the kind one achieves when a hard day's work is done than the pleasure of getting off work early with full pay. One has a sense of *affirmation*, of having done what is required, reestablished one's values, adhered to one's higher self, resisted impulses and urges, and been of virtue.

While pleasure and living up to one's moral commitments are not always or necessarily in conflict, they often compete in terms of their demand on resources (the time, energy, and assets dedicated to one are often required by the other as well—a major factor, say, in the life of parents who work outside the home). Also: quite frequently, pleasure-seeking acts and moral commitments are also incompatible in the behavior expected and rewarded (e.g., when managers are under great pressure to increase profits but also not to violate the rules of the game; the use of kickbacks or bribes to gain more business are cases in point).

Internalization: Turning Constraints Into Meta-Preferences

A most significant attribute that distinguishes moral commitments, especially of the absolute kind, from pleasurable activities, is that the values are "internalized." That is, individuals see these values as their own and not as external conditions to which they merely adapt. Internalization has been defined as part of the socialization process in which a person learns to "conform to rules in situations that arouse impulses to transgress and that *lack* surveillance and sanctions." (Kohlberg, 1968, p. 483, italics provided.) Once internalization has taken place, individuals pursue what they consider to be a moral line of behavior even in the absence of external sanctions (Hoffman, 1983. See also Meissner, 1981, p. 7). The process of socialization, in which a child becomes an autonomous person, is largely one of internalization of values, of building up self control rather than control by external forces. Hence, the behavior of properly socialized adults is deeply influenced by their absolute morality, aside from whatever expedient effects it has.

The concept of moral internalization marks a major difference between neoclassical and deontological psychologies. Neoclassical psychologies, in effect, deny that internalization of any kind takes place, moral or otherwise. They are highly environmentally driven: (1) They see people as responding to their situations (individuals will "behave" to the extent moral behavior is "expected," i.e., rewarded by social approval); (2) they see them as able to calculate these matters, and deal with them in a detached way, without value-judgments or emotional entanglements, like a Washington lobbyist figuring out which Congressional reception to attend.

In contrast, deontological psychologies assume that two kinds of behavior are possible: people may engage in expedient conformity or follow an inner sense of commitment. Most important, they will behave differently depending upon whether their choice is driven by the consideration of morality as an external constraint, or they are guided by their own inner values. Thus, the behavior of a person who feels he/she *ought* to work hard is different from that of one who feels it *pays* to work hard. The difference becomes apparent when the behavioral guidelines are not internalized: (a) when supervision is slack, if opportunities arise from shirking or faking, the persons involved will exploit these opportunities; and (b) when persons conform because of constraints, their behavior will be accompanied with resentment or alienation, feelings that are not present when the behavior is based on internalized values, holding constant the degree of pleasure or preference (Etzioni, 1975). In short *moral internalization turns constraints into preferences.* The reverse is true when moral commitments slacken; additional incentives or sanctions need to be introduced if the same level of compliance behavior is to be sustained.

Social scientists may well trace the origins of one's moral commitments to one's parents, culture, and peer or reference groups; but whatever their source, once internalized they become an integral part of the self. Thus, those who feel they ought to serve their country, God, or a cause, feel strongly—sometimes despite strong protestations from spouses, friends, and peers—that such actions are in line with their values, are their duty.

Empirical evidence that interalization takes place is seen in experimental studies of children showing that if children are mildly punished they are more likely to "behave" than if they are severely punished; studies of recidivism show a similar correlation (Dickens, 1986). There are several interpretations of these findings; the one compatible with the line followed here is that harsh punishment sponges off the guilt, while milder one leads to additional internalization of the particular value.

An example of the power of internalized values is that despite the high legitimacy that divorce attained in American society in the 1960s and 1970s, an informal survey suggests that extremely few spouses leave their husband or wife when they are afflicted with prolonged non-curable diseases, such as Alzheimer's Disease, incurable but slow cancer, severe paralysis following stroke, and so on—all diseases that are extremely taxing. The suggestion that the healthy spouse stays because of fear of social disapproval does not account for the very considerable dedication often revealed, nor does the notion that people can receive some satisfaction from being needed account for the magnitude of the suffering tolerated. It seems to reflect the strength of the moral commitment: People seem to persevere out of a strong sense that they ought to, "that it is the right thing to do" although not, by and large, an enjoyable one.

The preceding discussion draws on the concept of internalization as it has been widely used in psychoanalytical literature. It should be noted, however, that the concept has been abandoned by large segments of psychological literature as they have become neoclassical and focused on the role of environments (or constraints), playing down or ignoring the role of intra-personality processes and stuctures as well as that of values. Neoclassical psychologists argue that the evidence shows that there are no (or only very weak) personality traits (whether or not the result of internalization), because as people move from situation to situation their moral behavior changes. This is the often-cited finding of a highly influential study on why children lie (Hartshore and May, 1928, 1930). It also has been suggested that internalization is nothing but conditioning, reflecting prior rewards and punishments.

The reasons we nevertheless hold that internalization is a productive concept rest, in part, on re-examination of the data used to debunk it. The evidence actually does show that personality does make a difference in explaining why children lie. While the environment also plays a major role, personality accounted for 35 to 40 percent of the variance (Burton, 1963). This finding was replicated in subsequent studies (Nelson, Grinder, and Metterer, 1969). True, personality does not merely mirror internalized values; there are some internal developments and active responses to what is accepted. Still, all said and done, while the environment seems to account for more of the variance in behavior than personality, and while the values internalized are to some extent internally modified, internalized values have a significant impact on behavior.

As to the suggestion that internalization is merely the result of conditioning, the findings suggest that once individuals internalize guides to behavior these become *generalized* to a variety of situations beyond those in which the individual was conditioned, and are not merely a reflection of prior rewards/punishments. Further, they last well beyond what one would expect from prior conditioning.

Does all this mean that the pursuit of pleasure or self-interest is immoral? Not at all. There are significant areas within which such pursuit is judged to be legitimate, especially in economic activities. The reason why our discussion focuses on areas in which the two dimensions come into conflict is because it is in these areas that their distinct qualities stand out most clearly.

MORE THAN TWO?

The question has been raised, once the mono-utility model is abandoned, why limit the category of utilities to two? Envy, anger, achieving social dominance, conformism, novelty and xenophobia have been nominated as additions. Indeed, psychologists have made long lists of motives or needs. The point behind this challenge, advanced by neoclassicists, is that if there were a myriad "utilities" this would show the need for one supra-utility, to order all these sources of valuations; to abandon the reigning order would threaten anarchy.

In response we note, first, that utilities are not to be equated with specific needs, motives, goals, aspirations, preferences or predispositions; they are analytical categories that encompass numerous concrete manifestations. Just as the concept of a P-utility encompasses numerous specific pleasures—there is no separate utility for sports-car-pleasure and sitting-on-the-front-porch pleasure—so the moral "utility" encompasses numerous expressions. Moreover, a myriad specific needs, motives, goals, aspirations, preferences, and predispositions can be analyzed as reflecting various combinations of these two cardinal sources of valuations.

There is, however, no reason to argue that it is logically necessary, or productive, to assume that there are only two utilities (or main sources of valuation), and no others may be considered. One candidate for a third utility that has often been cited is affection. It is included in Adam Smith's theory of moral sentiments, in which he sees people as balancing their own conscience with demands of positive bonds to others.

The main question, though, is not whether one can discern a third (or fourth or fifth) utility, but whether one can keep the *number small*, to avoid over-determination, to preserve parsimony. And one must ask for *the criteria* for introducing into one's paradigm new utilities versus subsuming an observed motive, drive, or preference in one that is already a member of one's paradigm or theory.

In part, the answer is pragmatic. Utilities are not found in nature or on location in the brain; they are concepts we introduce to organize our thinking and the evidence we generate. The question is hence, in part, a matter of what "works," what is productive. For example, if we try to explain voting behavior in traditional utilitarian terms, as neoclassicists have repeatedly done, voting makes no sense because it entails efforts and yields no specific return. (A voter cannot reasonably expect to affect the outcome of the elections.) Neoclassicists deal with this "anomaly" by introducing ad hoc assumptions, suggesting that voters do "expect" to affect the elections after all, for various reasons. For example, they will turn out in larger numbers in close elections. (It turns out the correlation between turnout and closeness is weak, and hence the concept of "expected" closeness is added, which is difficult to measure. And still the correlations remain weak. Hirshleifer, 1985, p. 55.) A deontologist avoids these ad hoc additions and instead introduces another utility, expressing one's citizen's *duty*. There is a considerable correlation between the level of such a commitment and voting (Barry, 1978, p. 17; Godwin and Mitchell, 1982). One thus achieves higher predictive power, without any loss, indeed with a gain in parsimony, by introducing "citizen duty." And, the additional concept, which we shall see, often "works" elsewhere, adding to our explanatory power by bringing to mind factors the mono-utility concept tends to disregard. Thus, one criterion to be used in deciding whether or not a utility is to be added, is whether or not it *significantly* enriches our predictive and explanatory powers without overdetermination.

Another criterion is reducibility, i.e., the ability to account for a phenomenon by categories already in the theory. For example, to the extent that one can show that affection is part pleasure (enjoy your friends) and part obligation (the dictum to treat others like one's self and not as a medium of exchange), the case for introducing a new category is weakened. However, if a factor—say some emotion like hatred—could be shown not to be accountable by our knowledge of people's moral predispositions and quests for pleasure; say, if hatred drove people to do things that are both immoral and self-hurting (i.e., not pleasurable), a third category might be called for.

How can one fortell if these criteria will lead to conceptual anarchy, the result of the introduction of ever more utilities? Observing people's choices strongly suggests that while they are often subject to numerous forces, they experience them as the sum of a limited number of factors. Typically a person may feel that X would be pleasurable for two, three, or more reasons (a winter vacation in the South may be relaxing and comfortably warm) while moral considerations may include conflicting obligations to spouse, children, and even the community. Nevertheless, people's thinking and behavior reveals that *they* reduce these numerous forces to a small number in their considerations. Most people most times feel torn in just two or three ways; those that feel torn in upteen ways are considered mentally ill. These summary feelings can guide us in developing a theory of *utilities*.

No attempt is made here to formulate a list of utilities. Suffice it to establish that a multiple but small number is preferable to one, and to a larger list, and to indicate the ways such a list may be generated. For the balance of the discussion we have our hands full shoring up the distinction between the pleasure utility and the affirmation of moral commitments.

4

Some Evidence:
People Act Unselfishly

Now that we have explored what a moral act is, how common and significant are they, especially in economic behavior? At first one may wonder
"why document the obvious?" After all, does anyone really doubt that a
significant part of people's conduct expresses moral commitments? But
the fact is that neoclassicists have labored long and hard to show that
practically all behavior is driven by pleasure and self-interest. Altruistic
acts are accounted for as "really" being efforts to enhance one's reputation, gain social approval, and so on. To dismiss the role of moral factors,
several economists have extensively discussed even trivial behavior, such
as the observation that when on a trip out of town even neoclassicists
leave tips at restaurants they do not expect to ever revisit (Roberts, 1986;
Frank, 1987). The "reduction" and debunking of moral behavior is not
limited to neoclassical economists. It is a theme shared by a number of
major psychological theories (Wallach and Wallach, 1983). The neoclassicists follow a long tradition: When Thomas Hobbes was asked why he
contributed to a beggar, and was this not due to Christ's commandment,
he responded that he did so "with the sole intent of relieving his own
misery at the sight of the beggar." (Losco, 1986, p. 323.)

To the extent that the neoclassical paradigm has a place for authentic
altruism at all, it is said to be very limited in scope and hence one may
ignore it. "What is odd ... is the desire to derive everything from self-
interest as if that were a natural or necessary starting point. It is a peculiar feature of the sociology of the present-day economics profession that
this odd ambition should be so prevalent." (McPherson, 1984, pp. 77–
78.) "Exchange" sociologists, Public Choice political scientists, and New
Institutionalist historians also have taken up the same "odd" cause. Indeed, such efforts to explain away altruism have been advanced since the
ancient Greeks, since the Sophists. It seems each generation must answer
this challenge *de novo*.

To do our duty, we cite next several kinds of evidence (including experimental results, public opinion polls, economic data, and qualitative incidents) that suggest that many people often act on behalf of a moral "utility,"* and not merely to gain more consumption or pleasure, both in private and in public choices.

Many of the studies focus on what might be called authentic altruism, on instances in which the only and unmistakable motive is the concern and caring for others. However, from the viewpoint advanced here of the I&We, of codetermination, suffice it to show that moral commitments (which take many forms other than altruism) are operative, whether or not they are "mixed" in with other motives. Thus, persons who make donations to charity may act to enhance their reputation and their self-esteem, *and* also because it is the right thing to do. Why does it matter? Because those who do it in part out of moral commitment will behave differently from those who do it purely out of self-interest. For instance, all other things being equal, they will be inclined to make greater sacrifices, because they have more motivation; and they are more likely to continue in the face of opposition, because they internalized the values that justify their actions.

SOME EVIDENCE IN PRIVATE CHOICES

Incidents of Altruism

A considerable body of experimental data supports the existence of significant amounts of altruistic behavior. Several experiments show that many people mail back "lost" wallets to strangers, cash intact (Hornstein, Fisch and Holmes, 1968). In another study, 64 percent of the subjects who had an opportunity to return a lost contribution to an "Institute for Research in Medicine" did so (Hornstein et. al., 1971, p. 110; Hornstein, 1976, pp. 95–96). The costs are forgoing the found cash, as well as paying for postage, and going to the trouble of mailing the contribution. The reward? Chiefly, the inner sense of having done what is right.

In some situations, many individuals who see others in distress rush to help them without calculating the consequences for themselves when they feel responsible, as mothers do for their chidren when their houses are on fire (Janis and Mann, 1977, p. 27). In a set of experiments designed to study "costly self-sacrificing" behavior, people were asked whether they would contribute bone marrow for strangers (Schwartz, 1970a, p. 283). Of those asked, 59 percent said they would donate; an additional 24 percent indicated at least a 50/50 chance that they would if called upon; 12 percent indicated a less than even chance that they would make

---

*Two economists used the term "moral utility" in their study of investments influenced by social considerations (e.g., not investing in South Africa). See Barth and Cordes (1981), p. 235.

such a contribution; only 5 percent said they would refuse outright (ibid., p. 289).

Neoclassicists argue that studies of attitudes, of the kind where people are asked if they would make a contribution, do not provide firm predictions of behavior. This is generally a valid criticism. However, studies of altruistic *behavior* reach the same conclusion. Latane and Darley (1970) sent researchers requesting help into, of all places, the streets of New York City. High proportions of people who were approached for aid did assist individuals who they thought were in distress in a variety of ways. For example, an investigator who repeatedly fell down as drunk elicited help from passers by in 70 percent of the episodes (Piliavin, Rodin, and Piliavin, 1969). (For additional evidence and review of several of the studies cited, see Rushton, 1980, and Derlega and Grzelak, 1982.) People do things for the sake of others that they do not do for themselves. An older woman refused surgery to save her vision, until reminded of the effect her blindness would have on her children (Wallach and Wallach, 1983, p. 4).

In many situations (Wells, 1970, p. 47), gifts are not given to elicit reciprocal gifts nor adjusted "in terms of marginal utilities to the recipients," but to express a family commitment or bond (Cheal, 1984, p. 1; Cheal, 1985). Although cash is the most efficient gift, it is often tabooed. When cash is given (rather than an object), it is because this is defined, as proper by the values of the group(s).

Those who find the evidence cited so far less than overpowering might consider more compelling the fact that people who donate kidneys to their siblings or offspring do so because they feel responsible, that they "ought to." Indeed, throughout history we find people who risk their life for others and for causes, from a few Christians who saved Jews in Nazi Germany to thousands of freedom riders in the South (on behalf of civil rights).

A Factor in Economic Behavior

Neoclassicists may argue that the examples cited concern mainly social behavior. However, evidence shows that commitments to moral values also affect economic activities. Consider saving behavior. Neoclassical economists explain the level of saving mainly by the size of one's income (the higher one's income the more one saves), by the desire to provide for consumption in retirement, and by the level of interest rates. However, these factors explain only part of the variance in the amount saved. There are at least three moral values that also affect the amount saved: the extent to which one believes that it is immoral to be in debt; that one ought to save (for its own sake) and in order not to be dependent on the government or one's children; and that one ought to help one's children "start off in life." These moral commitments are affected in turn by the content and level of morality in society, by the values of one's subculture (for example, these pro-saving values seem stronger in small towns than in the big cities), and by other non-economic factors.

Economists have found that people save much more than can be explained by the desire to ensure their consumption after retirement. "At no age above sixty-five are Americans on average dis-saving." (Thurow, 1983, p. 221.) Attempts have been made to explain this "excessive" saving by the need to hedge the "risk" that one will live longer than expected, but this still leaves a sizable unaccounted "surplus." This, in turn, is explained by older people's enjoying the consumption of their offspring "extending through several generations" according to one economist, (Shorrocks, 1979, p. 416), and the "consumption of their [household's] descendants in all future generations," according to another (Laitner, 1979, p. 403). This seems an excessive attempt to stretch the consumption function; it is rather difficult to visualize how one can *enjoy* the consumption of the yet-to-be conceived offspring of one's offspring. It seems more plausible to assume that people have a moral commitment to help their children.

A neoclassicist suggested that the issue here is just semantic: neoclassicists say people enjoy the consumptions of their grandchildren, deontologists suggest that the same behavior reflects a moral commitment. However, the different concepts lead to different predictions. We saw already that those who rely on the pleasure principle (or P-utility) have a hard time explaining saving at all; it entails deferment of gratification, an act that is not pleasurable. And they must add odd assumptions in order to explain various levels of savings, e.g., that there is a fixed amount of total human desire to consume, which the more satiated it is—as income grows—the more people save. This leads to the prediction that the higher people's income, the more they will save, which is often not the case. Americans, for example, who have long enjoyed one of the highest income levels in the world, save comparatively little. If the position advanced here is correct, people in the same income group will save more the more these people are committed to certain values, for example, those associated with a conservative world-view.

In other societal contexts moral commitments may curb savings rather than enhance it, though of course they will still affect economic behavior. Kunkel (1970), p. 163) points out that in many historical societies saving was possible only if one was sufficiently withdrawn from kinship and tribal obligations to be able to accumulate any surplus. The same might be said about many first-generation immigrants to the United States.

Similarly, whether or not one considers buying on credit to be morally proper is a major factor in determining a nation's saving level. Longman (1985) shows how the fear of a new depression after World War II led to a concerted campaign to change the concept of thrift from a virtue into a vice. Soon, consumer debt (excluding real estate loans) increased from

$27.4 billion in 1952 to $190 billion in 1974 (Galbraith, 1984, p. 148).
Also, changes in public morality and perceptions made politically possible the increase in public debt, and persistent and growing trade and
budget deficits. True, other factors were also at work; for example,
changes in the banking system. However, it seems quite evident that
changes in moral values (and the resulting changes in legitimation) facil-
itated the changes in the banking system.

Phelps (1975, p. 5) notes that in the same world in which people sell
unsafe products, gouge, and short-weigh, one also finds "the prevalence
of altruistic behavior: a producer may advertise his product truthfully
when he need not, a labor union may refrain from breaking the law when
it could do so for a net gain, . . . a benevolent butcher may abstain from
short-weighing." Arrow (1975) goes a step further to argue that since it is
impossible to generate enough reinforcement agents and incentives for
many elements of the implicit and explicit social contracts that sustain
the market (e.g., trust in money), the whole economic system would break
down if it were not for these not-self-enforcing arrangements, i.e., those
based on government or morality.

The utilitarian (of the pro-pleasure variety) and methodological (need
for one common denominator) pressures, and the disregard of the role
of values, evident in the neoclassical economic theory concerning individual choices, are also very much in evidence in the theory of the firm.
Here, the concept of "profit" instead of pleasure is applied as the single
over-arching goal. Neoclassical writings often read as if the firm is nothing but an oversized individual who seeks to maximize the utility of his
or her investments, as if the firm embodies the entrepreneur or "the
owner."

Large amounts of research have shown that firms do not pursue one
over-arching goal, but that they have mixed goals; they do not maximize
any one utility, and are internally divided rather than acting in unison
(Herendeen and Schechter, 1977, p. 1514; Bailey and Boyle, 1977, p. 50;
Monsen, Chieu, and Cooley, 1968, p. 442). Among the goals that compel
executives are those prescribed as morally appropriate by their peers,
communities, and society as a whole. These are rarely limited to maximizing profit (Donaldson and Lorsch, 1983).

Many neoclassical economists acknowledge all this but continue to
hold to the mono-utility assumption. A common reason given for their
tenacity is that the orthodox theory of the firm is a powerful heuristic
device, and that they are not concerned with actual firms but with a theoretical concept that links inputs and outputs (Machlup, 1967, p. 9). A
multigoal and conflict-acknowledging model of the firm is more compatible with the bi- (or multiple) utility conception and the I&We paradigm.
Cyert and March (1963) and Pfeffer (1981), among others, provide solid
foundations for constructing such a model.

EVIDENCE IN PUBLIC CHOICES

Civility: Commitment to the Commons

The mono-utility conception is particularly strained when it is extended to encompass "public goods" and activities on behalf of the collectivity. "Public goods" is a term introduced by Samuelson, to refer to those goods that can be "used by many persons at the same time without reducing the amount available for any other person." (Alchian and Allen, 1983, p. 99.) Price mechanisms cannot work here to allocate resources rationally or to ensure "sufficient" supply, efficient production, or general welfare (Arrow, 1974). These "goods" include much of a society's culture, heritage, national defense, and environment protection, as well as pivotal economic elements such as major segments of scientific knowledge and of the nation's infrastructure. "Activities on behalf of the collectivity" refers to acts such as voting and doing voluntary work that serve shared needs.

Government coercion and inducements are a major method used to ensure attention to, and resources for, these public needs. Another major method, particularly important in view of the widespread recognition of the inefficiency and threats to freedom that emanate from excessive reliance on the government, is to build on moral commitments. Civility, the individual's moral commitment to shared concerns, is the concept used to refer to this factor that leads people to contribute to the commons (for additional discussion of the concept, see Benn and Gaus, 1983; Etzioni, 1983, pp. 56 ff.; and Janowitz, 1983). With the concept introduced at home, cultivated in schools, fostered by the news media, enhanced by voluntary associations and extolled from Presidential and other civic leaders' "pulpits," citizens of a nation feel obliged to contribute to the well-being of the community they share.

There is no question that civility exists; at issue is how encompassing and potent it is, and what accounts for whatever level of civility is found in various societies, and in groups within societies, at different points in time. Is it explainable in terms of a P-utility, or does it point to the force of moral commitments?

The Public Choice Positions

The neoclassical paradigm, we have seen, attempts to show not merely that there is an element of pleasure (or self-interest) in all seemingly altruistic behavior, but that self-interest can explain it all. In his 1986 presidential address to the Public Choice Society, Mueller (1986, p. 18) stated: "And, I submit, the only assumption essential to a descriptive and predic-

tive science of human behavior is egoism." When it is applied to the public realm, especially by the Public Choice school, its main thesis is that
collective action can be explained as nothing but the result of individuals
seeking to maximize their utility (Downs, 1957; Buchanan and Tullock,
1965; Riker and Ordeshook, 1968; Mueller, 1979), or their wealth (Barzel
and Silberberg, 1973, p. 51).

While there are differences among the members of the school,
Buchanan's work is typical. He received the 1986 Nobel prize in economics for his leading role in forming and advancing Public Choice. Buchanan views government decisions (for example, the level of spending
or deficits) as reflecting directly the personal, narrow self-interest "costs"
and rewards of politicians. For instance, Buchanan explains the level of
deficits by the fact that politicians find voters much more willing to
reelect them if the politicians increase spending for projects in their dis-
trict, and less so if they raise taxes or cut spending.

Downs, an early advocate of this line of analysis (1957, p. 28), writes:

> The politicians in our model never seek office as a means of carrying
> out particular policies; their only goal is to reap the rewards of holding
> office per se.

Tullock (1974, pp. 46, 140) argues that revolutionaries are *solely* motivated
by a desire for a good job in the new regime.

The specific propositions advanced by various members of the Public
Choice school follow:

(1). Individuals will not allot resources to public goods (unless "side
payments" can be provided to reward them individually for such investments). For example, because in most elections a voter cannot reasonably
expect that casting a vote will make a difference in his or her own life,
people are expected not to vote (Foster, 1984, p. 678). The advocates of
this approach point in support of their proposition to the "large number" of people who do not vote (Barzel and Silberberg, 1973, p. 53).

(2). People are expected to free ride whenever they can get away with
it. That is, they are expected to let others pay for a public good since
they can use it even when they do not pay for it. For instance, individuals
are expected not to contribute to public TV.

(3). People are expected to be more inclined to free ride in large
groups than in small ones, because here it is more difficult to tie efforts
to rewards ("shirking" is said to be easier). Members of a large group will
not contribute to activities on behalf of the collectivity unless coerced or
"unless some separate incentive, distinct from the achievement of the
common or group interest, is offered to the members of the group individually." (Olson, 1965, p. 2.) While Olson, to some extent, changed his
position subsequently, many others have continued to uphold the thesis
and seek evidence on its behalf.

(4). A less widely shared proposition is that individuals will not cooperate, even when this is in their interest, out of fear that they will "miss out" when they seek to cooperate if others will not reciprocate, a situation commonly referred to as the Prisoner's Dilemma. "When we all stand on our tiptoes to get a better view of the game, we see no more than if we all sat down, yet each of us would be rational to sit down only in those special cases where our example would lead the rest to sit down too." (Olson, 1984.)

(5). A thesis shared by several members of the Public Choice school and several other neoclassical economists is that individuals will lie, cheat, and violate other moral precepts and laws whenever they expect they can get away with it or when the penalty will be smaller than the gain. Williamson argues that rational actors who pursue self-interest are expected to act opportunistically, which often entails acting immorally. For example, those "who are skilled at dissembling realize transactional advantages. Economic man, assessed with respect to his transactional characteristics, is thus a more subtle and devious creature than the usual self-interest seeking assumption reveals." (1975, p. 255.) Becker (1976) explains the virtues of a person faking ("simulating") altruism, because then he can benefit from the altruism of others without contributing his share. Simulating is said to be limited mainly by the "transaction costs" of faking and the difficulty in being a completely successful faker (1976, p. 13).

Strong Counter-Evidence

The evidence runs strongly the other way: millions of people vote, support public TV, contribute to large groups without side payment, do not free ride, cooperate, and so on. No attempt is made here to review the evidence once more; it suffices to cite the conclusions of some of those who recently surveyed the field, and some illustrative evidence relevant to the present concern about the role of moral commitments. Margolis (1982, p. 1) refers to a "catastrophic" failure of the Public Choice model and its inability to account for the elementary fact that people vote, and do "not always cheat when no one is looking." (Ibid., p. 3.) No society could survive if its members were to free ride the way the model predicts (ibid).

A Harvard and a MIT economist, who reviewed the data about the behavior of politicians, concluded: "We find that approaches which confine themselves to a view of political actors as narrowly egocentric maximizers explain and predict legislative outcomes poorly." (Kalt and Zupan, 1984, p. 279.) A reviewer who examined the data base of Public Choice provides an odd compliment; in the process, he stands the Friedman thesis on its head: Public Choice, he writes, does not predict—but does "explain:" "Although existing theories [of rational actors as political participants] suffer from the deficiency of predicting behavior counter to that empirically observed, they do provide a means for basing an explanation of political action upon a theory of human motivation." (Uhlaner, 1986, pp. 551–52.) Never mind the facts; full speed ahead. Needless to say, this is not a widely held view of the role of theory.

The Olson reference to people's behavior at football games illustrates a point opposite to his own: Most people at most games most times do not stand up, and when they do, most times they heed a call to "sit down." The reasons are precisely those the Public Choice school ignores: Most people, at least in most American spectator sports, have internalized a set of values that define it as inappropriate to stand and to disregard a request to sit down.

Free Ride?

A large number of experiments, under different conditions, most of them highly unfavorable to civility, show that people do not take free rides, but pay voluntarily as much as 40 percent to 60 percent of what economists figured is due to the public till if the person was not to free ride at all. The main reason: the subjects consider it the "right" or "fair" thing to do. (For an article about these experiments, as well as a report of their own, see Marwell and Ames, 1981, pp. 295–310.)

An overview of the available evidence concludes: "The logic of the problem of collective action [as captured in the Public Choice school] is both compelling and illuminating. The problem with this logic, however, is that empirical evidence for its ability to predict actual behavior is either scant or nonexistent. The fact seems to be that under the conditions described by the theory as leading to free riding, people often cooperate instead." (Marwell, 1982, p. 208.) And, "in over 13 experiments we have found that subjects persist in investing substantial proportions of their resources in public goods despite conditions specifically designed to maximize the impact of free riding and thus minimize investment. The prevalence of such economically 'illogical' behavior was replicated over and over again. Nor do other experiments find their subjects behaving much differently (e.g., Bohm, 1972; Brubaker, 1975; Schneider and Pommerahne, 1979)." (Ibid., p. 210.)

Actually the findings of experiments conducted by Marwell and Ames are stronger than the preceding summary suggests. To support this point a pivotal feature of the experiments must be explained. The researchers allowed their subjects to choose whether to invest their resources either individually or in a group pot. In the first pot, the yield was independent of the action of other group members. In the group pot, individuals received a return based on a pre-set formula with the results depending on the actions of others. The formula was such that only if all invested in the group pot would each individual member come out ahead. However, an individual would do best by investing in the individual pot while everyone else invested in the group pot (Marwell and Ames, 1981, p. 297). Under these particular circumstances, the free ride proposition would lead one to expect no voluntary investments in the group pot. This expectation was confirmed by 5 out of 6 economists who reviewed the experiment's design. This version of the free ride hypothesis was completely rejected; in all the groups studied, investment in the group pot significantly exceeded the expectation. Hence, the research focused on the question why on average "only" 47% of the available resources were invested in the group pot. But there is no reason to expect that people will dedicate 100% of their resources to collective action. The question was studied largely because, working from the opposite assumption that people will invest nothing in the group pot (because no side payments are available), there was nothing to study: no subject behaved that way. (For one study that found that people's cooperative behavior does not persist, see Isaac, McCue, and Plott, 1985. The study, however, cites five other studies that point to the opposite conclusion [ibid., p. 69].)

Another series of experiments was specifically designed to show that egoistic incentives (reputation, reciprocity) are not necessary to create cooperation and altruism. Subjects made donations anonymously and side payments were explicitly ruled out. Pro-social behavior was common, and the sense of commitment was *easily* elicited, often in a 10-minute discussion (Dawes, Orbell, Kragt, unpublished, 1983; and see also Dawes, et. al., 1986). (For further discussion of altruism without "reinforcement," i.e., without reward or penalty, see Kahneman, Knetsch, Thaler, 1986. For additional discussion of "pro social" behavior and cooperation see Collard, 1978, and Derlega and Grzelak, 1982.)

Cooperative Prisoners

Prisoner's Dilemma experiments are similar to experiments that study free riding in that they too cast light on Public Choice: Will the quest of each individual to maximize his or her outcome lead to a beneficial *shared* outcome? They differ, however, in terms of the specific issue. The question is not whether to contribute to a public good without a pay-off, but how best to advance self-interest: Should one strike out on one's own, or take a risk for a potentially better outcome, following the cooperative route?

This question generated a sizable industry of over 1,000 studies. They vary greatly in design, details, and findings. Without going into the very numerous variations of experimental conditions and procedures it suffices to note here that *under most circumstances a significant proportion of the subjects do cooperate* without being coerced or paid. This is especially noteworthy because in most experiments the players are recruited as individuals, and are not tied by any group relationship or loyalty—not even the kind that exists in very large groups, let alone specific sets of values shared by those who regularly work together. They are like a bunch of individuals who pass each other in a railroad station for the first time. Moreover, very often extreme limits are set on the subjects' ability to communicate with one another: they are separated by partitions, and not allowed to communicate at all or only in some highly constrained manner (Rapoport, 1985, p. 148). And still, *many do cooperate.*

The proportion cooperating differs according to numerous details, especially by how many times the experiment is repeated with the same subjects. It seems that not being allowed to communicate, the subjects use the first runs to signal their willingness to cooperate, somewhat like bridge players use their opening bids to signal their partners. A not atypical finding runs as follows: "On the first trial, the proportion of cooperative choices is typically slightly greater than ½, but it is followed by a rapid decline in cooperation. After approximately 30 repetitions, cooperative choices begin to increase in frequency . . . , usually reaching a proportion in excess of 60 percent by trial 300." (Coleman, 1982, p. 116.) Some report still higher levels of cooperation: Lave (1962) found that 80 percent or more cooperated or tried to cooperate; others found lower levels, although these studies tend to deal with computer simulations and not actual experiments (Axelrod, 1984). However, no matter which way one interprets the findings, significant cooperation occurs despite highly unfavorable circumstances, and the Public Choice theory cannot account for it.

Other Evidence

Studies of voting behavior have attracted the attention of the Public Choice school, because among other reasons it involves a large number of individuals and hence readily yields to statistical and mathematical manipulations, unlike much other public behavior (from negotiation between the White House and Congress to rulings by the Supreme Court). An overview of the findings of Public Choice studies of voting compares the role of ideals and sentiments to that of self-interest. It concludes: "In general, symbolic attributes (liberalism-conservatism, party identification, and racial prejudice) had strong effects, while self-interest had almost none." (Sears, et al. 1980, p. 679.) Among the reasons people vote are their need to express their approval of the political system, their identification with their candidate and/or party, to be part of the event, and to express their moral commitments to the commons, their civility.

Various attempts have been made by Public Choice defenders to shore up their theory in view of such overwhelming empirical challenges. One attempt, that illustrates well the strained effort of many others, is the Public Choice argument that if people do vote, it must be because the election is close, or because voters, believing it to be so, feel their individual vote may make a difference. However, while there is a rather weak correlation between voter turnout and the closeness of an election, close-ness does not explain most of the variance (Hirschleifer, 1985). Obvi-ously, to all who care to note, millions vote whether or not the election is close. *The* explanatory and predicting factor seems to be a moral com-mitment, namely the intensity of their civility or sense of "citizen duty." As the following table shows, closeness of the election accounted for at most 9% of the difference, usually less; civility accounted for 30%–40% or more.

| | "Citizen Duty" Score | | | | | |
| | HIGH | | MEDIUM | | LOW | |
Expected closeness of election result	High P.D.*	Low P.D.	High P.D.	Low P.D.	High P.D.	Low P.D.
Close	91%	83%	85%	71%	65%	44%
Not close	86%	74%	77%	71%	62%	39%

SOURCE: Brian Barry, *Sociologists, Economists and Democracy*, The University of Chicago Press, 1978, p. 17. © 1978 by The University of Chicago. All rights reserved.

*P.D. = party differential, i.e., how much difference the respondent thought it made which side won.

Another problem for Public Choice: Even if people contribute to pub-lic goods for some selfish reasons, according to the theory they should contribute *less* the *more* others contribute. The opposite is typically the case—when the moral climate is favorable, many contribute more, and vice versa (Sundquist, 1985).

Attempts to defend the Public Choice school against a barrage of criti-cism draw on the I-Utility concept (see above, pp. 25–29). It is argued that whatever moral commitments motivate people, they are part of their util-ity. Downs introduces *deus ex machina*, a desire to preserve democracy (1957, pp. 266–71). Riker and Ordeshook (1968) simply add a "D" to the person utility, and operationalize it is a citizen's duty. The criticisms already made against this approach apply here. Thus, to state that politi-cians will serve their public either out of self-interest or out of sense of duty, but that there is no difference since they draw personal satisfaction out of doing their duty, turns an interesting if erroneous proposition (that they act only out of self-interest) into a useless tautology. As McPher-son put it: The Public Choice arguments "are balanced awkwardly be-tween tautology and falsehood." (1984, p. 77.)

Buchanan calls for a constitutional amendment to balance the budget as a way to curb self-seeking politicians, who cynically cater to voters who have nothing on their mind other than their own self-interest. But who is to pass such a constitutional amendment if not politicians and/or vot-ers? And why would they tie their own hands for the future and hurt their own pocketbook if they have no sense of public responsibility? Similarly,

Buchanan argues that deficits rose as the moral climate deteriorated after World War II (as liberalism spread, he elaborates). But his theory has no room for such a concept. The fact that he resorts to it as a central factor in his accounting of public affairs is one more indication, if one is needed, that a theory without a major moral category is woefully deficient.

In short, Public Choice is but an extreme example of a neoclassical theory that finds little support in the facts, and is widely contradicted, precisely because it does not tolerate moral factors as a significant, distinct, explanatory, and predicting factor.

CODETERMINATION AND INTERACTION EFFECTS

The Basic Position of Socio-Economics

The position advanced here is *not* the opposite of the Public Choice or the neoclassical position. The I&We paradigm does *not* hold that people simply internalize their society's moral code and follow it, impervious to their own self-interest, or allow it to be defined by the values of their society. The position is (1) that individuals are, simultaneously, under the influence of two major sets of factors—their pleasure, and their moral duty (although both reflect socialization); (2) that there are important differences in the extent each of these sets of factors is operative under different historical and societal conditions, and within different personalities under the same conditions. Hence, a study of the dynamics of the forces that shape both kinds of factors and their relative strengths is an essential foundation for a valid theory of behavior and society, including economic behavior, a theory referred to as socio-economics.

The moderate deontological, socio-economic codetermination concept is advanced as an alternative hypothesis to the reductionism of neoclassical economists, to the notion that people act morally only as long as it makes sense in economic terms: "Economic theory . . . tends to suggest that people are honest only to the extent that they have economic incentives for being so." (Johansen cited by Sen, 1977, p. 332; see also Cloniger, 1982.) Tobin has suggested that attitudes largely reflect objective economic realities (1972, p. 55). These statements conflict with much readily observable behavior. After all, most men and women refrain from part-time prostitution on the sly not because the pay is poor, the hours long, information on how to proceed is missing, the return on capital outlays is unattractive, or large capitalization or extensive R&D is required.

Once one recognizes that it is productive to treat moral commitments as a factor separate from the quest for pleasure, the next step is to ask what the relationship is between these two factors. It seems that *while both affect behavior, they also affect one another*. And these *effects flow both ways,* rather than moral factors only affecting economic factors or vice versa. While the relative weight of these two core factors, and the size of their interaction effects, is expected to vary under different conditions, in general *each factor is only partially shaped by the other;* that is, each factor has a considerable measure of autonomy. The following chart summarizes these statements:

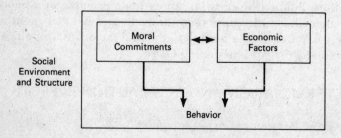

Studies of Codeterminations

A particularly illuminating study by Grasmick and Green (1981) deals with the role of deterrence (by use of punishment, i.e., cost) and of moral commitments in curbing crime. Respondents were asked if they committed various criminal and immoral acts in the past and if they thought they would do so in the future. Next they were asked to "estimate the chances *you* would be arrested by the police if *you* did each of these things." The question was worded as such because the authors believed that "to be consistent with the utilitarian perspective, measures of perceived *certainty* of punishment must be from the viewpoint of the respondent." (1981, p. 3.) Next, respondents were asked "how big a problem that punishment would create for your life," in order to account for the fact that the same penalty has different effects on different people. To measure moral commitment, verbal responses revealing the participants' attitudes toward a series of criminal acts were used; similar measures have been used in previous research (Grasmick and Green, 1981, p. 5). People were asked to rank the acts in terms of how wrong they considered them to be (never, seldom, sometimes, usually, and always). The result was that all three independent variables correlated, significantly. That is, *both deterrence and moral commitments affected the predisposition to commit a crime or to violate a moral value.*

The independent effects of values and prices were examined in energy studies. Sudden large increases in prices encouraged people to consume less energy. The effects of less drastic changes, in prices or other pecuniary incentives, such as tax credits for weatherization, were found to be more ambiguous. At the same time, values, such as the commitment to help others, had a significant impact (Stern, 1984, p. 72).

Bivariate Correlations Among All Composite Variables (N = 390)*

Variable	Certain	Severe	Moral	Violation P
Perceived Certainty of Arrest (CERTAIN)	—			
Perceived Severity of Punishment (SEVERE)	.31	—		
Moral Commitment (MORAL)	.21	.28	—	
Self-reported Past Violation (VIOLATION-P)	−.34	−.27	−.42	—
Estimated Future Violation (VIOLATION-F)	−.24	−.30	−.55	.71

*All correlations are significant beyond the .001 level.

SOURCE: Harold Grasmick and Donald Green, "Deterrence and the Morally Committed," *Sociological Quarterly*, Vol. 22, No. 1, p. 6.

The combined role of information and values was studied in a four-year field experiment with time-of-day pricing of residential electricity in Wisconsin. Individuals were experimentally assigned to a variety of electricity rate structures. Those individuals who believed that lowered demand in peak periods would be good for the community, for example, by allowing utilities to shut down inefficient and polluting power plants, and who also believed that households as a group could make a big difference in peak demand, felt a moral obligation to lower electricity use in peak periods (Black, 1978).

People who felt an obligation to change their behavior had lower electric bills than people who felt no moral obligation, but who were charged the same electricity rates. The effect of the obligation was greater than that of price differentials between peak and off-peak hours, even when these were as high as 8 to 1 (Heberlein and Warriner, 1983). Especially relevant to the issue at hand is a three-way path analysis run by Heberlein and Warriner. The first two simply correlated price ratio (peak to off-peak) to on-peak electricity use, and intensity of moral obligation and use, and found the "independent direct effects of both price and commitment." (Ibid., p. 123.) However, the authors felt that "still, level of commitment may be due in part to the price for on-peak electricity. If this were the case, a theory of moral attitudes and behavior may be simply subsumed by economic theory. . . ." To exclude this possibility a third-path analysis combined both factors in one model with price causally prior to commitment. They found that the influence of price on commitment was small, accounting for less than one percent of the variance, and statistically not significant (ibid., p. 124).

Another study correlates both income and social/moral attitudes with tax compliance (as measured by the propensity to evade paying taxes that are due). It found that income correlated somewhat more strongly with compliance than did moral attitudes, but only after the study lumped income from all sources together while separating alienation (a sense of rejection of the governing regime, policies, or values) into six factors. Even given this procedure, the correlation of compliance with income level was 0.3560, while that with "general" alienation was 0.3024, followed by a correlation with distrust of 0.2955, with suspicion ("others cheat") of 0.2788, and so on (Song and Yarborough, 1978, p. 447). Disregarding the question of relative strength, clearly both economic and moral attitudes are at work. Both seem to account for significant chunks of the variance, and not merely reflect one another.

5

The Irreducibility
of Moral Behavior

Examination of behavior shows that individuals who seek to live up to their moral commitments behave in a manner that is systematically and significantly different from those who act to enhance their pleasures. This chapter spells out these differences. True, behavior is often codetermined, reflecting both utilities. Hence a technically precise formulation is: People systematically and significantly behave differently to the extent that their behavior is motivated by moral commitments rather than pleasure. This distinctness of moral commitments was noted by one of the major utilitarian philosophers, John Stuart Mill, although he referred to them as "social." He wrote: "certain social utilities . . . are vastly more important and therefore more absolute and imperative than any others are as a class . . ." and these utilities are "guarded by a sentiment not only different in degree but in kind." (Cited by Nisbet, 1981, p. 42.)

Aside from documenting the differences in behavior, this chapter also supports the thesis introduced earlier that it is productive to view choices as multi-staged, multi-level events, in which moral and pleasure considerations are combined in complex manners. And the evidence strengthens the view that it is not productive to consider moral commitments as just one more source of consumer preferences, by suggesting that moral commitments are best viewed as a significant and "irreducible" category. Furthermore, the evidence suggests that objects subject to moral commitments and those that are sources of pleasure cannot be "exchanged" in the same way that various objects of consumption can be traded among one another, and that such exchanges, to the extent that they do occur, are poorly conceptualized by market models. Finally, we shall see that people seek a *balance* between their moral commitments and their pleasures (a judicious "mix"), rather than seeking to "maximize" either.

As we indicate from the onset, this work is one of paradigm development and theory building. Evidence presented is illustrative, not conclusive. The phrase "is expected" is used in the following discussion to remind the reader that the statements are hypotheses rather than conclusive statements.

TENACITY, LEARNING, AND TRANSACTION COSTS

The more individuals act under the influence of moral commitments, the more they are expected to persevere (when circumstances change). Conversely, the more individuals heed their pleasure or self-interest, e.g., by calculating costs and benefits, the less likely they are to persevere. As a result, moral commitments are expected to "stretch out" the learning curve and to increase transaction costs when changes favored by economic rationality are inconsistent with moral commitments.

The learning curve records the time lapse and the costs involved in improving performance. It reflects the fact that, unlike the assumption that earlier economists relied upon, and some still do, people who are provided with information do not absorb it instantaneously. The more sharply sloping the curve, the lower the learning costs; the more stretched out, the higher. The level of the learning costs, the shape of the curve, is determined in part by non-moral factors (for example, the complexity of the information to be absorbed). However, assuming all these factors are equal, it is expected that learning will be slower and more costly the higher the moral objections to what is being taught. A re-analysis of the Coleman data on American schools suggests that student performance is affected by how *legitimate* (i.e., morally appropriate) they consider the homework assigned to them, and how *fair* they feel are their teacher evaluations of their efforts (Etzioni, 1984b, p. 26).

The concept of "transaction costs" has been introduced by economists to help explain "stickiness," the fact that people do not modify their behavior even when such modifications are advantageous to them, if the costs of modification exceed the expected gain. Among the factors that affect the level of transaction costs are moral commitments. For instance, the stronger the moral commitment, the higher the return needed before the individuals involved will violate their implicit contracts in the face of the changed economic circumstances that favor such a violation, and they will absorb more of an economic loss in order to live up to their obligations. For example, it is considered "improper" for professors to accept an offer from another university in May to start teaching in September (because it is difficult to replace faculty so late in the academic year). This sense of propriety is said to be stronger in some universities (Ivy League?) than in others (Red Brick?). Hence, it is expected that it would take a larger salary differential to move a professor from the first kind of university than from the second kind, in May. That is, moral behavior is "stickier" than a-moral behavior.

Moral commitments reduce what economists call "moral hazards" (for definition, see Chapter 14, pp. 239–40). Specifically, *the stronger the moral underwriting of implicit contracts, the lower the transaction costs, resulting in less of a need to buy hedge protection* (in case resources are not delivered, or workers quit, and so on) *and to spend resources on legal action* (such as drafting explicit contracts, and litigation to enforce them). While reference here is to specific situations, for example to differences between those industries where one can ("usually") rely on one's word versus those where such reliance is less assured, the same point has been made about whole societies. It is common to note that because it is not possible to provide enough police, accountants, and inspectors to verify more than a small segment of all the transactions that take place, economies and societies require that most of the transactions be based on voluntary compliance. This, in turn, is significantly affected by the relative *level* of morality within a given society (or subsociety) in a given historical period. For example, when corruption in a society is high, it acts as a major drag on economic performance.

Unusually high resistance to change (unexpected low elasticity) is another indicator of the tenacity caused by moral commitments. This can be seen even in such daily activities as shopping. For instance, consumer demand for a given brand of coffee is typically quite elastic; however, when instant coffee was first introduced it was deemed "inappropriate;" serving it was considered a "lazy" way of treating one's spouse or guest. It required larger-than-usual promotion costs (an empirical measure of the resistance) to gain approval for instant coffee. (It still does not have complete approval.) For the same reasons, those who introduced cake mixes found it advisable to offer mixes that leave homemakers a step or two, say adding eggs, although a completely ready-to-use mix requires less effort and hence should have seemed more attractive. More recently, as husbands have become more sensitive to women's rights, resistance to executive relocation has grown significantly to the point relocation has become much less frequent. Many companies, which used to move their executives around once every three years, move them now much less frequently, bowing to the new values of inter-gender equality.

To put it differently, to the extent that moral commitments enhance the resources that can be dedicated to economic activity rather than to supervision and verification, a higher level of morality increases productivity and the GNP. (For evidence of the effects of employee thefts and other crimes on reducing productivity, see Denison, 1979.)

"DIRTY" PREFERENCES AND ENCUMBERED TRADES

Neoclassicists tend to assume that preferences are unequivocal ("clean"). Given a price and an item, a consumer at a given income level typically is expected either to prefer to buy the item or clearly to refuse. If offered an identical item at a lower price, assuming no transaction costs, the consumer is expected to switch to buy the lower-priced item, and so on. Evidence of the existence of *ambivalence*—whether its source is moral conflict with pleasure, competing moral claims, or competing pleasures—poses a difficulty for neoclassical economics. It is supposed to arise, in the "standard" model, only when consumers are indifferent among various combinations of commodities. The lead article in an issue of the *American Economic Review,* the official scholarly publication of the American Economic Association, is dedicated to the puzzle of people whose behavior is said to reflect at one and the same time *two incompatible preferences* (Schelling, 1984b). For instance, a host is approached at a cocktail party and informed that, when the guest becomes drunk, the host should refuse the guest's request for the car keys; what *is* that person's preference? If to drive drunk, then why ask to be refused the keys? And if not to drive drunk, then why ask for the keys? Many more examples are given, and considerable deliberation has been devoted to the dilemma (Ainslie, 1985, Schelling, 1985; and Elster, 1985a). It exists, of course, only because the theory assumes that people will have one clear preference, reflecting one utility.

In contrast, many psychologists expect people to approach *every act* with a mix of motives that are at least in part incompatible. Neoclassicists may argue that these various motives are "lumped" into one preference, revealed in the one thing a person in the end does under given constraints. This disregards (1) the state of mind and feelings that precede, accompany, and follow the act (e.g., how "badly" versus how "good" the person feels about the act), and (2) the fact that these often tend to have *behavioral consequences* at a later point in time. Our understanding of people's behavior, and our predictions, are expected to improve as these feelings are taken into account. True, the mix of motives may include conflicts other than the one we focus upon here; e.g., a conflict between two emotions. However, a divided-self model is particularly applicable to the moral evaluations of items because, as has been argued earlier, they frequently conflict with the pleasure evaluation that the choosing person accords to the same item. An important case in point is the attitude toward the "purchase" (the having) of children. Economists who compare children to durable consumer goods miss the deep ambivalence children evoke. Parents may perceive that having children is very costly, but also tend to be reluctant to think about these costs in view of the special moral value attached to children (Zelizer, 1985). (For similar discussion of other goods, see Douglas, 1979 and 1984, and Thompson, 1979.)

Our discussion next presents some evidence and further elaborates the general hypothesis that exchanges are multi-faceted, that this quality is in part caused by moral factors, and that it requires major modifications in the prevailing paradigm of behavior, especially of exchange behavior.

Guilt

Because moral and pleasure "preferences" are qualitatively different, items or means of satisfying them cannot be simply "traded off," or substituted for one another, the way various consumer goods can be. That they can be so substituted, however, is an essential assumption for the basic concept of the market as used in neoclassical economics. If my marginal utility tells me, under some given conditions, to buy more oranges and fewer apples, there is no after-taste (or residue) of guilt or shame, or the sense of affirmation, of having done the right thing, that comes, say, from having cared for the homeless. In contrast, *when people violate their moral commitments to enhance their pleasures, or forgo pleasures to live up to their moral commitments, such feelings are expected to precede, accompany, or follow their actions,* and these feelings in turn *have behavioral consequences.*

In experiments, people who were first induced to tell a lie were subsequently twice as likely to volunteer to carry out a chore than those who did not lie (Freedman, 1970, p. 156). Fifty-five percent of shoppers who believed they broke a camera in a shop offered to help another shopper in a staged incident, compared to 15 percent of a control group who did not help. (These and other studies are reviewed by Rushton, 1980, pp. 43–44). Subjects who thought they had shocked others (electrically) were subsequently three times more willing to help others than those subjects who thought they merely "buzzed" others with noise makers (Carlsmith and Gross, 1969). The relationship is often more complex: a single transgression may lead to some guilt, but only the cumulative effect of several incidents will lead to an act of remorse. If an economic analogue can be given to such behavior it would be akin to charging consumers, retroactively but irregularly, for a random subset of past purchases, or slapping on an additional charge for items they already consumed, or charging them "extra" in the same manner for some item other than the one they bought! (Guilt often spills over and attaches itself to other, seemingly unrelated, items.) Products turn out to be related in patterns that have nothing to do with substitutions, complementarity, or relative prices. For example, after several purchases of candy, a person might buy jogging shoes.

The behavioral consequences include sequences or cycles in which one or more illicit acts are followed by bouts of morally approved behavior, and/or an *increased search for or commitment to "rehabilitation" (or atonement) via morally approved behavior.* Several experiments have shown positive correlations between "pro-social" acts (e.g., giving to charity) and prior "transgressions," such correlations then being interpreted as the result of "guilt arousal." (Carlsmith and Gross, 1969, pp. 232–33; Sadalla and Wallace, 1966, pp. 187–94.)

Dissonance, Stigma, and Denial

Conflicts between pleasure motives and moral commitments, like other situations described by psychologists as governed by dissonance,* *are expected to lead to inaction*—as long as one is caught between the conflicting forces, until the dissonance is reduced—*and to denial* (one acts one way but pretends, or firmly believes, that one acts differently). A simple example of the effects of dissonance is found in changed attitudes toward installment debt. From 1967 to 1977 there was a sharp decrease in the proportion of Americans who judged installment debt to be "bad." It fell from 40 percent to 15 percent. However, there was next to no change in the proportion of families who actually used installment debt in the same period (Curtin and Neubig, 1979, pp. 1–2); their proportion rose only by 2 percent. All the others turned ambivalent, citing both merits and demerits (ibid., p. 2), and hence did not act, did not buy on an installment plan.

Maital (1982, pp. 142–43) points out that the success of credit cards and bank-check credit is attributable to the fact that they allow people to be in debt without having to deal with the dissonance between their feeling that "debt is wrong" and their desire to use credit. People do not perceive these debits as loans or debt. Dissonance affects the way people invest: Klausner (1984) notes that individuals who choose between two stocks will often proclaim the merits of the one they chose, ignoring its flaws, and belittle the merits of the other stock while emphasizing its disadvantages. The result is that the person is "cognitively widening the distance" that is perceived "to exist between the selection actually made and the one that was rejected." (Klausner, 1984, p. 73.)

Also to the point is Moffit's finding that large proportions of people eligible to receive welfare refuse it because of the stigma attached. Rates for participation in some programs are as low as 43 percent (AFDC-U), and 38 percent of those eligible for the Food Stamp Program.† He finds this behavior in violation of what is "perhaps the most basic assumption of the economic theory of consumer demand . . . that 'more is better than less' [and] the assumption that 'goods are good.'" (1983, p. 1023.) Moffit points out that for those he studied income is not simply income; it matters where it comes from. Stigma is attached to some money, making it

---

*On the term, see Festinger (1957) and (1964); for an application by economists, see Akerlof and Dickens (1982).

†Moffit (1983) p. 1023. Other factors besides stigma that are probably also at work include lack of information about how to enter the program, and deliberate hurdles set up by budget-minded authorities to deter enrollment.

less desirable than other money. Most relevant, the stigma is attached to the mere act of participation in the program; it does not vary with the amount received. (Moffit's attempt to treat this problem within a mono-utility framework is discussed below.)

An indication of denial can be seen in *the search for a less visible means of achieving a desired result*. For example, American sugar growers, most of whom subscribe to a conservative political philosophy, consider government handouts and subsidies a source of shame. Therefore, they fought for a less visible form of government support (*New York Times*, January 14, 1979). They obtained government loans for which they put up their sugar as collateral. If the price of sugar rises above an agreed level, the farmers sell their sugar and repay the loans; otherwise the government can take over the collateral but not sell it or even give it away. The higher cost of this program compared to the cost of outright subsidies provides a measure of the moral (stigma) factor. For instance, the cost of handling, storage, and transportation of sugar in FY1979 amounted to $2,521,403 out of a total program cost of $89,909,447. In the following years, when no sugar was added to storage, these costs continued to be incurred; for instance, in FY1981 they amounted to $1,166,305.* Moreover, the stored sugar deteriorated rapidly. (*New York Times*, January 14, 1979), depreciating the capital.

The conservative sugar growers did not simply opt for the more pleasurable higher income of government subsidies, preferably to the less pleasurable but morally proper take-no-handout position. They chose to make the government incur a still larger outlay to mitigate the guilt feelings which accompanied their decision to choose the pleasure of higher income over adherence to a moral principle, and to allow themselves to "deny" taking a government "hand out." That is, this choice allows for no clean trade-offs, and the complicating moral factor has a visible cost.

Stress: Diminished Capacity

Conflict between the pleasure valuation and the moral valuation of an item—whether the specific psychic mechanism that is activated to create a conflict is guilt, denial, or some other—*is expected to result in intra-psychic stress,* which in turn exacts costs that are not typical information or transaction costs: *they diminish the capacity of the actor.* A large body of research shows that under stress people's decision-making becomes less rational (if by acting rationally one means using information that is available, drawing proper conclusions from it, and so on). A major source of stress is "selling out" virtues that one believes in, and in doing so "prostituting" one's self. (For discussion of the concept of rationality, see Chapter 8; for discussion of the factors that determine the level of rationality, see Chapter

*Calculated from figures provided by Frank Briggs, U.S. Dept. of Agriculture.

9. Important work by Janis and Mann, 1977, showing the effects of anxiety on decision-making, is reviewed in Chapter 7.)

The discussion so far suggests that moral commitments cannot be exchanged for pleasurable acts without inner and behavioral consequences. It should be noted that many psychologists, from Sigmund Freud to Herbert Marcuse, have argued that the reverse also holds true: Basic urges or pleasures cannot be sublimated into moral commitments, or into socially approved behavior, with full success, without residue. This, of course, lends further support to the thesis that the two concepts refer to behaviors that are substantively different—not interchangeable, and not reducible.

Contextual Relations

While the preceding discussion offers some relatively clear and testable hypotheses, the following discussion refers to an effect—setting a context, creating a "climate"—that is more difficult to conceptualize and make operational; its discussion is included here because of its potential importance. Our starting point is the observation that moral values tend to generate *diffused* relationships between a broad contextual disposition and an open-ended list of specific behavioral items, a relationship that is radically different from that depicted in mechanistic models. The notion that one ought to be "fair" or "loyal" to one's employees serves as an example. A mechanistic approach assumes that there are sets of specific obligations that state, for example, that if an employee has worked for a firm for X years, and worked well (defined, say, as having achieved high ratings from supervisors), the company ought to do certain things for her, such as buy her a gold watch, or give her 30 days' notice if she is to be fired (although her contract calls for only 15), and grant her severance pay.

However, sociologists have argued that typically moral commitments are not structured this way but are "diffuse" and open-ended (Parsons, 1937). Thus, especially in small businesses, there is often an ill-defined, but nevertheless effective, sense that one has "some" obligations to loyal, long-time employees, and that one "ought to" do "something" for them. A large variety of behaviors, that differ greatly in price, can satisfy this obligation. Similarly, where there are explicit obligations, there is often a sense that one ought to do "more," and what constitutes "more," again, is ill-defined.

Many employer-employee relationships, especially for employees who are salaried, and employees who have de facto tenure, are actually much more akin to the contextual types we have just described than to a pure market relationship. The neoclassical paradigm does not easily accommodate such relationships; it tends to favor piecework and wages tied to performance, to reduce the possibility of shirking. However, many people work best, and feel less exploited, in contextual relations, in which they work *in part* out of moral commitment and are treated as human beings, and not merely as commodities (Etzioni, 1961, 1975).

Leibenstein (1976) points out that firms often buy the worker's *time*, but the relevant factor for productivity is the worker's *effort*. The result is dependent upon how *inner*-motivated the worker is, because time-based pecuniary rewards only set a context within which performance is dependent upon other motives—the X factor. Leibenstein estimates that ignoring this motivational consideration, by focusing on pecuniary reward systems, leads to considerable "X-inefficiency," resulting in significant losses.

Marital commitments are another case in point. Unlike Blue Cross coverage, there is no specific number of days of care that one spouse "owes" the other, nor is there a point at which the obligation will be exhausted; further, affection can be expressed through a large variety of items, from hugs to flowers, that vary greatly in their price but have a comparable context-reinforcing quality. Indeed, attempts to base marital relationships on explicit contracts typically fail, or cover only a few facets of the relationship, such as the division of assets in the case of divorce.

It should also be noted that there is a significant difference between explicit exchanges, of the kind that we typically associate with market transactions, and the notion that one does things because they contribute to a social system we consider as legitimate, or contribute to the general welfare, even if we perceive that we indirectly benefit from that well-being. For instance, a world in which blood is bought and sold over the counter, like any other product, may be indeed neoclassical. In contrast, a world in which blood is donated—in part out of sheer altruism, in part because one believes in the rightness of a voluntary system, in part because one feels it is fairer if we should need blood some day also to have donated it (although we know this is *not* required)—is a world in which moral commitments have a significant role. This is the case even if there is a vague sense of a reward for "good" deeds, especially if the reward is largely one of living in a world that is more moral (Titmuss, 1970; Kennett, 1980, p. 348).

Much gift-giving is contextual: Gifts often serve to reaffirm relationships. People do expect some return, but it is not the only or main reason for giving; and it is not a specific, tit-for-tat exchange, defined by the rules of transactions, but defined instead by the desire to uphold the relationship and whatever is considered a fair balance. What is considered fair is, in turn, morally defined.

Much economic behavior that entails trust (for example, between suppliers and customers) and loyalty (across ranks and within ranks) seems to be contextual: obligations are vague in details; items whose costs vary greatly seem to be interchangeable as long as they are comparable in their *symbolic* value (gold watches vs. severance pay); and obligations are diffuse although not without boundaries (e.g., there is a limit to how many sick days one allows a loyal employee, above those specified in the contract). That is, these relationships are not free from calculations of costs and benefits; however, these calculations take place within the peculiar framework and dynamics of contextual relations. Most important for our study: Moral values are a major contextualizing factor. They define, often loosely, what is within the range and what is beyond the pale.

STRUCTURAL DIFFERENCES

Irreversible, Lumpy, and Notchy

Guilt, ambivalence, denial, and stress concern feelings that precede, follow, or accompany choices and that affect individual behavior. In addition, the structure of many choices, in which moral commitments have a significant role, is systematically different from those in which pleasure considerations dominate. *Choices that are relatively heavily "loaded" with moral considerations, including many economic choices, are expected to be unusually difficult to reverse* (i.e., they are asymmetrical), *to be very "lumpy"* (or highly discontinuous), *and to reveal a high "notch-effect"* (a resistance to pass a threshold, that makes behavior sticky before it is passed; the reluctance is greatly diminished or lost once passage is completed). Take, for example, the decisions concerning pre-marital sex many women used to face. There were basically three morally recognized positions: virginity, being sexually active, and being promiscuous. Each contained a very large range of behavior considered to have the same basic moral standing; i.e., the decision was very lumpy. Also, once a woman "lost her virtue," or was known to be promiscuous, she found it almost impossible to reverse her moral status. Moreover, acts that had great value before passing the threshold (an incident of intercourse), have a much lower value, once a transgression occurred. Hence, there is no standardization of the item at issue.

The same basic observations can be made about joining welfare. Before one joins, a welfare dollar may be worth only 80 cents, but once one joins, and one is stigmatized as a "welfare client," the very next dollar may be worth 100 cents. And even if one gets off welfare and no longer receives stigmatized income, the stigma is likely to linger. Similarly, taking out the first loan, for people who feel that being in debt is a moral evil, is different from extending it or taking out a second one. Selling one's home, especially if it is the first move; moving to a different city, especially if it is the first relocation; and the first voluntary change of job may all reveal such a structure due to moral (and emotional) factors, all in sharp contrast to what economic transactions are assumed to be.

Non-Markets and Poor Markets

Some areas of behavior, we saw, are set aside as "sacred," either in the religious sense or in a secular equivalent. One empirically verifiable earmark of such separation of realms is the initial rejection of calculative approaches, such as a cost-benefit analysis. As a result, it is expected that *when moral commitments are prominent they in effect create non-markets in some areas, and rather poor ones in others.*

Take two extreme examples. Orthodox Jews will not consider buying or selling pork whatever the price, the opportunity costs, or potential profits; indeed, they are known to have given up their lives rather than consume pork. It is completely irrelevant whether, if offered $10 million, some would ingest some pork (showing that everyone has a price, and hence that the demand for pork among Othodox Jews is merely *very* inelastic). The point is that such trade is unthinkable among Orthodox Jews, and it is not fruitful to conceptualize their pork "purchase" behavior in typical neoclassical terms.

It might be said that this is a matter for some households, but as long as they are few, it will not affect the pork market (Kalt and Zupan, 1984, p. 281). However, there are important items that for most members of a given society, in a specific historical period, in effect are not subject to trade for moral reasons: human organs, for instance. It does not matter if there are a few individuals who think of selling one of their kidneys, or if a few physicians have offered to set up a profit-making organ bank. Tomorrow's *Wall Street Journal* will not carry the latest "bid" and "asked" organ quotes, nor, because of people's strong moral objections, is there any other place a market is made in these items. In the aggregate, human organs are not marketable in most societies, even if some isolated transactions do occur. Indeed, most people do not even consider the matter; it is unthinkable for them to market their organs. Similarly, most Americans do not consider sending their children out to panhandle, however large or sudden a shortfall in their income.

Some neoclassicists have studied the decision of whether or not to have children as though it were akin to buying a "durable" consumer good, or a "trade-off" for buying other goods (Becker, 1976, p. 169). It seems quite evident that, precisely because of moral considerations, the decision to have a child is very different from that to buy, say, a car. A car can be purchased to one's specifications in regard to desired mix of color, size, performance level, prestige and numerous other "options." If it is unsatisfactory, it can be returned, sold, traded, or junked. In "buying" a child, one engages in "biological roulette," and in an educational adventure, without control of the results and with a lifelong moral commitment to the "object." There are no recalls and certainly no warranties. This is not to deny that there are some analytic benefits to the approach of Becker *et al.* For example, money spent on children is not available for autos, and vice versa. The objection registered here is to the implicit and sometimes explicit suggestion that there are no significant differences *relevant to exchange behavior* when the analysis concerns items that have a specific moral standing as well as those that do not.

An economist who read a previous version of these pages wrote:

> *Cars and children* can both be lemons. The higher the probability of a car or a child being a lemon, other things being equal, the lower will be demand. There are analogies to sales of cars or even junking them: Parents of children with severe handicaps may institutionalize their children, parents may send out their children for adoption, or may even kill them. Van de Walle has argued that some of the decline in 19th Century infant and child mortality in France was due to improvements in the ability of parents to control family size. Child abandonment, sending children to Normandy for wet-nursing, dosing them with laudanum, and child abuse were common. He argues that these practices were methods by which parents coped with excessive numbers of children.

All this may be true, although different morals prevailed in different periods and societies, and may explain part of the difference in behavior. The question, though, is not whether economic factors affect the attitude to children as they affect the attitude toward autos, but whether there are no significant differences in the structure of the decisions, along the suggested lines: Do people trade-in their children, or otherwise exchange them for more desirable models? Do most parents dash into a burning house to rescue their kids but not their cars—even if both are insured? And so on.

The main point, however, is not that these extreme "limit" situations exist, but that in many areas in which moral commitments are strong, this seems one reason market models do not serve well. A prime "example" is labor markets. In fact, they are much more than an example: labor markets account for a large segment of all economic behavior, as indicated by the fact that labor costs account for three-fourths of all production costs, even in a highly industralized society. (Kuttner, 1985, p. 80.) The market model's difficulties begin with such elementary considerations as the fact that people cannot be bought and sold the way slaves were because of moral and legal factors; and that the way they are treated affects their motivation, the extent of their cooperation, and their productivity. (See McGregor, 1960; human relations school, Mayo, 1933; press reports on the success of Japanese labor relations techniques in the U.S., *Business Week,* July 14, 1986. On the quality of work life programs, see Kerr and Staudohar, 1986; Lincoln and Kalleberg, 1985. On the difficulties of using market models for labor economics, see Thurow, 1983, Chapter 7.)

All this holds even more strongly for those labor "markets" in which people are bound for long periods of time by implicit contracts, or by explicit contracts backed by moral commitments. Many workers, especially salaried, semi-professional, and professional employees, are not moved from job to job by some generalized price mechanism but are at most times effectively immovable. When they are moved, it is only after an individualized bargaining process, quite different from the market mechanism. Each "product" is treated as if it were unique. This non-market (or poor market), depicted by several economists (Baily, 1974; Azariadis, 1975), has "so puzzled" many (Bull, 1983, p. 658) that they have sought to explain it in various ways, for example, by pointing to the transaction costs involved in breaking a contract, or the damage to a firm's reputation. These factors surely exist. But it is also quite in line with experience and observation to assume that many individuals have internalized the notion that it is morally wrong to violate contracts. The question, how are these contracts enforced if they are implicit? (Bull, 1983, 1983; Hart, 1983) finds its solution here: under most circumstances, moral commitments compel people not to break contracts. Indeed, many explicit contracts are treated as if they are backed up by implicit ones that make it "improper" to try to "wiggle out" of them when circumstances change.

Neoclassical cost-benefit analyses of health, safety, and of public goods (such as environmental protection) run into severe difficulties. The root cause of many of these is the absence of markets for the items involved because it is considered immoral to trade in them. Since they have no price, economists "impute" monetary values to life, limb, and public goods such as clean air, on the basis of situations in which their prices are said to be indirectly revealed. For example, from the fact that houses which are closer to nuclear plants cost only a little less than comparable houses further away, economists deduce that the value people put on their life is relatively low. Other studies focus on pay for employees at various risk levels. The sense that such calculations are alien to the phenomena they attempt to model is reinforced by the finding that the same items, precisely because they are in a non-market realm, have highly divergent imputed "prices." For example, in 1984 life was valued at $3.5 million at the Occupational Safety and Health Administration; at $650,000 at the Federal Aviation Administration, and at $400,000 to $7 million at the Environmental Protection Agency (*New York Times*, October 26, 1984). The results are highly affected by the mode of calculation used. Measurements based on the earnings that a fatally-injured person would have collected had the person completed a full work life—a system that values life after retirement as zero, and also values at zero the lives of homemakers—yield relatively low estimates. Measurements that rely on awards by juries and on insurance payoffs yield much higher values. Still other methods yield still different results. Once a price has been put on lives and other items that are not typically bought or sold, neoclassical

80   *Beyond Pleasure: The Case for Deontological Social Sciences*

economists model them as if they were traded and attempt to predict behavior on the basis of these imputed values. The results are often quite dubious. The difficulties are illustrated by the finding that blood prices in the United States do not differ, although its quality—in terms of the probability that it contains hepatitis—may vary by a factor of ten (Kessel, 1980, pp. 75–76), a long way from what a market model would predict.

Goodin (1985) points out that economists tend to presume that if we can compensate people we can do "anything" to them. After all, they freely choose to accept the trade-off. This, Goodin writes, disregards two important distinctions: Those choices in which the state has legitimate "taking [sic] power" (no compensation expected), and those choices that are "impermissible" (even with compensation). Among those things the state can take morally, without compensation, is the freedom of criminals during their court-determined incarceration, the rights of owners of gas-guzzlers when the tax on gas is increased, and the rights of those precluded from building an office building where a house was declared a historical landmark. Impermissible areas are self-evident, from slavery to markets in babies. The furor over "trade" in the children of surrogate mothers highlights this point rather than refutes it. It would be outrageously silly to conclude that, because a few women "sell" their infants for $10,000, this is the typical market value of children, and to go on and conclude that parents are "inefficient" because costs vastly exceed the price of the product. There is also a world of difference between compensating for a loss caused inadvertently, and deliberately allowing it to happen, because of the morality of the intentions involved and the side-effects on the moral system. To compensate the family of a pilot whose plane collided with another is different from refusing to install collision-alert technologies (assuming no significant differences in costs).

True, these are historical and cultural matters. What is considered a fair exchange or proper trade and what is tabooed is, to a significant extent, a matter of the specific morals of a given society (or even a subsociety such as a class or region), and historical period. Blood is traded in the United States while it basically is not in Britain (Titmuss, 1970). We now are repulsed by the idea that draft exemptions could be bought, for $300, in 1863 (Walzer, 1983, p. 98), or absolutions in the pre-Reformation Church, but it seems in those days and places it was acceptable. And, while we argue that most American middle-class parents would not consider sending their children panhandling when suddenly faced with a financial shortfall, obviously this is not the case for parents in poor classes and countries.

An economist who systematically objected to the introduction of moral factors into the analysis of behavior wrote the author:

> I suspect that we do not observe these practices in the United States very much precisely because incomes do not fall sufficiently to induce such behavior, in part because of our welfare system which provides

minimum standards of living. Laws prohibit such activities and parents who sent their children out to panhandle would lose them. That is, their children would become wards of the courts. In the Philippines and India, child panhandling is common. The reason has little to do with morality; I am sure that Filipino Catholics are as moral as the Irish Catholics of Boston as are the Hindus of India. When family income without the contributions of children would be only (say) $100 per year and a child could bring in another $25 to $50 a year by panhandling, then the benefits of those contributions outweigh the costs.

About the military draft, the economist added:

Not all are repulsed by sales of draft exemptions. I rather suspect that many economists would find such a system attractive (if one did not already have a volunteer army paying a wage to attract a sufficient number of enlistees). There are both efficiency and equity arguments for allowing such sales.

A codetermination response to the preceding lines is: true, economic factors play a role; panhandling is expected to be more common the poorer the people and the more it brings in. However, within the same income group, even in the poorest of nations, most people do not send their children to panhandle, just the way in the United States most poor do not prostitute themselves or become muggers. (An excellent account of what the poorest in Calcutta would do is found in Dominque LaPierre's *The City of Joy*, Garden City: Doubleday, 1985.)

To reiterate, in any given society and period, certain items are not considered legitimate material for exchange. Walzer lists 14 major categories of "blocked exchanges." (1983, p. 97.) In this "domain of rights" (a term Walzer attributes to Okun) the 14 categories "are proof against sale and purchase." (1983, p. 100.) These include marriage (licenses for polygamy are not for sale), basic freedoms (one has them without needing to pay for them), and divine grace. Most likely, this means that up to a point they are not traded at all, and beyond that they may be traded once the taboo is violated, and only in encumbered ways described above. As a result, market models are expected to depict the relations poorly at best; socio-economic conceptions that include moral as well as economic factors are necessary. (For a preliminary attempt to evolve such a concept, see the discussion of encapsulated markets, Chapter 12.)

Morally Infused Markets

The neoclassical paradigm also ignores the role of moral values (as well as the role of power and of stratification) in that it depicts the market as an allocative mechanism, i.e., one that determines who gets what. To neoclassicists this is basically a matter of efficient allocations that "ought not" to be "distorted" by "extrinsic" criteria, such as people's values (other than those built into their self-serving, individualistic preferences). The implication is that the market rewards those who work hard and save, and punishes those who are inefficient or lazy (Okun, 1975). A "fair" allocation is viewed as that in which no one person's position can be improved without worsening someone else's ("Pareto-optimal").

This approach has been criticized roundly and often (see, for example, Kuttner, 1984, pp. 10–19). Here our discussion focuses on the ways allocations (and reallocations) are actually made; we discuss later the role of power. The role of stratification (the "prior" distribution of assets) is quite evident, for instance, in the effects of inherited wealth. Here the role of moral values is explored. They greatly affect what individuals consider as equitable or fair and what they are willing to accept, tolerate, or fight to change.

The role of values stands out clearly in the noneconomic "exchanges" neoclassicists have studied, for instance, love. They found that people seek equity; they fall out of love when they feel either exploited or exploiting (Walster, Walster, and Berscheid, 1978). In marriage, the exchange is said to be between spouses who choose to produce household services and those who work for the market (Heimer and Stinchcombe, 1980; Becker, 1981). A traditional wife, who worked in the kitchen and nursery the whole day, will fall out of love with a husband who does not "provide," and a traditional, hard-working husband will fall out of love if he comes home and there are no cooked meals, the children are neglected, and so on.

While there is a kernel of validity to this view, i.e., that even noneconomic relationships, love included, tend to contain elements of exchanges, it must be stressed that what is perceived as equitable is significantly affected by people's values. *The same exchange patterns,* that many in the past considered highly legitimate, in recent decades have come under severe criticism as being highly exploitative, because they required women to work at home, and other aspects of the traditional interspousal exchanges are now considered by many, but not by all, as highly unfair.

What is easy to see for exchanges within the family also holds for economic transactions, for instance among the subsidiaries or divisions of the same corporation. As Eccles (1985, p. 27) has shown, the costs of production and profit margins outside the corporation are but one factor for setting transfer prices—prices for transactions within a corporation. Another major factor is what their managers consider a "just" price.

Values also play a key role in transactions within the market at large. Many corporations do not cut wages during periods of severe unemployment, in part because their executives do not wish to be considered unfair. Sport and entertainment industries do not increase the price of tickets for highly popular events that are about to sell out, and so on. True, corporations may fear that customers or workers may react to what they consider "unfair" practices, and reduce their loyalties. But this only high-lights the question: what is considered fair? It is clearly a matter of people's value-judgments and is not economically determined.

Kahneman, Knetsch, and Thaler (1986) study this question. They find that people see certain levels of prices and profits as fair (reference points), and object to a firm that *arbitrarily* increases the prices. However, when people perceive that there is a legitimate reason to adjust prices and profits, whether or not objectively this is the case, the reference points are adjusted, and changes in prices and profits are considered legitimate. Thus, people object to a firm reducing the wages of its work-ers because new competitors pay less to their employees, but feel it is legitimate for the firm to pay less to *new* employees it hires (ibid., p. 730). People were found to legitimate steps to protect profits from reductions, but not steps to increase low profits, although economically there is little difference. Furthermore, people are willing to act on these feelings and "punish" those they consider unfair (for example by withholding busi-ness from them).

Values, other than a sense of fairness, that deeply affect transactions include the notion that the powerful (or lucky or privileged) "owe" the vulnerable members of the community, an idea sometimes referred to as the notion of social responsibility. For example, people who are termi-nally ill or old are "entitled" to receive and are *not* expected to recipro-cate (Gouldner, 1960). Experiments show that the more workers thought their supervisors were dependent on them (e.g., to gain a raise), the more they helped the supervisors, even if the workers thought their efforts were anonymous (Berkowitz and Daniels, 1963). And, despite all that has been written in recent years about the rising old "class" exploiting or depending on the young, old Americans contribute much more to their offspring than they receive, with no expectation of "later" pay offs (Cheal, 1986). Supply and demand are not the only factors that bring the groups together, organizing their exchanges; the values of each group and the values they share explain, in part, the relationships.

THE QUEST FOR BALANCE

Balancing vs. Maximizing

The concept of a single over-arching utility disregards a major human attribute observable in the behavior under study: people do not seek to maximize their pleasure, but to balance the service of two major pur-poses—to advance their well-being *and* to act morally. The quest for bal-ance is evident in that, as individuals advance one major over-arching concern, they continuously strive not to neglect the other.

A trivial example of the difference beween maximizing and balance is found in buying fruit. When one buys fruit with one goal in mind, say to maximize vitamins by the use of the allotted funds, one may buy only apples or only bananas or whatever mix of the two "maximizes" the one goal at hand. However, when one seeks to make a fruit salad, while there is no precise definition of the right mix, buying too many fruits of any one kind is not considered satisfactory.

If one examines people's allocation of resources among work, consumption, leisure, saving, and civility, a similar balance is evident. Juster (1986, unpublished) found, in contradiction to the neoclassical assumption that work is a pain, and leisure a pleasure (people must be compensated to work), that most people prefer a mix of work and leisure over leisure alone, and that work has great intrinsic rewards. Specifically, many people prefer a part-time job and more leisure to either full-time work and little leisure, or full-time leisure. However, as part-time jobs are scarce, people prefer full-time jobs and little leisure to full-time leisure, because being at work is valued positively in our society.

Similarly, most people feel they ought to keep some kind of balance between their private take and their public contribution (charity, voluntary work, help to neighbors, and so on). People do not simply free ride, or give it all to public "good;" they divide their time and monies between the two. Many people also feel they ought to donate some proportion of their income. Sometimes such rules are made explicit, for example tithing in the Mormon Church and in a Minneapolis "5 percent club," in which corporations are expected to donate 5 percent of their profits to civic causes. More commonly, such rules are implicit and imprecise, reflected in such decisions as how much to consume and how much one "ought to" bequest to one's children or donate to charity (see Collard, 1978, Chapters 10 and 15).

Expressing all of one's preferences (under given constraints)—moral commitments included—by one summary indicator, as the mono-utility theory does (typically in the price a person is willing to pay), distracts attention from the crux of the matter: the people's quest for a balance. To assume in this context a unitary preference is like calculating a score that combines the measurement of means and of standard deviations of a statistical distribution into one figure. Such a calculation can be completed but it sacrifices important relevant information about two highly distinct, independent components; in effect, it is a rather meaningless measurement. The same holds for combining pleasurable and moral "tastes."

An example from organizational behavior may help. Universities seek to enhance both education and scholarship. (Many advance additional goals; for example, service to the community, disregarded here). True, to some extent these goals are complementary, but often they are in conflict over resources and over norms for behavior. While there is no precise definition of the proper balance between activities serving the two goals desired at a particular university, there is (1) a strong sense that if one goal is neglected, the mix of activities should be altered to advance that goal, and (2) activities that advance one goal but undercut the other (e.g., research that takes professors away from the campus for long periods of time) are considered particularly undesirable. These, and a few other such rules, are much less unitary and tight than those suggested by maximizers, but we suggest that they do guide decision makers in organizations that pursue multiple goals.

When such organizations are studied, one might refer abstractly to a supragoal they pursue, say "academic goals," and attempt to formulate a unitary measurement for the advancement of such a goal; such an approach, however, would disregard an essential quality of behavior in such situations: the desire to protect the inter-goal balance, not merely to advance a total. To put it differently, while 5 units of research and 5 units of education (assuming the particular university weighs them equally) may constitute as much a contribution to a unitary goal as a distribution of ratios of 1 to 9 and 9 to 1, a balance-seeking organization will prefer a distribution that remains within the 7:3 to 3:7 range or some such pattern.

Stress is inherent in the deontological individual, in being a socio-economic person, because the balance between pleasure and moral conduct is not achieved once and for all. Rather as in riding a bicycle, individuals continuously "correct" tendencies to tilt excessively in one direction or the other. Also, circumstances affect the balance. For example, behavior is balanced at a quite different pleasure/moral ratio in a highly integrated community (in which there is a clear moral code, well-supported) as compared to a community that is in social and moral disarray (Banfield, 1958). Hence, one would look in vain for a fixed proportionality of "that much to Caesar, that much to God." While the sought-after combination is expected to change over time and among social contexts, (1) both elements are expected to always be present, and in non-trivial amounts; and (2) much is to be gained, both in explaining and in predicting individual behavior and the aggregation of it, once the factors that modify the balance are understood.

Various Multidimensional Models

To argue that people (and organizations) do not seek to maximize one utility but to advance two (or more), and that unitary measurements hence are misleading, does not suggest that such bi-utility behavior cannot be "modeled." Indeed, considerable work has been undertaken, both on the individual and organizational level, to develop such multigoal models. Some of these try to maintain that these multiple goals are but subgoals in the service of one over-arching one, others drop this assumption. Several volumes (Johnsen, 1968; Stokey and Zeckhauser, 1978,

Chapter 8; Lee, 1972, pp. 18–20) and major essays (Amemiya, 1981; Buckley, 1984; Goldberg, 1974, pp. 201–04; Keeney, 1973), have been dedicated to reviewing these numerous efforts. No attempt is made here to re-review them. A few examples are cited to indicate that (1) such modeling is possible, but (2) in so far as these models were formed for balances other than pleasure and morals, the proper model has not yet been developed.

For instance, one might look at the moral/pleasure conflict (when it is present) as a "tie-in sale," a term used when buyers desire one good but are forced by a seller to purchase with it specific amounts of some other good they do not desire (or desire less). One can then add the price of the other good to the cost of the first one, or deduct it from the benefit the first good entails. This basically what Moffit (1983) is doing; he treats stigma as akin to a toll. (Moffit found that the toll is fixed rather than varied, say, according to the amount of the welfare payment, or of other income, probably because the stigma is attached to joining the program, not to the amounts received).

Another approach reduces lumpiness—expected to be particularly high in choices strongly affected by moral considerations—by taking into account that what seem like highly discrete acts (e.g., buying/not buying a house) can actually be treated as much more continuous if one takes into account that people may also choose to buy smaller versus larger houses, lease or rent them, and so on. Presumably, moral choices could be treated similarly. For example, instead of the lumpy decision whether or not to maintain virginity, several degrees of "virginity" might be considered; for example, those who pet versus those who do not. (The term, "technically a virgin," is sometimes used.)

Still another approach treats certain considerations as constraints within which the final choice must be made. For example, in setting up a dieting person's program, such models take into account that the person needs X amounts of vitamins A, B, and so on, and then asks, within these constraints, what is the "best" buy? Presumably, one may view moral commitments as such constraints. And, models have been developed to view objects such as autos as bundles of attributes and "disaggregate" them, assessing the "utility" of each attribute separately (Lancaster, 1966). Presumably pleasurable and moral aspects of an act could be similarly treated.

An evaluation of the applicability of these and many other such modeling efforts to the issue at hand cannot be undertaken here because it would constitute a very considerable digression. It suffices to note that the treatments cited raise several issues that illustrate the problems that arise when models that have been developed for other purposes are applied to the modeling of the pleasure/moral mix and the quest for balance. Viewing morals as a toll disregards the fact that violating one's principles is an odd tax: it is being collected long after the income (or pleasure) has been exhausted. Guilt, as a wit put it, is the gift that keeps giving. The lumpiness-reduction measures do not deal with after-effects, side-effects, and the halo-effects (on other seemingly unrelated items) of moral transgressions. The tie-in sales and disaggregation approaches disregard the accumulation effects (several transgressions may accumulate to generate one act of remorse), and so on. The "diet" model does not deal with the fact that moral commitments are not fixed constraints and are highly lumpy.

These models may be adapted to take into account one or more of these attributes, and two or more of the models may be combined, or still others may be developed for the purpose at hand. However, no model is likely to be productive that assumes a unitary goal, and disregards the strength and non-reducibility both of utilities and of the quest for a balanced mix. In short, socio-economic behavior may well be subject to modeling, but not by those models that assume one over-arching utility or goal.

PART II

Beyond Rationalism:
The Role of Values
and Emotions

The nature of the human purpose ("utilities" or goals), the source of various valuations, has been addressed in Part I by drawing on ethics, social philosophy, and sociology. It led us beyond the utilitarian foundations of the neoclassical paradigm, to draw on deontology and point to the significance of moral valuations, above and beyond pleasure and self-interest. The question, how are the means selected to advance one's purpose, the focus of Part II, requires the assistance of psychology. We find that much of it, like mainstream economics, is imbued with neoclassical assumptions. Here we try to move beyond rationalism, to take into account the positive role of values and emotions in decision-making.

The Age of Reason advanced the image of a rational person, who chooses means on the basis of evidence and logic, free of the bondage of the superstition, prejudices, and biases that dominated early ages. *Homo-economicus,* rationalistic, isolated, and preoccupied with self-interest, is but one offspring of the Man of Reason; the offspring has a neoclassical psychological sibling. The sibling, too, is largely reactive, driven by inputs, is without personality, hedonistic and egotistic, a-social, devoid of affect (or emotions). Moreover, the sibling's value judgments are locked away into a forgotten compartment.

We are wiser now, at least we ought to be. The bloom is off our collective infatuation with the power of science and technology, and the bloom has also faded from our hope that reason will conquer all, replacing emotion-based and value-laden judgments with the conclusions of careful deliberations. As we grew familiar with the modern, reason-dominated person, the cardinal significance of moral commitments and the positive role of affect has been rediscovered. Unfettered reason now scares us; it evokes the images of Frankenstein, if not of Dr. Strangelove. We reject the notion that emotions are irrational, animal instincts that a mature, reasonable person sublimates and if necessary represses. The positive role of affect, such as to love and be loved, even when it sways reason, is increasingly acknowledged. Moreover, means are again assessed not only in terms of their instrumental contributions—how efficient they are— but also in terms of their normative standing. ("Normative" refers to the deontological prescriptive aspect of behavior, to *ought-to* statements, as distinct from positive, "are" statements. The reasons why the term "normative" is used from here on, rather than the related but less encompassing term "moral," are discussed in Chapter 6, pp. 105–6. Basically, moral values are universal, such as the taboo on murder, while normative values also include particular social values, such as conceptions of justice.) People, of course, never ceased to be affective and normative; it is the social sciences, and the intellectual perspectives that draw on them and feed them, that are re-recognizing these facts.

The main thesis advanced here is that the most important bases of choices are affective and normative. That is, people often make non- or sub-rational choices, first because they build on their normative-affective foundations, and only secondly because they have weak and limited intellectual capabilities.

Specifically, we shall see that in some matters normative-affective factors account in full for the choices made; in other matters these factors significantly affect the choice, although logical/empirical considerations play a secondary role. Finally, under some relatively infrequent conditions, when choosing among options that have comparable normative-affective standings (or none at all), people are open to logical-empirical, rational choices (so far, Chapter 6). It is at this point that actors are hindered by the severe limits of their intellectual capabilities and resources. They do not maximize *or* "satisfice;" they often make quite poor, sub-rational choices. While this position may seem pessimistic from the rationalistic viewpoint of the neoclassical paradigm, it is not nearly as pessimistic as the viewpoint that people are basically irrational, or only able to muddle through, as others have argued (Chapter 7). And, to reiterate, *some* limitations on rationality are highly functional if the full range of human needs is taken into account.

The concept of rationality itself illustrates the role of normative-affective factors. It reflects the values of those who advance the concept, and it is frequently defended with surprisingly aroused emotions. (Indeed, for most members of the Western culture, rationality is a positive label. To be told that one is acting irrationally is to be cussed out.) It should be obvious, however, that whether or not "man" is "found" to be rational reflects only in part what he or she is, or is capable of being; it is largely a matter of definition, of how quickly or loosely the definition grants the qualification of being rational.

There are numerous definitions in the immense literature on the subject. By some definitions, we shall see, it is nearly impossible—or even outright impossible—for people to act non-rationally, even when they pay stockbrokers for advice in markets that are random, ignore all the findings and insights of economics (say, by heeding sunk costs), or behave in ways mental health experts consider insane. However, we shall argue, such non-differentiating definitions are at most tautological, and at best highly unproductive. As they fail to differentiate between that which is rational and that which is not, they prevent theory from discharging one of its main duties: to explain. The theory's predictive power, we shall see, is not much higher (Chapter 8).

The definition of rationality followed here is that of actors who choose means most suitable to their ends; i.e., who choose on the basis of empirical evidence and logical reasoning (Chapter 8). By this definition, a high level of rationality is quite exceptional. Hence, our *base line* is the concept of a normative-affective, non-rational actor who is inefficient to boot. The special person and societal factors that move some individuals and communities above the base line, to make them rational to one degree or another, are also explored (Chapter 9).

Neoclassicists argue that individuals need not be able to deliberate; they may make rational decisions without deliberations of their own. They may draw on rules of thumb, heuristics, norms, or institutions that their culture provides. These, in turn, are said to be rational because either they reflect accumulated experience or evolutionary selection. We hold that while rules, heuristics, norms, and institutions sometimes do serve in the suggested manner, they typically reflect normative-affective factors (especially consensus) and power relations to a greater extent than knowledge. Empirical evidence about the use of rules raises many doubts about their merit; logically, we shall see, they *cannot* serve in the expected manner. Moreover, neither experience nor evolution is able to ensure rational rules, and rationality often benefits when such rules are violated rather than followed (Chapter 10).

In short, Part II constitutes an attempt to develop a decision-making model that is much closer to the way people actually make decisions than the one the neoclassical paradigm assumes; our model stresses normative-affective rather than cognitive factors. In the process, rather "old fashioned" psychological concepts are utilized, such as personality, affect (or emotion), values, and group. While these concepts may seem rather self-explanatory to many social scientists and to members of the intellectual community, it should be noted these concepts have been largely avoided by many psychologists in the 1960s and 1970s, although recently these concepts have enjoyed a comeback. They are used here because they are productive concepts, as the following discussion seeks to show. At the same time, there is no denying that serious problems remain in making these concepts operational. Fortunately some progress is also being made in this direction.

6

Normative-Affective Factors

BEYOND RATIONALISM

Intellectual circles in Europe were preoccupied for more than a century shadow-boxing with the ghost of Karl Marx, trying again and again to show that history is not dominated by economic or materialistic factors, that ideas matter. Similarly, social scientists and attending intellectuals, on both sides of the Atlantic Ocean, have been preoccupied—and still are—with extolling, questioning, and attempting to shore up the notion of Rational Man (or *homoeconomicus*). Indeed, even those who challenge this notion often define their position in terms of various deviations from the rational model. This is evident in the frequent reference to their concepts as dealing with a residual realm, the "non-rational," rather than a category that can, by itself, be positively defined. Moreover, non-rationality is often confused with irrationality and tends to carry a negative connotation. "The trouble is that once one starts to talk about rationality, it preempts the way we organize our views of human thought and behavior. We tend to think always in terms of default from a standard. . . ." (Abelson 1976, p. 61.)

Here an attempt is made to follow those who break out of the rationalist framework, by positing a different view of human nature: a concept of individuals governed by normative commitments and affective involvements, referred to as N/A factors. The central thesis advanced here is: (1) that the majority of choices people make, including economic ones, are completely or largely based on normative-affective considerations, not merely with regard to selection of goals, but also of means; and (2) that the limited zones in which other, logical-empirical (L/E) considerations are paramount, are themselves defined by N/A factors that legitimate and otherwise motivate such decision-making.

One of the virtues of the neoclassical paradigm is that it provides a clear, concise, and simple conception of the human nature it presupposes. Many of the social scientists who have demonstrated that this concept is extremely unrealistic, and have sought to posit an alternate view, have run into difficulties because the concept they have advanced has been complex and fuzzy, the result of their enriching the basic concept with numerous elaborations and qualifications. Here an attempt is made to provide a parsimonious deontological conception, although admittedly it is not as simple as the notion of a rational utility-maximizing individual, a notion whose excessive simplicity one may well not seek to match (Hirschman 1984, p. 11).

The concept of normative-affective actors, of actors whose choices are dominated by values and emotions, is an ideal type, a base-line concept. Once it is introduced, there is room to discuss the conditions under which behavior deviates from this basic concept. Neoclassical economists often referred to theorems about rational utility maximizers as akin to theorems about a frictionless slope (albeit, as a rule, they do not discuss the corrections the friction factor requires). The concept of normative-affective actors is our frictionless slope; friction is introduced later. Or, to push the point, since actors are viewed here as typically highly inefficient (though not ineffectual) persons, by the criterion of rationality (defined below), the baseline used here might be viewed as 100 percent friction; the corrections to be introduced later concern those factors that alleviate friction. N/A factors thus provide the context within which L/E considerations are employed.

In keeping with the preliminary approach, only an outline of the conception is provided; findings are cited merely as illustrations rather than to provide one more review of the literature.

At issue are largely means, not goals; only immoderate rationalists deny the role of normative-affective factors in the selection of goals or utilities. The main bone of contention is the role of normative-affective factors in the selection of means. A typical neoclassical argument (Stigler and Becker 1977, p. 76) claims that one cannot argue about tastes, preferences, or values. The desire to buy deodorants is not more "rational" (or irrational) than the desire to buy bread (let alone, white bread). The question, we are told, is whether or not, given two comparable ("homogeneous") deodorants, but one less costly than the other, the consumer will purchase the less costly one. That is, rationality enters when we come to the choice of means. The position advanced here is that *normative-affective factors shape to a significant extent the information that is gathered, the ways it is processed, the inferences that are drawn, the options that are being considered, and the options that are finally chosen.* That is, to a significant extent, cognition, inference, and judgment—hence, decision-making—are not logical-empirical endeavors but are governed by normative-affective (non-cognitive) factors, reflecting individual, psycho-dynamic and, we shall see, collective processes. For instance, N/A factors determine to a considerable extent which sources prople draw on for information (for example, whether or not they read newspapers or watch TV, and what they watch: news, sports, or soap operas), how they interpret what they see, and what they believe they ought to infer from what they think they have learned about the situation at hand.

The discussion in this chapter proceeds by first introducing a N/A based decision-making model. We then explore whether or not N/A factors are necessarily disfunctional to decision-making, as has often been stated. The chapter closes with an attempt to deal with three anticipated criticisms: by those cognitivists who "reduce" the concepts of emotions and values, by empiricists who argue these concepts cannot be measured, and by neoclassicists who maintain that N/A factors can be incorporated into their paradigm.

TOWARD A N/A DECISION-MAKING MODEL

A Radical Departure

The neoclassical decision-making model draws on one variation or another of the information-processing means-end scheme. Individuals are assumed to have ends (clear and orderly) and to set out to collect, process, and interpret information about alternative means to serve those ends, drawing proper inferences as to the most efficient means to render decisions. We radically depart from this model here and argue that the majority of choices involve little information processing or none at all, but that they draw largely or exclusively on affective involvements and normative commitments. Thus, for most Americans, the question of whether to work in the United States or in Mexico or even Canada is not mainly a question of relative wages or tax rates, but largely one of national, cultural, and social identity. Choices either entail no deliberation at all (the "right" choice is "self-evident"), or entail a rather different process, e.g., evoking a value or weighing among them. Thus, the question of whether a worker owes more loyalty to the work place or a labor union is not mainly or only one of relative costs and benefits, but of judging which loyalty is more commanding.

A minority of choices is based on L/E considerations, but many of these are infused to one extent or another with N/A considerations, as we shall see. One may wish to use the term "choice" to refer to all selections among options, however limited the scope of information-processing, deliberation, and other L/E considerations, while reserving the term "decision" for deliberative choices. This usage is followed here. (Additional reasons to support the distinction are discussed in Chapter 8. For other attempts to develop "moral" decision-making models, see Schwartz 1970a, 1970b; Simmons, Klein, Simmons 1977, pp. 237 ff.; and Latané and Darley 1970.)

The N/A L/E Choice Continuum

Normative-affective factors influence the selection of means in many areas *excluding* the role of logical-empirical considerations (i.e., choice is made exclusively on normative-affective grounds); in other areas, by *infusing* the deliberations in such a way that logical-empirical considerations play a relatively minor or secondary role to normative-affective factors; and in still others, by defining the areas in which choices may be made largely or solely on logical-empirical grounds, areas referred to here as normative-affective *indifference* zones. Together the three concepts—exclusion, infusion, and indifference—characterize three segments of a continuum of bases of choice, ranging from 100 percent N/A and 0 percent L/E to 100 percent L/E and 0 percent N/A. Note, though, that according to the thesis advanced here, (1) the zone high in L/E considerations is itself formed and defined by N/A factors, and (2) the segments are far from equal in size. For most individuals, in most societies, in most historical periods, the indifference zones are much smaller than the other two, and the exclusion zone is the largest in behavior in general, economic behavior included. As Katona (1975, p. 197) put it: "... there is hardly any knowledge lacking affective connotations." The three zones are next discussed in more detail.

Exclusion

One major way exclusion of L/E considerations takes place is by N/A-based fusion of a particular means to a particular end. When exclusion takes place, all other means that L/E considerations allow by objective standards are treated by the choice-maker as morally and/or emotionally "unthinkable" or irrelevant. To suggest that L/E considerations in this zone are seen as "unacceptable" is to understate the case, because it implies that they have been considered and rejected. Excluded options are not considered by the actors; they are blocked from conscious deliberation; their *consideration*—not merely their adoption—is tabooed. Thus, to use an obvious example, most shopkeepers do not consider bombing their competitors even when times are difficult. Or, only one course of action or means is deemed appropriate.

Such fusion of means to an end is often found when a means commands a symbolic significance, i.e., when it embodies, renders concrete, and illustrates a value.

When N/A fully excludes L/E considerations, actors choose a course of action without exploring alternatives, because they sense it is the right way to proceed. They inform interviewers that they did not deliberate, and observers see no signs that they did. When the house is on fire, the children are upstairs, their mother dashes in, without considering alternatives. Internalized moral values and emotions invested in the children fully form the choice. Studies of people who were asked to donate one of their kidneys to a sibling report that they responded positively and instantaneously (Simmons, Klein, Simmons 1977, p. 243): "Case 1: Donor (mother): 'Me? I never thought about it . . . I automatically thought I'd be the one. There was no decision to make or sides to weigh.' Case 2: You mean did he think about it and then decide? No—it was just spontane-ous. The minute he knew . . . it was just natural. The first thing he thought of. He would donate." Lest it be said that such "verbal responses" are unreliable, note that most of those studied acted on them by actually donating the kidney (Fellner and Marshall 1970, p. 1249).

The situations depicted so far are extreme; however, many daily eco-nomic choices are made in this way—impulse buying, for example. The same holds for the much more common habitual purchases. Evidence on the scope of such choices is presented in Chapter 9, and the argument that they are "rational" after all, because they save decision-making costs, is critically examined in Chapter 10.

Choices made exclusively on N/A bases have been discussed so far re-garding situations in which the actors perceive only *one* course of action, although from the viewpoint of the observer there are at least two. It might be said that a mother "chooses" between running and not running into the fire; indeed, all acts may be compared to the option of not act-ing; however, the actor perceives only one option; non-action is defined as "out of the question" by N/A factors. Beyond making the choice com-pletely, N/A factors often make the choice even when actors perceive two or more options. In a psychological experiment, subjects were given a choice between a classical and a modernistic print (i.e., both have the same cost, none). When the group climate prescribed one kind of print, the subjects chose it, without deliberating. Similarly, a typical American teenager will not require any deliberation to choose between a serving of snails and Perrier and an order of hamburgers and Coke.

In still other situations, N/A factors do not make the choice but ex-clude most options (rather than all), often by excluding from delibera-tion *major subsets* of facts, interpretations, and approaches that are L/E-accessible (as deemed by scientific observers). Here, N/A factors, instead of fusing a means to a goal, form what has been called a *tunnel vision* (Easterbrook 1959).

When the author suggested to a young, successful Wall Street banker that he look for a place to live in Brooklyn Heights (one subway stop away from his workplace) rather than in the much more expensive, distant, mid-Manhattan, the banker recoiled in horror: "To live in Brooklyn?!!" he exclaimed, rejecting out of hand the suggestion to "at least have a look." It might be said that the banker's choice was "rational" because the prestige loss and the restrictions on his social life that would result from living in Brooklyn would exceed the saving in real estate. However, as he refused to examine the Brooklyn option, and had no knowledge of the size of the saving in real estate, of how many singles roam the Heights, the comparative number of discos, and so on, we maintain that stigma prevented the option from being considered. Given the low cost of a trip to Brooklyn, we score such choices as dominated by N/A factors, and as not rational.

College, career, and job choices are often made only within N/A prescribed sub-contexts. For example, to begin with, whole categories of positions are not considered at all by most young people who plan their job education and career; these categories range from becoming street vendors to funeral parlor directors; similarly, traditional males did not consider work in "feminine" occupations. And people set on becoming white-collar workers do not consider blue-collar jobs, even when they pay more. (Neoclassicists may say this simply means that these people value the white-collar prestige higher than, say, the higher income some blue-collar jobs provide. Our point is that, blinded by taboos, some actors will not consider blue-collar jobs without ever finding out how much they pay.)

N/A Infusing

The partial exclusion of options establishes a context in that it sets a normative/affective framework within which L/E considerations may take place. N/A infusion, discussed next, affects the specific choice made within the N/A context, further narrowing the range of L/E considerations. (As a first approximation, the discussion here deals with the role of N/A factors, in affecting choices, as if they were a single factor. Additional elaborations require exploring the relations among N/A factors, which leads to issues that had been previously explored as substantive rationality (Weber 1921–22/1968), moral reasoning (Kohlberg 1981, 1983), and some aspects of what is called cognitive dissonance (Festinger 1957, 1964) but actually reflects N/A factors. These issues are not explored here).

In those behavioral zones in which actors are open to "search behavior," where they seek valid information and try to interpret it and draw inferences properly, their choices are often and extensively subject to N/A infusing. Such infusing takes two main forms: loading and intrusions.

Normative-affective factors *load* (or "color") various facts, their interpretation, and the inferences drawn from them, with non-logical and non-empirical "weights." Unlike exclusion, which precludes from consideration certain facts, interpretations, inferences, and hence options, loading only provides *differential normative-affective ranking* that orders options in ways that differ from their L/E standing.

For example, selling short a stock has the same basic L/E standing as buying one "long" (although there are differences in risk, and some other

L/E considerations concerning payment of dividends and interest charged on marginal accounts, and tax considerations). However, for long periods many Americans—especially small investors—believed that selling short was unpatriotic, "selling America short," not believing in its future. We expect, although we know of no such study, that the more a person was committed to this view, the less likely he or she would be to sell stocks short. This example illustrates, in an area of economic behavior, a situation where the actors do *perceive* two options as a way to improve their investments—buying stock A or selling stock B short. However, they treat one as less "acceptable" than the other, and hence choose B only if the return is much higher, although there is little or no L/E reason for such behavior. Other examples (Katona 1975, p. 272) include people who would rather use installment payments or credit cards, despite their higher interest rates, than take out a loan, because they are against "being in debt;" they do not perceive the use of credit cards as a source of borrowed money, but as "deferred payments." The well-known phenomenon of "money illusion," that suggests that people under some circumstances prefer seemingly higher nominal wages to wages that are actually higher but seemingly lower, is also, at least in part, explained by affective factors; high nominal wages may provide more self-esteem. That is, while both options are perceived by the actor, one option is valued as higher on non-L/E—on N/A—grounds.

Intrusions occur when N/A factors prevent the orderly completion of a specific L/E consideration. L/E considerations require the completion of a *sequence* that involves collecting facts, interpreting their meanings, and drawing inferences leading one to favor one option over others. Decisions often entail several such sequences, one or more for each option, aside from the task of weighing the options themselves. N/A factors—aside from limiting the options that are considered, or loading those that are—often cut short L/E considerations by skipping steps or inadequately completing them.

Interrupted sequences are found in many forms. In some, each step in the process of decision-making is cut short; in others, individuals (and organizations) collect numerous facts but underanalyze them, turning prematurely to conclusions. While L/E thinking is conducted "vertically," in sequences, N/A reflections often draw on "lateral thinking," "jumping" to the solutions. Other forms of intrusion have been established. For example, high stress has been shown to increase random behavior, increase error rate, generate regression to more "primitive" or simpler responses, induce rigidity, reduce attention and tolerance for ambiguity, diminish the ability to separate dangerous events from trivial ones, and cut one's ability to think abstractly (Torrance 1954; Korchin 1964; Holsti 1971).

Data about N/A-loaded choices are available from studies of the ways graduates of universities, including MBAs, choose among job offers they receive. One study reports that the graduates spend a long time comparing the first and second satisfactory offers they receive, in the process subjecting one of the two offers to an unfavorable perceptual distortion, as a way to make it easier to pick the other (Soelberg 1967). Two other studies report that such choices are made without much thought (Moment 1967; Nisbett and Grant 1965). It should be noted, however, that some other studies found a higher degree of reliance on L/E considerations (e.g., Glueck 1974).

Decisions are often discussed and studied as if they occur at one point in time. Actually, most decisions are composed of a series of steps, or subdecisions, or require repeated steps. A decision to stop smoking, for example, is rarely a once-for-all decision but a continuous one. For many, the decision to invest in a stock is not a one-time occurrence—buy it and put it away—but one that is frequently reviewed and, in effect, remade. According to Sjöberg (1980, p. 123), for such decisions there are often "relapses to non-preferred alternatives" as N/A factors undermine decisions previously made on L/E grounds, such as to diet, to stop drinking to excess, or to hold a stock despite short-term price fluctuations. (For additional discussion, see Elster 1985a, pp. 6ff.)

N/A factors also lead people to adhere to loaded decisions even when the L/E factors turn against them. Studies show that people tend to stick to their decisions once a commitment has been made, either publicly or even to one's self (Steiner 1980, p. 22)—they reflect a value that censures being "frivolously inconsistent." If new information that is adverse to their decision is introduced, people tend to deny they could have foreseen it (ibid., p. 24). Berelson and Steiner (1964, p. 575) hold that "The more a person is emotionally involved in his beliefs, the harder it is to change him by argument or propaganda—that is, through an appeal to intelligence—to the point of virtual impossibility." In short, N/A factors may intrude in many ways, but are rarely absent.

Various attempts have been made to incorporate N/A factors into the neoclassical paradigm by assuming that the actors are aware of these factors and respond to them in a calculating fashion, basically as if they were nothing other than one more set of external constraints (Fishbein and Ajzen 1975; Kelley and Thibaut 1978). It is hence necessary to reiterate that it is assumed here that while actors under some conditions treat N/A factors in that manner, these factors are often internalized, i.e., they are absorbed by the person, and shape the inner self. In the process, the N/A factor may well be modified by self, but when the process is complete the values and emotions are, at least in part, what the person believes, feels, prefers, and seeks—not something the person treats as external. (In other words, the fact that people to some extent choose what emotions to display or what values to pay lip service to, does not mean they have no others that they see as their own.)

Legitimated Indifference Zones

Normative-affective factors *define specific, often quite limited* zones as appropriate for, or even as demanding, a decision to be made largely (rarely exclusively) on L/E grounds. These zones are referred to from here on as *legitimated indifference zones**, to emphasize that they are set and protected—from N/A intrusions—by N/A factors. A familiar example from everyday life is when parents berate teenagers for impulsive buying; or, in the traditional family, when husbands (who often considered themselves to be more "rational" and budget-minded) berate their wives for "impulsive" buying. That is, values (for example, frugality) and affect (e.g., anger) are used to curb impulse- and habit-buying, i.e., to enhance rational buying. Similarly, in some homemakers' circles, there is peer pressure to shop wisely, i.e., rationally, by consulting Consumer Reports, engaging in comparative shopping, using coupons and discounts, and so on. The significance of these observations is that indifference zones do not simply exist; they are not the "normal" way people make consumer decisions, as neoclassical economics implies, but are set by N/A factors. The extent to which people "search" is thus not merely a function of information costs and potential savings but of the amount of normative tolerance for, or support of, search behavior. (Thus, in our time it is more legitimate to be concerned with costs and benefits when it comes to "heroic" measures to extend a life, than it may have been in earlier generations when the governing value was that one ought to do "all" one can for a "loved one.")

The limited scope of indifference zones even in the purchase of consumer goods (less N/A-loaded than other economic decisions, such as investment or job choice) is highlighted by studies of involvement. An overview of numerous studies of consumer behavior distinguishes between "high-involvement" products (for most contemporary American consumers) and "low-involvement" ones (Engel and Blackwell 1982, pp. 21–22). High-involvement goods are those that consumers consider not merely as products they may wish to use, but also as items that "send a message to the world" about the person, and that are tied to the person's sense of self-esteem. Choosing among them involves decisions that are more "complex" and prolonged and N/A-affected than deciding among items of low involvement, a decision entailing no risk to one's self-esteem.

The finding that is particularly significant for our model is that surprisingly numerous items fall into the high-involvement category. These include not only "big" purchases such as autos, houses, and most cloth-

---

*Barnard (1947, pp. 167–69) uses the term to denote an area in which an individual is willing to accept orders. Actions outside the zone violate the person's sense of what ought to be obeyed.

ing, but also coffee (the quality of which is viewed as indicating one's "ability" as a homemaker), buying generic drugs rather than brand name (which is perceived as "taking a risk with one's family"), and many other items (Engel and Blackwell 1982, p. 21). Low involvement items include ball-point pens, light bulbs, and aluminum foil and other such relatively trivial items. Other studies have come up with different lists, but the role of N/A factors and the limited range of indifference zones are evident in all of them (Furham and Lewis 1986, pp. 207ff; Morgan 1978, p. 61).

Similarly, it is common to note that in public policy matters one ought to draw on expert "inputs," but that, because of N/A factors, decisions are often made by policy-makers who draw on "other," especially on ideological-political, considerations. Only decisions of a highly technical nature are left to experts, typically only within the context of choices made, in part, on N/A grounds.

In other words, L/E considerations are allowed to dominate those choices in which none of the options is N/A-loaded, i.e., when all options have the same or a comparable N/A standing. Here, according to Janis and Mann (1977), individuals are "cool," and L/E considerations are allowed to govern. As we see it, all this is quite true, except that people are often not that cool. And, the extent to which they are is, in part, determined by N/A factors.

ARE N/A CONSIDERATIONS "DISRUPTIVE"?

Affect: A Matter of Personality Theory

How one views the role of affect in decision-making is framed by the personality theory to which one subscribes, if any. The phrase "if any" is introduced because in recent decades the great difficulties in agreeing on one personality theory, and in operationalizing such a theory, has led many psychologists to abandon the use of personality theory and focus instead on the study of specific cognitive processes. Without attempting here to review the immense literature on personality theories (the volumes on different interpretations of Freud alone would fill a small library), the points relevant to the issue at hand are briefly indicated.

Some personality theories, usually associated with Freud, see raw emotions (or the *id*) as wild forces that disrupt reason. While these forces can be "civilized," even used to energize the *superego* and *ego,* improper or incomplete socialization leaves some raw emotions lurking in the dark recesses of the personality. Sooner or later, these emotions break through, causing impulsive, regressive, infantile—i.e., irrational—behavior, or activating various unwholesome defensive mechanisms. In short, raw emotions are viewed as antithetical to reason. No wonder Freud's work is viewed as a grand challenge to the Age of Reason.

Implicit in the argument that L/E considerations are rational, at the core of the neoclassical paradigm, is the prescription that they are the correct ones to make. Indeed, it is widely acknowledged that neoclassical decision-making theories are much more prescriptive than descriptive. The role of affect, to the extent that it is not simply ignored, is depicted as negative, a factor that "twists" and "distorts" thinking. Elster (1985b, p. 379) holds that "When emotions are directly involved in action, they tend to overwhelm or subvert rational mental processes, not to supplement them." Sjöberg (1980, p. 123) refers to "twisted reasoning" by "emotional stress." Toda (1980, p. 133) sees emotions as having a "disturbing" role, as "noisome, irrational agents in the decision-making process." Still others see emotions as "desorganizing." (Four sources are cited by Isen 1984, p. 180.)

Literally hundreds of studies could be cited that support this perspective. A typical study establishes the role of affect in the estimation of probabilities. Wright and Bower (1981) tested the influence of mood on an individual's estimation of "blessed" and "catastrophic" events. Subjects were asked to evaluate the likelihood of various events on a scale of 1 to 100. They evaluated half the list in an induced happy state, the other half in a sad state. The control group evaluated the whole list in a neutral state. The neutral group evaluated the events as follows: Blessed .44; Catastrophic .43. The happy group rated Blessed at .52 and Catastrophic at .37, while the sad group rated Blessed at .38 and Catastrophic at .52. Thus, when sad, negative events are viewed as more likely and good outcomes as less likely than when the subjects are in a neutral mood. When happy, the subjects view good outcomes as more likely. In short, mood biases cognition. (For further evidence on the subjective editing of probabilities see Steiner 1980, p. 23, and Edwards 1954, p. 400.)

While the study cited here deals with an element of information-processing and decision-making (estimation of probabilities), Janis and Mann deal with the role of affect in the whole process. They found (1977, pp. 10–11) that it is very difficult to judge the efficiency of a decision maker by outcomes because the outcomes are numerous, and often difficult to measure quantitatively. Hence, they developed a process model of seven steps which efficient decision-makers go through, drawing mainly on the work of Etzioni (1967, 1968), Katz and Kahn (1966), Simon (1976), and others. The steps included "thorough canvassing of a wide range of alternative courses of action"; surveying full range of objectives; careful aligning of consequences; "search for new information"; and "open assimilation of new information." (Janis and Mann 1977, p. 11.) Jointly these steps are referred to as vigilant decision-making. Omission of any step will render a decision defective, and the greater the number of omissions, the more defective the decision.

Janis and Mann next reviewed numerous psychological studies to show that most decision-making is not vigilant, because all significant decision-making evokes anxiety—i.e., an emotional strain. People often fall into one of four defective patterns: inertia (sticking to a course, despite a challenge, without proper decision-making by the use of established criteria); an unexamined shift to a new course of action; defensive avoidance; and, lastly, hypervigilance. The study provides detailed analyses of each pattern and their antecedence. Anxiety is cardinal to all.

Freudian and other psychodynamic theories, that view raw affect as antithetical to reason, are usually contrasted with the work of Piaget, which focuses on cognitive processes. Even when he deals with moral development, at the core is the development of judgments, not of commitments. Cognitive psychology, in general, has in recent decades been strongly inclined to view emotions as an unnecessary concept, in Leventhal's words (1982, p. 126) to "treat emotions as the product of non-emotional processes, usually a synthesis of cognitive and automatic motor reactions." More on this below. However, the main alternative to Freudian and other such overarching positions on the role of emotions, is the position—found in the work of humanistic psychologists, for example Abraham Maslow—that says that affect provides a constructive basis for behavior and decision-making. Here, people are seen as motivated by the desire to satisfy basic human needs such as affection, self-esteem, and self-actualization. Affect is depicted as wholesome and "normal" rather than destructive. Indeed, some see excessive preoccupation with reason as problematic. Spontaneity is valued over extensive deliberations.

The main view followed here is that raw emotions often do curb reason, and that the socialization of emotions may never be complete. At the same time it is recognized that socialized emotions often, though not always, play significant positive roles, including enhancing decision-making. That is, whether affect is constructive or disruptive depends on the specific circumstances and the role it plays.

To illustrate: some studies suggest that the greater the emotional intensity, the more narrow is one's focus. For example, in an extreme state of fear, an individual will notice only the feared object. This narrowing is beneficial or detrimental depending on the nature of the task involved. The narrowing may exclude irrelevant facts and help individuals concentrate their intellectual powers. On the other hand, it may exclude highly relevant factors, preventing the proper analysis of available options.

While not all the findings point to the same conclusion, it is widely agreed that there is a *curvilinear* relationship between the level of affect and that of rationality. When affect is very low, decisions may not be made when it is rational to proceed. When affect is very high, it tends to disrupt deliberations. At moderate levels, affect is more likely to facilitate decision-making (Woodworth and Schlosberg 1954; Holsti 1971, p. 57).

Yerkes and Dodson (1908) found that the more complex a task, the lower the optimal level of emotive arousal. This was supported by several more recent studies. In one of them, a group of students was given a problem-solving test in which the problems became increasingly more complex. Prior to the test, while the control group was given an unrelated task, the experimental group was given a block-tapping test so difficult that it was impossible to succeed. This frustrated group (now more emotionally aroused than the control group) scored higher than the control group on the early part of the test. As the problems became more complex, the control group surpassed the frustrated group in performance. And students who were most frustrated by the block-tapping test did the most poorly on the complex problems.

Pieter and van Raaij (1987) provide a major review of the role of affect in economic, especially consumer, behavior. They list the following significant functions:

1. Affect serves as an information organization about one's own somatic functions (e.g., it informs self how hungry one is), and about the environment (e.g., how scared one is, say, about reports of a shortage).

2. Affect serves to mobilize and allocate resources (e.g., strong emotions mobilize or inhibit action).

3. Affect provides sensation seeking (e.g., to overcome boredom on an assembly line) and avoidance (to combat stress).

4. Affect serves as a communication system (showing one's feelings to others, say, regarding how much a fur is desired).

The authors proceed to review scores of studies showing these varying effects of affects.

In short, the notion that affect necessarily, commonly, or even typically subverts rational decision-making is rejected. Affect often plays a positive role, although it undermines rationality when it excessively restricts the context of decision-making, heavily loads one option compared to others, or interrupts L/E deliberations. Further work is needed to spell out the specific conditions under which affect is productive, and when it undermines rationality. This is preferred to assuming that it is either constructive or disruptive in nature.

The Role of Normative Values

Values are an overarching criteria people use to make choices. Values may be moral, personal, social, or aesthetic (Williams, 1968). Most values—all but the aesthetic ones in the preceding list—contain an affective element. It is the source of the commitment to the content of the value, the motivational force. Values that have lost their affective elements become empty shells, fragments of intellectual tracts or phrases to which people pay lip service but do not heed much in their choices. From here on only those values are studied that have an affective power, that prescribe behavior—values referred to as "normative."

Normative values differ from sheer affective involvement in that they contain a justification and define a wider claim (others to whom the same right applies), while sheer affective states contain no such statements and often are particularistic. (Love for mankind is a value; love for a particular person is an emotion.) Normative values may be internalized and thus become part of the actor's perception and judgment, or they may remain external, part of the constraints the actor faces. Judgments based on normative values may be used to curb emotions or to legitimate them. And normative values are at the core of the deontological paradigm.

The line that separates moral values (the focus of Part I) from the wider, more encompassing set of normative values is not sharply delineated. It is common practice, however, to refer to values that agitate against lying, stealing, and killing as "moral," and values such as equality, freedom, and justice as social values. Since the discussion in Parts II and III encompasses both moral and social values, the term normative values is used.

The relationships between normative values and rationality is in many ways akin to that of affect and rationality. Normative values may exclude some or most options, load others, and so on. For example, a study (Lefford 1946, p. 141) has shown that normative loading inhibits logical reasoning. Students were given 40 syllogisms. Half of these dealt with socially controversial material, the other half with neutral material. Subjects were asked to state the validity of the syllogism as well as whether they agreed or disagreed with its conclusion. Most subjects were better able to judge neutral syllogisms than charged ones, and their reasoning was biased in the direction of their convictions. Moreover, the group of students who were given the neutral syllogisms first, followed by the charged syllogisms, did better on both.

Normative values are also reported to lead to selective exposure to information. For example, during Watergate, McGovern supporters actively sought information about the event, while Nixon supporters avoided it (Chaiken and Stangor 1987, p. 10). Normative values influence the weight given to information in ways that bias judgment toward strengthening preexisting beliefs (Abelson and Levi 1985). When information conflicts with one's commitments, it may not "sink in," and will not be ingested (von Magnus 1984, p. 637). Anybody who ever debated or argued with a true believer, one who is committed to a religion or ideology different from one's own, is familiar with such behavior.

Abelson (1976, p. 61) discusses the many functions served by holding beliefs (a term often used as synonymous with or similar to normative values) ". . . other than in the service of rationality. Beliefs may be comforting, may protect against anxiety, may organize vague feelings, may provide a sense of identity, may be the prerequisite for participating in a cause, may provide something to say to avoid seeming uninformed, etc."

Last but not least, normative values, as factors that influence the choice of means, help ensure the primacy of ends. The preoccupation with means, with enhancing their strength, scope, quantity and quality, is the essence of industrialization, market economies and economics, technology and applied science, in short, of the modern age. However, this preoccupation, through a process known as goal displacement, tends to lead to the primacy of means over ends. Studies of organizations are replete with reports of organizations designed to serve a specific goal; however, when the design proved to be inappropriate, rather than adjust it, the organizational goal was replaced to suit the existing design (Sills, 1957). Multi-millionaires work themselves to a frazzle to increase their income. Executives work "for their families," destroying their family life in the process. Societies undermine their fabric in order to accelerate economic growth. This phenomenon has been referred to as irrational rationality, or mad rationality.

Dr. Strangelove provides a convenient symbol for the issue at hand. It is not a matter of ends. Dr. Strangelove, one may concede, may be truly dedicated to peace, but he does not see any limits to the means he employs. In his quest for ever "better" means of deterrence, "better" nuclear weapons, he may end up killing all mankind in order to ensure peace. The issue arises elsewhere. Totalitarian movements are frequently charged with a disregard for the normative standing of means. Castro believes that to make omelets (revolutions) one must be willing to crack eggs (or heads), while democracies hold that certain means defile the goals. Normative values serve as an antidote to goal displacement because they weigh-in against the use of certain categories of means (those that undermine ends) as well as excessive preoccupation with means (or efficiency), to the neglect of other values.

Within Western thought, the rationalist position—which tends to disregard the legitimate role of normative values in the selection of means— is reflected in a widely held position among scientific experts who bemoan the fact that politicians "do not comprehend" this or that L/E consideration; they also suggest that, once goals are chosen, experts should make the decisions. (In a more extreme form, they wish to draw ends from a scientific analysis. Hence the attempt to form a science of ethics.)

Medical research provides another example of the positive role of normative values. There is a need to continually assess new experimental interventions from moral viewpoints. True, occasionally the normative factors may set too tight a context; e.g., by unduly limiting experiments. However, in other situations, scientists are insufficiently restrained. The correct question hence is not: do normative values play a positive role in decision-making, but rather, under what conditions do they contribute to, and when do they undermine, rationality? (Fine material on these conditions is found in the organizational behavior literature. See Beer, Spector, Lawrence, Mills, and Walton, 1985, and Walton and Lawrence, 1985.)

It is tempting to suggest that with regard to both values and emotions,

N/A factors enhance decision-making when they set contexts (limits within which means may be freely chosen), and hinder decision-making when these factors infuse, and especially when they interrupt, L/E considerations. While such a statement may serve as a very crude first approximation, it must be noted that the "tightness" of context is another factor: the fewer options it legitimates, the more it limits rationality, but not all limits on rationality are disfunctional. Also, some interruptions of orderly decision-making—e.g., in an emergency, when emotions instruct us to escape rather than deliberate—are highly functional. In short, the specification of the relation between the role of values and rationality decision-making, like that of affect, is a task far from complete, but it is clearly established that both affect and normative values often play important positive functions, and that they are not merely hindrances to reason.

ON DEFINITIONS, MEASUREMENTS, AND ALTERNATIVE INTERPRETATIONS

Cognitive Interpretations of N/A Factors

Cognitive psychologists correctly challenged the notion that every deviation from rationality is due to an N/A factor. Indeed, they have provided robust evidence that L/E considerations are often limited or disturbed by *intra*-cognitive factors (discussed below). It is argued here, however, that the approach is sometimes carried too far when it is suggested that all or most limitations on L/E considerations are cognitive, and that N/A factors play no significant role. While we have no new evidence to present, the data available suggest that the role of N/A factors in affecting decision-making is far from trivial.

Most of the cognitive studies chose tasks for their subjects that have two features of particular relevance for the issue at hand: they have one unequivocal solution (at least within the framework of Bayesian logic), and there are no normative-affective loadings attached to any of the options. For example, when subjects are asked whether Xs or Os are more frequent in a random sequence (on which they tend to project a pattern), the correct answer—that both are equally frequent—is not hindered by an affective attachment to, or normative judgment of, either X or O. Hence, it is quite plausible that the source of the bias that subjects exhibit is intra-cognitive.

In contrast, many facts, inferences, and judgments that people make in real-life situations concern matters that have no clear-cut answers, and which include items that evoke affects and normative judgments. Typically, facts that individuals employ are more akin to those Americans have with which to gauge whether or not the Soviet Union is trustworthy, or what inflation and interest rates will be ten years hence—judgments that are anxiety-provoking (a mistake may cost one's home, or country). That is, while in some situations only intra-cognitive biases are at work, and in others both intra-cognitive and N/A factors are present, we suggest that most real-life decisions are of the second kind.

Indeed, in those studies conducted by cognitive psychologists that deal with real-life situations, the N/A factors seem to us to stand out and provide a parsimonious explanation. For example, psychologists find that people are, in general, overconfident in estimating probabilities that affect their lives. They believe they are better drivers than average drivers, more likely to live past 80 than the average, and also less likely to be harmed by products (Slovic and Lichtenstein 1982). This is explained as a matter of "availability," a cognitive phenomenon in which people respond more to "vivid" information than to "dull" statistics. Since people have little experience with major accidents, these events are said not to be "vivid" and hence are underestimated. This may well be true; however, it seems plausible that *part* of the variance is to be explained by N/A factors—such as people trying to protect or enhance their self-esteem ("I am a good driver"), and by cultural pressures to display confidence. (Thus, one would expect such responses to be more common in boisterous cultures than in those in which self-effacing is the accepted norm. Compare American attitudes to British, for example.)

The same point can be seen in the finding that most people's risk behavior defies the assumptions of neoclassical economics about such behavior. For instance, individuals prefer a sure gain over a much larger but less certain gain even when according to the probabilities the economic value of the second option is considerably higher (Kahneman and Tversky 1982, p. 160); i.e., individuals prefer the smaller return. Similarly, people violate the neoclassical assumptions that they will take a risk only if compensated for the risk. They prefer to gamble on a loss than accept a certain loss even if the gamble loss is much larger (of course, taking into account the difference in probabilities), and so on. All these findings are explainable *in part* in the relative loss to self-esteem (part emotion, part value) caused by some outcomes as compared to others. For example, the reason people prefer a sure, smaller gain over a less probable, larger one is explained by the observation that a small but sure gain avoids the possibilities of having to criticize oneself if the gain is lost, a prospect a person must face only if he or she goes for the larger gain. This N/A line of explanation, in addition to cognitive interpretation, may be validated if people with higher self-esteem will be found more inclined to take risks.

In effect there is a considerable body of psychological studies that tie cognitive biases of the kind discussed above to various ego-defenses, and specifically to self-esteem (Heider 1958; Jones and Davis 1965; Kelley 1967). For example, individuals often attribute success to their own efforts, and faults and failures to bad luck, or to other factors over which they have no control (in achievement tasks: Davis and Davis 1972; Feather 1969; Fitch 1970; Wolosin, Sherman, and Till 1973; in teaching performances: Beckman 1970; Freize and Weiner 1971; Johnson, Feigenbaum, and Weiby 1964). Similarly, the fact that people are much more willing to take a risk to avoid a loss than to make an equivalent gain seems to reflect, in part, N/A factors: a loss concerns what a person has; a gain yet to be made is not yet incorporated into one's self-concept. Compare, for example, the resistance to a wage cut versus gaining a smaller raise than expected. True, other factors are also at work; for instance, people may make financial commitments on the basis of what they have, commitments not made as readily for funds they hope to gain. But, even for those with ready credit, losses "hurt" more than forgone gains.

The difference in emphasis is highlighted in the discussion of prejudice. Nisbett and Ross (1980, pp. 237–42) attack the tendency to attribute racial or ethnic prejudice to motivational, emotional, or spiritual "defects," to a "triumph of the heart over the intellect." They see the cause of prejudice in various *cognitive* biases. For example, those in groups against which prejudice is held, those members who fit stereotypes are given disproportionately higher weight than others, and "vivid" incidents are used to "validate" the stereotypes (p. 240). Thus, according to this line of analysis, those who see a few lazy blacks, or loud Italians, and assume that all are, are simply over-generalizing. One may wonder, why do they not over-generalize positive attributes? Why do they so often focus their hostility on vulnerable groups? Emotional mechanisms seem at work. For example, people seem to split their ambivalence about others in such a way that negative feelings are projected on the out-group and positive ones to the We group.

Matters of Operationalization

The terms "affect" and "normative values" have been used in the preceding discussion despite the fact that in the mainstreams of recent psychological literature these terms are avoided, although in the 1980s the concept of affect (or emotions) had a measure of a comeback. (Not so, yet, for normative values.) Without going here into details of the complex matters involved, it is necessary to indicate briefly the reason the author draws on these unfashionable concepts.

Part of the answer lies in intellectual history. In the period between 1960 and 1980, mainstreams of psychology were preoccupied with establishing that intra-mind processes are valuable, and in overcoming the behavioristic notions that behavior is externally driven, formed by inputs from the environment, with the person being viewed as a "black box" that need not be explored internally (Norman 1980, pp. 1–11). The internal processes that were highlighted were characterized as strictly cognitive, as if the difficulty of introducing such an ephemeral concept as cognition were so great as to discourage any disposition to go even further and also reintroduce affect (Zajonc 1980, p. 152). Indeed, emotions were either "shown" to be an unnecessary concept or viewed as reflecting cognitive interpretations of unspecific psychological arousal.

The work of Schachter (1966, 1971) and his associates (Schachter and Singer 1962) is often cited to argue that emotions are nothing but physiological arousal, and a cognitive coding of the situation that generates the arousal. What the person "feels" depends not on the inner sensation, but on the situation that caused it, and on the ways the person appraises the situation. The *same* arousal may be experienced as joy or anger depending on the cognition brought to bear. We note that many criticisms have been made of the original studies, and that attempts to replicate them have not succeeded (Marshall and Zimbardo 1979; Maslach 1979), and that hundreds of studies have shown the role of affect (for a review work see Isen 1984).

Another major reason emotions have been played down is that they have been difficult to define. It should, however, be noted that there are similar difficulties in defining the term cognition (Holyoak and Gordon 1984, p. 62), and, of course, rationality. Hence, definitional difficulties should not be used to favor one concept over the other.

Finally, researchers have encountered considerable difficulty in finding empirical measurements of emotions. However, we believe that a promising approach to measure affect is to combine several measurements, thus correcting for the weakness of each single one. For example, self-reports ("verbal, introspective") of emotional states tend to be problematic because they are subject to rationalization. (People buy more of a product when the background music is to their liking, but, when asked, report they bought the product because of its qualities.) Physiological aspects of emotions are measured by electronic devices (similar to polygraphs), and indications such as flushing, breaking out in perspiration, trembling, are unreliable because they may reflect other factors, e.g., changes in temperature or in physical exertion. Behavioral measures, such as smiling (when happy) and frowning (when concerned), are similarly unreliable, when used in isolation.

However, when all three kinds of indicators point in the same direction, one may be assured that the affect is indeed operative. And when the measurements are incompatible, this may be used to form a typology of different kinds of affect, such as declared emotions (only self-reported), physiological arousal, and so on. Those, in turn, may correlate with various psychological observations. For example, emotions limited to one of the possible three levels, are expected to be less stable than those that encompass all three levels. For instance, a person who only declares an emotion, but exhibits no arousal or emotional behavior, may be expected to conform to social norms that have not been internalized (for example, one may salute a flag when one is actually quite unpatriotic). For additional discussion of definitions and measurements of emotions, see Izard, Kagan, and Zajonc (1984).

The concept of normative values may pose fewer problems than that of affect, but is hardly free of methodological concerns. The concept is often challenged on the ground that values as states-of-mind are not observable, and provide poor predictions of behavior. However, in recent years approaches have been developed that measure values closer to behavior than was previously the tradition (Schwartz 1977; Ajzen and Fishbein 1980; England 1967; England and Lee 1974; and Watson and Barone 1976). Indeed, studies that include such variables often predict better than those that do not include attitudes (Hoch 1985).

All this is not to say that the serious problems in defining and operationalizing affects and values have been solved. However, they also are evident in the other, widely used concepts, and there are some promising leads at hand.

Can N/A Factors Be Incorporated into the Neoclassical Paradigm?

Neoclassicists argue that even if all these observations about the significance of N/A factors are valid, it is still unnecessary to evolve another paradigm because these factors can be incorporated into the prevailing paradigm. N/A factors can be included in preferences (especially as they affect goals) and in constraints (especially as they affect the choice of means). Value commitments and emotional involvements are said to be simply two of the many factors "reflected" in one's preferences. Much of Part I of this volume is dedicated to the argument that such incorporation of values is excessively parsimonious, unproductive, and ethically unacceptable. Here additional arguments are brought to bear to support the thesis that N/A factors should be treated as a significant, distinct category, both of preferences and constraints (Etzioni, 1986a).

If N/A only curbed one's choice to a limited extent, these factors could be "modeled" as nothing more than one more factor that affects constraints, like adding a friction factor in frictionless slope models. This would be the case, for instance, if one studies a tribe whose members are prohibited from purchasing cows, but are free to trade in thousands of other items. However, the position taken here is that a good part of the choices made by individuals is made on N/A and not L/E grounds; i.e., N/A factors are not simply one more factor, part of a large batch, but explain a significant proportion of the choices made, and hence need to be studied separately if choices are to be explained.

Most important, neoclassicists treat preferences as stable and/or as given (see above). However, as N/A factors account for an important part of the variance among preferences and for changes in them, a productive social science paradigm must be able to identify the factors that form and that change affect and values. Hence, cultural change, social movements, the rise and fall of leaderships, societal strains and their resolution or reduction—all factors that explain N/A changes—must be included in the paradigm.

Also, as neoclassicists are stressing the merit of their approach because it is highly parsimonious, it should be noted that recognizing the role of N/A factors is especially parsimonious because they affect both preferences *and* constraints.

An example serves to illustrate all these points. From 1981 to 1986 in the USA there was a decline in the consumption of alcohol. A neoclassicist may seek to explain this trend by a change in constraints, such as rising costs, new taxes, increase in the drinking age, and so on. However, the price of liquor actually declined as compared to that of other products, and consumption declined even in states that did not raise the drinking age. The major reason was a change in preferences, the result of a neo-temperance movement (especially MADD and SADD) adding its influence to that of a rising movement for fitness and health. *These same factors* also affected the price:—they led to some increase in taxes—and of the drinking age.

7

How Inefficient?
The Scope of Intra-Cognitive
Limitations

THE SUB-RATIONAL POSITION

The Issues Outlined

Even in the zones in which N/A factors do not fully form the choice of individuals, and in particular in the zones in which N/A factors legitimate the primacy of L/E considerations, individuals are not necessarily free to render rational decisions. In these zones, decision makers are hindered by the limitations of their intellectual capabilities. We have already established the reasons we expect their emotions and values to lead them to drive high-powered autos in congested downtown streets, even when walking is cheaper, faster, and healthier. But once they are in their car, they seem unable to find the best route, or to follow it once it is pointed out to them.

There are numerous robust studies that support the conclusion that *intra*-cognitive factors, factors that are built into the individuals' intellectual capabilities, typically prevent people from making decisions that are fully rational. (For a definition of rationality, see Chapter 8, pp. 144–45.) That is, even when N/A factors do not hinder L/E deliberations, the actors' knowledge (of real-life situations) as a rule is not merely "imperfect" but quite limited, and their ability to analyze whatever information they do command, and to draw proper inferences from it, is rather low. They are *sub*-rational even within the L/E zones.

The real question is, how limited is individual thinking and decision-making? In attempting to answer this question the following analysis draws on a specification of Herbert Simon's critical breakthrough, the well-known abandonment of the notion of maximizing (or optimizing), and the introduction of the concept of "satisficing." What remains to be clarified is whether satisficing behavior is close to maximizing, or only to "quite good," or do most individuals settle (or, have to settle) for quite mediocre decision-making?

Once this question is answered the discussion builds on a second major breakthrough, that by the Prospect School, which has proven that the intra-cognitive heuristics used by decision makers are systematically biased. These are vision-distorting glasses that everyone wears. The question here is: Can these distortions be corrected, or do they constitute congenital limitations?

An examination of these two positions will show that while they serve as major correctives to the super-optimism of the enlightenment position, entailed in the neoclassical rationalistic position, they under-correct: people's intellectual capabilities are lower than is expected even by these important revisionists. The next step in the discussion is to examine polar opposite positions, to see if die-hard pessimistic positions are more appropriate. First we examine the disjointed incrementalists, led by Charles Lindblom. They assume no ability to accumulate systematic, comprehensive knowledge. Next we briefly discuss the subjectivists who are even more pessimistic, because they question the very possibility of a concept of an L/E validity or truth. We find these positions excessively pessimistic, though closer to the situation than the sanguine schools.

The position advanced here might be characterized as moderately pessimistic (as regarding ability to render L/E decisions). It is suggested that while, as a rule, people cannot successfully complete detailed analyses, they can combine the use of guidelines for broad overviews with some detailed analyses. This approach is referred to as "mixed scanning," was previously published (Etzioni 1967), and achieved a measure of support (for overview, see Etzioni 1986a).

Specifying Satisficing

Herbert Simon is the David who successfully dared the neoclassical maximizing giant, following generations in which he was merely peppered with criticism (for review of those see Papandreou 1952; empirical evidence in support of Simon, see Rados 1972, and Cyert and March 1963). It is well known that Simon concludes that "Man" is unable to maximize (for reasons cited below). It is much less often noted that because practically all the debate has been between maximizers and satisficers, the question has not been answered: How divergent are the two? Are satisficing decisions "quite good," albeit not perfect, if those actually made are compared to those that could have been made given full information and analysis? Or are they rather mediocre?

A development in Simon's own writing on the subject suggests the direction in which an answer might be found. In an early article, applying the concept of "satisfice" to the theory of the firm, Simon (1959, pp.

262–63) explains the notion in psychological terms. The motive to act, he writes "stems from *drives,* and action terminates when the drive is satisfied." This implies a quite satisfactory decision-making process: It is terminated only after solutions are found that attend to one's needs. However, Simon leaves the door open for less optimistic interpretations in the very next lines:

> If we seek to explain business behavior in the terms of this theory, we must expect the firm's goals to be not maximizing profit, but attaining a *certain* level or rate of profit, holding a *certain* share of the market or a *certain* level of sales. Firms would try to 'satisfice' rather than to maximize. (1959, p. 263, italics provided.)

The term "certain" level, "certain" share, etc. is quite open-ended. There is no indication whether actors or firms will come to rest at what, from the viewpoint of an objective observer, is well below the level of L/E decision-making they could attain, or quite close to it.

In a later writing, Simon (1979, p. 503) states:

> . . . one could postulate that the decision maker had formed some *aspiration* as to how good an alternative he should find. As soon as he discovered an alternative for choice meeting his level of aspiration, he would terminate the search and choose that alternative. I called this mode of selection *satisficing.*

Simon adds that aspirations will rise in benign environments and fall in harsh ones. Viewed in this way, the actors adjust their goals to what their decision-making can service. If the target is easy, aspirations rise; if difficult to fathom, they fall. For example, if economic policy-making cannot attain a 4 percent unemployment rate without inflation, rationalizations are advanced to explain why 7 percent is the proper goal, and immediately our policy-making capacity improves significantly. If this line is followed, decision-making will tend to be quite satisfactory from the subjective viewpoint of the actor, but an observer may find it rather inadequate, at least from the viewpoint of the goal the actor initially set out to accomplish.

Simon (1981, p. 139) comes closest to an answer in a recent book.

> We cannot within practicable computational limits generate all the admissible alternatives and compare their respective merits. Nor can we recognize the best alternative, even if we are fortunate enough to generate it early, until we have seen all of them. We satisfice by looking for alternatives in such a way that we can generally find an acceptable one after only moderate search.

The key phrase and hypothesis are contained in the notion that a typical search is a moderate one. That is, if a prolonged, all-encompassing, complex search is required, which most real-life decisions require, most actors most of the time will settle for a rather sub-rational course of action compared to that which an observer will deem is possible. The pessi-mistic interpretation of the concept of satisficing, we shall see, is compat-ible with the evidence.

The reasons actors are expected to be sub-rational decision-makers can be gleaned from Simon's examination of the intra-cognitive factors that severely curb their L/E considerations, beyond N/A factors. Basically Simon (1978, p. 13, italics provided) sees *"limited* information and *limited* computational capacity to deal with enormous problems whose shape we barely grasp." Simon (1979, p. 96) points out that

> the evidence is overwhelming that the system is basically serial in its operation: That it can process only a few symbols at a time and that the symbols being processed must be held in special, limited memory structures whose content can be changed rapidly. The most striking lim-its on subjects' capacities to employ efficient strategies arise from the very small capacity of the short-term memory structure (four chunks) and from the relatively long time (five seconds) required to transfer a chunk of information from short-term to long-term memory.

Steinbruner (1974, pp. 49–51) complains about those who expect tennis players to calculate whether to lob, smash, or rush the net, saying that they must deal with 4200 possibilities. Others came up with higher fig-ures. In a simple game of checkers there are said to be 10^{40} choices of moves. At 3 millimicroseconds per move, a computer would take 10^{21} centuries to calculate all possible options and resultant outcomes (Wal-drop 1984, p. 1280). The so-called "combination explosion" seems un-solvable even by high-power computers.

Elsewhere Simon stresses the limitations of *short-term memory.* While individuals can store large amounts of information in the deeper recesses of their memory, the bottleneck occurs in the rapid-access storage that uses short-term memory. People are able to hold only some seven items (or perhaps as low as three) in their immediate mental grasp (Simon 1981, pp. 74–75). Compare this to the hundreds of items a maximal deci-sion may require. And Simon calls attention to the great difficulties that individuals have in *logically combining* prior information with new inputs, which causes them to either grossly over-respond or under-adjust to new information (Simon 1979, p. 139). All said and done, one may conclude that while to "satisfice" somehow sounds as not too remote from to maxi-mize (indeed, some argued the two cannot be told apart, see the debate in Chapter 10 between Lanzillotti and Kahn), a closer reading of Simon implies a relatively weak performance compared to what it might be.

The Prospect School: Biased Heuristics

A second major breakthrough in dealing with the issue at hand is the result of highly robust and accumulative work on systematic biases in thinking by a group of cognitive psychologists who formulated the Prospect theory. Its key members include Daniel Kahneman, Richard Nisbett, Amos Tversky, Lee Ross, Paul Slovic, and Richard Thaler. Their main thesis is that given the limited ability of human beings to process information, and the complex world they face (as Simon indicates), people use various heuristic devices to simplify the complex world in order to be able to deal with it. However, while these heuristics help to some extent, they themselves introduce major systematic biases of their own which subvert human deliberations, and hence subvert decision-making.

The Prospect School focuses on major systematic biases that enter as people must deal with uncertainty in most real life decision-making, and hence assign probabilities to the expected outcomes of their interventions, and to events that might impinge on the chosen course of action. While early neoclassical writings assume actors act under certainty, in recent decades the fact is often recognized that actors must frequently choose among future outcomes and courses of events that are uncertain. A very sizable and rich body of literature has been developed which attempts to sustain the neoclassical paradigm (for review and reference see Hirshleifer and Riley 1979). Basically, this literature assumes that actors can estimate the probabilities of various outcomes of events, and use these to guide their own deliberations. Thus, instead of assuming that if they will drill for oil at cost X they will find Y barrels of oil, to be sold at price Z, the actors assign probabilities to these factors and thus make their calculations. The Prospect School findings that people cannot make these calculations properly hence knocks out the recently erected neoclassical defenses.

While numerous biases have been uncovered, three have received major attention and are briefly reported here for those unfamiliar with the findings. *Availability* refers to the findings that people systematically accord higher estimates to the frequency of events (or category of events) that they can recall more readily, than to those that are more difficult to recall. Events which are "vivid" (say, a personal experience) or highly publicized are estimated as being more frequent than others that are reflected in "dull" statistics, even when this clearly is not the case. For example, people believe homicides are more common than suicides because of the higher publicity accorded to murder, although the opposite is the case. While all physicians are aware of the statistical evidence about the danger of smoking, there is a clear correlation between the closeness of their specialty to lungs, and cessation of smoking. Mere publication of statistics on risk for breast cancer had little effect, but the publicized mastectomies performed on Mrs. Ford and Mrs. Rockefeller in the Fall of 1974 led to a flood of visits to cancer detection clinics (Nisbett and Ross 1980, p. 56).

The second systematic bias is that of *representation*. The question is, what are the chances that object X belongs to category Y? People judge the probability by a similarity principle: How much is X like Y? This is misleading because similarity and frequency often do not coincide. For example, when people are given information about the probabilities of certain events (e.g., how many lawyers and how many engineers are in a population that is being sampled), and then are given some additional information as to which of the events has occurred (for example, about a person who has been drawn from the population), they tend to ignore the probabilities and rely on the incomplete or even irrelevant information about the individual. Thus, if they are told that 70 percent of the population are lawyers, and if they are then given a noncommittal description of a person (one that could equally well fit a lawyer or an engineer), half the time they will predict that the person is a lawyer and half the time that he is an engineer—even though the laws of probability dictate that the best forecast is always to predict that the person is a lawyer (National Academy of Sciences 1986, p. 25).

The third systematic bias is referred to as *anchoring and adjustment*. People use a convenient starting point (the anchor) to estimate a magnitude. People often start with a wrong initial estimate ("prior") which is not as much of a concern, because they are expected to learn from experience (simulated by repeating the same experiment). However, the experiments show that people either dig in and refuse to adjust (see Simon 1978, p. 9), or grossly under-adjust (Anderson, Leper, Ross 1980; Kahneman and Tversky 1973). These experimental findings are substantiated in real-life situations.

> There is a famous case history that illustrates this point. A manufacturer put out a new ceiling tile without holes or perforations of any kind, and it could be demonstrated that sound absorption capability was markedly improved. Yet, consumers rejected the product on the basis that an effective ceiling tile must have holes. After a period of unsuccessfully fighting this misbelief through advertising, the manufacturer inserted the holes and thereby reduced the performance of the product. Sales then responded positively. (Engel and Blackwell 1982, pp. 14–15.)

As Nisbett and Ross (1980, p. 41) put it:

> ... once subjects have made a first pass at a problem, the initial judgment may prove remarkably resistant to further information, alternative modes of reasoning, and even logical or evidential challenges. Attempts to integrate new information may find the individual surprisingly "conservative," that is, willing to yield ground only grudgingly and primed to challenge the relevance, reliability, or authority of subsequent information or logical consideration.

Kagel and Levin (1985) conducted a series of experiments using MBA and law students. In these experiments students were given money to bid in a series of auctions. Their gains were added to their capital available for subsequent rounds, and were paid out at the end of the series;

their losses were deducted. A sound strategy of bidding was available to the students (ibid., p. 20), but they did not avail themselves of it. In all the 11 series of auctions conducted, the subjects initially grossly overbid. In latter rounds, after experience was gained and bankruptcy had eliminated the most aggressive bidders, the subjects lowered their bids but still placed them well above what was considered rational. The suggestion that the poor "priors," slow and poor adjustment, were due to a lack of guiding "rules of thumb" in the experimental situation is belied by the availability of a sound strategy and by the fact that oil companies, in real auction markets, behave quite the same way as the subjects. They exhibit the same "winner's curse:"

> Bidders naively bid an amount near their estimate of the value of the item so that the winner tends to be the player who most overestimates the value of the item. As a consequence, the winning bid tends to be too high, often substantially exceeding the value of the item, and resulting in below normal, or even negative, profits. (Apen, Clapp and Campbell claimed that this phenomenon was responsible for the low profits earned by oil companies on offshore oil tracts in the 1960's.) (Kagel and Levin 1985, pp. 1–2.)

Many other systematic biases have been found to be built into people's cognitive apparatus. People assign a higher probability of success to a lottery number they picked than one given to them, say by a computer (Langer 1982). They see patterns where none exist, which may explain why they pay for stock advice even if the market is random (Lichtenstein, Fischoff, and Philips 1982). People systematically underweigh opportunity costs and fail to ignore sunk costs (Thaler 1980). Individuals are affected by the way probabilities are expressed, rather than by what they are (Kahneman and Tversky 1982, pp. 166–67). People have a very hard time in judging low-probability events correctly. An often-cited example is their refusal to buy flood insurance even when the government extensively subsidizes the insurance (Kunreuther et al. 1978). Hogarth (1980) reports 27 kinds of systematic error and bias in human beings. A listing and brief review by Winterfeldt and Edwards (1986) of numerous systemic cognitive biases ran to thirty printed pages, backed up by a nineteen-page list of references.

Some economists have argued that these experiments do not provide people with economic incentives, and that hence people make no efforts to be correct (Grether and Plott 1979). However, when the experiments were repeated with economic incentives, no important differences were found (Grether and Plott 1979). Whatever differences were discerned, they indicate that people act a bit less rationally when given monetary incentives.

How Congenital?

The extent to which one considers the findings of the Prospect School as indicating severe additional limitations of the L/E capabilities of individuals (above and beyond the effects of N/A factors) depends, in part, on the question of how curable these cognitive biases are. If they are easy to correct (say by including statistics in high school curricula or by raising the awareness of decision-makers to these biases) the handicap is obviously limited. On the other hand, if these biases are very difficult to overcome, if people persist in making these systematic errors even if properly trained, the handicap is much more severe.

There is no ready answer to this question because the matter is much less studied than the existence of the biases themselves. Einhorn (1982) finds that while people in theory can learn to correct these biases, in *most* situations they do not, because there is no well-structured feedback. Lichtenstein et al. (1982) found that most people *remain* very overconfident.

Physicians are obviously much more educated than the average citizen, yet their judgments—in their area of specialized training—are subject "to all the flaws of human reasoning," a review of the literature concludes (Borak and Veilleux 1982, p. 1939). This led to the suggestion to introduce training in quantitative analysis into medical schools. However, such training improves their decision-making rather little (Nisbett and Ross 1980, pp. 286–94). A study, specifically designed to examine this matter, concludes: "Among physicians with greater knowledge of statistical principles . . . probability estimation, although somewhat more adequate, was still largely dominated by logical inconsistency and failure to apply basic concepts of probability" (Borak and Veilleux, p. 1941). In effect, "sophisticated physicians" did not perform significantly better than nurses and non-professional hospital workers, even when dealing in medical issues (ibid.). Similar findings are reported for experts in other fields (Dawes and Corrigan 1974; Einhorn 1974; Radner 1975, p. 253). Stein (1986, p. xi), who has been referred to as "a pioneer in honest ignorance" (McCloskey 1986, p. 1), argues that "1. Economists do not know very much. 2. Other people . . . know even less. . . . These beliefs do not provide a platform from which to make strong pronouncements about economics or public policy."

There is a tendency in psychological writing to treat the deliberations of common people as akin to those of scientists, to see people as logical-empirical thinkers, as "lay" or "intuitive" scientists. Much that is appealing is implied in the suggested equality of the great unwashed masses and the scientific Brahmins. The question is whether *either* the masses or the scientific Brahmins are that scientific. Indeed, if one can show that even scientists cannot abide by the canons of science as the rationalists depict them, it will come as no surprise that lay people cannot abide by them either. *Thus, rather than see people as lay-scientists, we see scientists as only somewhat more endowed,* equipped, trained, and cool *than the laity,* but still sub-rational.

In effect, the problem runs deeper. Beyond the congenital limitations of scientists, there are built-in limitations in science, the body of knowledge that scientists use. These deserve attention in view of the central role of the non-rational belief in the rationality of science, which dominated the Age of Reason and is still with us. We turn next to argue that science does not provide the kind of clear guidelines to decision-making, the keys to the truth, that the rationalists implied they would. We try to progress beyond merely showing the limits of the scientific approach, by asking what adaptive mechanisms people use to make relatively less sub-rational decisions.

The Limits of Science

Science, as an empirical/logical endeavor, contains a relatively confident element, logic, and a much more tenuous element, evidence. True, even logic is a matter of definition; what is logical in one framework is not in another (e.g., Pascalian versus Baconian). (Cohen 1979, argues that the reason many fail the cognitive tests set up by the Prospect School is that they are based on Pascalian logic while people act on Baconian logic.) And, the steps one must undertake in logical derivations are not at all as self-evident as the uninitiated tend to presume. I.e., even logic does not provide a simple, reliable guide to inferences.

However, logic provides a very much firmer foundation for inferences than empirical evidence. It is not only that both the laity and scientists experience great difficulties in determining what is a fact (because of N/A loading and intra-cognitive biases); science, as an accumulative collective endeavor, is hampered by the relativist nature of all observations (they depend on the paradigm within which they are made), by the tentative nature of all findings, and by the great difficulties in bringing together the findings of induction and the conclusions of deduction.

Some philosophers of science despair of even defining scientific truth. Instead, they prefer to discuss science as a mode of editing statements; i.e., replacing one statement with another that seems sounder, without confident assurance that it is (Popper 1961). (See also the attack on Positivism by Rorty 1979, and, its specific application to neoclassical economics by McCloskey 1985).

Subjectivists reach the same basic conclusion via different routes. The basic issue is as old as Plato's analogue, comparing the shadows (appearances) to whatever they reflect or "represent" (reality). Science is to a large extent based on this dualism, on the expectation that our hypotheses can be compared to the "real" world. Subjectivists have argued for many centuries that one cannot reach beyond appearances, one cannot reach the world; our total existence is one of shadows. Many contemporary schools, from phenomenology to deconstructionism, in effect are founded on this basic position (see, for example, Schutz 1967; for studies of organizations that stress the role of a shared sets of meanings and interpretations of experience, see Donnellon, Gray, and Bougan 1986).

A leading social anthropologist, Shweder (1986) captures well the essence of the subjectivist position. He compares the experience of visiting a Hindu temple in India to attending a seminar at the Institute for Psychoanalysts or one of Marxist studies. In the Hindu temple it is taught that ancestral spirits must be fed daily, that souls transmigrate, and so on. These observances seem ridiculous to a Western outsider, but make sense if one looks at them from *inside* the Hindu paradigm. And, what psychoanalysts or Marxists state is not more realistic, valid or true; it is also only sensible for those who share the internal premises of these paradigms. Similarly, what neoclassical economists say makes sense only if one buys their core assumptions.

Most important, *each* of the paradigms has its own criteria of validation, of reality-testing, which sustain it, and none has validity if tested by the criteria of the other paradigm! I.e., as the subjectivists see it, *all reality is intra-paradigmatic.* Shweder (1986, p. 170) cites Horton approvingly: "that the goals of religious thought 'may not be unlike goals of scientific thought' to explain and influence the works of everyday world by discovering the constant principles that underlie the apparent chaos and flux of sensory experience." He goes on to state that "the doctrine on the kingdom of Satan provided people in the Sixteenth and Seventeenth Centuries with a powerful explanation of illness and suffering, . . . the doctrine was constantly being tested against 'reality'." Most important: "It is conceivable that the sense of objectivity invested in religious beliefs is not fundamentally different from the sense of objectivity invested in scientific beliefs, and that to describe other people's beliefs as religious or supernatural and our own as scientific is merely to disguise a prejudice in favor of our own conceptions of natural laws over theirs." (P. 107.) Those who have not been around this issue may exclaim: "but a scientific theorem can be tested"; and Shweder (p. 173) answers with a quote from Kuhn: "There is, I think, no theory-independent way to reconstruct phrases like 'really there'."

The intrinsic limitations of science (and all other forms of knowing, of the L/E orientation) have often been spelled out and hence need not be further elaborated here. There is, however, a second major reason why science does not provide a guide for rational decision-making, as to how to act within the world (as distinct from seeking to understand it); this reason is not often explored and hence is discussed here in some detail.

It has often been noted that scientific analysis requires abstraction. Unique features of various incidents of the same phenomenon are deliberately overlooked in favor of generic features. It is much less often taken into account that scientific analysis also proceeds by fragmenting the phenomenon under study. Instead of all the facets of a phenomenon being studied, many qualities, including generic ones, are deliberately and systematically ignored in favor of focusing on a few selected attributes. A chemist may focus on the process of photosynthesis of flowers; a geneticist, on the various chromosomes; an economist, on differences in the flowers' prices; a social psychologist, on the meaning of giving various kinds of flowers.

Scientific work progresses by grouping information (or findings) about a slice of the phenomenon under study, into analytic categories. Analytic theories are constructed by grouping variables of one kind, either chemical, or genetic, or economic, and so on. Propositions are derived within these segregated frameworks and are compared to data organized within the same categorical confines. Scientific knowledge is accumulated and transmitted within these frameworks.

Little attention has been paid to the problems that scientific fragmentation poses when one seeks to act within the world, as distinct from seeking to comprehend it. Under many circumstances, *action requires dealing with all the main elements of the phenomenon* which are intertwined. Hence, when the findings of one analytic science are applied directly, one in effect seeks to base action on knowledge of a *subset* of variables. This can result in effective action only under rather specialized conditions.*

Typically, we deal with a complex and changing world and need to apply more than one set of specialized variables; decision makers as a rule need to deal with all the relevant factors that account for a significant portion of the variance, as well as with the result of their interactions, disregarding the disciplinary compartments to which variables that characterize the phenomenon belong. Otherwise, the variables ignored will come to haunt the actors, as is the case when the psychic implications, or the social, cultural, and political prerequisites of economic policy are ignored. This happens, for example, when without regard to the stability of a government, austerity programs based on monetarist theories are introduced into developing countries in order to curb inflation,

---

*When the dynamics of the phenomena are governed by variables, all members of the same analytic subset (e.g., physics or biology or chemistry) and the phenomena are separated from all others, for example, the movement of the planets from radioactive decay on earth. Or when only a low degree of precision is sought (the "imprecision" is the variance accounted for by the other factors not encompassed); when the other variables affecting the phenomena change very slowly (e.g., values), or the time studied is short, which allows greater prominence to a subset of variables which is the focus of the application. However, under all other conditions action based on one analytical discipline will lead to an erroneous knowledge base for policy making.

causing governments to be overthrown and the policy to be thrown out together with the policy makers (Diaz-Alejandro 1981; Nelson unpub.).

When one seeks to apply the knowledge of basic sciences to complex phenomena, the prescribed way to overcome the problem posed by fragmentation is as easy to depict as it is difficult to procure. *The proper way is said to be to resynthesize the findings of the various relevant analytic disciplines before one seeks to act* in the concrete world. (This notion is implicit in the "unity of science" movement, which saw the advancement of "all kinds of scientific synthesis" as one of its main purposes.) The resynthesized flower would contain all the relevant information bearing on the flower and the variables which account for changes in the observed data. It would include the relationships and interaction among these variables, not merely within one discipline but also across disciplines. For example, it would record that excessive plasmolysis of cellular fluids will result in wilting, decreasing the flower's price, and reversing its symbolic connotation.

Why not then combine relevant findings of several analytic disciplines? For two reasons: resynthesis is infrequently attempted and never successfully completed (for complex systems, which include most real-life situations). First, complex phenomena require a renaissance mind capable of encompassing the variety of variables, and combining data about their status and their effect on one another. Merely combining the data of two disciplines, such as chemistry and biology, often proves quite taxing. Encompassing resynthesis is typically overwhelming. (Computers may help in dealing with the data, but so far seem not to have proven very useful in the conceptual integration required.) And when resynthesis is not encompassing, some major relevant variables are likely to be left out.

Second, to construct the analytic disciplines, assumptions are introduced about the nature of the world and the processes within it. These assumptions are specific to each discipline, and often incompatible with those made by others (Hammond, McClelland, and Mumpauer 1980). Much of economic theory tends to assume that people are basically rational and will act to advance their own self-interest. In contrast, major segments of psychology, sociology, and social anthropology assume that people are largely governed by non-rational forces, such as values and emotions, and will act to advance shared goals quite readily. Moreover, physiology tends to treat people without assuming either capacity.

In short, at least in the practical future, resynthesis will remain elusive. To urge people to straighten out their act and follow scientific procedures in their inferences and decisions is unduly rationalistic. Science does not provide such guidance. Ask any policy maker who called in a team of scientists to seek guidance. True, other difficulties arise: policy makers are concerned with political and N/A considerations; scientific advice is not. Politicians often are more risk-averse, and so on. However, even when politicians are open to scientific counsel and able to follow it, an honest scientific advice should be well hedged: We at best know only a fragment of the world.

The *scientific model, suited for building up analytic knowledge* through an endless process (in which the ultimate truth is elusive), *is not a suitable model for decision-making and policy-making.* It is not only because the actors are highly affective and normative, because their indifference zone is rather small, and their capabilities and resources are limited, but also because of the inner fragmented structure of science. Various adaptive mechanisms that have been developed to cope with the limitation of the decision-maker *and* of science are discussed below. They allow one to cope with but not to solve the dilemma: It is not possible to act rationally in complex situations, even when one is backed up with scientific knowledge and methods.

Disjointed Incrementalism

The severe and congenital cognitive limitations of individuals' ability to engage in L/E decision-making led several scholars to develop a decision-making theory that assumes little and asks for less from decision makers. The approach is referred to informally as "muddling through," or more technically as "disjointed incrementalism." Lindblom (1965, p. 144) summarizes the primary requirements of this approach as one in which the decision maker, rather than attempting a comprehensive survey and evaluation of all alternatives, focuses instead only on those policies that differ incrementally from existing policies. Only a relatively small number of policy alternatives are considered. For each policy alternative, only a restricted number of important consequences are evaluated. Thus, there is no one decision or right solution but a "never-ending series of attacks on the issues at hand through serial analyses and evaluation." The term "disjointed incrementalism" is used to emphasize the lack of major direction, policy, or course-setting capacity. The incrementalist fate, wrote Kenneth Boulding, is to stumble through history, putting one drunken foot in front of the other (Boulding 1964, p. 931).

Lindblom (1965, pp. 138–43) identified seven reasons why people are doomed (my term) to incrementalism, and which in his view render the rationalist ("Synoptic") model of decision-making "useless." These reasons are briefly listed for those unfamiliar with them:

(1) People's limited intellectual capabilities make full deliberation of all options and consequences impossible. People simply are unable to obey the Synoptic Ideal's edict: "Be comprehensive!" There are too many things to consider.

(2) Information is inadequate and (3) analysis is costly. Many facts cannot be obtained. Decisions must be made in the absence of relevant facts.

Often, the cost of gathering and analyzing even those facts one might gather before the decision must be made could outweigh the benefits of the decision. There is also a link between people's limited intellectual capacity and the general inadequacy of information: the more information one commands, the greater the strain on one's intellectual capability. The further one gets from the first constraint, the closer one gets to the second.

(4) There is no satisfactory set of criteria by which to judge outcomes. Goals cannot be clearly set and systematically tallied. Further, there exists disagreement on values; and the existence of agreement on means is *not* indicative of an agreement on values (e.g., there are those in the U.S. on both the right and left extremes who call for greater decentralization of power).

(5) There is a close relationship between facts and values. They do not exist in separate containers. Examination of the facts is often accompanied by examination of one's values. Values in turn direct one's choice of relevant facts. This interdependence of facts and values implies a constant shifting between empirical and value elements in decision-making.

(6) The system of variables examined has a high degree of openness; it is difficult to create a closed system of variables for making a decision. Unlike the simple closed system of experiments, the systems of variables in the real world are characterized by a high degree of openness.

(7) Problems arise in diverse forms. One cannot easily isolate "the problem." Rather, "the problem" is actually a part of a myriad of interlocking problems with interdependent solutions.

Under the incrementalist approach, one focuses on the *increments* by which alternatives and consequences differ. This enormous reduction in the range of options to be examined is an adaptation to people's limited cognitive capabilities, the inadequacy of information, and the costliness of analysis. Attention is further limited by simply disregarding many alternatives and outcomes even if this elimination involves the accidental or deliberate disregarding of important alternatives and outcomes. As Lindblom states: "Decision makers must choose between errors of omission and errors of confusion." (1965, p. 146).

Incrementalists argue that an option chosen on the basis of a simple analysis that suffers from errors of omission is certainly incomplete, yet is correct within its limits. For example, if one studies the effects of tobacco on health by simply examining the effects of cigarette smoking, one's solution is correct within its proper limits (the effects of cigarettes) and is incomplete (it ignores the effects of cigars, chewing tobacco, and so on). An option chosen on the basis of a complex analysis suffers from errors of confusion; striving for completeness may lead to a totally incorrect option.

Incrementalists further maintain that their approach involves serial analysis and evaluation: A problem is attacked over and over again.

Therefore, there is no need to search for the "right" solution. And incrementalist policy involves a reconstructive analysis: There is no single specification of "the problem." Rather, ends are constantly adjusted to the means; "the problem" is redefined in the search for solutions. Rather than endlessly pursue an unsolvable problem, it is redefined to make it more manageable.

ADAPTIVE APPROACHES

One can reject the rationalist approach as a guide to decision-making without turning as pessimistic as the incrementalists are. Various adaptive strategies have been developed (Katona, 1975, prefers the term "coping" to adaptive). None of these can "solve" the problem of decision-making; they merely endeavor to formulate relatively more effective decision-making strategies than incrementalists. The approaches, so far quite undeveloped, are advanced on three levels: development of bodies of knowledge; isolated guidance rules; and decision-making strategies. Together they constitute the beginnings of a less pessimistic approach than incrementalism, without turning nearly as optimistic as rationalists are.

Medicine as a Case Study in Adaptation

Medicine (as a discipline taught to practitioners) provides an opportunity to study the ways one may adapt to the fact that one often commands rather poor knowledge and limited decision-making capabilities. How does medicine allow its practitioners to render complex decisions despite their limited ability to resynthesize? First, medicine draws on several analytic disciplines simultaneously but without seeking to integrate their findings or assumptions, in what might be referred to as a mechanical, as distinct from a chemical, combination. For instance, when faced with patients who report severe and persistent headaches, established medical procedure requires the physician to test first for organic causes (e.g., order a brain scan), and only after the search for those is exhausted are patients to be referred to psychiatrists. This combination of two radically different approaches to the diagnosis of severe headaches is based on the practical consideration that the organic causes (e.g., a tumor) may require urgent attention, while psychic causes can wait. Such sequential diagnosis, based on a practical setting of priorities, "will do" for treatment purposes. In contrast, comprehension requires a much higher level of knowledge, often not available to physicians; e.g., what (if any) are the interaction effects between organic and psychic factors in causing headache? Are there headaches caused by psychic factors alone? Can those be distinguished from those caused by organic factors? This is but one of the numerous items which could be cited in which medicine pieces together various kinds of analytic knowledge, sufficient for service purposes but not for full comprehension.

The example also illustrates the reason medicine draws on several analytic disciplines. The causes may be genetic, chemical, physiological, or psychic. Medical diagnoses based on one analytic discipline are likely to prove unsatisfactory in a high proportion of the cases medicine seeks to treat. Second, because even the combined analytic knowledge is not sufficient, medicine benefits by also drawing on knowledge gained from experience, case studies, statistical relationships (without a knowledge of mechanisms or causes), and other sources of practical knowledge. For example, it is quite useful for a physician to know that studies show that there is a strong correlation between smoking and lung cancer, even if science has not established as yet how smoking causes cancer. Estimates vary for how much of the knowledge currently contained in medicine is of the practical kind (and the proportion varies among the subfields); however, estimates run as high as 50 percent (Inglefinger, Erlman, and Findland 1966; Schon 1983).

Finally, to adapt to the need to act within complex and only partially known systems, physicians acquire, as an integral part of their discipline, certain guidance rules and decision-making strategies for making decisions in the face of high uncertainty, utilizing only partial knowledge.*

Examples of Adaptive Guidance Rules

Probably the most widely used procedure for adapting to unknowability might be called *focused trial-and-error*. It combines knowing where to start the search for an effective intervention with checking outcomes at predetermined intervals to adjust and modify the intervention, and to make up for the limited ability to anticipate future outcomes. This approach differs significantly from what should be called *outright* trial-and-error, in which no prior knowledge is assumed, and from *fine-tuning* searches, that ought to be attempted only when knowledge is high and uncertainty is low.

It cannot be stressed enough that focused trial-and-error is an adaptive

---

*The term "partial knowledge" is used advisedly, to contrast it with the often used term "imperfect" knowledge. Imperfect knowledge implies that we know most of what we need to know to act rationally. Hence we can almost ignore, or correct later, the imprecision that will result from the imperfections, and act largely as though we had full knowledge. This is not the case in numerous, if not most, medical interventions. At the same time medical knowledge as a rule is not so deficient as to suggest the application of procedures appropriate when knowledge is nonexistent or minimal; e.g., random interventions. We thus cannot follow the procedures that fully rational behavior requires, nor need we follow procedures appropriate for situations in which we are nearly or fully ignorant. Special procedures are available to guide action when the knowledge available is but a fraction of what is required by fully rational decision making.

procedure, but not a rational one. It assumes that there are major segments of the world that are not known to the actor but that the actor must deal with in order to proceed. Hence it is not a matter of "correctly" understanding the world and logically inferring what is to be done on the basis of facts, and so on. It is a question of how to proceed best, knowing that the decision-maker lacks major chunks of the needed facts, cannot review many options, and so on.

Another major adaptive rule draws directly on the understanding of the limits of the actor's understanding: it urges *procrastination,* delaying a decision as long as possible. The delays allow for some more evidence to be collected, for more data to be processed, for new options to present themselves, or for the problem to recede, untreated, on its own, before action—which is likely to be faulty—is undertaken. A corollary rule is to *stagger a decision* as much as possible (rather than render it in one fell swoop). One reason central banks (like the Federal Reserve System in the United States) typically raise or reduce their interest rates a fraction at a time, often repeating their act in subsequent periods, rather than introduce the "right" degree of change at once, is that they do not know what the correct amount is. They fear overdosing; hence the wisdom of staggered decisions.

Hedging bets is another example of an adaptive guidance rule. Obviously if one knew with certainty (or relatively high certainty) which stock would do best by whatever investment goals one pursues, for the period one is interested in, the investor would put all his or her funds into that stock. On the other hand, the less one knows about a specific stock, the wiser it is to spread one's investment among several stocks. Similarly, if one is less sure about stocks, spreading one's investment among several investment instruments is called for (bonds, real estate, and so on). Economic theory, especially portfolio theory, lays major claims to provide models that inform investors how much to spread, claims that cannot be evaluated here. Most decision-makers, especially those dealing with options that are difficult to quantify, may find the models that economics provide difficult to apply. Hedging their bets is still likely to improve their long-term yield and security, even if their investments will be far from maximal.

These are but some examples of adaptive guidance rules (for additional discussion of adaptive rules see Quade 1982, especially pp. 217ff.). While other rules come to mind, the task of developing these and testing their efficiency under different circumstances, and for actors whose capabilities and resources differ, remains largely to be carried out.

Mixed Scanning: An Adaptive Strategy

The adaptive guidance rules reviewed so far are isolated rules; they are advanced one at a time. Mixed scanning offers a full-fledged decision-making strategy and a way to derive numerous adaptive rules. Mixed scanning refers to a descriptive model of decision-making as well as to a prescriptive model; i.e., it guides to more efficient and effective decisions. Those who engage in mixed scanning combine wide ranging but not deep (detailed) scanning of facts and options with more detailed but less encompassing scanning of selected subsets of facts and options. The way the World Bank and LDCs make investment decisions (Leff 1985), illustrates the mixed-scanning strategy. First, these institutions designate high-priority sectors, and *within them* select promising projects. The "optimal" project might be in a lower-priority sector, but to find it would entail studying all projects, which mixed scanning assumes cannot be accomplished.

Mixed scanning is easiest described in terms of a contrast between the two prevailing models of decision-making—rationalist and incrementalist. The rationalist model requires full scanning of all the relevant facts and options. It has been often and soundly criticized as impossible to heed because it requires knowing consequences that are far away in time, the amassing of enormous amounts of facts, and the use of analytic capabilities that actors do not command. As the defects of the rationalist approach have been extensively discussed above, they are not explored here.

A major defect of incrementalism, and one that points toward mixed scanning, are the incidents of fundamental decisions, such as the declarations of war. Incrementalists do not deny their existence, but treat them as exceptions. While it is true that incremental decisions greatly outnumber fundamental ones, the latter's significance for decision-making is not commensurate with their number; it is thus a mistake to ignore non-incremental decisions on the ground that they are exceptional. Moreover, fundamental decisions often set the context for numerous incremental ones. In other situations, fundamental decisions are "prepared" by several that are incremental, so that the final decision is less of an abrupt change; still the decisions are relatively fundamental. The incremental steps that follow cannot be understood without them, and the preceding steps find their meaning in fundamental decisions to which they lead.

Thus, it is not enough to show, as Fenno (1966) did, that Congress makes primarily marginal changes in the federal budget (a comparison of one year's budget for a federal agency with that of the preceding year showed on many occasions only a 10 percent difference), or that for long periods the defense budget does not change much in terms of its percentage of the federal budget, or that the federal budget changes little each year in terms of its percentage of the Gross National Product (Polsby 1964, p. 86). These incremental changes are often the unfolding of trends initiated at critical turning points at which fundamental decisions were made. The U.S. defense budget jumped from 5 percent of the GNP at the beginning of the Korean War in 1950 to 10.3 percent in 1951. The fact that it stayed at about this level, ranging between 9 and 11.3 percent of the GNP, after the war ended (1954–60), did reflect incremental decisions to engage in the Korean War (ibid.). Fenno's own figures show almost an equal number of changes above the 20 percent level as below it; seven changes represented an increase of 100 percent or more, and 24 changes increased 50 percent or more (Polsby 1964, p. 83). Recent nonincremental decisions include the 1986 Tax Reform Act, not paralleled in scope in seventy years, and President Reagan's additions to the federal deficit that exceed those generated by all his predecessors combined.

It is clear that, while Congress or other decision-making bodies do make some cumulative incremental decisions without facing the fundamental one implied, many other decisions that appear to be an incremental series are, in effect, the implementation or elaboration of a fundamental decision. For example, after Congress set up a national space agency in 1958 and consented to back President Kennedy's space goals, it made "incremental" additional commitments for several years. Initially, however, a fundamental decision had been made. Congress in 1958, drawing on past experiences and on an understanding of the dynamics of incremental processes, could not have been unaware that once a fundamental commitment is made it is difficult to reverse it. While the initial space budget was relatively small, the very act of setting up a space agency amounted to subscribing to additional budget increments in future years. (For a powerful application of mixed scanning to the study of court decisions, see Snortland & Stanga 1973, pp. 1021–31.)

Incrementalists argue that incremental decisions tend to be remedial; small steps are taken in the "right" direction, or, when it is evident the direction is "wrong," the course is altered. But if decision-makers evaluate their incremental decisions and their small steps—which they must do if they are to decide whether or not the direction is a correct one—their judgments will be greatly affected by the evaluative criteria they apply. Here, again, one must go outside the incrementalist conception to ascertain the ways in which these criteria are set. Thus, while actors make both kinds of decisions, the number and role of fundamental decisions are significantly greater than incrementalists state, and when the fundamental ones are missing, incremental decision-making amounts to drifting, to action without direction.

A somewhat more active approach to decision-making requires two sets of mechanisms: (1) high-order, fundamental policy-making processes that set basic directions, and (2) incremental processes that prepare for fundamental decisions and specify them after they have been reached. Both kinds of decisions are encompassed by mixed scanning. Mixed scanning thus is much less complete and demanding than rational decision-making, but more encompassing and innovative than incrementalism. It is an adaptive strategy in that it assumes inability to know more than part of what we need to know, but an ability to cope rather than proceed blindly.

A significant part of the works that followed the first publication of the mixed scanning conception (Etzioni 1967), spelled out mixed scanning in systematic rules, rules that can be used as a guide for decision-makers, as a starting point for a computer program, and as a basis for research designs. Etzioni (1968, pp. 286–88) started this elaboration:

a. *On strategic occasions* (for definition see d below) (i) list all relevant alternatives that come to mind, that the staff raises, and that advisers advocate (including alternatives not usually considered feasible).

(ii) Examine briefly the alternatives under (i) (for definition of "briefly" see d below), and reject those that reveal a "crippling objection." These include: (a) utilitarian objections to alternatives which require means that are not available, (b) normative objections to alternatives which violate the basic values of the decision-makers, and (c) political objections to alternatives which violate the basic values or interests of other actors whose support seems essential for making the decision and/or implementing it.

(iii) For all alternatives not rejected under (ii), repeat (ii) in greater though not in full detail (for definition of scale see d).

(iv) For those alternatives remaining after (iii), repeat (ii) in still fuller detail (see d). Continue until only one alternative is left, or randomize the choice among those remaining (and ask the staff in the future to collect enough information to differentiate among all the alternatives to be reviewed).

b. *Before implementation* (i) when possible, fragment the implementation into several sequential steps (an administrative rule).

(ii) when possible, divide the commitment to implement into several serial steps (a political rule).

(iii) When possible, divide the commitment of assets into several serial steps and maintain a strategic reserve (a utilitarian rule).

(iv) Arrange implementation in such a way that, if possible, costly and less reversible decisions will appear later in the process than those which are more reversible and less costly.

(v) Provide a time schedule for the additional collection and processing of information so that information will become available at the key turning points of the subsequent decisions, but assume "unanticipated" delays in the availability of these inputs. Return to more encompassing scanning when such information becomes available and before such turning points.

c. *Review while implementing.* (i) Scan on a semi-encompassing level after the first sub-set of increments is implemented. If they "work," continue to scan on a semi-encompassing level after longer intervals and in full, over-all review, still less frequently.

(ii) Scan more encompassingly whenever a series of increments, although each one seems a step in the right direction, results in deeper difficulties.

(iii) Be sure to scan at set intervals in full, over-all review even if

everything seems all right, because: (a) a major danger that was not visible during earlier scanning but becomes observable now that it is closer
might loom a few steps (or increments) ahead; (b) a better strategy might
now be possible although it was ruled out in earlier rounds (see if one
or more of the crippling objections was removed, but also look for new
alternatives not previously examined); and (c) the goal may have been
realized and, therefore, need no further incrementation. If this occurs,
ask for new goal(s), and consider terminating the project.

d. *Formulate a rule for the allocation of assets and time among the
various levels of scanning.* The rule is to assign "slices" of the available
pie to (i) "normal" routines (when incrementing "works"); (ii) semi-
encompassing reviews; (iii) over-all reviews; (iv) initial reviews when a
whole new problem or strategy is considered; (v) a time "trigger," at set
intervals, to initiate more encompassing reviews without waiting for a
crisis to develop; and (vi) an occasional review of the allocation rule in
the over-all review, and the establishment of the pattern of allocation
in the initial strategic review.

Janis and Mann (1977, p. 37) introduced a major improvement of the
program. They point out that while in the initial scanning, all those options that have no "crippling objections" are held over for closer scanning (which amounts to a "quasi-satisficing" approach), "each time the
surviving alternatives are reexamined, the testing rule might be changed
in the optimizing direction by raising the minimum standard (from crippling objections to more minor objections)."

They also expanded the range of decision-making to which mixed
scanning may be applied: "Although intended for policy makers, the
same program, with minor modifications, could be applied to an individual's work-task decisions and to personal decisions involving career,
marriage, health or financial security." (Ibid., p. 38.) For such applications, they indicated, step a(i) must be modified: the staff and advisers
would be replaced by family or friends.

The detailed or incremental decisions are best made within the context of fundamental ones, although empirically one encounters numerous incremental decisions made without attention to a context or to a
fundamental direction. The virtue of putting incremental decisions into
a fundamental context is not derived from the assumption that fundamental decisions can be made on sheer L/E grounds, but from the assumptions that they provide the focus part of the ongoing trial-and-error
processes and hence enhance reality-testing. They are like working-
hypotheses (of a very young "science"), rather than sources of definitive
answers.

The question arises: what are these contextuating, fundamental decisions based on? In part they reflect L/E considerations, past experience,
prevailing theories, and so on. In part, though, they are the bridges that
lead from the limited L/E zones to the N/A contexts. There are few funda-

mental decisions that do not reflect some N/A factors; many are made largely on N/A grounds. In short, one other way of showing the limited role of L/E considerations, and the difficulties of completing them on cognitive grounds, is to see the relationships between detailed, incremental decisions (that may be relatively open to L/E considerations) and the fundamental decisions, that are much less so. Mixed scanning, we suggest, improves decision-making over disjointed incrementalism; however, it does not provide a basis for rational decisions. Ultimately, cognitive inability to make fully detailed decisions—the reason there is mixed scanning to begin with—is a clear indication that even within the zones set aside by N/A factors as legitimate L/E zones, decision-making tends to be sub-rational.

8

What Is Rational?

The answer to the question: "how rationally do people choose means?" depends in part on how one defines rationality. Obviously, if one defines rationality in a way that makes it easy to meet the criterion, many more people will be found to make rational decisions than if one uses more stringent criteria. Thus, if one defines rationality as using whatever facts one commands, by whatever rules of inference one believes in, even heeding the counsel of astrologers turns rational. On the other hand, if one defines rationality as applying high-power scientific or analytic procedures, say advanced forms of calculus, most people—including quite a few scientists—will be found to act not rationally. What is a productive definition of this much-used concept?

In searching for a productive definition we found it necessary to explore the normative (value) foundations of the concept of rationality; it is hardly a neutral term. Neoclassicists imply, for reasons to be discussed shortly, that one must assume people to be rational or one undermines their liberty. In this chapter, we argue that one can acknowledge the severe limitations of human rationality, as commonly defined, and still be as committed to liberty and individual rights as neoclassicists are.

Once the normative foundations of the concept of rationality are disclosed, the discussion turns to the definition of the concept. While there are at least sixty definitions of rationality (for a fair list, see March 1978), in effect most of those who use the term have in mind the concept of an actor who acts wisely, and who chooses efficiently the means that advance his or her goals. This concept of *instrumental rationality* sees it as based on openness to evidence (no N/A barriers to new information or adherence to obsolescent data) and openness to reason (no N/A *a priori* assumption, and/or opposition to any given line of reasoning, e.g., secular). This is, in effect, the concept of rationality that many authors use even if they start their discussions with different definitions of the term. It is also the concept of rationality that is deeply ingrained in our culture. Furthermore, we shall see that this is the concept of rationality that is most defensible from a methodology viewpoint, because it meets a major criterion for productive concepts: it differentiaties; it allows one to tell the rational from the non-rational, and to ascertain various degrees of rationality.

Rationality, in the neoclassical paradigm, is tied to the individual following his or her self-interest. Actually, we shall see, one may serve the commons rationally. There is no necessary connection between rationality and self; an activity that serves the I, the We, even Them, any activity—including one that seeks to advance the commons—can be examined as to its degree of rationality. We shall argue, however, that rationality in all activities entails deliberations; it is not automatic or non-conscious.

LIBERTY WITHOUT RATIONALISM

Practically none of the voluminous writing on the concept of rationality and its various meanings acknowledges its normative nature. ("Normative" refers to the implied value judgment of the merit of acting rationally, not to the distinction between prescriptive versus descriptive decision-making models.) Many seem unaware, and others ignore the fact, that the concept is deeply rooted in a particular political philosophy and ethics. In effect, the concept of rationality is closely linked to that one notion of liberty that stresses individual freedom and individual rights (Chapter 1, pp. 9–11). The deeper reason neoclassicists assumed that individuals "must be" rational, "must be" able to form their own judgments, and that their choices must be perceived as basically morally correct, is because neoclassicists believe that any other position would justify a curtailment of individual rights.

The idea that individuals know what is best for them is widely expressed throughout neoclassical (and other Whig, especially libertarian) writings, and is at the core of the pivotal notion of "consumer sovereignty." Economists explain that at most an actor may "sometime" "imperfectly" perceive what is good for her or him. But to get at these imperfections one would need to interview a person's spouse and/or psychiatrist. Practically, they argue, it is best to assume that individuals know their own mind.

Most important, neoclassicists maintain, to assume otherwise, is to assume that people make unwise or morally deficient choices, and to suggest that they can be manipulated (West and McKee 1983, p. 1110); this systematically opens the door to government intervention, if not to totalitarianism. Moreover, whatever surrender of individual freedoms that is needed to provide for the commons (especially, for shared security), it is assumed, can be arranged by free individuals. In short, the neoclassical concept of rationality is rooted in a Whiggish concept of society and of liberty.

The trouble lies not in the deep commitment to liberty. One may share it in full but still recognize that the neoclassical paradigm lacks the concepts and perspective required to understand the sociological and psychological conditions under which people are free, and liberty is preserved. Individuals can reason best, and are least subject to manipulation and to government intervention, when they are members of a community, when they can rely on their bonds to their fellow citizens, on their We-ness, for psychological anchoring and social support in resisting outside pressures. That is the reason the Founding Fathers feared the rule of the mob, a mass of "free," unrelated individuals, whipped into a frenzy by demagogues. That is why, from Alexis DeToqueville (1840) to Eric Fromm (1941), the observation has been advanced of the merit of a society in which individuals are members of viable communities and voluntary associations. This is the often discussed merit of pluralism. This is why the mass society, one in which individuals have lost their place in a social fabric and are on their own, "atomized," has been found to be vulnerable to totalitarian movements, and subject to manipulation by charismatic leaders and the mass media (Kornhouser 1959). In short, to be free requires individuals that are not socially isolated, cut off from one another; they must be linked to one another and bound into a community, to form a We, and to be able to sustain one another's emotional stability and inner security. It is on these psychological and sociological foundations that people fully develop and freely express their individuality. When the commons are experienced as oppressive, the group as a They, people can still assert their individuality, but never as fully and as free from distortion as they can when, by transforming their commons from a They to a We, they turn it into a responsive community.

Last, but not least, by assuming that preferences are stable and are those of individuals, the neoclassical paradigm avoids all questions of ends (value) formation. It states that people "have" preferences; it does not matter where they come from, or what they are, and it assumes that they are "stable." However, once it is recognized that ends can be changed and are subject to manipulation, that they are in part "imported," we realize that the neoclassical paradigm's focus on the efficient use of means is too narrow, too parsimonious; a productive theory must also deal with proper processes for the formation of ends (e.g., participation versus imposition), and protection of the primacy of ends over means. To be efficient may be only as good as the goals that are efficiently implemented. We cannot escape judging goals, not in simple terms of according them merit and demerit points based on *our personal* preferences or values, but in terms of an ethic whose criteria can be justified, and in terms of exploring the *sources* of these goals: to what extent are they formed freely by members of a community or imposed by powerful actors, whether it is the government, a foreign power, a corporation or a labor union?

For this reason we are concerned with the positive and not just the disruptive, role of normative factors in decision-making (see Chapter 6) and study the role of the We—next to the I—in the decision-making process (see Chapter 11). In this context, the term "instrumental rationality" helps us to recall that rationality is not an ultimate value; it is desirable to act efficiently—but only in pursuit of worthy ends.

METHODOLOGY CONSIDERATIONS

Differentiation as a Criterion

Once the concept of rationality, and the question of how rational individuals are, is freed from the Whiggish assumption that people "must be" rational, one is ready to ask by what criteria is one to decide which concept of rationality is *productive* for a social science paradigm? In the literature on the subject, much attention is paid to the question of whether or not the neoclassical assumption of rationality is "realistic," and whether or not it is proper to use unrealistic assumptions as long as they generate predictions and provide a parsimonious theory. We, too, share these concerns but add a consideration usually neglected in these discussions, the merit of using a *differentiating* concept.

For a variable to be productive, it must generate a distribution among the various points (or "scores") on the continuum most variables generate. The distribution of the incidents among these points does not have to be even, bell-shaped, or to take any other particular form, but it ought not to be very heavily skewed toward one point. For example, for most purposes there is little merit in a sex typology that puts man and woman in one category and "all others" into another.

From a methodological viewpoint, inclusive statements—that characterize a whole species as having certain shared attributes—when made in other disciplines, are regarded as preliminary, poor first approximations, because science builds not on characterizations that apply to all the incidents of a category under study, but on recognizing variations, on variables (Nisbett and Ross 1980, p. 8; Musgrave 1981). Thus, it is of little interest to note that people's blood is warm unless one compares them to some species whose blood is cold. When one studies people, interest focuses on differences in temperature, not on the shared range.

Drawing on this general view of the way scientific knowledge advances, it seems productive to treat rationality not as a trait all people share, but to ask to what extent the behavior of various groups (subaggregates) of people is rational, and under what conditions their behavior is more versus less rational. That is, it is unproductive to ask whether or not people "are" rational. Rationality is best viewed as a continuous variable; people are more or less rational depending on their abilities, the strength of the activating forces (discussed below), and the environmental circumstances that help or hinder these forces. Thus, from a methodological viewpoint one reaches the same conclusion one arrives at from a normative viewpoint: it is not helpful to assume all people *are* rational; it is more productive to assume that under some conditions their rationality is well protected and enhanced and relatively high, while under other circumstances it is low and undermined.

Neoclassical Definitions

The trouble with the neoclassical concept of rationality is that it either does not differentiate at all or differentiates very poorly. It either defines individual behavior as rational (which is achieved by crafting full-blown tautologies), or it defines rationality in such a manner that most behavior of all actors qualifies, recognizing only limited exceptions that can be disregarded as an insignificant residue, as in the concept of "imperfect knowledge"—an unproductive near-tautology.

Typically the question is not put in terms of how rational people are, but people are said "to be" rational and arguments are advanced against those who maintain otherwise. Leckachman (1976, p. 108) reports: "Everybody in this prosaic universe [the world according to economists] is rational." And Tobin (1971, p. 18): "Economic theory is usually predicated on the premise that, given their schedules of preferences for goods and services and leisure, individuals behave consistently and 'rationally'." Williams and Findlay (1981, pp. 18–19) agree: "Economics ... the discipline is founded on the rational man premise.... Even most non-'mainstream' economists who are uneasy with both the methods and conclusion of neoclassicism unhesitatingly adopt assumptions about human behavior that are increasingly questioned elsewhere...." Neoclassicists often argue that all kinds of behavior, that at first seem to be non-rational, in effect are rational. Some even include pathological behavior, because psychoanalytical literature "explains the patient's illness in terms of the functions it performs for him." (Simon 1978, p. 3.) It has already been pointed out (Williams and Findlay 1981, p. 23) that "unfortunately, such a generalized definition of rationality makes madmen rational." Thus, all-encompassing definitions deprive the concept of its differentiating power and of meaning.

Rarely are attempts made to empirically verify the assumptions introduced. Thus, if a car buyer stops looking for a better deal after visiting only two dealers, it is argued that the buyer "must have" calculated that additional search costs would exceed potential savings, rather than that he may have acted non-rationally. Typically, no attempts are made to establish whether or not buyers made such calculations, or are able to make them, or whether the costs of additional search that the actors did not conduct would indeed exceed the potential savings, and that the value put on time and effort in the occasion at hand is consistent with the way buyers usually value their time and other resources.

In the rare instances the neoclassical theorem at hand is sufficiently specified to be empirically tested, and the test uses straight data (instead of data rearranged by adding various assumptions and regression analyses), the findings are clearly incompatible with the thesis. Telser (1973, p. 46) suggests that it would be rare to find a price range exceeding 50 percent between two shops or suppliers in the same market. This is a rather weak test because while a 50 percent savings may not amount to much for individual consumers when they deal with low-cost items (saving ten cents on a stick of gum will not compensate most buyers for the "costs" of comparative shopping), the profit mark-up is so high on a volume of sale that it should attract competitors to reduce it, if the neoclassical economic theorem is valid. In effect, a study of middle class consumers found, within their shopping area, not only a price difference of 408 percent for low-cost aspirin, but also 286 percent for tape recorders. For a sample of twenty-five products, the price difference of nineteen (76 percent) was higher than the Telser test of 50 percent. Indeed, for 44 percent of the products, price differences were 100 percent or more, including for substantial purchases such as bicycles and life insurance (Maynes et al. 1984, pp. 187ff).

Mueller (1986, p. 13) recounts another telling example:

> Both Arrow (1982) and Heiner (1983) have noted the seemingly irrational behavior of many individuals when faced by decisions with very small probabilities of very large payoffs, citing the refusal of most individuals to purchase flood insurance at rates below its actuarial value as reported by Howard Kunreuther, et al. (1978). While this behavior, if it were rational, would imply an extreme willingness to take risks, other behavior with infinitesimal probabilities and large payoffs suggests extreme risk aversion, for example, when couples with children fly on separate planes to avoid the possibility that both parents would die in an airplane accident, or the measures taken by some recently to avoid contact with those with AIDS. While information costs might explain some of these anomalies, as Arrow notes with respect to flood insurance, "the information seems so easy to acquire and the stakes so large that this hypothesis hardly seems tenable" (1982:2).

When all else fails, some factors that are difficult to measure are added, especially psychic costs, to somehow argue that the action, however absurd on the face of it, is rational (Thurow 1983, p. 16). The result is often rather strained argumentation of the kind usually encountered less in scientific literature than in scholastic, Talmudic, or Marxist writings. The argument that advertising is informative rather than containing persuasive elements is a case in point. Thus, it has been argued that when Joe Namath endorses a pair of L'Eggs (women's stockings), and Muhammad Ali endorses a pest killer, this is not persuasion but information!

How? Because the fact that the advertiser spent large amounts on obtaining such expensive endorsements is said to inform the consumers that the products must be of high quality (Lindsay 1984, p. 205).

Cross (1983) comes to the rescue by arguing that at any point in time decisions may not be rational because actors have not yet adjusted to various feedbacks of the outcomes of their previous acts; the implication is that in the longer run they surely will. The trouble with this line of argument is that people are constantly "off," if only because their circumstances constantly change and they never have a chance to catch up, even if this would be theoretically possible. In any event, if people are constantly "off," whether "temporarily" or existentially, the "off" state should be the focus of our study, not how they behave if one day they will make it to rational behavior.

The great difficulties in defending the neoclassical notion of rationality has led to numerous attempts to redefine the concept. In the resulting sizable literature, esoteric definitions are compared to other esoteric definitions, and hairs are split on the ground that this or that authority in the field said such and such. Little attempt is made to show the productivity of this versus that definition. Here no attempt is made to review, argue with, or add to these defintions, because none of them is in wide use, and hence one must assume they are not productive. (Among the positions not discussed, the most interesting is the repeated suggestion that there are several kinds of rationality, say, economic and political. See Mannheim 1949; Diesing 1962; Parsons and Smelser 1956.) The discussion here focuses on a few definitions widely used by neoclassicists and provides the methodological reasons for the particular definition followed here.

Consistency: Neither Valid nor Differentiating

Neoclassicists often define rational behavior as consistent behavior, behavior that is stable and transitive. That is, people who choose X over Y (if it is a single item or a basket) will choose the same an instant later, and if they prefer X over Y and Y over Z, they will also prefer X over Z. This is a very widely used definition, as Becker (1976, p. 153) points out: ". . . everyone more or less agrees that rational behavior simply implies consistent maximization of a well-ordered function, such as a utility or profit function." Some argue that this definition is completely test-proof, in the sense that it cannot be verified or falsified empirically (Sen 1977, p. 325). Others amassed evidence that shows that people do not behave consistently (Kahneman and Tversky 1982, p. 162).

Despite the rather simple nature of this definition, it is very difficult to specify the conditions under which it can be tested, because when people act inconsistently neoclassicists say they must have changed their preferences after all (Sen 1977, pp. 322–23). In this way all behavior can be made to seem consistent. The "Rhine-wine" case highlights the extremes to which some neoclassicists will go to defend their paradigm. The case concerns a person who does not consume wine in general and hence has no intention of purchasing any particular brand of wine, but who yields to an impulse and buys and consumes a bottle of Rhine-wine. Croce (1953, p. 177) uses such behavior to distinguish rational from non-rational behavior, because he sees in the purchase of the wine an act in contradiction of the person's purpose, an illogical act. However, neoclassicists argue that the notion of an *a priori* plan or commitment is inappropriate; after all, it does not "exist," it is just in the mind. Ends are revealed in behavior. Hence, if the person did buy Rhine-wine, never mind what the person set out to purchase; the purchase is deemed to be rational because it is said to serve that person's goal—as revealed in the buying act. (Argument is by Tagliacozzo, cited by Kirzner 1976, pp. 169–70.)

As we see it, consistency is at best a necessary but not a sufficient condition for most behavior that is commonly referred to as rational, referred to here as instrumental rationality, because consistency does not necessarily involve reason, or even being conscious (Becker 1976, p. 7; March 1978, p. 593). Indeed, low species, say worms, whose behavior is determined by genetic codes, might be much more consistent than human beings. There seems to be little merit for a concept that cannot differentiate between the intellectual capabilities of low species and human beings. For the same reason, the findings that rats behave rationally by neoclassical criteria (Kagel et al. 1975), is actually a source of concern. At issue is a study of how sensible and wise human decision-making is. To reiterate, if the concept cannot distinguish stupid from brilliant decision-making, rat from human, what does it tell us? All it does is to prove the paucity of the definition, and hint at the normative commitment to defend rationality at all costs. It is difficult to improve on Samuelson's (1983, pp. 91–92) conclusion: "The result can very easily be circular, and in many formulations undoubtedly is. Often nothing more is stated than the conclusion that people behave as they behave, a theorem which has no empirical implications, since it contains no hypothesis and is consistent with all conceivable behavior, while refutable by none." We need a concept that is more differentiating.

Parsimony versus Over-Determination

When presented with the suggestion that one should recognize N/A, non-rational, bases for making choices, and incorporate these factors into one's paradigm, neoclassicists argue that their approach is more parsimonious and hence ought to be preferred over "over-determined" theories. In such writings the concept of parsimony is used as if parsimony was a simple, objective, easy to verify criterion that allows one to determine which theory is more parsimonious than another. Actually, it is quite difficult to determine the extent to which a theory is parsimonious. For example, pray tell how many assumptions are there in Parsonian functionalism, Levi-Strauss structuralism, or Marxist economics? And is there a single neoclassical economist who would drop her or his paradigm and embrace, say, institutional economics—not to mention Marxist economics—even if it were to be proven that these other paradigms are significantly more parsimonious?

Also, while neoclassical economists often start with very few assumptions, numerous ad hoc assumptions are often added in the process of bringing their positions and the data together (Blaug 1985, pp. 242–43). A somewhat more complex paradigm, but one that encompasses all major necessary assumptions, is preferable to one that has few assumptions that are integral to the paradigm (if this can be established), but requires numerous assumptions that are ad hoc. Hirschman (1984, p. 12) already made the case for some increase in complexity: "Like any virtue, . . . parsimony in theory construction can be overdone and something is sometimes to be gained by making things *more complicated*." We shall see below the specific additions that are required to retain the concept of rationality and turning it into a differentiating concept.

Instrumental Rationality

The definition of rationality we find most productive is one that characterizes decision-making when it is based on deliberation, i.e. on the collection and processing of information, and on the drawing of proper conclusions from it. That is, rational decision-making is based on openness to evidence (an empirical orientation), and on sound reasoning (logic). The more the actor is open to reason and evidence, to L/E considerations, the more rational the actor. To assume a deliberating and a hence conscious actor, indicates that automatic choices, based on subconscious hunches, feelings, or intuition, may be effective—but are not rational. Similarly, decisions based on rules provided by others, or previously set by the actor, and that are not reexamined if they suit the occasion, may be fully rational but are not necessarily so. They are determined by culture or habit. (These points are elaborated below.)

The term *instrumental* rationality is used because the definition views the actor as pursuing goals, to which he or she is committed for reasons irrelevant to the definition. Instead, the definition focus is on the selection of means. The information amassed and utilized is used in finding efficient, "suitable," means. This facet of the definition of rationality is important for the deontological position: to stress that the decisions are and ought to be in the service of other considerations, and that the decisions ought to be "instrumental," not dominant. That is, rationality has a limited role, albeit an important one.

The author was asked at which point, by this definition, people cease to act non-rationally? After all, all decisions may fail to be rational when made by an objective omniscient observer, who commands all the information and unlimited processing capabilities. Indeed, by the definition given, decisions *are* never completely "rational" (except, maybe, when dealing with extremely simple situations) or "not-rational," but are rational (and by the same token non-rational) to varying degrees. This "result" of the definition is a major reason in its favor: it differentiates. Its productivity is documented below (Chapter 9).

The view of rationality as open behavior, open to logical-empirical selection of means, is, of course, the way Max Weber (1947) used the term when he differentiated *zweckrationalität* from *wertrationalität*. (See also Parson 1937.) It is sometimes referred to as calculative rationality or intentional rationality (March 1978, p. 589) or procedural rationality (Simon 1976, p. 131). A careful reading of numerous usages of the term rationality, which need not be retraced here, suggests that this is the meaning most often implied when the term is used (Simon 1976, p. 130, 179; Kunkel 1970, pp. 62–64; Lee 1972, pp. 6ff).

So far the distinction between instrumental rationality and the concept of rationality typically used by neoclassicists has been highlighted. However, there is the opposite, subjectivist definition. Subjectivists argue that decisions are not to be considered non-rational when they are made without the use of all the information available, as seen by an objective observer, but only when decisions are made disregarding information to which actors have access; they further argue that decisions are non-rational only when actors misinterpret the information available by *their* rules of inference, not by established logic.

The "cargo cult" is often used to illustrate the subjectivist's view of rationality. During World War II, the Japanese captured the coastal towns of New Guinea. The Americans parachuted commandos in the interior mountains to harass the Japanese. Cargo planes dropped boxes full of goods the natives had never seen before, from clothing to guns. When the planes stopped coming, the natives built mock airplanes out of sticks and clay and worshipped these in the hope of restoring the manna. Subjectivists argue that the cult worship is rational because, given the information accessible to the New Guineans at the time, and given *their* rules of inference and believe in magic and so on, the act makes sense (Shweder, 1986).

In contrast, the concept of instrumental rationality used here assumes that actors' decisions are compared to what they might have been as viewed by an objective observer. That is, actors who do not search, or who search little, when the conditions (including costs) call for an extensive search, and who stick to their prior beliefs despite present evidence to the contrary, are not viewed as having rendered rational decisions. The reasons for preferring this approach are that (1) the subjective definition of rationality constitutes a near if not a complete tautology; whatever a person decides can be said to be based on what he or she knew and/or interpreted it; (2) it does not differentiate between poor decision-makers and more efficient ones; everyone might simply be said to pursue their beliefs; and (3) it flies in the face of the substance of the term, as it is commonly used. All said and done, one may ask: If the cargo cult is rational, what is a person to do for an act to qualify as non-rational? More generally, we seek a differentiating concept. Instrumental rationality, which compares the results *and* processes of the actor's deliberations to those of an objective and omniscient decision maker, with unlimited capabilities, is such a concept.

DELIBERATIVE, EFFICIENT, BUT NOT SELF-CENTERED

Key attributes of the definition of instrumental rationality are explored next: What is the goal or goals it serves? How is this form of decision-making different from other forms of behavior? And must the process of selection of means be undertaken consciously?

Rationality Not Equal to Self-Interest

The neoclassical core concept of rational utility maximization, in effect, fuses two concepts: one concerns the goal, the other deals with the means. In this concept, the goal of a rational act is to maximize the actor's utility, i.e., his or her self-interest (Mueller 1986, p. 18; Wilde et. al. 1985, p. 406; Brandt 1972). The rational person is out to enhance *his* or *her* goals. Means, according to neoclassicists, are chosen and resources are allocated in such a manner as to maximize the *actor's* utility. As we see it, there is no necessary connection between the self-serving goal and the efficient use of means. The best way to see the difference is to examine service to some other goal, say, the production of public goods. Obviously resources may be used efficiently (or inefficiently) to serve the community as readily as one's self. Hence, the definition of rationality ought to focus exclusively on the selection of means, not on the nature of the goal. (Goal selection is a matter of ethical or value judgments.) To imply otherwise is to introduce a utilitarian value judgement that those who serve the public, or serve others for others' sake, act in inexplicable or non-rational ways, a judgment we do not share.

Purposive

To ditch the concept of utility as self-serving is not to deny that rational behavior is purposive. That is, we share in the assumption that the person, organization, or society at issue are committed to one or more goals (states of future they seek to realize, to which there is a significant measure of commitment of psychic energy and resources).* Behavior which is merely "functional" but not purposive, that is, behavior that is useful as judged by observers but unbeknown to the actor, nor deliberately sought by the actor, is not rational in the terms used here and by many others. Thus, a person who bats his eyelashes "in order" to remove a particle of dust, a reflexive act, is not engaged in rational behavior. The reason behavior that is only "functional" but not purposive is excluded is that otherwise all behavior becomes rational, because all behavior can be shown to be useful by some criteria or another in some time frame or another, thus depriving the concept of its differentiating power.

The goals used in the defining criteria, those that are sought by the actors, can be observed empirically (they are reflected in the minutes of board meetings, organizational charters, budget allocations, and so on). No theological reasoning is involved† because we do not "assume" purpose, but measure it empirically independently from the action taken.

Before the discussion continues, a major limitation of the concept, that has often been noted before, must be reported: The definition assumes a clear distinction between goals and means, itself a rationalistic distinction. Often, goals are in continual flux, as means are chosen, and decision-makers do not set out with clear goals (let alone, clearly ranked goals), but discover what they are after as they proceed. Thus, many young individuals embark on a college education without knowing what they will major in, and keep trying different majors until one becomes their chosen vocation or avocation, in the process clarifying—if not finding out—many of their life's goals. Some days full-time homemakers, people of leisure, and weekend vacationers go out "to shop" *without* a clear agenda, often inviting impulse buying. Also to the point is the finding that once a person chooses to work for company X, he or she finds the company more to their liking than before they made the choice, and the company not chosen less to their liking than before (Vroom 1966; Soelberg 1967). It might be said that this is a matter of obtaining more information about the chosen company, but that would assume that the original guess was always right. More likely, people adjust their "taste" to what they have chosen. Similarly, saving and investment in part may be non- or *pre*-purposive; people with "surplus" income may put some funds aside, to consider later to what use to put the funds, as well as whether or not they ought to continue to save or spend, given their evolving goals. By the definition followed here (and often followed by others), all such behavior is neither rational nor irrational but of a third kind, the *pre*-rational if one wishes, or normative (goal-formation or clarification), because if goals do not exist or are to a significant extent in flux, means typically cannot be well chosen.

*The last part of the definition is necessary to exclude lip service.

†cf. Miller and Starr 1967, p. 42.

Not Implemented

Reference is to decision-making, not to implementation; for instance, to the decision of which plant to build, not to the job of construction, to what some psychologists call "reasoned action" (Ajzen and Fishbein 1980). The distinction is stressed because well–thought out decisions may run into unexpected events (e.g., oil price "shocks"), which in retrospect may make a decision seem non-rational even if, at the time it was made, all the available information was used, and the proper conclusions were drawn. And poor decisions may luck out of trouble. That is, a stock bought on a whim may rise; but such an increase will not make the decision to buy it rational. *Instrumental rationality is not judged by the consequences but by the processes of decision-formation.*

True, in a model world, in which all future events (or at least all significant future events) can be anticipated, the distinction between decision-making and implementation may become irrelevant. But for decisions that deal with matters more real and complex than the tossing of coins, or with highly contrived situations in laboratory experiments—i.e., with most decisions—the distinction is essential.

The deeper source of the difference between rational decision-making and implementation is the realm in which they take place. Decision-making takes place within a person's mind, at corporate meetings, in computer programs—in the realm of intellectual processes and symbolic transactions. Implementation takes place within the world of nature and society, of objects and people. There are significant inherent differences between these realms: the symbolic one can be much more easily restructured, manipulated, and rationalized than the other (albeit not necessarily easily). One can readily think about a horse with wings; to breed one is a rather different matter. (For additional discussion, see Etzioni 1968, Chapter 2.)

In the preceding discussion of instrumental rationality the term was deliberately defined in reference to decision-making. While it is possible to refer to rational behavior, such usage actually means behavior "in line with rational decision-making." More than a technical quibble is at issue: If decisions are hardly ever very rational, implementation is much less often so, because numerous unforeseen factors intervene to affect the outcomes, other than the intentions of the actor; this is a major point rationalism tends to ignore.

Pivotal Deliberations

The definition of instrumental rationality brings out the pivotal role of deliberations. Rarely does information per se point to the decision to be followed. Typically, it must be evaluated, and integrated with other items of information the actor already possesses; projections and interpretations must be added, and conclusions drawn.

Neoclassicists frequently state that it does not matter whether or not the actor is deliberating (or calculating), whether or not decision-making is conscious. Becker (1976, p. 7) states: ". . . the economic approach does not assume that decision units are necessarily *conscious* of their efforts to maximize or can verbalize or otherwise describe in an informative way reasons for the systematic patterns in their behavior." (Italics added. See also March 1978, p. 593; Wilde et al, 1985, pp. 404ff.) To a large extent, this position is based on very loose definitions of rationality, to ensure no act will be left out. Thus, if one uses the minimalist criteria of being consistent, not just the nonconscious, automatic behavior of people, but even the choices made by rats (Kagel et al. 1975) qualify as "rational." "The people who will appear in this book are, if you like, no less rational than pigeons," states Homans (1961, p. 85). "If it be rational of pigeons to learn and take the shortest of two paths to a reward, so it is of our men. . . ." Homans goes on to acknowledge that "such rationality . . . may not amount to much." (Ibid.) We argue that it amounts to less.

Another way automatic behavior may be made to seem to reflect rational decisions is to point to situations in which physical limits (or their imitation in experimental situations) force nonconscious choices into a mode that seems rational. Thus, given a fixed amount of resources, a shopper buying more of an item will buy less of some other item (if leisure and savings are included), whether or not the shopper deliberates. And given that there are only 24 hours per day, women who work outside of their home will "allot" less of their time to their other activities.

While it is possible, as has been just illustrated, to remove the element of deliberation (or consciousness) from the definition of rationality, the result is an undifferentiating—or at best a poorly differentiating—concept, and a loss of many interesting issues. For example, to what extent can the rationality of decisions be improved by enhancing the ability to deliberate? Or, when individuals buy less of X, granted they will transfer the freed resources to non-X, will they distribute them efficiently among all the numerous non-X items? And what role do deliberations play in forming such reallocations?

To support the claim that the level of instrumental rationality in decision-making is associated with the extent and quality of deliberations, it suffices to conduct the following mental experiment. Imagine a person under observation engaged in a decision-making process, say reviewing a list of stocks with an eye to decide which stock to buy on the basis of information provided to the person about recent developments. The person's veins are hooked to an IV and alcohol is dripping. There seems to be little question that gradually the person's ability to pick stocks in line with the evidence and criteria previously agreed upon will deteriorate, indeed, eventually be wiped out. Other drugs that modify consciousness; fatigue, lack of proper nutrition, emotional stress, and moral commitments, all have a similar effect. It suffices to compare an impulsive, harried, uninformed, low-IQ shopper, to a meticulous, unhurried, informed, high-IQ shopper to see the point. It seems difficult to understand why a factor that seems *that* seminal would be left out of one's paradigm, unless it is because of the normative commitment to keep everyone rational by definition, even if they act without the benefit of forethought. (For further discussion on the pivotal role of consciousness in rational decision-making, see Brunsson 1982, p. 29; Simmons, Klein, Simmons 1977, pp. 237ff.)

We seek to move into the opposite direction because of our concern with finding differentiating concepts, and the deontological concern to keep intentions and consequences clearly distinct, stressing the significance of intention. To highlight the point, the following terminological distinction has been suggested: The term *choice* should be used to encompass the sorting out of options, whether conscious or nonconscious. Deliberate choices are to be referred to as *decisions* (i.e., all decisions, by definition, entail deliberations), and the other choices may be referred to as non-deliberative. Equipped with these distinctions, we inquire in the next chapter about the forces that enhance or retard deliberation, and thus (all other things being equal) raise or lower the level of instrumental rationality.

9

Instrumental Rationality: Supportive Conditions

RATIONALITY AS A PRODUCT

The thesis that people are to be viewed as commanding varying degrees of instrumental rationality, rather than as being either rational or non-rational, leads one to ask which conditions enhance and which hinder instrumental rationality, a productive question as we shall see. Moreover, several significant "anomalous" bodies of findings find a systematic theoretical home once this approach is applied, accomplishing one of the purposes of moving toward a more encompassing paradigm.

Basically it is argued here that *rationality is antientropic*. That is, the natural or baseline state of human choice is assumed to be *not* rational; often, means are chosen on N/A grounds, and those L/E considerations that are introduced are deficient. For *choice to be rational even in part, forces must be present or activated to pull the choice in the rational direction.* These forces can be identified, and their role in promoting varying measures of rationality can be empirically "validated." Moreover, following such an activation, choice behavior "strives" to return to the entropic state*. *Hence, to act rationally, requires a continued investment of resources and effort.* (The analogue of non-rationality to entropy is limited to one major point: It takes special forces to pull the situation or behavior away from its natural state. Otherwise there are many differences between entropy in nature and in behavior that need not to be discussed here.)

To put it differently: *non-rational choice is natural; rational decision-making is artificial;* it must be manufactured. Support for this position is introduced in this chapter by drawing on various well-known bodies of data that are compatible with the thesis advanced here, and by referring to a well-established fact—that rationality must be continuously manufactured, like other perishable goods, *at a cost.* The fact that resources must

---

*For a previous well-known attempt to relate economic theory to entropy, see Georgescu-Roegen (1971).

be sacrificed to gain even a measure of rationality provides empirical evidence that instrumental rationality is a product, and often a costly one.

The position undertaken here is far from a radical departure from widely held positions in social sciences. Williams and Findlay (1981, p. 17) concluded their 1981 review of the relevant social science literature with the statement that "it is becoming increasingly obvious from the research conclusions of other [non-economic] disciplines (psychology, philosophy, political science, and sociology in particular) that the simplistic notion of *'economic man'* posited so often in economic literature, is more fancy than fact." Lovejoy (1961, p. 64) found that "man's 'reason' has, at most, a secondary and a very small influence upon his conduct and irrational or nonrational feelings and desires are the real efficient causes of all, or nearly all, of men's actions." Many others have taken similar positions (for extensive bibliography see Williams and Findlay, 1981). Cohen (1976, p. 148) and Johnson-Laird (1982) are among those who approached the concept of rationality as a matter of degrees or levels, rather than assume that people "are" rational (or non-rational). Also highly relevant is Leibentein's (1966, 1976) concept of X-efficiency and the various factors that affect its level (for literature review, see Alessi 1983, and Frantz unpublished).

In comparison, the position taken here is rather moderate. It is not assumed that rationality is elusive, only that it is often costly, and, when "bought," it is typically purchased only in rather small quantities. At the same time, it is true that when the needed resources are available and dedicated to the development of science and technology, the efficient organization of production and distribution, and a professional public administration (often over many decades) considerable zones of relatively rational behavior are established, in what is known as the process of modernization (or development).

From a methodological viewpoint, since non-rational behavior is the common natural state and the starting point for those unsocialized, we shall see that it is more efficient to use it as the baseline and explain whatever level of instrumental rationality is attained, rather than proceed the other way around, that is, by assuming that people are rational and wondering why their behavior does not always reveal this predisposition (cf. Day 1967; Wilson 1970; and Elster 1979).

RATIONALITY EQUALS EFFORT

To seek the most efficient means to advance one's goals, to act rationally, entails effort. The term "effort" is used here in a broad sense to include the commitment of resources, energy, time, and dedication. (It is much broader than the term "costs," at least as both terms are usually understood. "Effort" encompasses such elements as developing self-discipline, and the mobilization of self or of the collectivity.) In contrast, entropy, the state of nature, is effortless. It involves no setting of goals and hence no selection of means; ongoing processes are not deliberately interfered with, but proceed like rivers flowing downhill. Similarly, to act impulsively in line with one's prejudices, urges, or habits, in disregard of information, and without analysis or deliberation, requires little effort.

The efforts that rationality entails are of three kinds: (1) the search for effective means (including preparations for searching), to be referred to as *cognitive work*; (2) the development of *personality, organizational, and societal foundations* that are required to be able to undertake extensive search, and search that is relatively free from irrelevant constraints and interruptions; and (3) combining the *maintenance* of the appropriate resources, procedures, and institutions (e.g., computers, software and R&D staff, legitimation of science) with *adaptation* (the "updating" of the resources, to keep them responsive to the ever-changing environment). The differences among these three kinds of effort are briefly indicated for individuals, organizations, and societies before evidence is cited about the corelation between effort levels and rationality levels.

Cognitive Work

One kind of effort expected to be associated with the level of rationality is the *commitment of resources to cognitive work* that is needed to assemble, analyze, and apply relevant information. Cognitive work encompasses efforts expended directly on search behavior (for example, how many dealers an individual visits before he or she buys an auto) as well as efforts entailed in preparations (for instance, a new investor in the stock market may participate in an investment workshop before setting out to "search" which particular stock to invest in).

Cognitive work for a person may entail gaining access to specific items of information (for instance, purchase of a technical report), to general sources (for example, permission to use a library), or to information-processing technologies. For a corporation it may involve increasing its investment in R&D, or changing the staff-line ratios to increase the relative size of the staff. For a society it may entail increasing the reliance on a professional civil service, and reducing the role of political considerations in the selection of means.

The approach advocated here is one of subaggregation. Instead of attempting to answer the question of how rational "Man is"—the way the question is still often posed—the discussion here focuses on the extent various subcategories of people, organizations, and societies are more or less able to select means efficiently. A simple example, is that individuals with more education, especially technical training, are on average more able to render instrumentally rational decisions (in areas in which their special qualifications apply) than those with less preparation. Other find-ings cited below are less self-evident, but follow the same basic pattern of subaggregation, of correlating various psychic or social attributes with varying degrees of instrumental rationality.

Personality and Societal Development

The observation that personality and societal developments provide major noncognitive foundations for rational behavior is a major observa-tion that one may draw from psychological, sociological, and anthropo-logical works. That is, rational behavior does not take place in a vacuum; it requires appropriate personality and societal context and structure. Their specific nature is explored below; the term noncognitive simply indicates that the issues at hand concern other attributes than intellec-tual capabilities.

Although all individuals may well have the same potential to learn to act rationally, people are not born with the necessary motivation and personality traits to actually act rationally. Indeed societies differ signifi-cantly in their tolerance for rational decision-making. In some societies, decisions are governed by N/A factors expressed in myth, tradition, famil-ial and tribal obligations, or in politics; in others, the size of the legiti-mated L/E indifference zones are relatively considerable. Max Weber's well-known comparative study of Western Europe, China, and India ([1904–05] 1930, [1915] 1951, and [1916–17] 1958) is of course focused on this issue.

As personality and societal development affect one another, it is useful to discuss first a situation where the societal context has already been "rationalized" (i.e., a modern society) but new persons (children, or im-migrants from less-developed countries) are yet to be introduced to the relatively more instrumentally oriented culture and society. These per-sons will have to acquire the noncognitive capabilities that instrumental rationality requires. Such an acquisition entails more than acquiring the appropriate cognitive skills, say, learning to read a blueprint. It also en-tails gaining the ability to resist impulse and prejudice, to maintain or-derly sequences, to keep N/A factors from excessively infusing one's L/E zones by building up the required psychic traits and social relations—for example, a measure of "coolness" and distance from the family when at work. The difference between the cognitive skills and the noncognitive personality foundations is illustrated by people who realize they have reasons to suspect they may have cancer. A study found that people who recognize symptoms of cancer are not more likely to act on them than less knowledgeable persons (Goldsen et al. 1957, op. cit.). Those who were able to act rationally, and to consult a physician, were those who had more than the needed information—they had the capacity to over-come anxiety (ibid, p. 5). A good part of the literature on the psychological and sociological conditions under which entrepreneurship rises is also relevant to this line of analysis (Casson 1982).

There is no agreement in the literature about psychic foundations of rational decision-making, about the specific nature of required capabilities or how they are evolved. Without attempting to review the enormous literature on the subject, the following merely illustrates the nature of what, lacking a better term, is referred to as the noncognitive foundations of rationality. According to one line of work, the ability to engage in instrumentally rational decision-making is developed first at home, and later further advanced in school. Specifically, the hypothesis is that the ability to do cognitive work is associated with the ability for self-mobilization (as distinct from acquiring specific skills, such as to calculate). To be able to think logically, to process and to absorb evidence, to heed the cues it provides, and to interpret them properly, a person must be able to follow a set of procedures and rules, follow "steps," rather than rely on "snap judgment" or "intuition," or follow what is "typical" or traditional. Parents and educators help develop within the child a generalized capacity to control impulse, a kind of psychic stamina for intellectual efforts.

In modern societies those parents who conform to their society's main values (as distinct from those of deviant subcultures) invest considerable effort in developing in their children the capacity to mobilize self. Kindergarten, schools, and even colleges, further contribute to this development. This takes place when, for instance, the ability to work on one's own, to plan one's work, and to work on schedule are rewarded. In a reanalysis of Coleman's data about American high schools, we found that high performance was correlated with homework. Homework is valuable because it allows a person to develop self-discipline, especially when it is done because the assignments are considered properly assigned and fairly evaluated (Coleman et al. 1982; Etzioni 1983, Chapter 6, 1984b).

The main point for the thesis at hand is that certain kinds of personality development—prerequisites for rational action—require considerable investment by the family and by the schools. The counter-hypothesis is advanced by some radical critics of institutional education. Illich (1971) maintains that it would be best to close schools and allow children to follow their parents through their day of work. Holt (1972, p. 2) writes: "Children are by nature smart, energetic, curious, eager to learn and good at learning." In an earlier writing (1970, pp. 70–71) he would leave educators quite passive: "We teachers can see ourselves as travel agents. When we go to a travel agent, he does not tell us where to go. He finds out first what we are looking for. . . . Given some idea of what we are looking for, he makes some suggestions. . . . He does not have to take the trip with us." While even this approach is not necessarily effortless, the efforts involved, especially for others than the learners themselves, are minimal.

To turn now to societies, they, too, may undergo developments (economic, educational, cultural) that allow those societies that develop their instrumental institutions as collectivities, to choose more rational policies. The conditions under which a society's instrumental foundations and L/E zones develop have been analyzed in a vast literature that has shown little tendency to reach a consensus. Most approaches, though, clearly show that such developments (often encompassed in what is referred to as modernization) require massive efforts. One school of thought emphasizes the need for capital formation. Typically this entails deferring consumption in order to enhance the productive capacity of society, which strains the people of those countries, especially when consumption is low. In contrast, to the extent that development is based on foreign aid or can be financed from the gains of expanded trade, comparatively few sacrifices are required. There is, however, little reason to expect that, as a rule, development is to a significant extent achieved in this way.

Another school of thought stresses the role of education, training, and R&D, that is, the role of investment in "human capital" in achieving modernization. Because of the longer lead time between this kind of investment and the desired yields, the effort development entails according to this thesis is even greater than the one assumed by the capital formation school.

A significant body of literature is dedicated to the question of which specific organizational arrangements promote rather than hinder rationality. Williamson's (1975) work, and several which followed it, in effect address the question under what conditions does the market provide a less efficient mechanism than "hierarchies" with which to organize division of labor and transactions? Other studies explore which specific organizational arrangements foster or undermine various L/E based activities. (For additional discussion see Chapter 11, pp. 196–98.)

Max Weber ([1921–22] 1968) dedicates much attention to the question of under what conditions rationality can be "institutionalized." Stinchcombe (1986), who recently has been surveying various arrangements, begins his list with the following (p. 157): The person making a judgment is required to justify his or her decision to other experts in the field. "Thus, when, a scientist announces that he or she (tentatively) believes a certain thing in a scientific paper, an explanation of the reasoning and evidence leading to the belief are required." Other examples are appellate court decisions; second opinions in medicine; and auditors, if their view of the firm's finances differs from its accountants. In effect, a fair measure of required explicit accounting is found not only in appellate courts, but in all courts that have to justify their judgments rather than merely pronounce them, and in most expert advice. Indeed, Weber expected all administrators and executives to be required to account for their decisions, and to be protected from N/A pressures of the community and politics so that they could make their decisions on objective, logical grounds. Bureaucracy for him was not a derogatory term but a designation of an institution that enhances people's ability to follow rational rules rather than passions. An institutionalized civil service was the example that stood before his eyes in contrast to a feudalized service.

Maintenance and Adaptation

Rationality is not a habit which, like swimming, once acquired, tends to be maintained without *continued* effort. On the contrary, it is our hypothesis that *rationality is not a self-sustaining attribute.* If no maintenance efforts are undertaken, the capacity to act rationally will diminish over time. In addition, the changing environment requires the adaptation of existing patterns of cognitive work, capabilities, even personality and societal foundations, if a given level of rationality is to be sustained. Physicians must attend workshops, follow journals, etc., to update their knowledge and skills. Corporations must dedicate resources both to maintain their computers and to purchase "state of the art" software. Societies must appropriate budgets to educate and train the new generation, both to transmit the stock of existing knowledge and to develop new knowledge. While early studies expected that inventions (or R&D work) will cause investments, investments have been established as leading to inventions (Schmookler 1972, pp. 74–76).

The typology of efforts just outlined is an analytic one; that is, specific resources are not exclusively dedicated to cognitive work, development, maintenance, *or* adaptation. The same resource, a school for example, may serve all three kinds of efforts. The classification of a resource draws on the ways it is mainly used. Kindergartens tend to be used relatively more for personality development, high schools for cognitive training, and so on. However, one must keep in mind that such classifications provide mere approximations, not a full account.

All said and done, while there are counterhypotheses to the thesis advanced here, and while the voluminous research on personality and societal development does not speak to one conclusion, most lines of work point to a correlation between extending efforts and acquiring, maintaining, and adapting rationality.

THEORETICAL HOME

Several significant lines of development of neoclassical economics, that attempt to cope with major "anomalies" that the paradigm has encountered, find a theoretical home in the thesis about the antientropic nature of rationality. In discussing these developments our purpose is not to do justice to the many important works on each subject, but only to point

to theoretical links. At the same time, the discussion affords us some opportunities to further support and extend the thesis itself.

Information Costs

In early economic works, and in some recent work (especially that by
the school of "rational expectations"), it was common to assume that information has no cost. This notion is implicit in the basic concept of a
market. It assumes that all the buyers and sellers have uninhibited access
to the information about all offers to buy and sell.

Economists have come to recognize that information is not free, and
have gradually moved to integrate information costs into their analyses.
Information costs have been incorporated into the rationality model by
suggesting that the "correct" point for terminating the search is reached
when the marginal cost of additional learning equals the expected marginal improvement (Stigler 1961, pp. 213–215). Leaving aside the question of whether most actors most times can make such a calculation, one
must note that these approaches treat the costs of the search in cavalier
fashion (Simon 1978, p. 101; Radner 1975, p. 253).

More is involved than traveling from one auto dealer to another.
There are emotional "costs" (such as the need to agree with one's spouse
about the demerits of each option rejected), and normative ones (e.g.,
check each item considered against the values of one's group or groups),
among others. That is, deliberations activate a wide range of complex
N/A considerations, far beyond mere price comparisons (cf. Stigler 1962).
It follows that information costs are considerably higher than is often
assumed. It further follows that search behavior will often be much more
limited than is assumed by neoclassicists. High information costs suggest
that much of behavior, including economic behavior, will be unresponsive to various changes, including changes in prices; and that the areas
of choice-avoiding behavior will be sizable.

A conceptual clarification is necessary here. Information costs and
transaction or implementation costs are not to be viewed as synonyms.
Transaction costs include, aside from information costs, implementation
costs. (This is implied by Nicholson 1978, p. 32, and Kamerschen and
Valentine 1981, p. 246). A search, that costs X, might lead to the conclusion that an investor ought to switch from instrument A to instrument
B, but if to implement the decision (say, for a small investment) involves
proportionally high brokerage costs, this may make the transaction not
worthwhile. Indeed, implementation costs, especially in labor markets,
are expected to often significantly exceed information costs. For example; Detroit workers may buy Houston newspapers to learn about jobs in
Texas; but the costs of moving to the job are obviously much higher than
the cost of the newspaper. It hence seems sensible to see transaction costs

as the more encompassing category which includes both information and implementation costs.

The preceding discussion deals with information costs only. In contrast, price dispersion, widely used as an indicator of *information* costs (Stigler 1961, 1962; Marvel 1976), reflects both kinds of costs. (Cf. "Price dispersion is a manifestation—and, indeed, it is the measure—of *ignorance* in the market," Stigler 1961, p. 214. Italics provided).

If one focuses on information costs alone, it should be noted that information costs are higher in some areas of economic activity than in others; for example, they are expected on average to be higher in deciding which R&D activities to fund than in deciding on purchasing equipment, if the same size of investment is involved. Decisions in areas in which information costs are relatively higher will tend to be less rational. This requires some elaboration.

Market models typically assume that all participants have the same easy access to information. However, information asymmetries are common; often, one side of the market (buyers *or* sellers, management *or* workers) has much lower information costs than the other (Akerlof 1970). That is, the ability to overcome entropy is not equally distributed among all actors. For example, most sellers of used autos command more of it than most buyers, because most sellers know their car better than most potential buyers (ibid.). Market models that assume free information serve relatively poorly in these situations, and models that take into account differential information costs are far from adequately developed (Riley 1979; Crocker and Snow 1985).

In short, the very existence of information costs is compatible with, or "derivable" from, the antientropic thesis. To act relatively rationally requires, among other things, to use information. One reason why it requires effort to act rationally is that information is not a free good. A positive correlation is to be expected between the degree of rationality and the amount of resources invested in rational deliberations and preparations. Large amounts of resources allow an actor to purchase a larger (and/or better) quantity of information and processing capabilities. Information costs are often high, and while it may be rational not to pay them, (1) the actors often have no way of knowing how much the information is worth, and (2) given the often high cost, must often resort for their decision-making to bases other than information processing and deliberations.

The Learning Curve

The learning curve is another phenomenon that engineers, operation researchers, and economists have discovered, which finds a theoretical explanation in the antientropic nature of rationality. Moreover, our observation that rationality typically requires efforts, and often sizable ones, helps explain the particular shape of various learning curves. Basically the curves reflect the fact that cognitive work and preparations, relevant personality and societal development, maintenance and adaptation are not free goods.

Early economic theory, which assumed information to be freely available and instantly absorbed and utilized, expected learning to be instantaneous and effortless. This was often not explicitly stated, but was reflected in ignoring the time and costs that learning entails (MacRae 1978, p. 1245). Specifically, the disregard of the learning curve can be seen in the notion that the unit production costs (of the same product) will remain constant over time (assuming, of course, no change in input costs, such as labor and capital, and in technology). It was noted as late as 1964 (Hirschmann, p. 125) that "although learning curves have been recognized in industries other than aircraft, they have not been as widely accepted. Instead, predictions are usually based on assumptions of level performance and constant costs." This is despite the fact that industrial learning curves have been observed as early as 1925, in the production of airplanes (Wright 1936), and that it was well established that, as management and workers gained experience with production based on new technologies, unit costs declined significantly. The same was observed for other products (Andress 1954). True, not all the gain was due to learning; in part it was due to increases in the size of production batches over time (Goddard 1982); but the learning factor is clearly significant.

What accounts for the graduated pace of learning, for the curve, is, in part, the cost of rationality. A new or modified technology or technique is rarely introduced in its fully developed stage into a plant. Experience (a major source of knowledge) forces numerous modifications. Resources must be dedicated to train the workers and to motivate them to learn. Structural changes in relations among workers, between staff and line, and between levels of management, are often necesasry, but do not come about without effort. For example, R&D staff often have an interest in trying new techniques, while production managers frequently resist such innovations, and hence are "bought off." (Dalton, 1950.)

The fact that learning has costs supports the thesis that rational behavior is not free; the fact that learning is often slow and partial suggests that the cost of rationality is often high. This is one reason most people will not be fully, or even highly, "learned" most times, especially in a rapidly changing environment; that is, they will not act very rationally.

Thurow (1983) points out that neoclassical economists assume an equilibrium which, if disturbed, will seek to reestablish itself. Hence, they in effect argue that one cannot learn about the "normal" situation from periods of disruption. He wonders, however, whether one can retain these assumptions about the working of the economy in a world of rapid changes in which learning is ever present and equilibrium is never approximated? In such a world, which we agree is the world we face, behavior will be substantially less rational than the equilibrium theory assumes.

Habit versus Prices and Efforts

The most common way individuals, organizations, and societies choose is not by deliberating but by following inertia or habit. Habits have been defined as routine behavior without cognition or evaluation, (Verhallen and van Raaij 1985, p. 5). Evidence is cited next on the wide role of habits in choosing. The argument has been made that habits are actually rational, that they reflect past experience, or reflect socially aggregated knowledge. This position is critically evaluated below; suffice it to note here that the formation of habit often reflects N/A factors (e.g., a tendency to be other-directed, or an excessive desire to conform), and habits often persist because of emotional investment in the status-quo and resistance to learning.

In contrast to the assumption that actors rationally decide what to purchase, and how much to save, and that they otherwise act rationally in economic matters, evidence has been accumulating that often this is not the case. People use credit cards and installment payments, even at 18 percent interest, when they have cash on hand (Katona 1973, p. 27). People buy out of habit, on impulse, and out of what has been called "brand loyalty." "Habitual behavior occurs much more frequently, and, whatever the origin of our habits, they do not exhibit the major features of rational behavior," observes Katona (ibid., pp. 218–19). "People act as they have acted before under similar circumstances, without deliberating and choosing. Routine procedure and an application of rules of thumb by consumers as well as businessmen exclude the weighing of alternatives." (Ibid.)

Studies of the purchase of major household appliances—i.e., expensive and enduring items infrequently bought and of relative importance—show they are acquired with relatively little deliberation (Katona and Mueller 1954), even "in a careless way." (Katona 1975, p. 220.) For other items, for example new sport shirts, deliberation was found to be even more limited (Katona and Mueller 1954). Factors governing the purchase were found to be a sense of an urgent need preventing careful deliberation (say, one's refrigerator broke down beyond repair), and/or a sense of satisfaction with a similar article previously bought. (The fact that a product was satisfactory is, of course, no proof that it is either the best or that a superior item has not become available since the last one was purchased.)

A classic study of the subject is by Houthakker and Taylor (1970), who analyzed consumer expenditures for 82 items. Fifty items were found statistically to be subject to habit formation. These 50 accounted for 58.4 per cent of the total expenditure. In contrast, commodities subject to inventory adjustment accounted for 28.2 percent of total expenditure. As Houthakker and Taylor point out, prices (at many income levels) are relatively unimportant, and so leave habits as the main explanation of why people (within a given income level) spend what they do. Houthakker and Taylor concluded (ibid., p. 164) that "habit formation quite *clearly predominates* in the United States consumption." (Italics added.) (For a challenge which uses different time units, see Sexauer 1977.)

While habit buying seems more common than impulse buying, the latter is far from uncommon. For operational purposes, impulse buying is defined as purchases undertaken without a need to buy having been consciously recognized, or a buying intention having been formed prior to entering the store (Engel and Blackwell 1982, p. 552). Such purchases are reported to represent over 33 percent of all purchases in variety stores and in drugstores according to several studies, and a still higher percentage of purchases in liquor stores (Hansen 1972, p. 338). Still another study found unplanned purchases ranged from 38.7 percent in a department store to nearly two-thirds of all purchases in the supermarket (Engel and Blackwell 1982, p. 552). It should be noted that serious conceptual and methodological problems arise as to what is defined as impulse buying, which are not explored here.

When one moves from regular consumer items to other purchases, rational behavior is even less common. Katona (1975, pp. 222–23) points out that "Even people who are accustomed to buying cars on credit are often not able to say what the minimum requirements for down payment or the costs of credit are, . . . lack of information on life insurance is extensive, for instance, about the differences among different kinds of policies and their costs."

Addictions to cigarettes or alcohol, for instance, are an extreme example of habit formation. This has been reported in the form of a "kinked" demand curve. If these goods were not affected by habit formation, one would expect the demand curve to be smooth and the curve for the elasticity of demand to be symmetric. However, for goods affected by addiction, the demand response to price is a-symmetric; response to price increases is smaller than to price decreases. Demand is inelastic to price increases and relatively elastic to price decreases (Scitovsky 1978; Young 1983).

Habits affect not merely purchasing. Changes in fiscal policy, for instance cuts in income tax, frequently are found not to have the expected effects on motivation to work (Lewis 1982, p. 4) "because the public may persist with previous economic behavior as though it were ignorant of these fiscal changes." When Americans were offered a free "energy audit" (to establish how they could reduce their energy waste and hence expenditures) only a very small fraction of the public accepted the offer (Stern 1984, p. 62).

The saving rate in the United States between 1951 and 1981 remained "surprisingly constant within a range of 16 to 18 percent of GNP," states Bosworth (1984, p. 62). This, despite the fact that in the period under study numerous changes were introduced in tax policies which presumably made it "rational" to change one's saving behavior, including significant changes in the general level of taxation and specifically in taxes levied on capital gains. While the lessons of evidence concerning the post-1981 years is still being debated, it seems that supply-side tax cuts also did not change this basic conclusion.

All this is not to suggest that changes in prices, in interest rates, or tax incentives have no effect. However, we hypothesize that (1) "no effect" (or a trivial one) is more common than having an effect, which supports the thesis advanced above that the norm (or ideal type) should be non-rational behavior. (2) The size of the change (in prices, incentives, and so on) needed to bring about a change in the frequency and magnitude of a response, provides a measure of the relative costs of "producing" a specific level of rationality in a given area of behavior as compared to others, and for a particular group of individuals (say, middle class) as compared to some others.

All this supports our suggestion that the base line assumption for the study of rationality ought be "no effect," and the thesis that when effects do take place, there are special circumstances that account for them. For instance, when price changes are comparatively large, and highly publicized, or otherwise administer a "shock," they are more likely to initiate search behavior than a series of small or routine changes (Heberlein and Warriner 1983).

Thurow (1983) gives examples of inertia by the economy, not merely by individuals. When President Johnson decided to finance the war in Vietnam without raising taxes or cutting domestic spending, as his economists advised him, since the economy was already at full employment, inflation was expected. However, it took three years, much longer than his economic advisors had expected, before inflation rose from 2.2% in 1965 (when Johnson acted) to 4.5% in 1968 (pp. 53–54). Thurow discusses a similar slow reaction to deflationary measures (ibid., 54–55, 66). One major reason routine changes in prices, wages, tax incentives, and so on typically are unlikely to have an effect is that habit and impulse buying, continued saving at the same level as in the recent past, and brand loyalty require no cognitive work, preparation, development or adaptation; i.e., they have no rationality costs, although they clearly exact economic ones. And, by the same token, the relative infrequency of highly rational behavior in buying, saving, and so on attests to the considerable efforts, and high costs, that even relatively rational behavior entails.

THE "QUALITY" OF INFORMATION

The preceding discussion of the conceptual association (or correlation) between the *amount* of effort invested and the relative level of rationality attained by individuals, organizations, and societies, provides only a first approximation. The next step is to drop the assumption that, simply by increasing the efforts invested, the level of rationality will automatically rise. Obviously, the law of declining marginal productivity is expected to apply to this factor, as it does to others. Adding ever more computers, engineering, R&D, and so on, is expected to yield ever lower marginal improvements in rationality.

Less obviously, the "quality" of the inputs is expected to affect the outcome. Economists often discuss information and efforts (or resources) in terms of the amounts available (as the author did up to this point in the discussion). However, studies show that other attributes have a significant impact. To develop a list, or a theory of these attributes, is beyond what can be accomplished here. The purpose of the following is only to illustrate the significance of the quality of information, such as the extent to which the information is credible or seems to those who receive it. Studies of life insurance purchases show that the majority of buyers do not compare the costs of different policies; have difficulties in determining whether they get their money's worth out of their purchase; and do not use a buyer's guide that government regulations require they be given. Trust in the selling agent accounted for significantly more of the decision to buy than any other factor (Collesano, Greenwald, Katosh 1984). (Trust, in turn, was based on feelings about the agent, not some kind of inter-agent competition.)

Price changes are often depicted by economists as market signals, as conveying information to which a rational actor will respond. The National Academy of Sciences conducted a study of consumer responses to information about the availability of financing to improve one's residential use of energy (e.g., through insulation); it found non-financial features were much more important than the size of the financial incentive. Given the same finance information coupled with different non-financial attributes (such as simpler versus more complex implementation procedures; varying degrees of protection against shabby work) caused very large differences in response (in effect, sales) ranging from less than 1% of households' approval to more than 40% in one state; and from 8% to nearly 90% in another state (Stern 1984, p. 55). Using a poor information "format" caused the consumers of Duke Power to select a combination of conservation measures that was less than half of the most efficient available to them, spending $230 to $300 more than necessary to achieve a $252 annual saving (Magat, Payne, Brucato 1986, p. 29).

It might be ill-advised to refer to these attributes as "qualities" of information, because this implies some aspects that are difficult to measure, like the quality of food or of education, as distinct from amounts of calories or years of education. Our main point is that information is multi-dimensional: Often more than one attribute must be measured to assess the input. Thus, one needs to know not merely how much information a person was given, but also how reliable it is. True, *some* of these "additional" attributes are qualitative or relatively difficult to measure, but many others are not.

Finally, one must examine the relationships between various attributes of the information acquired, and the relative capabilities of the actor processing it. For example, obtaining more information of relatively low reliability without additional or more effective processing facilities will create overloads; that is, it will diminish the marginal effect, reducing the rationality of the decision. Very little research has been done in these matters, both because information is often treated as a relatively simple asset, and because of the neoclassical focus on inputs and outputs coupled with a tendency to neglect the intermediating processes. Here little more is achieved than putting the subject on the agenda.

10

Thoughtless Rationality (Rules of Thumb)

THE ROLE OF RULES

Followers of the neoclassical paradigm argue that individuals may render rational decisions without processing information or deliberations, by using "rules of thumb."

> Cognitive capacity is a scarce resource like any other.... To gather the information and do the calculations implicit in naive descriptions of the rational choice model would consume more time and energy than anyone has.... Anyone who tried to make fully-informed, rational choices would make only a handful of decisions each week, leaving hundreds of important matters unattended.
>
> With this difficulty in mind, most of us rely on habits and rules of thumb for routine decisions. The habits or rules themselves are of course nonrational by definition: Regardless of the costs and benefits specific to each case, they spit out a fixed response. Most of us shop at the same supermarket each week, even though some other market will often have lower prices. We know many of our decisions will be inferior to those a fully informed, rational agent would have made. And yet we have no better alternative. Given scarce cognitive resources, to rely on habit and other nonrational decision rules is fully rational. (Frank 1987, p. 23.)

These rules are provided to individuals by their culture and their organizations, or else are a product of their previous experience.

No formal definition of the concept of rules of thumb is provided in the small literature on the subject. Examples of rules of thumb, referred to in the literature, are mainly from rules used in everyday life (take an umbrella on a cloudy day, rather than "research" the weather forecast). Some writers list more explicitly pronounced rules, used in corporations and other organizations, such as "always set your prices higher *before* you announce a sale." Still others focus on cognitive patterns such as heuristics or "routines;" for example, the use of abbreviations as memory aides. The same thesis is also extended to societal institutions, value systems, and norms of conduct, ranging from those that define one's table manners to the Constitution. All these rules are said to "inform" the individual on how best to behave, without any necessary calculations or forethought (March and Olsen 1984; Heiner 1983, p. 573). In the following discussion the term "rules" is used to refer to all these informal, ready-made, decision-making aides. There is only one book that lists rules of thumb (Parker 1983); it is used below as our main source. (While this compilation seems to contain typical rules, representativeness is difficult to ascertain in the absence of a clearly defined universe.)

A neoclassical colleague suggested that a definition is necessary to distinguish rules of thumb from other personal or collective rules, say religious norms. He suggested a definition, "perhaps tautological," that rules of thumb are those rules that are used in the guidance of action in order to save the costs of detailed calculations. However, we do not wish to define away the issue—do such rules "save?" Do they enhance rationality? Nor are we confident that these rules are used with a deliberate purpose in mind rather than are choices made habitually. Nor are they necessarily clearly set apart from religious or any other norms. We hence see rules of thumb as informal rules that actors use to simplify their choosing, drawing on ready-made guides. (Scientific theory and logic do not qualify; their rules are formal in the sense that they are accountable components of a system and use explicitly defined terms.)

Neoclassicists argue that rules of thumb are rational because they reflect an accumulative experience or are the beneficiaries of evolutionary developments: those who follow non-rational rules are driven out by those who adhere to the rational ones. Hence, non-rational rules will be swept aside by rules that are rational.

The discussion here focuses on the merits of rules of thumb (and other devices for which the same neoclassic arguments have been advanced). It is suggested that (1) the empirical evidence about the rationality of these rules is dubious, and that (2) they logically cannot serve as a basis for rational conduct. A person who abides by rules of thumb may be somewhat less or somewhat more rational than those not so guided, but not very rational by the criteria applied here and widely accepted elsewhere (as discussed in Chapter 8).

AN EMPIRICAL TEST: PRICE SETTING IN FIRMS

The most detailed empirical testing of the extent to which rules that are provided are rational has taken place with regard to price-setting in firms. It has been often observed that business executives do not set prices at the place a simple profit maximization theory states they ought to, where marginal costs equal marginal revenue. Instead, prices are set where firm policies tell executives to set prices. But do these rules (corporate policies), guide executives to the same maximal point?

One of the earliest and most influential studies on the use of rules is that of Hall and Hitch (1936). They surveyed 38 British firms and found that in 30 the executives said they used full cost pricing rules. Full cost pricing rules basically add a "normal" or target profit margin (or a percentage return on invested capital) to an estimate of unit costs to establish a product's price. When the executives were asked why they used such rules, they provided three responses: to deal with the uncertainties in the estimates of demand functions; to avoid charging too high a price (and driving away customers) or too low a price (in an oligopolistic market); and to avoid the great burden imposed by calculations for marginal cost pricing, on businesses that sell thousands of different items.

Machlup (1952) takes issue with Hall and Hitch's conclusion that full cost pricing does not lead to profit maximization. Using Hall and Hitch's data, Machlup argues that executives observed full cost pricing only as long as it was consistent with profit maximization. Further, Machlup notes that the answers that the executives provided shows that demand was in fact considered in pricing. Several executives admitted that they would change price in periods of exceptionally high or low demand. Additionally, Machlup (ibid., p. 71) points out that the answers executives provided to the question of why they used full cost pricing—fear of competitors and demand being unresponsive to price—show that they were taking into account demand elasticities "which to the economist is equivalent to marginal revenue considerations." Further, he points out that respondents were using demand signals, though the term elasticity might not have been used.

In their influential study, Cyert and March (1963) in effect support Hall and Hitch. Cyert and March were able to predict prices at a large department store with great accuracy by discerning three rules for pricing in different situations: normal pricing, sales, and markdown. While normal prices and sales prevail at regularly scheduled times, markdown is a contingency employed in the failure or the perceived failure of these two other rules. For each situation a common procedure is used which determines price by the application of a predetermined, rule-based markup to a cost.

Using these rules, Cyert and March were able to predict prices in a normal pricing situation down to the penny 188 out of 197 times (a 95 percent success rate). In regard to sales pricing (ibid., p. 139) "pricing is a direct function of either the normal price (i.e., there is a standard sales reduction in price) or the cost (i.e., there is a sales mark up rule)." They were able to predict the prices correctly down to the penny 56 out of 58 times (a 96 percent success rate).

Markdown is a situation employed when feedback indicates an unsatisfactory sales or inventory position. Even though markdown is a contingent situation, rules were still found to govern the ways it is treated. First, prices are not to be set below cost except as a last resort. Second, prices were to be reduced by one-third and carry the result down to the nearest 85 cents. With these rules and few others, Cyert and March were able to correctly predict prices down to a penny in 140 of 159 markdown situations (an 88 percent success rate). It should be noted that such a high level of prediction is practically unknown in economics or in other social sciences; hence, this study should be regarded as very compelling empirically.

It would seem that pricing policies like the aforementioned only take into account the cost side, not studying the demand side at all. It hence would seem that profit maximization is not taking place. However, Nicholson (1978, p. 275) argues that despite the fact that the rules appear to consider cost alone, demand is ultimately considered as well.

> R. M. Cyert and J. G. March spend considerable effort in analyzing the feedback that the market provides for the pricing of a product. Even though prices and profit margins may initially be set without adequate reference to demand, the reaction of the market provides information on the true demand situation, and prices are adjusted accordingly.

In short, Nicholson is trying to do to Cyert and March what Machlup did to Hall and Hitch: Use their own data to argue that rules are rational. Other studies provide additional ammunition—to both sides of the debate.

In a study that examined a group of companies over nine years, Lanzillotti (1958) found that companies followed various pricing rules. These include pricing to achieve a target return on investment, seeking price stabilization, pricing to realize a target market share, and pricing to prevent or meet competition. About one half of the companies indicated that their pricing policies were based mainly upon the objective of realizing a particular rate of return on investment in a given year, over the long haul, or both. The question has been raised whether a firm is maximizing profits when it sets a target rate of return, or is merely setting a "satisficing" goal? Lanzillotti points out that actual returns over a nine year period (1947–55) were greater than the target returns used in setting the prices. Hence, he concludes, prices could be hardly set at the maximization point.

As to how the profit target was set Lanzillotti (1958, p. 931) notes:

> The most frequently mentioned rationalizations included: (a) fair or reasonable return, (b) the traditional industry concept of fair return in relation to risk factors, (c) desire to equal or better the corporation average return over a recent period, (d) what the company felt it could get as a long-run matter, and (e) use of a specific profit target as a means of stabilizing industry prices.

In regard to pricing for stabilization Lanzillotti (1958, pp. 931–32), develops the concept of corporate *noblesse oblige* which scarcely coincides with profit maximization, but is more like the Marques of Queensbury rules:

> The drive for stablilized prices by companies like U.S. Steel, Alcoa, International Harvester, Johns Manville, duPont, and Union Carbide involves both expectation of proper reward for duty done, i.e., "proper" prices, and a sense of *noblesse oblige*. Having earned what is necessary during poor times to provide an adequate return, they will refrain from upping the price as high as the traffic will bear in prosperity. Likewise, in pricing different items in the product line, there will be an effort (sustained in individual cases by the pricing executive's conscience) to refrain from exploiting any item beyond the limit set by cost-plus.

However, Kahn (1959) argues that Lanzillotti's data can be used to support the thesis that even large corporations try to maximize profits. He notes the widespread use of target pricing,

> which is really an aspect of full cost pricing, provides their [Lanzillotti et al.] principal evidence against profit maximization in general and the marginality description thereof in particular. This misconstruction is in confusing procedures with 'goals'. Actually the target return seems above all to reflect what the executives think the company can get; and as to the extent actual earnings diverge from the target it is because the market turns out to allow more or less. (Kahn 1959, p. 671.)

In a response to Kahn's criticism, Lanzillotti (1959) states that the concepts of target return and target market share seem far more helpful in predicting and understanding the price behavior of large corporations than any notion of profit maximization. Lanzillotti suggests that target rates of return are useful quantifiable measures corporations strive for, while profit maximization, given its ambiguity, is likely to be an ex post rationalization. Lanzillotti (p. 682) also asks ". . . whether by stating that the target return is really another name for profit maximization Kahn has explained anything about the pricing policies of large corporations."

Katona conducted one of the few studies of the use of rules for decisions involving investment rather than the setting of prices. He notes (1975, p. 323) that decisions on plant building, location of plants, and acquisition of new equipment are enduring and nonreversible. They in general involve large sums of money; hence, one would especially expect rational behavior in these decisions. "In fact, even casual observation reveals numerous instances in which rules of thumb prevail and business investment appears to be the habitual or even automatic result of certain conditions rather than the outcome of careful deliberation." One example is the "follow the leader" principle: In various industries one firm is often looked upon as a leader whose decisions are imitated by other firms, whether or not it was justified in view of intra-industry differences.

For instance, decisions to introduce new technology often seem to have a fad-like quality.

Without attempting to explore further the ins and outs of these studies, their respective merits, let alone review still others (a task undertaken by Scherer, 1980, pp. 187–189), it is clear that the same data are interpreted by some as indicating that rules can be used to maximize, i.e., that they are fully rational, and by others to show that rules cannot so serve and in effect perpetuate poor practices. The obvious conclusion is that *the rules are not sufficiently specified to allow either their rational application or their study.* Luckily, we shall see shortly, the empirical question need not be answered in order to reach a conclusion on the merit of rules.

ORGANIZATIONAL CASE STUDIES

Organizations of all kinds, from armies to churches, from public schools to prisons, promulgate large numbers of rules. While these rules change over time, their adjustment to changed realities is frequently slow and far from sufficient to ensure rational adaptation as indicated by the term "bureaucracy" often applied to organizations (Argyris 1985). An overview of the relevant literature (Stern 1984a, p. 110) concludes: "Rules are broadly adaptive, but there is no guarantee that they reflect optimal, or even acceptable, solutions when new problems arise." Adaptations of rules are also reported to be limited to the "local" problem area and not be used organization-wide.

When executives are faced with unfamiliar, new, complex situations, they tend to break them into components and deal with those elements that are or look familiar. Perrow's (1981, p. 17) case study of the nuclear accident at Three Mile Island near Harrisburg, Penn., concludes that "it is not feasible to train, design, or build in such a way to anticipate all eventualities in complex systems where the parts are tightly coupled. They are incomprehensible when they occur. That is why operators usually assume something else is happening, something that they understand, and act accordingly." During the accident at Three Mile Island signs of danger were not communicated to key personnel because operators did not believe them. Thus, the rules (in the sense of "routines") delayed proper response to the novel situation because people misinterpreted the situation and did not recognize it as novel. Perrow (ibid., p. 25) notes: "This is the significance of the widely reported comment by the NRC commissioners that if only they had a simple, understandable thing like a pipe break they would know what to do."

Other studies show that organizational rules for collecting information tend to result in information overload in which important items go unnoted. It is a problem common to many intelligence services. This is one main reason the warning about an imminent attack on Pearl Harbor was "lost" on its way to Washington (Wohlstetter 1962). When new auto-matic gates closing railway crossings were introduced in Britain, a major train disaster, known as the Hixon disaster, followed. It was established later that slow-moving trains could not clear the crossing in the allotted 24 seconds (allowed before the gates reopen automatically). This fact was duly noted in a long technical manual provided to every police station as the new gates were installed, but it was "lost" in the avalanche of infor-mation the manual contained (Turner 1976; see also Neustadt and Fine-berg 1978).

Nutt (1984) studies 78 decision-making profiles of predominantly ser-vice or voluntary organizations. He finds that managers violate all the rules advocated by academics for "good" (rational) decision-making. The managers assume away uncertainty and treat causation and desired re-sults as clear and specific, thereby creating a false sense of security. Nutt further reports that managers have a predisposition to focus their rule search very narrowly, as they have a "low tolerance for ambiguity and a high need for structure." (Ibid., p. 446.)

Cyert and March (1963, p. 121) note that the search process is based initially on two simple rules, that are hardly rational:

> (1) search in the neighborhood of the problem symptom and (2) search
> in the neighborhood of the current alternative. These two rules reflect
> different dimensions of the basic causal notions that a cause will be
> found 'near' its effect and that a new solution will be found 'near' an
> old one.

An example of how such a limited search leads to a non-rational re-sponse is provided by Hall (1976, p. 201) in his study of the decline of the old *Saturday Evening Post.* Hall points out that when the managers of the *Post* faced rising production costs due to excessive expansion, result-ing in depressed profits, they responded by substantially increasing the subscription rates. This proved to be the *Post*'s undoing, for their read-ership growth leveled off and their profits were further depressed, as a significant amount of funds had to be spent on promotion merely to hold readership steady. The *Post* thus staggered into the circulation wars of the 1950s in poor financial shape, and never recovered. Hall argues that the *Post*'s decision is a typical result of a narrow rule-search strategy that led to an increase in the subscription rates rather than attacking the "underlying causal structure of the problem (namely, the loss of control of the annual volume and the consequent increase in production costs)."

Sometimes rules, rather than change inadequately, fail to change at all. Historically developed rules continue to be applied long after their usefulness has been lost, and when more efficient alternatives are readily available. For example, despite the obvious fact that real prices are the best measure of economic activity, nominal prices are very widely used in financial reports, contracts, and government studies (Baran,

Lakonisnk, and Ofer 1980). Cyert and March (1963, p. 138) report that frequently the mark-ups with an industry remained the same for 40 or 50 years. Further, rules that may be rational in the abstract lead to poor decisions because their guidance is insufficiently specific (Sproull 1981; Britan 1979).

Finally, the study of rules as rational assumes there are clear goals, or at least some set goals, even if they might be somewhat unclear. However, this is often not the case. A study of OMB under President Kennedy depicts the difficulties the agency had in formulating specific budgets because the President failed to set the total outlay targets (Mowery et al. 1980). Indeed, for many organizations, not just the situation is in flux but also the goals (Sills 1957) rendering the use of most rules non-rational. This is a problem often encountered in evaluation studies: By the time performance is measured by the initial organizational goals, the goals have changed.

RULES CANNOT BE USED RATIONALLY

We have seen, so far, that the empirical evaluation of the use of rules seems inconclusive. Despite several sizable studies, conducted over decades, it is not possible to draw a firm conclusion whether or not rules enable their followers to act rationally, because the theory is insufficiently specified. While several case studies of organizations provide considerable plausibility to the thesis that the application of rules often leads to non-rational behavior, such studies, by their very nature of being "cases," are not fully compelling. There is, though, a way to resolve the issue because it is possible to show that rules in many situations *cannot* provide rational guides. It is a matter of logic, not of empirical evidence. Thus we shall see that rules typically deal with one factor at a time, while most choices deal with multi-faceted situations; and that rules that advocate a certain course of action also advocate the opposite course, and so on. We hence need not study the effects of such rules; they just cannot work, on the face of it.

The discussion turns next to provide several reasons in support of the position that the use of rules is *a priori* non-rational in many circumstances.

1. Rules are typically advanced in *isolation* from one another rather than as parts of a comprehensive system. As a result, rules tend not to take into account that, in the real, complex, world, an efficient response to most challenges requires taking multiple considerations into account.

At the same time, there is no reason to deny that in some instances some simple rules prove very useful. The IRS is using numerous guidance rules, collated into *Classification Handbook IRM 41(12)0*. For example, the IRS pays special attention to children claimed as exemptions by separated parents, because they are often claimed by both, while only one claim is proper. Hence, while—because of the *a priori* reasons provided above—one may expect that rule-guided behavior will often be quite non-rational, this generalization is not expected to apply in every instance. As to the question, under what conditions the application of rules is relatively more rational? This seems to be a matter about which relatively little is known, which is one more reason why relying on them is not rational.

2. When individuals are provided with more than one rule, those rules often *conflict with one another.* For example, investors are advised to "buy low and sell high" (an ambiguous rule by itself, because no definition of either "high" or "low" is included, and hence the rule invites investors to project their feelings on to the situation). Sometimes "high" or "low" refers to P/E (price/earnings) ratios. However, what is a high ratio is not agreed upon, and people are advised to invest in stocks of "high-growth" corporations despite the fact that their P/E ratios are often infinity because they initially show no profit at all. Investors are also advised "not to fight the tape" and to "let their profits run but cut their losses short," two rules that suggest that if the price of a stock moves up, investors ought to expect the price to move still higher, while if it falls— and hence is relatively low—investors ought to sell it. The rules are obviously incompatible with the one cited first. Add to this "no price is too low for a bear or too high for a bull," a dictum from *Barron's* (November 10, 1986, p. 16) and the confusion is complete.

3. Rules are typically formulated *as if they were universal truths,* applying to all circumstances, to all times, and to all people. Three examples illustrate the fallacy of universality: Rule number 810 from the only book exclusively dedicated to "rules of thumb" (Parker 1983, p. 124) reads: "Don't pay more than twice your average annual income for a house." It neglects to mention if gross or net income is at issue, and the effects of one's tax status. For example, given current tax laws, it makes much more sense for a person with a high income but few other deductions to violate the rule than for one with lower income or many deductions. Also, different tax laws apply to those who are 55 years or older; for instance, older Americans benefit from a one-time exclusion of capital gain (to $125,000) from the sale of their house. Hence, rules that might serve the young are misleading to their elders, and vice versa.

Rule number 96 (ibid., p. 16) warns those who go on a political campaign trail that "a certain percentage of voters will be for or against you based purely on party affiliation. Only a small percentage of voters are truly independent and will consider you without bias." Aside from the fact that the rule uses vague terms such as "certain percentages" and "truly," in view of the fact that political affiliation is much less important than it used to be, the rule holds much less now than, say, twenty years ago.

When the value of the dollar on foreign exchanges dropped 20 percent early in 1985, many economists feared that this would exacerbate
inflation in the United States because a 10 percent drop was expected to
add 1.5 percent to 2 percent to inflation. But James E. Annable, chief
domestic economist at the First National Bank of Chicago, stated that
this would not be the case because "rules of thumb that applied in the
1970s don't apply in the 1980s." (*New York Times,* March 31, 1985.) He did
not elaborate if the rules must be adapted every decade, or more often,
or how one tells before the fact if they still apply.

Ample examples of the application of rules out of context is found in
the frequent use of neoclassical economics in policy making. Much of
neoclassical economics is formulated on the assumption that the relationships that are studied take place in a fully competitive market. However,
in the real world such markets do not exist, and are not even approximated. Yet economists recommend and policy makers apply rules formulated for full competition, to these fundamentally different situations.

4. When rules conflict with one another, people tend to follow the
rule that coincides with their *subjective estimates,* emotions, and values. For
instance, a less risk-averse person may follow Parker's rule #102 (1983,
p. 17): "Don't enter a poker game unless you have forty times the betting
limit in your pocket". The more risk averse may pick rule #103: "Don't
enter a poker game unless you have sixty times the betting limit in your
pocket."

Another pair of conflicting rules is discussed by Kindleberger (1985,
p. 1) in his essay on the social responsibility of corporations. He writes:
"The least of the issue is the clash between 'When in Rome, do as the
Romans do,' and 'To thine own self be true'." "Look before your leap,"
and "he who hesitates is lost" is another pair of rules that float in our
culture, for decision-makers to draw upon according to their mood.
Many a corporation chooses between those two not according to some
cost benefit study but in line with its established set of values.

5. Another way to see that rules that the culture offers are not rational
is to see that they are often *not sufficiently specific* to provide guidance.
Barron's publishes a weekly pool of the "sentiments" of traders in Trea-
sury bonds and bills, expressed in percentage "bullish." But it always
adds a note that "high readings usually are signs of market tops, low ones,
market bottoms." Neither high nor low (or "usually") are defined. Hence,
in effect, the weekly table provides a typical two-faced, highly if not completely ambiguous, rule. If bonds go up, the poll is "validated;" if not, the
note is. Together they provide at best a very vague guide.

Editing and writing are taught by rules, but, as anybody who took such
a class can attest, these rules are often quite bewildering. Norman Mailer
regularly violates every rule taught in courses on the writing of proper
English, but is considered a very crafty author (reference is to style, not
content). Kenner (1985, p. 1) writes: "The plain style has been hard to

talk about, except in circles. . . ." Swift, Kenner reports, refers to it as "proper words in proper places," but Kenner points out that Swift does not explain "how to find the proper words or to identify the proper places to put them into." (Ibid.)

6. Psychologists (Chaiken and Stangor, 1987) have shown that people often evaluate the validity of messages using rules such as "length implies strength," "consensus implies correctness," "expert's statements can be trusted." The knowledge that people are vulnerable in that way, in turn, is used to fashion persuasive advertising—for example, by asking actors who impersonate doctors to "recommend" over-the-counter drugs to buyers who hardly need them. That is, rules that people follow in their decision-making are *used to deflect* them from rational decision-making, rather than to enhance their decision-making ability.

7. Rules tend to *ignore interaction effects.* For some people it might be advisable to drink a glass of milk each day and to take antibiotics under certain circumstances. However, few note that the combination of the two things, each "good" in its own right, is not necessarily positive. Milk may negate the effects of the antibiotics.

A colleague wrote: "Just because some rules are silly does not mean they all are." Fair enough. Some rules are useful. However, we argue that (1) *many* rules constitute poor guides for decision-making, for one or more of the reasons discussed above; and (2) that individuals experience great, if not insurpassable, difficulties if they seek to distinguish useful rules from all others.

All said and done, rules that are informally formulated, that in effect invite individuals to project their subjective interpretations, emotions, and values onto the rules, and rules that often conflict with one another, typically provide a highly irrational guidance to decision-making, useful though they might be on some occasions. Hence, the thesis that people neither deliberate nor need to make rational decisions—that they may instead rely on prefabricated rules—seems highly implausible.

EXPERIENCE AND EVOLUTION

While Darwinism is not an integral part of the neoclassical paradigm, it is mobilized when the going gets tough. Accordingly, people are said to drop non-rational rules and retain rational ones, as their personal or collective (shared and accumulative) experience teaches them which are the rules that work. "Fit" rules survive while unfit die away. Actually the users of rules cannot judge or evaluate them any better than the options they face to begin with (and which lead them to use rules), for basically the same reasons they very often cannot make a highly rational decision to begin with: limited intellectual capabilities and a very complex subject. (Winter 1975, made the same point about information costs.) It might be said that there are many fewer rules than options, and hence that rules are easier to "process." However, the evaluation of most rules is much more difficult than the evaluation of most options. Compare, for example, the dilemma of a chess player who must decide how to proceed in a particular game and specific situation versus judging the rule, say, that one ought to develop one's forces (how long?) before one attacks. Compare determining at what level to set the price of a specific product in a specific market, to determining which pricing policy is the most effective. We saw already the difficulties professional economists have in coping with the latter question after decades of study and argument.

It should also be noted that the Prospect School has established that heuristics, themselves considered rules of thumb, and used in evaluating rules of thumb, are systematically biased and hence constitute a poor guide to decision-making (see above, pp. 117-20). Evidence that people learn only slowly and poorly from experience is seen in that people keep making the same numerous systematic mistakes in evaluating probabilities, using the same biased heuristic, over the course of a lifetime. That is, their experience does *not* suffice to teach them to modify the rules (Tversky and Kahneman 1974, p. 1130). In effect Skinner provides a rather compelling model for how rules may be reinforced even when they are quite incompatible with the evidence. By feeding pigeons at brief random intervals, Skinner reinforced certain items of behavior. Whatever activity the pigeons happened to be performing before feeding—for example, bobbing their heads—was reinforced. Soon the pigeons acted as if they believed that bobbing their heads was a way to obtain food (Skinner 1948).

Rules that are collectively provided by society, and carried in the culture, are said to be rational. As Toda (1980) puts it, much learning takes place on the "species" level rather than on that of the individual. One reason given is that individuals—who are rational—created these rules. Heath (1976, p. 63) points out that "Norms and institutions were presumably created by men ... and there is no *a priori* reason to suppose that these men were any the less rational when they were constructing institutions than they were in the rest of their daily lives." For the viewpoint presented here, the same statement is to be read in the opposite way to the one the author intended: People are sub-rational in their daily life; there is no *a priori* reason to believe the rules they promulgate will be more rational. As Cross (1983, p. 17) writes: "it is one thing to observe that choice making in practice seems to be governed by simple and inexpensive decision rules; it is quite another to show how those rules that are in use have come to be selected in preference to all of the other simple rules that could have come to be used instead." And however wisely rules may have been originally formulated, as we have seen, they tend to ossify and lag behind changes in the environment.

ORGANIZATIONS (AND INSTITUTIONS) AS RULES

Rules that organizations promulgate have been studied above. It should be noted that organizations (and institutions) themselves are depicted by neoclassicists as mechanisms that limit the need to choose by providing a rational context for decision. Traditionally, organizations—especially firms—have been viewed by sociologists as social units that evolve in part in ways the participants are unaware of and their founders and leaders do not desire. Originally, an organization *may* have been designed as an efficient means to implement its particular goal or set of goals. But organizational studies show, that as rules get entrenched and vested interests in them evolve, politics intensify, informal cultures arise, and organizations as a result cease to be efficient tools, if they ever were.

The evidence cited above seems amply to support this view. However, in recent years, neoclassicists have formulated a New Institutional Economics drawing on a Coase (1937) article and the work of Williamson (1975, 1985). The Whigish, neoclassical paradigm here conflicts sharply with the Tory paradigm, and with the We factor within the I&We paradigm. The collectivist Tory school sees institutions as preceding any individual in time, power, and rights, and as reflecting the embodiment of the society's values and authority the way the church embodies Christ and secular states—their founders' values. The institutions are the starting points, and they have a dynamics of their own. Individuals are studied to determine under what conditions they accept, deviate, rebel, or—rarely—change institutions. In contrast, New Institutional Economics (and the Public Choice school) study institutions as if fully competent individuals, in rational pursuit of their self interests, designed the institutions to suit those purposes. The institutions are assumed to reflect an aggregation of the individuals' preferences. For instance, hierarchies are introduced, firms are formed or expanded, as the need for supervision and information-processing grows, and hence hierarchies are most efficient than the market. Accordingly, firms arise when it is efficient for them to arise: when organizing production through the price mechanism (or market) becomes too complex and hence too costly. The hierarchical structure of firms is viewed by this approach as a response to the need for more supervision, more information collection, and more processing than the market can handle, when transactions are numerous or complex (Williamson 1975). Most of the writing along these lines is highly deductive: "Firms must have arisen, because. . . ." Empirical evidence is scant. The very fact that rather inefficient firms exist right next to quite efficient ones, in the same industry, for long periods of time, casts grave doubt on this approach.

Some neoclassicists have extended even further the view of rules as efficient guides to decision-making, from organizations to whole polities and even societies—and on to the march of history. They have ceased to take institutional arrangements as given, the result of historical and sociological forces no one understands in full nor controls, and turned to view them as rational responses to specific economic needs, as if they were designed by an all-powerful God dedicated to the utility maximization of consumers and entrepreneurs. For example, North (1981) argues that states are akin to firms in a market: They seek to maximize revenue growth subject to various constraints (such as, technical knowledge). The rise and fall of states is next studied in terms of changes in constraints. For instance, states will increase taxes up to the point where the costs of the transactions involved become too high, or citizens' allegiance (said to decline as taxes are increased) becomes too low. Further, states develop various mechanisms (for example, the farming-out of tax collection to private parties) that reflect efficient adaptation to the constraints they face. (For further discussion and critical review of this approach, see March and Olsen 1984; Simon 1983, pp. 78ff; Perrow, 1986, Chapter 7; and Douglas and Wildavsky 1982.)

Heiner advances the thesis that rules, on all levels, from thumbs to societies, are rational due to evolutionary selection. He explains (1983, p. 560): ". . . evolutionary processes have long been interpreted as one of the key mechanisms tending to produce optimizing behavior, or conversely, optimizing behavior will predict the behavior patterns [or rules, AE] that will survive in an evolutionary process. . . ." And "appropriately structured behavioral rules . . . will evolve to the extent that selection processes quickly eliminate poorly administered behavior." (Ibid., p. 586.) Field (1984) argues that there is a limited universe of possible norms (or rules). Members of social groups, organizations, and societies work out together—using game theory strategies—which rule to share, and which rules are the most efficient. See also Ullmann-Margalit (1977).

For the viewpoint advanced here, the notion of a state of nature, in which there are individuals before rules existed—individuals who are not only fully formed and able to render decisions, but who also employ sophisticated game theory strategies, and hold their emotions and values in abeyance—that notion is rather flawed, not only historically but also as a heuristic. Individuals are not well formed unless they are members of collectivities, which in turn contain rules (see earlier discussion of the I&We). While there is little to be gained by pursuing the question of who was first at the creation of the human realm, an I or a We, if the question must be broached, the anthropological literature leaves little doubt that collectivities within which there were little or no individual identity awareness and autonomous action preceded individual self-awareness and action. In other words, collectivities can hardly be the product of rational individuals who preceded them.

Moreover, the conditions for the evolutionary selection of rules often do not exist. Among most types of organizations there often is no competitive market; good schools do not shove poor schools out of business; poorly run nursing homes are found next to others that are well run, and so on. Even the existence of competition among economic organizations is historically rare, and, even in the West, its scope is much more limited than is often claimed (see Chapter 13). And the environment, to which firms and other organizations must adapt, is largely composed of other firms like themselves, not a set nature. Also, as Simon argues, evolution leads to local or sub-optimal selection; there is no reason to suppose leads to optimal rules (Simon 1982, pp. 53ff).

What holds for organizations holds even more true for societies. There obviously is no market of societies in which the efficient ones drive out the others. Societies with extremely inefficient institutions or regimes, such as the Soviet mega-bureaucracy, survive for decades. Very few societies ever collapse; instead, they change but often very gradually and continue to be quite inefficient even if they give up some of their most inefficient features, without acquiring worse ones. Clearly evolution is not working on this level either. The argument that it takes a long time for evolution to sort out the rational units that survive from the others (North 1981, pp. 113ff) is rejected for three reasons. First, because it renders the hypothesis tautological. If after whatever time, even decades, non-rational institutions still exist, the evolution hypothesis is insufficiently specific. Second, if non-rational institutions survive for decades, and if there are numerous non-rational institutions and, people cannot distinguish among them, then institutions—like rules—do not provide a reliable guidance to rational decision-making. Last but not least, given so many "temporary" non-rational institutions for extensive periods, we need a theory that will encompass the factors that explain how these institutions function and influence choices, a theory of non-rational choices.

In short, the argument in favor of automatic or collectively provided rationality, one in which individuals need not deliberate yet can act rationally, is poorly supported by facts and is logically untenable. The fact that it is continuously to be advanced is itself an indication that rules, at least in the form of theorems, survive for reasons other than that they are logical or empirically supported.

PART III

Beyond Radical Individualism: The Role of Community and Power

Radical individualism, which is imbued in the neoclassical paradigm, leads it to focus on one level of human activities in its study of human purpose and its instruments: on that of myriad individuals. The paradigm evolved here sees a great deal of the explanation of human achievements—and what holds them back—on the collective level of historical and societal forces. Individuals *do* play a role, but within the context of their collectivities. These are pivotal even for those individuals who challenge their collectivities and work together to change their We-ness. Moreover, the collective level is not an aggregation of myriad individual decisions, transactions or actions, but has a form, a structure, of its own, which affects all behavior significantly. Individuals must either act within the constraints imposed by the structure or learn to change it. Hence to understand choice, and to seek to expand its scope, one must study the collective level, the forces that form it, and those that might transform it.

The first step in exploring the collective (or macro) level of the I&We paradigm is to show that usually collectivities are more consequential in forming the choices of individuals than the individuals themselves; collectivities are *the* decision-making unit (Chapter 11). That is, decisions of the kind economists routinely study—what people buy, how much they invest, how hard they work, and so on—largely reflect their society, polity, culture and sub-culture, class, as well as collectivities to which they used to belong, and changes in these all. This, of course, is in contrast to the neoclassical paradigm that sees free-standing individuals as the decision-making units.

The next step is to critically examine the widely held notion that collectivities, or more precisely, their decision-making instruments, from committees to organizations, often referred to as bureaucracies, are less rational than those of individuals. Actually, we shall see, in many areas (albeit not in all) collective thinking and decision-making are more rational (although often *not* highly rational) than that of individuals (Chapter 11).

Aside from enhancing the rationality of decision-making, in the sense of increasing its L/E content and reducing the knowledge costs, collectivities often provide the organization that "coordinates" millions of individual choices (and transactions). The basic neoclassical position is that no collectively provided organization is necessary. The market (viewed as composed of individuals, or households and firms treated as if they were individuals) is self-regulating; as each individual seeks to pursue his or her "utility" rationally, they find it is to their interest to exchange; rather than chaos breaking out, harmony is the result. Occasionally, neoclassicists mention the need for externally provided rules of the game, in terms of values or governments; however, the basic neoclassical paradigm does not include these factors, nor does it account for the processes that provide the needed rules, above all—ensure their adequacy.

In contrast, the paradigm advanced here assumes that if competition is left on its own it will escalate into a destructive, all-out conflict. Hence, those who see virtue in competition must recognize that it is nothing but *contained* conflict, that it can be sustained only within a moral, societal, and governmental context which ensures that conflicts remain confined within prescribed limits. True, the same contextual elements may also unduly restrict the scope of competition. The question hence, is how to provide a context that is strong enough to contain competition but not so powerful to undermine it, rather than disregard the role and dynamic of the moral, social, governmental contextuating factors (Chapter 12).

The set pattern of collective relationships, the structure of the collectivities, is a major factor in determining whether the context of competition will be duly supportive or unduly restrictive. While collective structures have many facets, one major facet is explored here to highlight the kind of analysis needed: relationships between economic transactions and political power. Neoclassicists have pointed out that competition is undermined when some competitors accumulate economic power. Accumulation of political power by economic actors, which is quite common, is similarly disruptive to competition. Hence, aside from seeking to ensure that the contextuating government will refrain from exercising its power to intervene unduly in the market, those who favor competition must establish the conditions that prevent powerful economic competitors from using their *political* power (power over the government) to undermine competition. For instance, to prevent large corporations from pressuring legislatures to modify laws in ways that advantage them in competition with smaller corporations. Developing structures that are able to limit the political power of competitors turns out to be as important to sustaining competition as preventing large concentrations of economic power (Chapter 13).

Once this line of analysis is much extended, we shall be able to understand the conditions under which individuals, working with one another, can recast the collectivities of which they are part (their We's) and render them more responsive to their needs and aspirations.

11

Collective (Macro) Rationality

MACRO-RATIONALITY INTRODUCED

The neoclassical paradigm celebrates the individual; neoclassical economics assumes that individuals are the decision makers and that they ought to be. The decision-making unit (D.M.U.) is a person. The role of historical and societal forces and the significance of the community and that of other collective (or macro, "emergent") factors is largely ignored by this approach. The paradigm stipulates ". . . the theoretical primacy of individual actors rather than of social collectivities. . . . the individual acting unit is taken . . . [to] exist prior to and independent of larger social institutions and is understood as the autonomous generator of its own ends. Social reality is understood as made up of many such individual actors. . . ." (Ashley 1984, p. 243.) And Crouch states (1979, p. 24): "to explain human behavior, attention must be focused on the individual. It is always an individual who makes choices and takes action." Similarly, neoclassical psychologists tend to limit their attention to individual behavior; and, to the extent that they seek causability at all, they look for it within the individual. Thus, typically, studies of congenital defects in people's ability to reason focus on intra-cognitive, individual, biases.

In contrast, it is a core assumption of socio-economists that social collectivities (such as local communities, ethnic and racial groups, and social movements) are pivotal actors; and that the qualities of most decision-making *and* deliberation—the collection of information, its processing, the drawing of inferences, and formation of judgments—are deeply affected and can be explained to a significant extent by collective processes and structures (institutions and organizations). Moreover, individual decision-making and deliberation largely take place with collectively set contexts, although infrequent genuine individualistic departures (including modification of collective structures, and the formation of new ones by individuals) are of disproportional significance to their

185

small number. Above all, much causality, much power to explain, we shall see, lies on the macro, collective level. Thus, if one asks for the reason why individuals prefer this or that product, why they "expect" some events to be more likely than others (e.g., inflation to rise rather subside), or why they choose a particular risky or risk-averse decision-making strategy, the answers are to be found to a significant extent in differences among, and dynamics within, various social collectivities to which these individuals belong. Even exceptional individuals, such as innovators or entrepreneurs, who break away from their collectivities, must be seen against the background from which they break away. In short, *social collectivities are major decision-making units, often providing the context within which individual decisions are made.* (It should be noted that as startling and objectionable as this theorem is to neoclassicists, so elementary and unsurprising the theorem is to followers of many other paradigms, for instance the paradigms used by traditional sociologists and anthropologists.)

Once the significance of collectivities is duly recognized, the question "How rational is Man?" must be restated to include the question: How rational are social collectivities, or how rational can they be made to be? True, collectivities *per se* do not deliberate or decide. However, many social collectivities have an organized sector that provides "its" collectivity with capabilities. For example, societies have governments, and the governments routinely make decisions for the societies. Moreover, governments are frequently restructured, among other reasons, to render them more instrumentally rational and also, by implication, the societies they serve. Similarly, ethnic groups have associations, and occupations have trade or professional organizations. Many firms are, in effect, collectivities (or sub-collectivities), each equipped with an organized governance. In effect, most collectivities have one or more organizational instruments, which are used to deliberate and to decide (in board meetings, staff conferences, and so on). We suggest, for reasons indicated below, that despite the widely held views to the contrary, by using organizations as instruments, *collectivities are* (or at least can be made to be) *more rational than their individual component members*, in most areas of decision-making, those concerning economic behavior included.

While neoclassicists have vastly overemphasized the ability of individuals to render decisions on their own, some students of social collectivity have put too much emphasis on the role of groups and that of other collective factors. Just as the neoclassical concept of individuals is undersocialized, so that of collectivists is over-socialized; individuals are perceived as submerged into a We, merely reflecting their groups, or even unable to separate reality-testing from group conformity, an extreme version of what has been called "groupthink" (Janis 1972; Longley and Pruitt 1980). A survey of social science findings argues: "For a population as a whole, there appears to be little lasting development of opinions, attitudes, and beliefs that is independent of parental, group, or strata predispositions and is based mainly on 'objective' data or 'rational' analysis of information and ideas." (Berelson and Steiner 1964, p. 574.) The position advanced here is that in many areas collectivities (if properly structured), can (1) render more rational decisions than their individual members (albeit, to reiterate, not necessarily highly rational ones), and (2) that collectivities account for more of the variance in individual decision-making than do individual attributes. However, individual attributes do matter; they merely are secondary rather than being the primary—let alone all-inclusive—explanatory factor.

It is necessary to repeat that the following discussion attempts to provide a first approximation, the charting of a paradigm, and a research agenda. On many of the issues explored below there are vast bodies of research and theoretical literature. There are numerous elaborations and qualifications that can be added to each point. However, the purpose here is merely to suggest a general approach. Avoiding these secondary matters, as important as they are, is essential if the task undertaken here is to be advanced.

COLLECTIVE THINKING

The Relevant Decision-Making Unit

In practically all of the rich and important series of studies conducted by the Prospect School, the subjects involved are studied individually and are studied one at a time, leaving their "normal" group bonds behind. (In the few studies where aggregates are involved, it is a misnomer to refer to the ad hoc combinations of individuals as groups.) As a result, the subjects must perform the assigned cognitive tasks and render decisions without the cues they typically draw on—those provided by the social collectivities of which they are members. This is somewhat like studying the direction a fish swims after isolating one from its school. Villagers cannot confer with their elders, teenagers cannot consult their peers, employees cannot dialogue with their coworkers. Little wonder the individuals are so disoriented and perform poorly: Aside from whatever intrinsic limitations they clearly have, they are deprived of the social foundations of their thinking and decision-making. True, to a significant extent individuals internalize the frameworks, procedures, and heuristics of their collectivities. Hence, they are able to render decision-making seemingly "on their own." But, aside from the fact that they draw heavily on internalized, collectively provided, guide lines, they continuously seek—and are accustomed to getting—additional cues about what to think and what to choose, and reinforcement to assure them that they are "on the right track," in step with their collectivities.

Are we suggesting that the individual who decides with the help of his or her group will be able to hold more than eight facts in his or her short-term memory, and be able to calculate probabilities correctly, etc? No. But they will find other collectively based ways to deal with their cognitive defects. Their spouse will remind them of part of what they forgot. Group members will correct some of the grossest errors. ("You know," they say to those who have a fear of flying, "it is safer than riding in a car.") That is, individual cognitive defects are "corrected" *in part* by groups (although in some other situations, they are exacerbated by groups).

Moreover, differences in collectivities account for an important part of the differences in what people know, how many options they examine, and so on. Thus, in some groups people are expected to calculate (e.g., do comparative shopping, or consult manuals), or are provided with "expert" help, while in other groups more impulsive behavior is legitimated. That is, *the point at which one is "satisfied" is largely socially determined.* In short, the question of how well or poorly people think and decide must be repeated, studying people within their natural *collective* habitat.

Of the very rich body of literature that supports the preceding points a few illustrative findings follow. A well-known, often-cited study concerns the movement of a light. The experiment draws on the fact that when a point of light is projected on the wall or a screen in a dark room, it will seem to the human eye as if it bounces around, although it does not move at all. When individuals are asked to estimate how much the light moves, they are greatly influenced by what their group members (in many experiments, collaborators of the person who conducts the experiments) tell them (Sherif 1952; see also, Asch 1958).

A National Research Council committee, reviewing findings about the effects of groups on changing energy consumption behavior, concluded:

> Social group memberships are also important as sources of innovation and of energy information. A homeowner may get the idea to install a clock thermostat from seeing one in a friend's or neighbor's home; the decisive information about whether the investment is a good one may come from the experiences of that friend or neighbor. When this happens, the action is most accurately described by the metaphor of social contagion, even if the individual rationalizes his or her action in terms of expected financial return. Since such action is not the outcome of detailed search for information and may not produce the maximum expected benefit, it is not rational in the formal sense. It may not even approximate formal rationality—individuals may rely on sources that can add no accurate information whatever. (Stern 1984a, p. 63.)

People in smoke-filled rooms were less likely to report an emergency when other subjects (stooges) did not react versus when they were alone. That is, even the perception of danger to self is socially affected (Latane and Darley 1968).

The neoclassical paradigm refers to the transmission of information to individuals as if the facts could speak for themselves, as unmistakable "objective" signals, often viewed as embodied in the price. In effect, numerous studies have established, beyond reasonable doubt, that the sources of communication that people choose to expose themselves to (newspaper or TV, sports or business pages), and the message they hear, and the way they interpret what they have heard after they hear it, and the conclusion they draw, are all highly subjective and, to a significant extent, socially shaped. (Holz and Wright 1979; Wright 1975; Katz and Lazarsfeld 1955. For studies of the effects of groups on whether the satisfaction of a new consumer good is perceived as high or low, see Johnson and Andrews 1971; on group effects on risk perception and risk taking, and on negotiating and bargaining, see an overview of studies by Myers and Lamm 1976). Indeed, whether or not people sense they have a choice to make—what psychologists call "the attribution of choice"—is itself to a large extent socially and culturally determined (Steiner 1980, p. 2). Even what is perceived to be *self*-interest is group shaped.

Isolated individuals who command information that strongly suggests, on rational grounds, that they follow a straining or stressful course of action—i.e., one that requires a high level of motivation—often ignore the information. This is the fate of most health warnings, for example. (Heavy smokers *know* smoking is harmful.) However, once the recommended course of action is also given *social support,* of the kind provided by Alcoholics Anonymous, heavy drinkers, heroin addicts, compulsive overeaters, and gamblers are often successful in overcoming their dependency *and* repeating the correct decision by again and again resisting temptations to violate their new, health-oriented course. (For evidence and literature overview, see Janis 1983.)

Collectivities are not "externalities" or environments that fully formed, autonomous individuals face, free to calculate whether or not to heed their signals. The collectivities discussed here are integral parts of the selves of those involved, as they themselves are of the collectivities. The collective effects work, in part, via internalization and by providing the N/A contexts that people use to form their deliberations and decisions. Individuals *in addition* may often also be aware of some facets of collectivities as external forces. However, as a rule, individuals do not realize that, even as they consider how to deal with those parts of the social world they do perceive, other parts of the same social realm shape what they see, how they query, and so on. Thus, a person may calculate whether or not to move with coworkers he or she is close to, when their plant relocates, taking into account the value of the camaraderie. However, how much weight is put on it, as compared, say, to the needs of one's children, and whether the risk entailed in refusing to move is considered acceptable, and so on, these decisions are unconscious and socially shaped. That is, collectivities "work" on individual decision-making at least in part via N/A processes, and—in part—in ways individuals are not aware of, and are unable to control.

Finally, it should be noted that there is ample evidence to show that when individuals, for one reason or another, are cut off from all collectivities and isolated, their thinking quickly become highly disoriented (Srole 1975; Berelson and Steiner 1964, p. 252; Kinkead 1959).

The Social Realm

The discussion so far provides a first approximation, a deliberate simplification. It is a socio-economic equivalent and counter-assumption to the concept of an individual who is a rational utility maximizer of neoclassical economics and its psychological sisters. A closer approximation to actual behavior would require adding several significant complexities. One concerns the fact that many individuals are members of more than one social collectivity and these may guide thinking and choosing in ways that are incompatible. The resulting crosscues may, under certain circumstances, allow for a relatively high degree of individuation (gaining degrees of freedom by drawing, not necessarily consciously, on one collectivity to stave off the others). More commonly, though, such conflict causes stress and further reduces the rational behavior of the individual. A common response is decision-avoidance.

Another source of complexity and individual differences lies in the effect of non-membership collectivities, referred to as reference groups, groups on whose values and cognitive standards individuals draw without being members (Hyman 1942). A recent study shows the ways these groups influence judgment. Groups of students were provided with poll data purporting to report the views of groups to whose membership the students aspired. The students modified their attitudes to conform to these groups' viewpoint (Hall, Varca, Fisher 1986. See there too for varying definitions of the concept and a review of findings about other effects of reference groups). The reason reference groups further complicate the social world is that an individual, who belongs to one or more membership groups (say, first generation immigrants, blue collar workers), may aspire and relate to conflicting reference groups (second generation, middle class). Hence, to understand "individual" choices more fully, both memberships and reference groups must be taken into account.

The role of reference groups is highly relevant to socio-economics, including its study of the motivation to work, save, and consume; these are all actions in which individuals are driven not only by "real" quantities (the amounts they earn, save, and so on), but where they are also affected by who they compare themselves to. A $1,000 raise is high if "everybody" gained only a $500 raise, but rather small if all others achieved $2000. It comes as no surprise from the conception developed here that when split pay was introduced for the same work (e.g., new versus veteran flight attendants, working together), this generated large amounts of resentment (Mason 1987). The same, of course, holds for women and men and black and white once they work together and aspire to comparable, if not identical, reference groups.

Reference groups also help explain the well-known Easterlin (1974) paradox. Easterlin found that "happiness" (the subjective side of the neoclassical paradigm's super-goal of utility or satisfaction, see above) is *not* related to income or wealth. People in poor countries are about as happy (or unhappy) as those in much richer ones. For example, Easterlin notes that West Germany in 1957 had a rating of personal happiness of 5.3 out of 10 and a real GNP per head of $1,860 while Yugoslavia, with a three times smaller real GNP per head in 1962 of $613, had a comparable personal happiness rating of 5.0. At the other end of the scale, India with a real GNP per head of only $140 in 1962 had a personal happiness rating of 3.7, much higher than the Dominican Republic's rating of 1.6, even though the Dominican Republic had a real GNP per head at $313. Within each country, however, the higher the *relative* income, the happier are those individuals who are relatively better off. These observations find an explanation in that reference groups are typically nationally bounded rather than reaching across nations. Easterlin's findings are further supported by Duncan (1975): In the Detroit area, in a sample whose real income rose 42 percent from 1955 to 1971, there was no significant increase in happiness, because the reference group income rose as did that of the referring individuals.

A still fuller theory of individual deliberations and decision-making would include not merely contemporary but also anteceding collectivities such as those of origin. These include collectivities in another country in the case of immigrants; in different parts of the country, in the case of geographic mobility, say from Detroit to Houston; and in the case of social mobility, say, from working to middle classes or vice versa. (Additional complexities include various psychological explanations, especially the concept of relative deprivation. On these see Kaptyn and Wansbeek 1982, and works cited by them. For attempts to explain the same phenomenon within the neoclassical paradigm, see Abramowitz 1979, and Frank 1985.)

In short, a socio-economic analysis of deliberation and choosing starts not with the individual but with the social collectivities of which he or she is a member. It seeks an explanation of differences in the ability to render rational decisions in differences among collectivities, and in changes within each collectivity over time. Individual differences are etched in on these collective backgrounds.

If one follows the line suggested here, it cannot be stressed enough that one assumes that major locus of much causality is on the macro, collective level. To the extent one is merely descriptive, one may depict choosing as if it were largely aggregative-individual. For example, one may report that millions of Americans between 1980 and 1985 bought less liquor (although the price declined relatively to the prices of most other items) and more health food (although health food prices seem to have risen), as if this behavior was the result of an aggregation of numerous individual decisions. However, if one seeks to explain or predict such trends, the role of public health authorities, social movements, public education, the government, and the mass media—all macro factors—cannot be ignored: they are key explanatory factors.

Innovation: The Great Individual?

Nowhere is the myth of the individual as thinker and decision-maker more enshrined than in discussion of entrepreneurship, creativity, and innovation. Those activities are depicted by neoclassical economics, by much of psychology, and by the attending popular literature as individual actions par excellence. The images of Alexander Graham Bell and Thomas Edison tinkering in their laboratories and coming up with new products, from telephones to record players, are deeply ingrained both in the neoclassical paradigm and in the popular mentality. According to Schumpeter (1934, p. 93) the entrepreneur has three motivating factors: "... the dream and the will to found a private kingdom ... the will to conquer: the impulse to fight. ..." and "... finally there is the joy of creating, of getting things done. ..." Colorful individuals, from John D. Rockefeller to J.P. Morgan, from Cornelius Vanderbuilt to Henry Ford, play a key role in the literature on economic history.

There is an empirical element in these vivid images: Exceptional individuals do play a role in innovation. However, they do so much less than is often attributed to them. And the conditions under which innovators abound or largely fail to emerge lie very much in N/A and other societal factors, in the structures of social collectivities. For example, the lower the culture ranks adaptive functions (such as economic growth and productivity), efficiency, technology, and science, and the higher it ranks social cohesion, stability, and religion, the less innovative activities are expected. Japan's relative lack of innovation has been tied to its social structure of high collectivism and authoritarianism, and its tradition of respect for elders and tradition.

To state that legitimation plays a key role in determining the level of innovation is not to deny the role of economic incentives, such as the level of taxes on capital gains, and tax credits for investment in R&D. However, such economic incentives themselves reflect legitimation: For instance, the value attributed to these pursuits is a major reason legislatures agreed to lower the tax rates. Moreover, the special tax status constitutes not merely a "price" signal but also signals legitimation. Thus, tax benefits may provide both direct economic incentives and signals of social values.

Also, innovation often requires collectively provided resources, well beyond the means and efforts of most individual innovations. True, some innovation occurs merely in the mind, in a kitchen sink, or a garage (e.g., the invention of the prototype of mass production of personal computers, the Apple). However, most innovation, especially in advanced industrial societies, occurs in specialized collective settings, by teams and not by individuals, drawing on a concentration of resources, such as at Bell Laboratory (Schmookler 1972).

Last, but not least, without collective approval and collective support, innovations—even if some individuals come up with them—do not take off, in the sense of an idea or prototype leading to a product that gains acceptance. Often, the mere accumulation of new knowledge or of technical breakthroughs is insufficient; approval by the community is required. Indeed, *innovations are often to a significant extent changes introduced into the N/A context and structure of one or more collectivity.* For instance, the introduction of "Japanese" participatory work management styles entailed changes in the relations between those lower and higher in rank in corporations, and the introduction of automated data banks reduced the role of middle management.

In short, the activity often said to be the most individualistic of all economically relevant activities, innovation, seems to occur largely in favorable N/A contexts and collective structures. And, the fate of all innovations—including those conceived at random by maverick individuals rather than collectively planned and provided for—depends on favorable collective "take off" conditions.

COMPARING COLLECTIVE AND INDIVIDUAL RATIONALITY

Decision-making of organized collectivities is akin to that of individuals in that they, too, are deeply affected by N/A factors. Thus, a collection of authoritative studies of intelligence services in different countries and periods found that, in case after case, assessments of the enemy's capabilities and intentions, and inferences drawn from these assessments, were deeply influenced by prejudice and wishful thinking (May 1984). Information was often at hand but was disregarded when it did not suit national pride or prejudice, elite commitments, and other such N/A factors. Thus, General Henry Wilson, director of military operations for the British Army before 1914, reported to his government that six British divisions would have a decisive affect on the French-German war, while admitting in private that six were probably "fifty too few." (May 1984, p. 15.) The war in Vietnam was frequently plagued, among other things, by doctored intelligence assessments, a key issue in the CBS-Westmoreland court case.

, Second, the L/E bases of collective decision-makers are often quite limited. We have no quarrel with the numerous studies that show the subrational or worse quality of government decision-making (see, for instance, Stein 1984; Wildavsky 1979 and 1984), and that of various private organizations, including corporations (see studies cited in Chapter 10).

With this background, we are ready for the question: given that both kinds of actors—individuals and organized collectivities—are rather N/A dominated and low in L/E capabilities, whose instrumental rationality is lower? The question is not merely a theoretical one: It goes to the heart of, the balance between public policy and private decision-making. (There are other reasons one may prefer private decision-making than efficiency; however, the argument that private decision-making is efficient is often advanced in its favor.)

One reason one may expect that organized collective decision-making may be éven more deficient, on average, than that of individuals is that there often are significant differences within collectivities concerning the selection of goals that are to be served, and the values that provide the N/A context and load of the selection of means. We have seen that individuals are not the unitary, orderly, internally consistent bundle of preferences that neoclassicists assume; they are internally conflicted, ambivalent, and changing. Collectivities are often more so because, aside from containing these intra-individual conflicts, there are differences among sub-collectivities that hinder decision-making. This is evident in that those collectivities that have a relatively high consensus as to the goals to be pursued—and as to the N/A factors to affect the selection of means— are much more able to render decisions than more conflicted collectivities. A case in point is the difficulties labor unions encounter in dealing with management when they are internally divided, either because of a strife among factions or conflicts between two or more unions, each appealing to the same collective base.

On the other hand, there are several reasons to suggest that organized collectivities can deliberate and decide more efficiently in *many* important *sub*sets of issues (albeit not all) than the average individual, and possibly more efficiently than most individuals. These follow:

(1) When executive committees, managers and their support staff, corporate boards, and other such decision-making bodies deliberate and decide, they more often *curb each other's impulses* than exacerbate them, in part because it takes time and effort to gain group action, and in part because they have incompatible (hence, mutually curbing) proclivities. While a charismatic leader may whip up a mob frenzy and then feed on it, this is rare in organized collectivities.

(2) Divergent members bring to the decision-making process larger amounts and varieties of knowledge than any of the individual members

commands as a person. Also, groups are able to consider more options than an individual. While each individual may be able to retain only four to eight facts in their short-term memory, a decision-making group can bring to bear many more.

The suggestion that the attention span of organizations is as limited as that of individuals (Stern 1984a, p. 112) seems to us untenable. Thus, it makes a difference, say, in a busy airport control tower, whether there is one controller, or several who divided the skies into sections that each one focuses on, with still another serving as a supervisor and coordinator, and others standing by as trouble shooters or strategic reserves, to be mobilized when a particular sector is over-loaded.

(3) Organized collectivities can institutionalize distinct considerations through *intellectual* division of labor and of attention. Thus, if a decision requires several highly specialized skills, a team—especially if the division of labor is structural rather than ad hoc—is likely to render a more rational decision than most individuals. Moreover, considerations that tend to be overlooked by an individual can be made the specific responsibility of one member of such a team. For example, in many corporations there is a tendency in top management decision-making to neglect ethical considerations and those of public affairs. The appointment of special board committees—for example, internal audit committees—enhances attention to these considerations. (Audit committees are composed of directors independent of management, and exist to assist the board of directors to meet their oversight responsibilities in financial reporting and internal control. The practice grew in the post-Watergate period due to increased pressure on management to raise corporate ethical standards). Similarly, considerations of public affairs are less likely to be overlooked when they are institutionalized in a separate division, especially if the head of the division is included in the top decision-making bodies.

While there are only a few studies of organized collectivities from the viewpoint of the issues discussed here, there are very many experimental studies of small groups that focus on the issue at hand. Their findings are diverse and influenced by details of design. However, to the extent that a common finding can be gleaned from these studies, it is that when there is no one putatively correct answer, when judgment is called for, "groups tend to do 'better' than the average individual, but less well than the 'best' member." (McGrath and Kravitz 1982, p. 203.)

Groups are also reported to be better at cross-checking errors, where tasks can be subdivided, and in solving problems that require a variety of skills, as well as those in which the quantity of "production" is significant (McGrath 1978, p. 660). Similarly, a 1983 survey of 241 investment clubs showed an annual earnings rate over nine years of 28 percent, seemingly better than that of many individuals (Power 1984). In most R&D work, the necessity to rely on research teams rather than on finding individual "geniuses" is well established. (A detailed framework for conceptualizing the role of group processes in affecting the level of group performance, and an extensive review of numerous findings, is provided by Hackman and Morris, 1975.)

There are some subareas in which individual performance has been found to be superior. Groups are inferior to individuals working alone, in finding "creative" solutions and in solving "Eureka" problems—defined as problems for which there is one clear correct answer, but once found—is intuitively compelling (Laughlin 1980). But all said and done, decision-making by organized collectivities seems to exhibit a higher level of instrumental rationality than that of average and of most individuals.

THE STRUCTURE OF RATIONALITY

The neoclassical paradigm, whose radical individualism is reductionist in that it denies the role of collectivities, also ignores the significance of structures and chooses to look for aggregates of individual decisions instead. (See, for example, the discussion of the origin of rules, above, pp. 178–80). In contrast, the position evolved here is of deontological-structuralism, because it is productive to assume that there are significant, non-reducible macro-properties, among which the structure of collectivities is pivotal. Structures are lasting patterns of relationships among component parts (or members) defined by attributes of the whole. Thus, the relations among individuals who work in steep hierarchical relations differ significantly from those who work in highly decentralized (or "flat") structures, not according to their individual attributes, but by virtue of the systematic ways in which power, assets, and access to information are distributed among them by the organization.

Structures are common in the social realm. In nuclear families they provide a form for relations between spouses, and between them and their children. They affect the relations among ethnic groups, races, and classes in the community. They deeply influence the balance between the I's and We within any particular society and historical period. And we shall see that they deeply influence the role of markets within society and the polity, as well as the inner working of the market.

Here, the relationship of structure to rationality is explored in a very preliminary way. No attempt is made to specify the relationships, but as a first approximation, findings are cited to illustrate that the ways collectivities are structured deeply influences the level of macro-rationality. R&D activities are used to illustrate the general thesis.

The discussion assumes that R&D activities seek to enhance rationality by finding more efficient ways of serving existing goals. True, not every single R&D act is rational in the sense used here (for example, some are exercises in image building). However, if the R&D efforts are viewed in toto it seems proper to classify them as efforts to enhance instrumental rationality.

What determines the level of R&D performance? Studies in the early 1950s focused on individual attributes, including personality traits (e.g. Roe, 1952), IQ, and personal goals (Barth and Vertisky 1975). As of mid-1960, attention shifted to benefits of conducting R&D work in research groups or teams (Farris 1978). However, as Cheng (1984, p. 161) points out, much of this research concerned itself with "researchers in team settings rather than that of research teams as such," i.e., rather than with the role of structure. Only in the mid-1970s did attention focus on structural factors, resting on "the premise that contemporary research activity is no longer an individual enterprise." (Cheng 1984, p. 162; see also Cheng and McKinley 1983, p. 86.) The structural factors that have been found to correlate significantly with R&D performance are patterns of control (degree of hierarchization), communication, and coordination. They are next discussed one at a time.

Challenging the universal applicability of the Weberian notion concerning the virtue of hierarchical organization of complex division of labor, the studies suggest that for structures to be efficient the *patterns of control* must be varied to match the specific nature of the task and the environment in which it is carried out. Thus, typically, when uncertainty is high, information needs rise. Under these conditions, hierarchical structures tend to become overloaded because of their limited information processing capabilities. Hence the need to rely on relatively "flat" (non-hierarchical) structures that increase the information intake and processing capabilities (Galbraith 1973; Daft and MacIntosh 1981). Presumably, under the opposite conditions, more hierarchical structures will do.

A study of 13 research teams in a large industrial laboratory shows that, the higher the *level of intra-team communication,* the higher the research performance (Katz and Tushman 1979). The same finding is reported from a study of 1,131 scientists working in eleven different academic, industrial, and governmental laboratories (Pelz and Andrews 1966). Communication, in turn, is not random. It is affected by the way research teams are structured. While there are numerous findings on the subject, the one that stands out is the poor performance of centralized channels (in which communication must flow from each point to a center and distributed from here to other points) as compared to lateral channels, in which information flows freely from point to point (Shaw 1964; Glanzer and Glaser 1961).

One major study of *coordination* covers 127 research teams from 33 research organizations including academic, industrial, and government. The relations between coordination and quality of output is examined in teams where tasks are judged to require varying degrees of interdependence. Both quality and quantity of R&D output are found to correlate strongly with the level of coordination; and, the relationship is stronger—the higher the degree of interdependence (Dailey 1980).

These findings are far from surprising. On the contrary, they tend to confirm everyday observations about the merits of decentralization, communication, and coordination, especially for intellectual tasks. The significance, however, seems to require some highlight: The findings illustrate that the structures that collectivities provide for intellectual work affect the level of their instrumental rationality.

12

Encapsulated Competition

THE ENCAPSULATION THESIS

Free competition (the market) is the core macro concept of the neoclassical view of the economic world. It is typically viewed as free-standing and as self-perpetuating. Behind various formal definitions and mathematical notations there is a well-known idea: Adam Smith's notion that as each actor in the market pursues his or her own goal, the result will not be destructive conflict, but, on the contrary, an automatically harmonious and self-perpetuating system. Moreover, the exchanges—which is what the market is all about—will organize the use of resources in a maximally efficient manner, without outside intervention. Maintaining stability and order either has been "implicitly assumed and hence entirely ignored; or alternatively order is explicitly taken as given." (Schott 1984, p. 2. See also Thurow 1983, p. 231.)

In contrast, the I&We paradigm sees competition, the market, indeed the economy, as a subsystem nestled within a more encompassing societal context. And it assumes that competition is not self-sustaining; its very existence, as well as the scope of transactions organized by it, is dependent to a significant extent upon the contextual factors, the societal "capsule," within which competition takes place.

To put it differently, neoclassicists have valiantly tried to deal with the need for rules of the game—i.e., of competition—by generating them internally, by viewing them as having emerged from rational, self-maximizing individuals, who are seeking to improve their relationships. However, as indicated above, there is no historical or logical reason to assume that fully formed individuals preceded the community or shared rules. Indeed, it was argued that the individuals would not exist, if there were no community and no rules. And, far from being set by individuals, the formation of the rules and their change is, in large part, determined

199

by collective factors and dynamics. These must be studied in their own right and cannot be derived from the aggregation of microprocesses.

We view both the societal capsule and competition as differentiating concepts, as variables in the sense that, unlike perfect competition— which either exists or is absent— encapsulated competition (like instrumental rationality) exists in varying degrees and forms, some of which are more constructive than others. To explicate this socio-economic concept, the factors that constitute the capsule are examined below in some detail. First, though, the significance of the neoclassical search for "second best" concepts of competition must be briefly indicated.

NEOCLASSICAL QUEST FOR "SECOND BEST"

Very large proportions of neoclassical economic analysis assume that the transactions contemplated, and the relations explored, occur within the context of perfect competition (Marris and Mueller 1980, p. 32). However, the actual worlds in which economic transactions take place, and economic policy advice is given, are not perfectly competitive. Those unfamiliar with the "second best" studies may feel that one can apply soundly the findings, lessons, and insight developed for the perfect competition "world" to less competitive worlds, to reality; the conclusions would simply need to be adapted. For example, if one assumes that, in a "world" with perfect competition, firms that set prices above the market will be driven out, in a less competitive world one may expect them to linger on for a while. However, this is clearly not the conclusion of neoclassical economics, at least to the extent that it heeds the "second best" studies. This deserves some elaboration.

Economists, from the early work of Walras ([1874–77] 1954) to the later accomplishments of Debreu (1959), have been concerned about specifying the prerequisites of perfect competition. Although lists vary about what is required, the following elements are often included: The largest firm in any given industry is to make no more than a small fraction of the industry's sales (or purchases). The firms are to act independently of one another. Actors have complete knowledge of offers to buy or sell. The commodity (sold and bought in the market) is divisible, and the resources are movable among users (Stigler 1968, pp. 181–82. For a formal discussion of the Walras model and related points see Malinvaud 1972, pp. 138–43. See also Bohm 1973, pp. 128–42).

Economists long have recognized that the prerequisites of perfect competition may never be satisfied, and—most important—that when even one of them is missing, the benefits of perfect competition may not be available. The point has been highlighted by an often-cited, masterful article by Lipsey and Lancaster (1956). They posit that the ability of a market to achieve perfect competition is dependent upon its meeting all of the conditions of the Paretian optimum. And they add (p. 11): "It is well known that the attainment of a Paretian optimum requires the simultaneous fulfillment of all the optimum conditions." Lipsey and Lancaster also indicate that if one of the conditions cannot be met, "the other Paretian conditions, although still attainable, are, in general, no longer desirable." (Ibid.) A different pattern or model is then necessary.

It follows that when an economy moves toward perfect competition, say as the result of the deregulation of one industry, one cannot assume that such a step will yield some of the benefits of perfect competition. Competition is either perfect or it is not; like pregnancy, it cannot be had in degrees. Or, to put it differently, many processes in the real world seem to follow a curvilinear, not a linear, trajectory. That is, the roads that lead to the land of perfect competition often do not ascend in a straight line, but are full of ups and downs. For example, one may well incur some losses as one moves, say, from a highly regulated industry to one that is less regulated. The expected benefits of deregulation can be soundly assumed to be found only once the blessed state is reached. Hence, the frequently made argument in favor of deregulation of this or that industry, in the name of the benefits of the free market, is valid only if one assumes that deregulation of the industry at hand will be followed in short order with deregulation of all others, *and* the introduction of all the other elements of a free market. The often stated promise that the specific industry, its customers, or the economy, will benefit—regardless of what will happen elsewhere in the system—is not supported by economic theory.

The same points are illustrated by studies of international trade. Advocates of free trade argue that if some trade barriers are reduced this would lead to improvement in the world economy. However, studies by Ozga (1955) have shown the opposite effect. Ozga (1955, p. 499) concluded that

> in a world consisting of several countries, each with its own system of tariffs, the removal of some tariffs, no matter whether they are preferential or not, may lead either toward or away from the optimum allocation of the world's productive resources. And this means that it is impossible to say on a priori grounds whether in the world of today the establishment of a free-trade area in a part of it, for instance, in western Europe, or a general reduction of tariffs by one country, for instance, the United States, not followed by the complete removal of all tariffs and universal free trade, would lead to a greater or smaller income for the world as whole.

Viner (1950) had reached the same conclusion.

Championship of free trade is the policy item economists agree upon more than any other item (Kearl et al. 1979). It is an article of faith both within the discipline and with large segments of the public at large. The thinking on the subject, though, suffers from a confusion between trade that is free—i.e., in a fully competitive world-wide system—and one that is relatively less managed, free*er* trade. There is little, if any, foundation within economic theory for the argument that trade that is, say, three-quarters free is going to be more efficient than trade that is half-free, and so on. It may be, but then again it may not. The model of perfect competition simply does not deal with partial situations. Other economists have made the same point for other economic activities, including public finance and monopolistic competition (Chamberlin 1948, pp. 214–15). Recent work lends further support to the same thesis (Newbery and Stiglitz 1984).

Lipsey, Lancaster, and others conclude that it is not possible to derive the attributes of "second best" systems from the perfect competition model. They are not simply composed of "less" of the constituting elements that result in a perfect system; they have their own inner logic and states of equilibrium. It follows that "second-best" models must be found or formulated in some other way. Various attempts have been made by economists to evolve such models, under labels such as "workable competition," "monopolistic competition," and "contestable markets." None of these has been developed with anything even roughly approximating the detail and sophistication of the perfect competition model. The latter continues to be very widely used not only in theoretical exercises but also in attempts to deal with real-world situations that are far from perfectly competitive. The term "imperfect" competition is sometimes used to suggest that reality is "close enough" to *the* model to allow one to ignore these imperfections; but in effect we shall see that much more than small deviations are common. In other words, a different model is necessary. So far it has not been found within the confines of the neoclassical paradigm; we attempt next to contribute to the evolution of such a conception—drawing on previous works in sociology, political science, and economics—by studying the societal capsule and its relations to the market.

ENCAPSULATED COMPETITION INTRODUCED

The socio-economic concept of competition is a social science, cybernetic, system theory (Etzioni, 1968). Here, too, behind formal terms and theorems lies a core idea: that *competition is a form of conflict, namely contained conflict*. In contrast with Adam Smith's assumption of an invisible hand, socio-economics assumes that the divergent interests and pursuits of various individuals do *not* automatically mesh together to form a harmonious whole. Hence, specific mechanisms are needed to protect competition, to keep conflicts within limits, and to prevent conflict from escalating to the point of self-destruction.

To put it differently, just as we saw in our discussion of individual level decision-making in Chapter 6 that L/E considerations are carried out within N/A contexts, so we see on the macro-level that competition (as a realm of instrumental rationality and means) takes place within a societal (ends-setting and means-limiting) context. And competition serves to advance social organization as long as it remains within the context and does not become the context, just as rationality may improve the selection of means, but is not an end in itself. And, just as on the individual level N/A factors that affect the selection of means are not merely "constraints," nor a cost (see above, pp. 105–8) but play a positive role, so the societal context that limits the scope of competition is not merely a source of market constraints but also a precondition for its ability to function.

The within-context, hence *subsystems*, at issue are assumed to be neither fully competitive nor uncompetitive, but to vary in the scope of behavior organized by competitive rules. For example, these rules govern more relations among strangers than among kin, and are considered in many societies to be more appropriate for commerce and sports than for social relations. Within the contemporary American economy, competition is stronger in some sectors (for example, within the restaurant industry) than in others (for instance, among electrical utilities). And, societies differ in the effectiveness of the mechanisms that contain and sustain competitive behavior.

To develop a workable conception of competition, one must move beyond the conceptual opposition between "free competition" and "government intervention," which implies that all interventions are by a government, that all interventions are injurious, and that unshackled competition can be sustainable. Dichotomies are the curse of intellectual and scholarly discourse. Typical is the notion that competition is "voluntary" and hence "good" (disregarding that most exchanges occur among non-equals in economic, social, and political power, hence are partially coerced), and that government is "coercive" and hence "bad" (disregarding that the government is often persuasive or uses economic incentives rather than force *and* that the capsule is only partially governmental). Competition, like rationality, ought to be treated as a differentiating concept; the question is what levels of competition (especially as measured by the scope of activities it encompasses) are efficient, and in line with one's values, rather than destructive.

Second, according to the socio-economic line of argumentation advanced here, competition (as a mode of conflict) can be preserved only within some collectively set limits or context. This is true for all modes of conflict (for instance, national values that agitate against civil wars set the boundaries for "tolerable" intra-national political strife), including economic competition (for example, values prohibit the use of violent means among competitors, or illicit means such as industrial spying). The specific mechanisms that limit competition to prevent it from self-destructing will be explored shortly.

At the same time one must also establish the conditions under which the very same factors that sustain competition, by keeping it within bounds, themselves infuse the realm defined by society as the legitimate zone for competition (akin to the legitimate L/E individual zone discussed earlier), violate its autonomy, and undermine the ability of actors within the zone to follow its logic. In short, like a nuclear reaction, properly bounded competition may be viewed as a major constructive force; when unleashed, as highly destructive; and when repressed, as likely to lose its power, or even be extinguished. The line of analysis advanced here draws on previous sociological analyses that treat the economy as a whole (and not merely competition) as a subsystem "bounded" by, or "embedded" in, a social system (Polanyi 1944; Parsons and Smelser 1956, especially p. 21; Granovetter 1985; Swedberg 1987; and Etzioni 1965).

The socio-economic theorem evolved here is illustrated by a treatment of deregulation. Neoclassical economists tend to support deregulation, drawing on the notion that if the market is less intervened with, the economy will be more efficient. The "second best" studies should have given these economists pause, because there is no reason to hold that partial deregulation (of some industries, in a few countries) will have the expected benefits; total, or even near-total, deregulation is quite unattainable. Moreover, if full deregulation would somehow miraculously be achieved, the perfect competition model still would not apply because of numerous *other* restricting factors. Moreover, the more unfettered competition becomes, the more keenly one becomes aware of the need to be concerned with the capsule, with the rules of the game. This, in turn, leads to the question of which factors explain the relative strengths of the capsule, because economic actors do *not* automatically follow rules that they somehow discovered serve their self-interest in the longer run. And deontologically, one recalls, service of values other than efficiency— safety, for instance—cannot be left to the market place.

To stay with the example at hand, the notion that economic actors will not undermine safety (and other such public goods) because such disregard would increase their longer-run costs—e.g., accidents will jack up their insurance premiums—ignores the fact that unless regulations require the purchase of insurance, many economic actors do not acquire it. Inattention to safety is particularly evident in the trucking industry since the 1980's deregulation; trucking corporations put pressure on their drivers to drive longer hours and to drive faster; they also under-maintain the trucks. When major accidents occur and the driver's license is revoked in one state, the drivers use licenses from other states. In short, weak or inadequate regulation allows economic actors to escape the economic consequences of acting against the common good.

The same principle can be illustrated by studying common complaints about the distorting effects of issuing insufficient numbers of licenses to taxis ("medallions") in New York City. In the 1920s and 1930s there was no such regulation. There was a surplus of taxis that clogged the streets and engaged in price wars that kept fares so low the drivers barely made a living, and owners could not afford insurance or maintenance (*New York Times,* March 10, 1985). In short, often when public goods are involved, *some* measure of regulation seems called for.

Beyond this, rules are needed to preserve not merely the competition but also the competitors. Fully unfettered competition—all-out conflict—tends to self-destruct. Such competition leads corporations to cut short their investment in R&D, capital assets, and maintenance, and puts pressure on them to employ illicit or illegal means (or both). This could lead to either a catch-as-catch-can "war" that forces the community to re-intervene, or to the destruction of numerous competitors, as well as "innocent" third parties. Such a "war" would thus result in a concentration of economic power, and the end of free competition. Those who are committed to competition in the longer run, must therefore support its being a partially limited, rule-governed, conflict.

For those who maintain that preferences are revealed in behavior, the fact that people support considerable degrees of government regulation should have no less status than their preference for other items. People seem not to mind "privatization" of garbage collection and some other such municipal services, but they would rather not privatize fire and police departments, air safety, and the FDA. Why are these preferences to be heeded less than their preferences for deodorants, plastic surgery, and tattooed toe nails, let alone liquor and cigarettes?

Does all this constitute a call *for* rule-setting? It calls for a recognition that the world is more complex than allowing only two alternatives: either a simplistic endorsement of unfettered competition, or a blanket support for rules. Socio-economic analysis ought to focus on the question: How many rules are beneficial, and which facets of which economic activities can be rule-less without undermining values the commons are committed to, including that of maintaining competition? Among the dichotomies that hinder serious intellectual examination few are as detrimental as the notion that free markets are "good" and governments are "bad," both because some measure of rule-setting and enforcement is clearly needed, and too much is harmful. The proper question is not: Which ideal-type state wins your endorsement? but rather: What is the most productive mix, given various value (goal) assumptions? A main way to form and sustain rules is to build on and build up the moral values and commitments of a community, not to expand the government.

THE MECHANISMS

The principal mechanisms that constitute the competition-sustaining and containing capsule are normative, social, and governmental. Each of these mechanisms contains numerous specific processes that interact with the two others in complex ways. They have been analyzed frequently, and are discussed here as a conceptual effort, to help formulate a model of encapsulated competition, not as a report of new findings.

Normative Factors and Encapsulated Competition

All societies have value systems that define what members consider legitimate conduct. These include general normative principles governing the propriety of engaging in commerce, manual labor, entrepreneurship ("making money"), and applied research (in contrast to "scholarship"). In addition, there are specific norms and attitudes that define, for example, the levels of interest that is considered usury, and "color" the ways members of the society see multi-national corporations.

The most important contribution that normative principles provide to the competitive system is the legitimacy they offer to a sphere of activities within which L/E considerations can guide choices, relatively free of external N/A and power considerations. Within the context provided, an inner logic can be followed, allowing the payoffs to participants to be determined by the outcome of competition among them, rather than by political power, moral standing, or societal status. Max Weber's well-known work applies here if one interprets it to mean that certain religions provided a stronger legitimation to economic competition than did others. (Most of his arguments lead elsewhere, demonstrating that certain religions favored other capitalist features such as the work ethic, initiative, and saving.) Obviously, capitalist societies value competition more than feudal, traditional, and Communist societies do, but also more than social democratic societies such as Israel and Scandinavia. And within capitalistic societies, the legitimacy of competition changes throughout their history.

Undoubtedly, some normative principles, exogenous to competition, directly sustain it. Primary is the belief in the moral virtues of competition in general; Americans, for instance, believe that it builds character. There is also the belief in the virtue of economic competition, of the "free market," not merely among philosophers and economists, but also among the overwhelming majority of political leaders, voters, and the public. Americans tend to endow "the market" with numerous virtues, from efficiency and protection against tyranny to a source of welfare for all: "When the tide rises, all the ships rise." (Novak 1982; Lipset and Schneider 1983, pp. 286ff.)

Just as laissez-faire conservatism legitimates competition, so a number of socialist ideologies, humanist psychology (for instance, the works of Abraham Maslow), and counter-culture writers in the United States provided rationales in the sixties and seventies for greatly narrowing the scope of behavior governed by competition (e.g., justifying various public policies and regulations that limit its scope; for example, by favoring automatic promotion into schools). It was also suggested that competition could be limited by legitimating outcomes achieved via non-competitive mechanisms (e.g., Affirmative Action), and by challenging the merit of the competitive spirit and system. (See, for example, Hirsch 1976 and Hirschman 1982, pp. 1463–84.)

The sociological question is not whether these normative considerations are raised, but to what extent they are endorsed and followed, and what effects they have. Thus, for instance, during the height of the counter-culture, its values were endorsed to one extent or another by many more Americans than actually defined themselves as hippies, and competition lost some legitimacy in the United States. The proportion of Americans agreeing that "government should limit profits" of corporations rose from 25 percent in 1962 to 55 percent by 1976 and to 60 percent by 1979 (*Public Opinion*, 1980). This was also roughly the period in which regulation of the economy for social purposes (social justice; consumer, worker, and environmental protection; and scores of others) was greatly expanded. That is, loss in the legitimacy of competition was accompanied by political penetration of the competitive context in order to set some outcomes by exogenous criteria.

Beyond these general normative positions, there are specific norms and attitudes that help to either sustain or undermine the capsule of competition. An obvious example is the endorsement of competing fairly, "by the rules." Then the statement "it does not matter whether you win or lose but how you play" is in conflict with the notion that "winning is not the important thing; it is the only thing," immortalized by Vince Lombardi and embraced by Richard Nixon, among others. There are numerous other norms, characterizing as "unfair"—or as quite proper—this or that form of competition (e.g. "cut throat") or means of competition (e.g. price wars). Together they either provide a specific normative underpinning for a specific range of competition, or favor that it be curtailed, or argue for its expansion, in varying degrees. (For additional discussion, see Lodge and Vogel 1987; McCraw 1984; and Zaid 1979.)

Aside from periodic changes in the content of these norms, systematic changes occur in the extent to which they are followed by actors in different segments of the economy. These changes, in turn, deeply affect the level of competition within these segments. While the author is unaware of a systematic study of the matter, common knowledge of American society suggests that competition among most illegal dealers in controlled substances is less contained by normative values than competition among most computer sales personnel; is less contained among such persons as compared to that among most professionals; and is less contained among marginal doctors and lawyers than among core members of these professions.

Also, norms of the kind under discussion affect the level of competition by influencing special elements on which sustained competition draws. For instance, certain norms help keep transaction costs down. If dealers in contraband do not trust one another, they must have body-guards, armored cars, etc.; transactions must be paid for in cash, rather than with checks or financed with credit; and long-run planning is diffi-cult. In contrast, most transactions among actors in legitimate businesses are based upon trust. Typically, agreements are made in oral communi-cations; only few, proportionately speaking, are recorded; and of those that are recorded, only a fraction is scrutinized by lawyers. But trust is a continuous and not a dichotomous variable; it is higher in some indus-tries, subcultures, and societies than in others. The weaker the relevant normative factors, and hence the weaker the trust, the higher the transac-tion costs (Arrow 1974, p. 23). Indeed, trust is reported to be low in many economies of less developed countries (ibid., p. 26; Hirschman 1958). The high costs of bribery are known to increase the costs of conducting busi-ness in many countries. (Some distinguish between a low level of bribery, say up to 5 percent of total costs, that merely strains a system, and a ruinous level of bribery, that adds 100 percent or more to other costs of conducting business.) In the area of labor relations, Denison reports that theft by employees is a significant factor affecting the productivity of American corporations (Denison 1979, pp. 73ff). In short, normative val-ues are not merely principles to which people express commitments; they have specific behavior consequences that sustain or undermine competi-tion, and expand or limit its scope.

Social Bonds: Hidden Bases of Competition

The perfect competition model assumes that the relations among the actors are impersonal, as the actors proceed independently of one another in an anonymous market. "The fortunes of any one firm are independent of what happens to any other firm: one farmer is not bene-fited [sic] if his neighbor's crop is destroyed." (Stigler 1968, p. 181.) One might add: or, if his neighbor's crop thrives. And each actor is out to maximize what he or she can gain. This orientation is not problematic in the neoclassical paradigm of perfect competition because it is assumed that self-interest will sustain the system. It is problematic, however, in other paradigms, which acknowledge conflict, recognize the significance of positive, mutually supporting *social* bonds, and in which actors treat each other as persons, as ends, and care for one another, as contributing to the continuity of *economic* relations.

A well-known illustration of the conflict limiting role of social bonds is found in a political arena, that of the U.S. Senate. Senators are re-ported to be keenly aware that they are members of one "club;" that although they are in conflict on some issues, they soon will have to work together concerning others. Hence, they endeavor to limit the scope of their conflicts; for instance, personal attacks are considered highly improper.

Similarly, among traders in the market there are social bonds that help to sustain the relationships of trust (by and large, people trust those they know much more than they do strangers), and to limit conflicts. This observation has been referred to as the pre-contractual base of contracts. This is a point sociologists have made at least since Durkheim. His work (1947) shows that contracts, while on the face of it being voluntary calculated deals among uncommitted individuals, in effect draw on prior shared bonds which are not subject to negotiation, and of which the parties are often unaware. Without such bonds, contracts are nearly impossible to formulate and their enforcement costs would be often so high, that they would be impractical (Granovetter 1985). Phelps put it especially well. He first states (1975, p. 3) that "altruistic phenomena are equally crucial to the functioning of markets." He then elaborates: people do not behave in the maximizing way the perfect competition model implies; many corporations do not deceive in their advertising, pay fair wage rates, keep their word and so on. This, he adds, "contributes to economic efficiency. Certainly it reduces the risks and anxieties of being cheated or exploited. Beyond that, it tends to improve market resource allocations by lowering the transaction costs." (Ibid., p. 5.) One major reason the Japanese economy and society are reported to function significantly better than the American is that the nationalist, island-bound, homogenous society has stronger social bonds on all levels than does the United States (Vogel 1979). Among other things this is reflected in that Japan has many fewer lawyers (who increase transactions) and more engineers than the United States.

Although social bonds and normative factors are frequently mutually supportive, they are independent factors and are not to be viewed as one variable. Social bonds tend to unite people through positive mutual feelings, often enhanced by compatibility of background (social bonds tend to be stronger among people of similar ethnic class and educational background than among those of highly divergent ones), by compatible or complementary personalities, and by shared social activities (from golf to bowling). Such bonds are not inherently normative; they bind as readily a group of thieves as they bind police officers sharing a beat (Etzioni, 1975, Chapter 8). That is, they constitute a distinct category.

Social bonds exist on both micro—one to one, or small group—and macro, society-wide, levels. Micro-bonds help transactions between brokers and their clients, sales representatives and their customers, suppliers and manufacturers, and numerous others. Socio-economic analysis need not deny that *in part* the incentives for investment in such bonds, as distinct from trying to garner maximum benefit from every transaction, are due to "enlightened" (long-term) self-interest. However, it maintains that (1) social bonds, that precede and accompany economic relations, say among members of a work crew, generate economic benefits; and (2) that they bind people to some extent even when the social bonds exact some economic costs in the short *and* in the longer run (as for example if, in order to stay in the good graces of a group, one must regularly contribute to a given charity).

The relative strength of social bonds is often reported to be a significant factor in determining the nature of work relationships between supervisors and workers (and between other ranks), affecting the level of cooperation, productivity, the quality of work, and satisfaction derived from work. In organizational literature this is often referred to as the addition of human relations (or Mayonian) considerations to those of "scientific management" (or Taylorism).

The pivotal role of social bonds in affecting the level of competition has been recognized somewhat uncharitably by Adam Smith, in his well-known observation that whenever businessmen meet socially they never fail to use their "cabal" to limit competition. A study of commodity exchanges provides a highly illuminating case in point. Theoretically the "pits" provide an ideal situation for perfect competition to develop: All buyers and sellers are present; all are privy to the same bids to sell and to buy at the same time, and transactions take place in the open, indeed are shouted out. In effect, Baker (1984a, 1984b) shows, using strong observational as well as statistical data, that traders who are permanent staff of one pit, draw on their social bonds to drive out sellers and buyers from other pits. Low bids by these outsiders are deliberately ignored and prices are manipulated to undercut the capital of outsiders, to restrict the trade to members of the group (see also Abolafia 1984). What holds for the highly competitive trade in commodities exchanges is expected to hold many times over for trades that are less public, less visible, and less competitive; that is, for most trades.

Both minorities and women object to the existence of white male social clubs, among other reasons because they sense that social bonds built in these clubs provide useful business contacts. That is, members of the club will not search the field for the best bid, but tend to look for bids among members of the club. We saw already that because search costs are often high, searches are often limited. The clubs provide a rule of thumb for limiting the search; not at all the best one from the viewpoint of instrumental rationality, if the goal is to enhance the profits (the lowest bids may well be by non-members) but a rule that is followed for other, social, reasons.

On the societal level, social bonds exist among regions, races, classes, and generations. In the United States macro-social bonds were quite weak between the South and the North, but strengthened after the Civil War during the Reconstruction Era. And, while during the nineteenth century and well into the twentieth, American workers were treated as socially unfit, gradually their social acceptance grew. This greater acceptance is often cited as one reason that American labor is much less radical, and more accepting of the political and the competitive economic system, than its European counterparts. Strikes and violence are reported to be less common in the United States.

The next step in developing this part of socio-economic theory is to take these observations (often made, but also often overlooked) and to render them more specific. To specify them, measurements of various attributes of the social bonds have to be tied (or correlated) to the scope (and other attributes) of competition. *A curvilinear relationship is hypothesized to exist between social bonds and competition.* All things being equal, when the bonds are absent or very weak, the capsule that contains competition is expected to be insufficient, with competition showing signs of threatening to break down the containing capsule, leading toward all-out conflict. In labor relations, long and destructive strikes, shut-outs, wild-cat strikes, acts of sabotage and violence, and use of strike breakers are indications of such a tendency. In contrast, when various ranks of the employees consider themselves as one social community, a one We (as they are said to do at Delta Airlines), labor relations are expected to be much more harmonious. (This is not to suggest that labor conflicts are caused only by weak social bonds, but that weakness of bonds is a contributing factor, or indicates the weakness of other factors that might contain conflict.)

At the opposite extreme, where social bonds are very powerful, encompassing, and tight, economic competition is likely to be restrained, if not suppressed. For example, members of a close knit family find it difficult to charge one another for services rendered, and to engage in economic transactions and competition. This is one reason market economies tend to be limited, if not absent, in small, highly communal, tribal societies.

Accordingly, *competition thrives not in impersonal, calculative systems* of independent actors unbound by social relations, as implied by the neoclassical paradigm, *nor in the socially tight world of communal societies, but in the middle range,* where social bonds are strong enough to sustain mutual trust and low transaction costs but not so strong as to suppress exchange orientations. Aside from being of middle strength (more than between total strangers, but less than between kin and close friends), social bonds support competition when they distinguish relatively clearly between behaviors that are socially offensive (e.g., cheating), and those that are acceptable or at least tolerable (e.g., trading). This is the point at which social bonds and normative factors are intertwined. But, before such points of interaction are considered, the third component element of the capsule is introduced.

The Competition-Building Role of Governments

In the perfect competition model, the government is a distorting factor because the economic system is assumed to be self-regulating. Whatever government does here is properly termed "distorting" or "intervention" because it pulls the system away from its pure, "natural," Paretian-optimal state. On the other hand, it is sufficient to observe that all societies have some measure of government to conclude that a "second-best" competition model must be found. Whigs, who are philosophically attuned to Adam Smith's economics, tend to argue that the government should be minimal and limited to non-economic functions, especially to defense. However, defense requires a revenue-raising mechanism. And however government is constituted, even if it taxes only consumption and only individuals (neither capital nor firms), it still "distorts" the system, breaks the Paretian mold, and points to the need for a different model.

In contrast, the model of encapsulated competition requires some governmental activities, while it defines some other governmental activities as undermining the proper balance between intra-capsule activities—those organized by the rules of competition, and those that constitute the capsule. Government is required to sustain the capsule because conflicts are assumed to be endemic to the system, and gaining resolutions cannot rely only upon normative commitments and social bonds because actors can violate those. It follows that an institution that commands coercive power must be the ultimate arbiter of conflicts (e.g., by jailing violators of a court decree in order to force compliance). Moreover, the fact that the competitors themselves might resort to violence necessitates an institution able to disarm them, or at least able to deter the competitors from using their resources in violent clashes.

On the other hand, competition is undermined when the government goes beyond sustaining the capsule, trying to affect the outcomes of competition by favoring some competitors. This might be justified by values other than sustaining competition, such as social justice. In addition, to the extent that the government helps formerly excluded competitors to participate on an equal footing, such help legitimizes the system. Nevertheless, when these values are achieved by externally determining the outcomes of competition, instead of improving the ability to participate in the competition, competition is undercut.

Analytically the competition-sustaining and the competition-undermining roles of government are clearly distinct. Some government acts, such as laws that protect private property and the currency, or prohibit fraud and violence, are clearly supportive. Other acts obviously have other primary purposes; for instance, those that regulate the size of billboards to enhance "highway beautification." However, many other government actions need to be studied before they can be appropriately classified. For instance, laws that prohibit shops opening on Sundays, or after agreed hours, or laws prohibiting stores that sell the same items from being situated too close to one another—such laws may be used to sustain the capsule (by avoiding ruinous competition), or to favor white

Christian shopkeepers over racial and ethnic minorities, thus cutting the scope of competition by limiting the number of competitors.

Interaction Effects

Although the three mechanisms that constitute the capsule have been discussed individually, they are present simultaneously in the working of encapsulated competition, and affect one another as they affect the scope of competition (the range of areas of behavior governed by competition versus those in which it is deemed inappropriate). For instance, the stronger the moral prohibitions against violence and the stronger the social bonds, the less need there is for government action. This is a point of considerable significance. In much of the Whig literature on the subject, the government is contrasted with the individual, as if the only collective, community voice is that of coercion. However, the first line of defense of the commons, of the We, is the normative voice of the community. It appeals to individuals' commitments, and commitments that are based on values rather than on force, although it leaves the ultimate decision to the individual in the sense that he or she is asked to comply but is not coerced. One can hence be greatly concerned about the scope of government coercion and still uphold the need for a collective role and voice. Indeed, the more one is concerned with curbing coercion, the more one should recognize the value of the normative mechanisms of the community because, to reiterate, the more effective they are, the less there is a need for a government. At the same time, it is true, that in a normatively weak system, the government may, to some extent, replace the normative mechanisms, although at much higher costs, both in economic terms (a need for more police, courts, jails) and psychic ones (alienation). The capsule is, therefore, best considered an intertwined set of normative, social, and governmental mechanisms who each have a distinct role but also can, within limits, substitute for one another.

POWER RELATIONS

The perfect competition model assumes that actors have no power over one another. This point is usually expressed by saying that no firm has an ability to affect the market. Disregarding the "second best" insight, numerous economists have favored, and policy makers have attempted, nudging the economy toward such a model, for instance by favoring antitrust policies. The fact is, though, that in numerous industries there are at least some differences in the economic power of various actors (see Chapter 13). Indeed, power is so pervasive in the economy that socioeconomics assumes that for all intents and purposes *there are no transac-*

tions among equals. This is reflected in the real "exchange rates," i.e., amount of labor and resources one actor must invest to produce one unit of whatever is being exchanged, compared to the investment by the other party in the transaction. Such exchange rates can be calculated between countries (e.g., the United States and Panama), kinds of countries (e.g., developed and developing), and any two (or more) actors (e.g., major banks and major corporations versus major banks and small business).

As the scientific co-determination approach would lead one to expect, such calculations show two kinds of factors at work: the kind "modeled" by neoclassical economists, supply and demand, and the kind political scientists have traditionally studied, power differentials. Thus, General Motors can inform its small suppliers that it will not increase what it pays by more than X percent in a given year, and they as a rule have little choice but to cut their profit margins, while General Motors cannot do the same, say, to Citibank if G.M. needs to renegotiate its credit. *Prices, in general, reflect supply and demand* and *relative power.* True, in some areas, the relative weight of power is low, but in many it is quite high; it is rarely if ever, insignificant. These points are familiar to neoclassicists from their discussion of monopolistic behavior. However, they tend to assume that it is exceptional, and hence that the free market models can be applied. We shall see below the reasons and evidence that lead us to hold that, far from being exceptional, such behavior is quite common, and points to the need for a theory that encompasses power differentials and struc- tures as a basic building block (Coleman 1984).

The concept of encapsulated competition introduces a major new di- mension to the issue at hand: actors are assumed to vary not merely in their economic power (their ability to affect the state of the market), but also in their political power (their ability to affect the government that is part of the capsule, which, in turn may affect the outcome of transactions within the capsule). Concentrated economic power may thus be con- verted into political power and exercised to thwart the neutrality of the capsule-sustaining mechanisms, and to use the government to favor one actor (or group of actors) over others (for instance, favoring big business over small business).

It follows that the power prerequisites of encapsulated competition are the dispersion of economic power and/or the separation of economic power from the polity, so that economic power cannot (or, is difficult to) convert into political power. This requirement is not absolute, as it is in the perfect competition model; everyday experience clearly indicates that encapsulated competition can work despite some power concentra- tion. However, a high concentration of economic power undermines en- capsulated competition not only because it reduces the number of com- petitors (a point emphasized by the neoclassical theory of competition), but also because the higher the concentration of economic power the more likely it is to be a source of political power which, in turn, undermines the capsule (a point not encompassed in neoclassical economic theory).

Second, encapsulated competition requires segregation of political from economic power, whatever its degree of concentration (e.g., abolishing property-weighted franchises and poll taxes; prohibiting campaign contributions by corporations and labor unions. Etzioni 1984a, pp. 131ff). The more effective the segregation of political and economic power, the better is encapsulated competition able to withstand concentration of economic power, although even under complete segregation (difficult to imagine) a high concentration of economic power would have some debilitating effects. Finally, encapsulation requires maintaining a normative prohibition, built into the codes and traditions of the executive branch, enforced by the courts and legislatures, against the use of the capsule-sustaining power to affect the outcomes of competition.

These prerequisites are to be viewed as variables in that they are rarely, if ever, perfectly met or completely absent, and in that whatever their specific scores, they still affect the various attributes of encapsulated competition. For example, a rather weak government will permit a relatively high degree of monopolistic behavior and a high level of political corruption in the sense of political power being captured by private interests. Such behavior will tend to undermine the capsule because some participants in the competition will be able to neutralize, deflect, or make work in their favor the very mechanisms that are supposed to be applied evenly to all participants. This, in turn, will tend to weaken the legitimization of the capsule. A very powerful government will tend to act in areas in which it was not granted a legitimate role, and will thus constrict the scope of activities set aside for competition, undermining the instrumental rationality of the system and potentially its legitimacy. Only when the various variables are within the proper ranges can competition be both sustained and contained.

The issues discussed here appear in the political science literature, and in somewhat different terms in the polity and public parlance, but the issues, at least as the author sees them, are basically the same. One issue is the role of interest groups. While the public tends to condemn them, many political scientists tend to see them as part of the pluralistic society, a source of extra-constitutional representation. Indeed, some political scientists go so far as to deny their ability to formulate a shared public interest, and see the polity merely as an arena in which various interest groups vie for their share (for further discussion and references, see Etzioni 1984a).

From the viewpoint of the theory evolved here, pluralism requires a countervailing factor of unity, a community or nation-wide We, to balance the multiple particular interests, the group-level Me-isms. There is, hence, both a plurality of particular interests and a general, public, interest. Both are legitimate, as long as they do not invade each other's realms.

The same basic issue is addressed in the sociological literature on conflict (or class) theories versus community (powerless) ones. Conflict theories stress the significance of the struggle among various collectives, and often reject the concept of a shared society just the way some Whigish political scientists see no justification for the concept of the public interest. In contrast, the community approach stresses the role of shared values and sees well-formed societies in "equilibrium" (the way neoclassicists see the unfettered market), and view all other forces as "divisive" and "disruptive." We see room for conflicts *within* a community; classes *within* society. And while any one societal structure or equilibrium may be upset, society as a community needs to be maintained as a context for the particular collectivities, to encapsulate conflict, to avoid total war. In short, structures may be changed but society can not be avoided.

IN CONCLUSION

The search for socio-economic models of competition draws on a core idea: actors are not necessarily in harmony with one another; and competition is actually a form of conflict—contained conflict. The containing capsule, within which competition is free to range, is composed of normative, social, and governmental mechanisms each working on its own and interacting with the others. Their strength varies from being too weak to discharge their mission, to being too powerful, going beyond limiting conflicts to suppressing competition. The conditions under which the capsule is appropriately potent, without being excessively restrictive, are only beginning to be understood. The internal structure of the system is clearly a key factor. Power relations among the contestants in realms other than those in which the contest takes place—the polity rather than the economy—is a key element of the structure, a subject the discussion focuses on next.

13

Political Power and Intra-Market Structures

The economic literature is replete with references to distortions the government causes in the market. Comparable attention should be paid to manipulations of the government by participants in the market, and the effects of these manipulations on the internal structures of markets. A major way these manipulations are carried out is for corporations, banks, farmers, and labor unions to use their *political* power to significantly and systematically affect the outcomes of market transactions. Aside from being a significant factor in its own right, explaining a good part of what happens in the market, we shall see that the same phenomenon also serves to illustrate a major contribution of the deontological I&We paradigm to socio-economic theory: calling attention to the significance of structures (in contrast to aggregates); in the case at hand, to the structure of power relations among the market participants.

The observation that powerful economic actors use their power not only directly in the market, but also indirectly, by influencing government interventions in the market, has been made in several areas of economic behavior. Schattsneider (1935) finds that tariffs were set not in line with some economic logic, but that they reflected the results of a political struggle between some businesses and others that were less politically adept. Stigler (1971) argues that the regulatory policies of a government often represent not the public's needs but those of powerful economic units. A significant body of economic literature has further substantiated and developed this thesis (Peltzman 1976; Pashigian 1984, pp. 1–24; Toma 1983, pp. 103–16; and Kim, 1984, pp. 227–39). Finally, a literature on "rent"-seeking (Tullock 1967; Krueger 1974; Posner 1975; and Buchanan, Tollinson, and Tullock 1980) analyzes the societal costs that are caused by economic actors seeking favors from the government: Above and beyond distortions that government interventions cause in the market place, resources are wasted in competing over who will gain governmental favors.

217

Here, this line of analysis is extended to the study of power relations within the economy, among corporations, between them and banks, labor unions, farmers, and so on. Specifically, we shall see that the manipulation of the government by powerful economic actors generates *pseudo-concentration* effects; i.e., effects comparable to those caused by a concentration of economic power, by monopolies, or by oligopolistic collusion —without there being necessarily any actual concentration of economic power or collusion among economic actors. By contrast, the neoclassical literature on the subject focuses almost exclusively on intra-economic, and not on political, means for gaining monopolistic profits. In short, to understand the transactions *within* the economy one must understand its inner *political* structure—the power that various economic actors have over one another because they are able, more effectively than other actors, to mobilize the government to help them in their intramarket relations with others.

In the following discussion we show, first, how the neoclassical paradigm leaves out half of the story: The use of political means for monopolistic goals. This "interventionist" power of powerful economic actors is then systematically explained and its relations to economic power are explored. This leads us to ask to what extent the American economy is competitive, once one takes into account the application of both economic *and* political power. The chapter closes with an analysis of the means suggested to enhance the encapsulation of the market, and to protect it from the political power of its own players, not just from that of the government.

THE STRUCTURE OF ECONOMIC POWER IN THE NEOCLASSICAL PARADIGM

In the neoclassical paradigm there is no room for the concept of power. Says Stigler (1968, p. 181): "The essence of perfect competition is . . . the utter dispersion of power." He adds that power is "annihilated . . . just as a gallon of water is effectively annihilated if it is spread over a thousand acres." (See also Swedberg et al. 1985, p. 21.) However, even neoclassicists recognize, in the literature on what they call "industrial organization," that in conducting analysis of economic transactions in any system that even remotely resembles the real world, one must take into account that some sellers or buyers have varying measures of economic power. This is often defined as an ability to raise prices above marginal costs and hence attain a larger profit than would be possible in unfettered competition. The resulting so-called monopolistic profits are described either as the consequence of economic power or an indication that it is present.

The ability to control the market (i.e., to set prices) to one extent or another, is referred to as "industrial organization," meaning concentration of economic power. While a small firm cannot command economic power, a buyer or seller who is large, as compared to the total market size, can. Blocking the entry of potential competitors is often listed as an important corollary power to the ability to set prices; without it, control of market shares may not last long, especially if entry costs are low compared to potential profits (Baumol, Panzar, Willig 1982; Shepherd 1982, p. 616; Greer 1980, pp. 111–12; and Needham 1969, p. 84).

When there is only one single seller or only one single buyer—i.e., when one actor commands 100 percent of the market—they are said to command monopolistic or monopsonistic power. When there are but a few buyers or sellers, they are expected at least to command such power *in potentia* (depending on whether or not they collude). Indeed, when a group of oligopolistic firms actually collude with one another they are sometimes referred to as a shared monopoly. Most studies of oligopolistic behavior proceed from these starting points to examine the strategies that lead some firms to cooperate while others do not, and also to examine the means used to cooperate as well as to block new entries into "their" market.

The strategies and means typically studied tend to be intra-economic: they are employed by economic actors using economic means to economic ends. Strategies are devised and applied by corporate staff (executives), or those retained by them (e.g., their lawyers). The means employed may entail predatory pricing, price leadership, advertising campaigns, "early" marketing of new products, overt and covert agreements, rule of thumb pricing, and so on (Scherer 1980, Chapter 6). An excellent study of the means used by "dominant" firms emphasizes the role of non-price strategies, including product proliferation, R&D, vertical integration, diversification, and distribution channels (White 1983). Even the heretical analysis of Galbraith (1967) focuses on the intra-market power of large firms, which are said through advertising and planning to shape and control consumer demands rather than respond to them. In short, *although the study of "industrial organization" (or economic concentration) moves neoclassical economic analysis from the models of perfect competition closer to reality, it still basically treats the economy as a world set apart, free from political factors,* in the transactions and relations among the economic actors.

Moreover, the government is typically considered in this context as the source of antitrust policies, that is, as a force that seeks to limit the concentration of economic power in order to foster competition. McConnell (1975, p. 102) points out that "the government assumes the task of providing the legal framework and certain basic services prerequisite to the effective operation of a market economy." And according to Navarro (1984, p. 7) "A second model, that of market failure, is the proud child of economists. It portrays the government as a benevolent *deus ex machina* [whose role is] ... to correct these imperfections or 'market failures'."

The government in such discussions is typically not considered as a main source of "industrial organization" (beyond such legal acts as granting patents and issuing license and some effects of government procurement), nor as a major means that corporations use to form and to maintain economic concentrations, a way of forming monopolies and oligopolies. In contrast, we shall see that the government provides a commonly used and highly effective way of capturing and holding on to market shares, of curbing the entry of competitors, and an avenue for collusion, to make some economic actors powerful. (The term "powerful economic actors" hence refers to economic units, whether they be firms, labor unions, or trade associations, who command power over the market, whether its source is economic or political; it contrasts with competitive economic actors.)

To the extent that the use of the government by powerful economic actors is ignored, the analysis also disregards one of the most effective ways of gaining so-called excessive profits, *not by setting prices above marginal costs,* but by charging market prices and *using the government to acquire one or more input factors at costs substantially below those that competitors must pay.* These include gaining capital at below the market interest rates, for instance via industrial development bonds; tax exemptions or tax credits that are tailored to a particular firm or industry; cheap labor via government financed "work-study," training, and other such programs; and exemptions from laws or regulations such as those concerning the minimum wage or immigration; out-right subsidies; rights to benefit commercially from government financed R&D; purchase of government assets at fire-sale prices, and accelerated depreciation schedules which favor some industries over others (e.g., capital intensive versus service).

Reference is not to the frequently discussed market "distortions" but to the use of the government by some powerful economic actors to enhance their profit as compared to that of those who are weaker. Typically, 84 percent of the billions in tax benefits provided by the Domestic International Sales Corporation (DISC), to encourage exports of American manufactured goods, accrue to corporations whose assets exceed $100 million (Lang 1977, p. 7). Gaining "excessive" profits in this way, rather than by driving prices up, makes the gain less visible, which is desirable for the beneficiaries of such power in the political intensive economy. (For similar reasons, direct subsidies, which economic analysis prefers to tax exemptions, are considered politically less advantageous).

Last but not least, the focus on intra-economic means to the neglect of political ones, causes one to reach erroneous conclusions about the extent to which an economy is competitive. For example, when concentration ratios are used as a measure of the competitiveness of the American economy, it is possible to argue that it is largely competitive. However, when one also studies the use of political means to curtail competition, the picture, we shall see, changes significantly.

INTERVENTIONIST POWER

The vast neoclassical literature on the ill effects of government interventions in the market pays relatively little attention, for good reason, to the forces that drive the government to intervene. For many analytic purposes it does not matter if the government intervenes in order to enhance beauty or justice, or to help some corporations in their competition with others; the resulting market "distortions" are the same whatever the motive (with the important exception, said to be limited in scope, when the government acts to correct free-market "failures"). It is hence common to refer to the government without asking who drives it.

To the extent that there is discussion as to who is behind the government's interventions, it tends to focus on emerging social groups, such as minorities and women, and their inflationary demands (Bell 1975, p. 100; Friedman 1982, p. 23), politicians and bureaucrats (Downs 1967; Niskanen 1971), and special interest groups (Olson 1982). And the studies typically seek to explain the scope of government activities, and the distorting effects such activities have on the market, rather than their effects on the relations among economic actors (see, for example, Epstein 1969). Important exceptions are the work of Schattsneider, Stigler, and some others who studied the use of government tariffs and regulation by powerful economic units to their economic ends.

Political power is the ability of non-governmental actors to guide the government. The term assumes that the direction the government takes is *in part* determined by external factors. (Internal factors include values and goals to which the government or its staff are committed for moral or ideological reasons, and also include the self-interests of politicians and bureaucrats.) In naive democratic theory, political power is assumed to be evenly distributed among all citizens: "one person, one vote"; however this is hardly the way the political system actually works (Lowi 1969, Ornstein and Elder 1978). In all polities, political power is unevenly distributed within society and among economic actors. In democracies each person may have a vote; however, various economic actors command large parts of the resources necessary to inform, educate, persuade, and mobilize the voters. Most importantly, numerous government decisions are made between elections in consultation with and under the influence of economic interest groups, unbeknown to most voters and not subject to their approval.

While it is true that to some extent the various wielders of political power neutralize one another because they pull in opposing directions, it does not follow that therefore political power will have no net effect

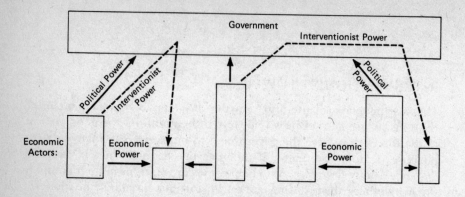

(cf. Key 1958 and Thurow 1980), or mainly a stalemating one (Riesman 1950, pp. 244–48). *No two groups have the same amount of political power, and hence a net tilt results from the tug of war among the various groups. Moreover, often a group has hegemony in one limited area:* for instance, the National Rifle Association over gun control, and farm lobbies, for many years, over farm subsidies.

The scope of the usages of political power is vast. It may be used to support various items of the so-called social agenda (such as abortion), foreign policy (such as support for the IRA), and scores of other matters which are basically not economic in nature. At issue here is the use of political power by *economic actors* for *economic purposes*. When one refers to political power, conventions of the language lead us to think of the power used by the government, or power used to influence the government. To keep attention focused on the use of governmental power by economic actors for their ends, the term *interventionist power* may be used. Corporate interventionist power refers to the use *of* the government *by* corporations to interfere in the economy in line with their goals. The term applies equally to other interest groups, so one can speak of the interventionist power of labor unions, farmers, and of associations of consumers (see chart).

Most of the literature on the subject deals with the political power that corporations and other economic interest groups exercise on behalf of ideological goals (e.g., supporting conservative candidates), and policies generally favorable to business (e.g., lower taxations on corporations), rather than specific *economic* goals that advantage the particular corporation in the market. (For a rich review of the literature see Salamon and Siegfried 1977. See also Epstein 1969.) And not all of the few who study the use of political power for economic ends find clear-cut effects. The findings of those who established effects are illustrated by Jacobs (Jacobs, forthcoming) and Salamon and Siegfried (1977, pp. 1035–36) who found correlations between the political power of corporations and the attainment of special tax rates.

ECONOMIC CONCENTRATION AND
INTERVENTIONIST POWER

The two most important observations about the application of interventionist power are: (1) its exercise generates *economic* consequences comparable in magnitude to those gained through the exercise of economic power (by one economic actor over others), and (2) interventionist power can be applied *whether or not the actor commands economic power.* Thus, the term calls attention to the ability of a firm to control large shares of the market without its being a large or dominant firm; to a firm's ability to block the entry of competitors into a market even though the powerful firm is not a monopoly or an oligopolistic firm; and to a firm's ability to generate "excessive" profits without raising prices above those that would be set by perfectly competitive markets. In short, *economic actors can, by the use of political means, achieve various effects often attributed to concentration of economic power.*

The theorem just stated is in opposition to the Marxist notion that political power merely or largely reflects economic power. While it is true that if an actor commands economic power it might be converted into interventionist power, economic power is *not a prerequisite* for interventionist power, and interventionist power is often the *source* of economic power. While many actors command both kinds of power, there is *no necessary* correlation between the two.

There are three basic forms of distribution of interventionist power: pluralism, oligarchy, and hegemony. Pluralism occurs when political power is more or less evenly distributed among a large number of actors. Democracy is said by many political scientists to be pluralistic because the government responds to the demands of a large variety of politically active groups. Pluralism occurs in an industry in which there are a large number of firms, and none commands significantly disproportionate political power. For example, if all might give roughly the same campaign contributions or have comparable lobbyists working for them, and so on. Under these circumstances, little or no interventionist power is generated because all the actors command the same (or similar) ability to "direct" the government and hence none can use it to disadvantage the others. (Theoretically it is possible for an industry to be without internal power differences but still be powerful in its acts as a group vis-à-vis other industries. Actually this rarely happens and this possibility is not further explored in this preliminary effort. The same holds for other possible differences between intra- and inter-industry "organization.")

Oligarchy occurs when political power is concentrated in the hands of a few actors. The church, army, and the aristocracy in nineteenth century authoritarian societies were oligarchic. Interventionist oligarchy exists when a small number of economic actors command most or all the political power generated in a specific area. For instance, to the extent that large oil corporations command most of the political power of the industry (Engler 1961), while little is in the hands of numerous small independent producers, this industry's interventionist structure is that of an oligarchy.

Hegemony exists when political power is largely concentrated in the hands of one actor (Keohane 1984). Such an actor is often referred to as the power elite. Interventionist hegemony occurred in earlier ages, when an exclusive right was granted to one economic actor to issue currency (frequently, a private bank), or to collect taxes.

At first it would seem that these interventionist modes—of singular, selective, and dispersed power—parallel those of well-known concepts of economic power, monopoly (and monopsony), oligopoly (and oligopsony), and competitive markets. However, according to the thesis advanced here, *there is no necessary correlation between the three forms of economic power and those of interventionist power;* all nine possible combinations are encountered (see following table). Moreover, variations in the specific combinations yield specific predictable dynamics.

(1) *Economic and intervention based monopolies.* In line with the analysis advanced here, there are three quite different kinds of monopolies: those based on economic power (type #7); those that are based on government intervention gained by one economic actor among many (type #3); and double-based monopoly that draws on both kinds of power, economic as well as interventionist (type #9). (Firms that are economic monopolies but share their interventionist power with a few other economic actors— e.g., relations between monopolistic firms and closed-shop labor unions, type #8—raise issues not pursued here.)

A situation in which an economic actor is in a highly competitive business with little or no economic power, but commands interventionist hegemony (type #3) is illustrated by an account of the business of one arms dealer in Libya. Edwin Wilson was selling weapons to Libya for numer-

A Typology of Power

	Interventionist Power		
	PLURALISM	*OLIGARCHY*	*HEGEMONY*
Economic Power			
Competitive Markets	1	2	3
Oligopoly	4	5	6
Monopoly	7	8	9

ous years at a 100 percent to 200 percent mark up despite the fact that many other arms dealers were bidding for the business of the same generals, and it was relatively easy to enter the business: No production capacity or weapon stockpiles or a track record were required (Goulden 1984). Nor was there collusion among most of the dealers. When a single buyer faces numerous independent sellers such a profit is not the expected outcome. Wilson was able to garner such profits because he had won and kept the support of the general in charge of acquisitions. Bribes were paid or offered by many dealers; Wilson's bribes were not lavish; at best they were "competitive." The suggestion that it was "rational" for the general to pay millions above the market because he knew Wilson as a reliable source flies in the face of the fact that Wilson regularly delivered junk. His powers were those of persuasion and of a con man. For the delivery of certain categories of arms, Wilson may be said to have created a pure *intervention-based monopoly.* (The term legal monopoly is avoided because the means used are often illegal or non-legal.)

The standard account in economic literature of how a monopoly is created and maintained deals with type #7, the monopoly based on economic power; according to Demsetz (1974, p. 164) it "conceives of monopoly power as producible by a firm or an industry without any substantial aid from the government." While it matters little to economic analysis how monopolies are actually historically formed, a heuristic tale is often used. It concerns the first mover: In a situation in which a new product or service requires large capital outlays, whoever makes these investments first is said to be likely to incur monopolistic profits. (For discussion of "the advantages of being first" and reference to several other works, see Glazer 1985. See also Smiley and Ravid 1981.) Other ways of forming or maintaining a monopoly, whether or not by moving first, are said to include controlling essential raw material. (Alcoa controlled the sources of bauxite in the United States and was the sole producer of aluminum from the late nineteenth century until the 1940s; Browning and Browning 1983, p. 305.) Another way is to build up consumer loyalty to a product (Kamerschen and Valentine 1981, p. 309).

Such intra-economic developments of monopolistic power do occur; however, they seem to be much less common than is often implied. As we see it, initially one of many competitive economic actors gains a monopolistic position by political means. For example, labor unions gain the exclusive right to represent the workers in a given firm, via elections supervised by a government agency (NLRB), drawing on a right that the state grants and enforces, which in turn is the result of political pressure by organized labor on the government. Obviously, the ability to monopolize the representation of labor in a firm or in an industry is much lower when this right does not exist.

Competition over gaining a cable TV franchise is potentially fierce precisely because once a firm lays its wires it is rather difficult for another firm to enter the market, and the profits are high. It is widely believed in the industry that many of the cable TV franchises accorded by local governments in the United States over the last two decades were awarded on the basis of illicit political deals, the most common of which is bribery. It is said typically to take the form of granting a hefty legal fee to a law firm with which the mayor (or another city authority) was affiliated before taking office, while only minimal legal work is entailed.

While theoretically all those who seek such a franchise might compete over who bribes the most, and a market of sorts would be created, in effect many firms refuse to engage in such business practices (Phelps 1975, pp. 3ff.) and others do not know the local ropes. Often only actors are "acceptable" who can be trusted, on the basis of close personal and social ties, or a long history of illicit deals. When only one of several competing firms "qualifies" to bribe, we face a situation of interventionist hegemony *without* prior concentration of economic power.

While interventionist power is often considerable on the national level, it tends to be higher on the state and local level. One may debate how much political clout the auto industry commands in Washington, but it is obviously higher in Michigan, and still higher in Detroit. Similarly, the DuPont power in Delaware is considerably higher than it is in the national capital, and so on. This is the case both because there are fewer "countervailing" forces on the local than on a national level, and because of the relative size of large corporations to a state versus their standing in the nation. In addition, corporations are frequently able to extract significant benefits from state and local governments by threatening to leave or by promising to move in. An indication of the higher susceptibility of local and state governments to interventionist power, as compared to the federal government, is seen in that many corporations prefer that safety, health, and other regulations be locally set and/or enforced than for them to be federally imposed.

Many monopolies that have been politically initiated, and that also acquire the economic features of a monopoly, constitute double-based monopolies (type #9). For instance, a firm that commands much political clout may expand its share of the market to the point it can also deter potential competitors by keeping prices low, or by committing a large amount of resources to raise the entry costs for competitors (say by heavy advertising), or by using other economic means to further enhance its power, rather than relying only on government interventions.

The different types of monopolies seem to differ systematically in their stability. Economic actors who rely exclusively or largely on either economic or interventionist power tend to find their preferred position relatively unstable, while the position of those that command both kinds of power seems to be more sustainable. As a result, *economic actors that command only one kind of power are expected to seek to acquire the other.* Those intervention-based monopolies that gain no or little economic power are expected to be inherently unstable because a change of those in office, or the entry into their markets of new politically powerful actors, will break their hegemonic power. This is the case when a firm has an exclusive franchise to operate a gift shop, bookstore, hotel, or restaurant in a given public territory (e.g., national park) but there is relatively little investment, or the capital goods belong to the institution. Under these circumstances, the authorities in charge can quite readily drop one firm, either at the end of a contract period or following notice, and award the franchise to another.

When their are pure economic monopolies without an interventionist base, their monopolistic profits are expected to be particularly difficult to sustain, and hence the pressure builds to move from this type to the double-based monopoly. Indeed, the author is hard put to find examples of pure economic monopolies so often described in economic literature. All those examined seem to rely on at least some measure of interventionist power, at least in some stage of their development.

Public utilities, for example, are often referred to as natural monopolies (because of the high capital costs), and also as regulated monopolies. To the extent that regulation limits their ability to raise prices (or rates) or curb their profits, these utilities might still be conceived as economic, and not as political-economic, monopolies. In these situations, political power is used not by utilities to secure their monopolistic position, but by the public, to curb it. However, regulation is also used to maintain the monopolistic status. Indeed, Stigler (1962) first developed his "capture" theory (i.e., that regulations are "captured" by special interests) in a study of public utilities. In short, "pure" economic monopolies (type #7) are logically possible but seem rare and unstable; on the other hand, monopolies based on political and economic power are common and stable.

(2) *The Interventionist Powers of Oligopolies* (# 4, 5, 6). Neoclassical economists have concerned themselves with the question of under what conditions oligopolistic firms collude rather than compete with one another. In the first case, they are likely to behave more like monopolies; in the second case, more like small firms. The strategies and means oligopolistic firms use are scrutinized in efforts to discern the factors that lead toward collusion versus conflict. However, these typically include only non-political means. Scherer (1980, Chapter 6) lists overt and covert agreements, price leadership, "rule-of-thumb pricing," "focal points and tacit coordination," and manipulation of the level of backlogs and inventories. Koch (1980, pp. 375–85) focuses on price leadership and basing-point pricing.

The present analysis suggests that the kind of interventionist power that firms command *as a group,* compared to other politically active actors, is a key factor in determining the outcome. From this viewpoint there are three kinds of groups of oligopolistic firms: those with little or no interventionist power (type #4); those with some interventionist power that they must share with some other such group or groups (type

#5), and those with interventionist hegemony in their particular industry or economic sector (type #6). All other things equal, the first kind are least likely to reap monopolistic profits, the last are the most likely, and the middle—an intermediate level, because the lower the level of shared interventionist power, the lower the ability to use the government to ensure special privileges, subsidies, and so on—the source of "extra" profits.

To illustrate: A major way oligopolistic firms block entries into their markets, secure monopolistic profits and collaboration with one another, is by jointly inducing the government to limit imports (by introducing quotas, tariffs, trigger prices), or by eliciting voluntary quotas from exporting countries. The extent to which this is achieved is in part a matter of a *group's* relative interventionist power. Thus, in the United States, oligopolistic auto makers had more political clout and hence were more able to limit imports (through "voluntary" import quotas) in 1984 than copper makers (although the latter's arguments per se are reported also to have been weaker). As a result one would expect the auto industry to garner more "monopolistic" returns than the copper industry. (While neoclassical economists tend to treat firms as autonomous, others have stressed the role of interlocking directorships as a way to generate the equivalent of collusion, to enhance coordination and profits. (Useem 1979; Burt 1983.)

(3) *The interventionist powers of firms in competitive markets* (types #1, 2, 3). The mutually supportive nature of pluralism and competitive markets, between free markets (free, among other things, from economic concentrations and from government intervention) and political freedom (free from political oppression), has been frequently pointed out (Friedman 1962; Novak 1982; Berger 1986). However, being a small firm in a big market does not ensure that such a firm will behave as expected, will compete efficiently, or be wiped out. Some firms that are small and command no economic power still use their interventionist power to generate oligarchies or gain hegemony by forming or joining groups of firms, or even by acting as individual firms. This may be one reason the correlation between economic concentration (as measured by size) and the level of profits is rather weak (Demsetz 1974, pp. 168ff): industries that economists consider not concentrated nevertheless gain "excessive" profits by the use of political means. Farming is a case in point.

Farming is often cited as a highly competitive industry. In a discussion of the attributes of perfect competition Stigler (1968, p. 181) writes: "The fortunes of any one firm are independent of what happens to any other firm: one farmer is not benefited if his neighbor's crop is destroyed." Using several measurements, especially market shares and concentration ratios, Shepherd (1982, p. 618) scored American agriculture, forestry, and fisheries as 86 percent competitive in 1980. Indeed, many farms are, economically speaking, small. However, it is well known that farmers use their political power to set prices and improve their return by gaining subsidies, and credit below market terms, and by limiting entry into their markets (via import quotas). They clearly have much power; only, it is political, not economic.

Whether farms are to be classified as interventionist oligarchies (type #2) or an interventionist hegemony (type #3) is largely a question of the extent to which the main farmers' organizations pull together, or under-cut one another. In either case there is little difference between a mass of small farmers acting together as one political body (or two) and a mo-nopolistic firm, according to an often-applied criterion to determine the existence of a monopoly: the ability to set prices and to block entries. (The fact that farmers, and other monopolies, may not garner high profits but merely stay in business when they otherwise would be driven out, or merely ensure themselves a disproportionate return, is a technical point.)

Similarly, hiring and promotion quota-systems that are politically im-posed tend to generate interventionist oligarchies (type #2), in that dis-persed categories of individuals who have little economic power—such as women and minorities—can gain, via Affirmative Action, preference in access to certain categories of jobs. Agreements, whether formal or informal, to allot staff positions among professionals in a hospital ac-cording to quotas (X to physicians, Y to nurses, Z to nurses aides) to the exclusion of others (midwives, medics, and chiropractors) are another case in point. Such allocative agreements may be due in part to non-political considerations such as proven medical merit and relative cost; interventionist power is at work to the extent that such allocations reflect relative political clout, and that what is affected is economic outcomes.

ECONOMIC AND INTERVENTIONIST POWER COMPARED

So far the use of economic power and that of interventionist power have been treated as interchangeable and/or complementary means to the same ends. Thus, a firm may use its resources to block the entry of another firm by launching a major advertising campaign, and/or by sup-porting politicians who will pass a law to a comparable effect. The discus-sion turns now to examine systematic differences between the two kinds of power. The most important difference is that legitimization and non-economic actors are much more important in the polity than in the economy.

Legitimization refers to a deontological factor, the role of values. While legitimization is a factor in both intra-economic activities and in those that are political, it is much stronger in the polity. Public officials are held to more and higher standards than are corporate executives. For instance, high-level public officials must disclose the sources of their income, are strictly limited in accepting gifts, their perks are often care-fully scrutinized, and so on.

Noneconomic actors, who actively and effectively participate in the polity, are groups whose *main* status base, association, and organization are social, cultural, or political activities. These include religious organi-zations, ethnic and racial associations, lobbies for senior citizens, and scores of others. These actors attenuate economic power in the political realm.

As a result of both factors, *in the polity a less inegalitarian distribution of benefits is considered preferable to a more inegalitarian distribution;* there is a tendency to provide at least some benefits or pay-offs to actors who com-mand neither economic nor interventionist power. That is, *when a transac-tion is carried out within the polity as compared to in a concentrated sector of the economy, on average the benefits are more widely and more evenly distributed.* For example, says Stigler (1971, p. 7), "small firms [in a regulated industry] have a larger influence than they would possess in an unregulated indus-try." Wilson (1980, p. ix) adds that not only smaller economic powers are cut in, "but if the 'capture' theory is correct—at least in some cases—it is unreasonable to assume that only business firms would be able to cap-ture an agency." Environmentalists, civil rights activists, and even aca-demics, occasionally, "capture" parts of the government's manna, that is, use their political power to extract benefits for their group.

Because of the higher visibility of the average interventionist (political-economic) acts as compared to intra-economic ones, garnering a dispro-portionate amount of benefits tends to have a higher cost in the polity than it does in the economy. In the economy, at least until concentrations become very large, they are considered legitimate by most; indeed, econ-omies of scale are viewed, up to a point, as necessary for modernity and as a reward for risk-taking, investment, and hard work. However, in the political democratic realm, the value of "one-person, one-vote" is widely held, and the ideal is upheld that all players will be treated equally, or the weakest be advantaged. Hence, in the polity more than in the economy, a concentration of power or of benefits tends to raise criticism and pres-sures to "level" the distributions.

The normative censure attached to extensive submission to interven-tionist power is reflected in the following observations: Members of Con-gress who are known for unusual integrity or who are especially opposed to private financing of election campaigns, a major source of interven-tionist power, limit the campaign contributions they will accept from any one source to $25 to $50. Some others set the limit at $250. Similarly, many corporations do not form PACs at all, in part because of their con-troversial nature. Thus, while it is quite legal for a corporation to form a PAC, a major way to elicit favors from politicians by raising campaign contributions for them, there were fewer than 4,000 corporate PACs by 1987; that is, most corporations did not form any. (PAC-less corporations included numerous corporations comparable in the kind of business, size, and many other attributes to those that did form PACs. I.e., these interests are comparable to those that form PACs but their political posture is different, for reasons not explored here, but seemingly due to their differences in corporate "culture" or values.) Of those corporations that do form PACs, most try to keep a low profile by contributing to politicians less than the legal limit. Large contributions call attention to themselves. Newspapers, Common Cause, and Congress Watch (a Nader group) regularly publish lists of the largest PACs (most of which are economic actors, such as defense contractors, banks, select industries, and labor unions).

The question may be raised: why would those who command a great measure of economic power resort to the polity at all, if they are relatively disadvantaged in this realm? In part, the polity provides ways to build up and to protect their special position, ways that are not available within the economy. Also, up to a point, *interventionist power is comparatively inexpensive and can be highly effective in cost/benefit terms.* The costs of lobbying and organizing a PAC for a politically active corporation are much lower than costs of R&D advertising campaigns or other economic means that may be used to attain comparable purposes, and often seem to be highly effective in comparison.

Because of data limitations one can gain only a rough estimate of the comparable costs of interventionist and economic power. One can still reach a judgment because the amounts involved are of a very different order of magnitude. For example, in 1979 the Carter Administration introduced a bill aiming to cap hospital costs and physicians fees. It was expected to reduce health expenditures by $40 billion. There was a high correlation between the members of Congress who received campaign contributions from the PAC of the American Medical Association and those who voted against the bill and defeated it. Of the 50 members who received the highest contributions, 48 voted against the bill (Etzioni 1984a). In toto, those who voted against the bill received 3.5 times more contributions than those who favored it. However the total costs to the PAC were very small: $1,647,897. Even if one would double or triple the estimate of the costs involved, they still would amount to less than a fraction of one percent of the revenues at stake. (The fact that members of Congress had other reasons, philosophical for instance, for supporting the AMA are irrelevant; these reasons had no cost for the AMA and were believed by the AMA not to suffice by themselves.)

Subsidies paid to dairy farmers under the price support system in FY 1982 amounted to roughly $2 billion. A 1981 proposal to reduce those benefits by $600 million over four years was defeated. Those who voted against the bill in the House received eight times more contributions from the principal dairy PACs than those who favored it. While the average contribution to those who voted against the bill was only $1,600, the total amount was $385,260 (Public Citizen's Congress Watch 1982, p. 6). The costs to Chrysler for a $1.5 billion federal loan guarantee without which it almost certainly would have had to declare bankruptcy, the costs to American auto makers for the $6 billion in revenues they gained in 1984 alone as a result of "voluntary" important limitations, and the costs to get $13 billion tax forgiveness for exporters (Brown 1983, p. 158), amounted to less than one percent of the added revenues to the extent that the size of such costs can be estimated. In short, despite the rapidly rising cost of politics, it is a dirt-cheap business. Compare, for instance, the costs just cited to the R&D or advertising costs, two major economic ways to create or maintain a monopoly. The R&D or advertising costs of several of the larger *single* American corporations exceed the total amounts raised to finance the primary and general 1981–82 election campaigns for both the House and the Senate, from all sources (individuals and interest groups) which amounted to $356.7 million.

While the unit costs of interventionist power are low, it has a sharply declining marginal benefit; indeed, negative returns can quickly be reached. Otherwise why would oil companies, fighting in 1974 to reduce a windfall profits tax initially estimated to run to near $400 billion over ten years, spend only a few million on lobbying and campaign contributions, instead of a billion or two, which would have exceeded spending by all other sources combined? The answer seems to be that the oil companies gained a hefty tax cut (initially, $228 billion; lower levels later) at a low cost, and that a higher exercise of interventionist power would have raised the risk of a public backlash. It hence seemed prudent to accept the remaining tax and not to endanger the gigantic cut already in hand. That is, to reduce visibility, and to maintain their claims to be "legitimate" interests, economic actors tend to participate in the polity at a low level.

THE COMPETITIVENESS LEVEL OF THE AMERICAN ECONOMY

How competitive is the American economy? The answer to that question changes significantly when one takes into account the effects of interventionist power in addition to that of economic power. Shepherd's study serves as a useful starting point for such a comparison. Shepherd (1982, p. 624) concludes that by 1980 competition was "pervasive" in the American economy. Pure monopoly and dominant firms accounted for about 5 percent of the economy; "tight" oligopoly for about 20 percent, "while the effectively competitive markets now [1980] account for over three-fourths of national income."

While Shepherd uses several criteria for categorizing each industry, he seems to give more weight to the concentration indicators that are relatively easy to measure, than he does to the efforts to block entry or to "excessive" profits, items that are more difficult to assess. (The weight he gave to various indicators is stated to be his judgment; 1982, p. 617.) As the first indicator is largely intra-economic, the other two reflect the result of both economic and interventionist power; according more weight to the first will tend to make the American economy seem more competitive than it actually is.

An examination of Shepherd's data suggests that the gaining of monopolistic profits by means of interventionist power have been insufficiently taken into account. For instance, "agriculture, forestry, and fisheries" are categorized as 86.4 percent competitive, but this disregards the farmers' interventionist power cited earlier. For example, the ability to keep sugar prices at levels *three times* the world market is bound to have a significant effect on the returns from cane and beet farming.

Steel, auto, and textile interventionist power in 1980 was also quite substantial. However, Shepherd classifies the manufacturing sector in 1980 as 69 percent competitive. Similarly, in view of the high extent of regulation and other forms of restraint of competition, an analysis that would take into account interventionist power is unlikely to classify transportation and public utilities as 40 percent competitive. Indeed, once the effects of interventionist power are added to those of economic power, much of the American economy is unlikely to be classified as highly competitive.

Shepherd (1982, p. 624) also argues that there was a substantial increase in competition from 1958 to 1980, and suggests that this should be reflected in higher economic performance "in the next decade or two." Rather than wait until the year 2000, it might be noted now that in the decades competition is said to have substantially increased, the growth of American GNP slowed, productivity growth declined sharply, and inflation and unemployment increased. This is more compatible with the thesis that whatever progress was achieved on the economic front, in reducing economic concentration and thus economic power (e.g., by some deregulation), that progress was more than offset by the increased use of interventionist power to restrain competition via the polity.

Adding consideration of the role of interventionist power in sustaining monopolistic behavior to that of economic power may also serve to correct a neoclassical view of the ease by which new entries are achieved into "contestable" markets. In recent years some neoclassicists have argued that monopolistic tendencies are curbed, and the need for anti-trust policies is significantly reduced, because monopolistic firms must "price at cost" or close to it to keep potential competitors out, under various economic conditions not discussed here (Baumol, Panzar, Willig 1982, pp. 4–8; Brock 1983, p. 1055). Others have argued that while new entries can be hindered by economic means (e.g., predatory pricing), these are costly and hence often cannot be maintained for long, and that if the monopolistic profits exceed the entry costs, new competitors will rush in. This line of analysis either disregards the low costs at which political protection (blocking of entry) often can be purchased by powerful economic actors, or erroneously assumes that the market in political protection is highly competitive, while actually it too is a concentrated market.

Aside from being of considerable interest to those concerned with understanding their society or acting within it, the extent to which the economy is not following the rules of competition is of significance for the application of economic theory. Neoclassical economists frequently argue that the economy is sufficiently competitive to apply perfect competition models (ignoring the "second best" findings). If, however, many economic sectors are in considerable measure monopolized and run by oligopolies, while some others are more competitive sectors; if, that is, there is a "mixed" economy even in the United States, and not just in the so-called social-democratic countries, then a rather different model of the economy is needed, and much of prevailing economic analysis and policy recommendations must be reformulated.

ANALYSIS OF CORRECTIVES

Reduce Economic Concentration and/or Interventionist Power

The most often repeated policy recommendation for curbing monopolistic tendencies has been to reduce the concentrations of economic power, to break up big economic actors (AT&T, for example) and to keep economic actors small. (The flat power profile of "democratic industrial society" is analyzed by Grossman 1974, p. 170). This, in turn, has led to a considerable literature on the specific features and effects of various antitrust policies. Without delving into this literature it seems that the recent consensus of many students of antitrust policies is that (1) all said and done, antitrust policies have not been effective in preventing economic concentration, and that (2) other non-governmental, intraeconomic factors have been more effective in enhancing competition; for instance, the rise of international competition. General Motors, it is typically argued, might have dominated the auto market when it was an American market, but with the advent of major foreign auto makers General Motors commands but a small share of the relevant world market.

A different approach to the problem is to reduce interventionist power by insulating the public sector from the private one (Etzioni 1984a, Chapter 7). Such insulation is achieved by reducing the ability of economic actors to generate political power. For example, public financing of election campaigns (which prohibit the use of private funds) reduces the obligations of elected officials to economic (and other) private powers. A similar effect is achieved when, as in Britain, the amount of money one can spend legally on election campaigns is strictly limited. Laws already on the books in the United States, that limit the direct use of corporate and labor union funds in election campaigns, and laws that require discloser of all contributions, already have some of the needed effect. Without going here into the numerous issues raised by these and other suggested reforms, it is clear that the less economic power can be converted into political power, the less the government can be made to back up powerful economic actors or be used to help generate monopolistic gains. That is, the lower is the level of interventionist power, even if the concentration of economic power is not reduced.

The two policy approaches are not mutually exclusive; indeed, they complement one another in one obvious and one less obvious way. Obviously the less economic power is concentrated the less it can be used to generate interventionist power; and, the more concentrated economic power is prevented from being converted into interventionist power, the less sustainable, we saw, is the concentration of economic power.

The less obvious connection is that both antitrust policies (to curb concentration of economic power), and various reforms to reduce the interventionist power of powerful economic actors, are themselves political acts. Hence, to the extent that the concentration of interventionist power is high, it tends to prevent both kinds of reforms from being carried out. That is, because of the suggested measures to enhance the capsule are subject to the same forces that caused its weakness in the first place, significant changes in the capsule hence may well require the rise of a new political power. Such a power was marshaled by the Progressive movement in the United States between 1900 and 1917.

Less Government

A rather different approach to the problem at hand is to reduce the scope of government intervention in the economy (and, hence its payoffs or "rent"), and thus reduce what interventionist power can deliver to powerful economic actors. It is argued, that to the extent that economic actors will be unable to reap billions through subsidies, tax exemptions, regulatory relief, and so on, they will concentrate their efforts on intra-economic activities. The scope of government, to be reduced, includes (aside from public expenditures), taxes and deficits, the amount of credit the government provides, the number of regulations it imposes, the talent it hires, and so on. However, as recent experience in the Reagan and Thatcher Administrations strongly suggests, a significant decrease of the scope of government is unlikely to occur. Between 1980 and 1986, the first six years of the Reagan Administration, the rate of growth of government expenditures was slowed to some extent but there was no overall reduction. While regulations were cut back or less enforced (Tolchin and

Tolchin 1983), this has led to a growing interest in re-regulation in several areas. It seems hence that for the foreseeable future interventionist power too is unlikely to be curbed by significantly reducing the scope of government. Thus, the importance of attempting to reduce the ability of economic actors to amass interventionist power to ensure greater separation of the polity from the economy, both to curb monopolistic profits and to enhance democracy.

14

In Conclusion: Policy and Moral Implications

POLICY IMPLICATIONS

Normative Factors and Economic Policies

Paradigms, and theories formulated within their context, have two major usages: To *understand* the world (to provide a conception of the part of the world they focus on, to explain it) and, to help those who *act* within the world (to provide a framework for decision and policy making). Thus, for example, to explore where one ends up by following the theoretical assumptions that information travels cost free and instantaneously to all participants in the market, is quite different from arguing that insider trading is harmless and should be legalized, because information, in effect, actually travels with the speed of light *(Business Week,* August 25, 1986, p. 114). Moreover, theories that seek to understand the world deal with slices of the phenomena, segregated for the convenience of analysis. Thus, many neoclassical economists treat tastes, preferences, and values as exogenous (as given) and as stable, and focus on change in constraints, while many deontological psychologists and sociologists study the formation and changes of tastes, preferences and values with little or no attention to constraints (e.g., prices) or income. Similarly, neoclassicists tend to study the market, or even the economy, as if it was worlds apart from the polity, culture, and society, while some other social scientists study the latter as if there was no economy at their core. Because theories seek to explain only the relations among variables that characterize a particular slice of the world that they define as "theirs," the difficulties that analytic segregation poses are often relatively limited. However, when one turns to act within the world, rather than merely study it, one must deal with the world-as-it-is, with its complexity, and must concern oneself with all the major relevant factors, conditions, and constraints. Here, encompassing paradigms are more effective than very parsimonious but highly focused ones. (For additional discussion see Chapter 7 and Etzioni 1986a.)

The deontological I&We paradigm, and the socio-economic theory based on it, are less parsimonious but more encompassing than the neoclassical paradigm and neoclassical economics. Hence, whatever its limitations as a scientific way to understand the world, socio-economics seems promising as a guide for action and hence for *policy analysis*. Here the advantage of a theory that draws on a more encompassing paradigm is evident. Policy makers must deal with all the major relevant factors; socio-economics, by incorporating economic, social, psychic, and political factors, obviously is more encompassing than mono-disciplinary approaches. To illustrate, the discussion turns to explore the role of normative factors in economic policies. It should be recalled that normative factors, as we see it, play a pivotal role both in forming preferences, ends, or goals (as discussed in Part I), in the selection of means (as explored in Part II, especially Chapter 6), and in forming the societal capsule (as we saw in Part III, especially Chapter 12).

Socio-economics suggests that whenever the goal of a policy is to change behavior, such as to encourage people to save more or pay their taxes more fully, both normative and economic factors should be considered as policy levers, taking into account the relative power of each of these factors in the particular situation. In contrast, policy analysis based on neoclassical economic theory tends to draw on pecuniary incentives such as tax incentives, raises, and bonuses, and to disregard or down-play the role of moral education and leadership (for example, from the White House "pulpit").

A case in point was President Carter's appeal to consumers in March 1980 to use less credit on patriotic grounds; the response seems to have been considerable (although, because interest rates were also increased at the same time, it is difficult to establish the relative effect of his appeal). True, not all presidential exhortations have a massive effect, but when presidential and other public leaders help set the society's moral climate, for instance, in favor of saving, of "buying American," or of some other economic goals such as labor peace, whatever effect is gained is achieved at much less a cost than exclusive reliance on economic factors.

The difference in the policy implications of the two paradigms is further illustrated when tax policy is examined. Neoclassical policy analysts focus on the effects of various tax rates on collected revenue, the opportunity for evasion, and the risk involved. Deontologists will note that another key factor is the public judgment of the legitimacy, i.e., the moral standing, of the tax laws. Studies have found a relatively close association between the sense that taxes are fairly imposed, the sense of the legitimacy of the government and the purposes for which revenues are used, and the extent of tax evasion. (For an encompassing review of available evidence and detailed discussion, see Lewis 1982.)

In the early 1980s in the United States, in a climate celebrating private initiative and profit, lower tax rates are reported not to have resulted in people's abandoning their tax shelters, as supply-siders had predicted, but they motivated at least some individuals to seek riskier shelters that would provide the "old" amount of tax avoidance (or a near sum) at the lower tax rates (Kwitny 1984; Glassman 1984, p. 202). The change in moral climate (more entrepreneurial) seems to enhance people's preference for risk, which offset the lower marginal benefit from tax avoidance due to the new rates. From a policy analysis viewpoint, it follows that steps to enhance the legitimacy of a tax system, say through the introduction of a flat tax, may well do much more to raise revenue than lowering the rates but keeping the loopholes.

Moral factors play a significant role not only in public economic policy but also within each corporation and work place. A typical neoclassical treatment of the subject is properly entitled "motivating workers: incentive pay" (Ehrenberg and Smith 1982, p. 312) because it sees various compensation schemes as the only ways to motivate workers. Numerous other treatments of the labor force by neoclassical economists, whether they deal with productivity, labor mobility, acceptance of hazardous work, or other such topics, focus on economic incentives, either ignoring or slighting other considerations (Levitan and Johnson 1972; Thurow 1983, Chapter 7). However, there is considerable evidence that changing the corporate culture, including its informal moral codes, frequently can deliver a significant part of the desired results, at a much lower cost (Kilmann et al. 1985; Deal and Kennedy 1982). Granting workers more opportunity for participation in decision-making, greater social acceptance, and more dignity, is a major source of motivation for employees to work harder, reduces turnover, and curbs absenteeism (Greenberg and Glaser 1980). It also enhances the quality of work and increases the effectiveness of management due to a better upward flow of information. Much of the economic success of Japan is attributed to a management culture that provides for more worker-involvement and participation, an approach which is reported to have been successfully applied by Japanese managers in American factories (*Business Week,* July 14, 1986).

Several neoclassical economists suggest that "shirking can be minimized by close supervision." (Ehrenberg and Smith 1982, p. 312.) There is, however, strong psychological reasoning and some evidence to suggest that close supervision is particularly alienating, and that employees perform best when they are not closely supervised but properly socialized, especially when the work requires initiative, extensive use of knowledge, or care about quality (Etzioni 1975).

Another illustration of the difficulties in policy implications of the two paradigms can be seen in matters concerning insurance. Many neoclassical economists assume that people will act at their worst under conditions referred to as "moral hazard." The term refers to risk-sharing under conditions in which individuals can take private actions that affect the probability of the distribution of the outcome (Holmstrom 1979, p. 74). This situation arises when people buy insurance policies and then (neoclassicists assume) become more careless about their driving, about locking their doors, installing smoke detectors and so on, if not actually resorting to arson, or filing false claims (Varian 1984, p. 298; Layard and Walter 1978, pp. 382–83). With this assumption in mind, neoclassicists recommend close monitoring of those involved (Holmstrom 1979, p. 74). The next step is to search for combinations of deductibles and coinsurance policies to insure proper monetary incentives so the people will not exploit the situation (Heimer 1985). The fact that many, if not most, individuals do not act in this way is ignored, as are the effects of treating them all as potential liars and thieves instead of looking for ways to recognize and to enhance their moral behavior.

Neoclassical economists who do recognize the significance of moral values, tend to explain them in intra-economic terms: "Economic theory in this, as well as in some other fields, tends to suggest that people are honest only to the extent that they have economic incentive for being so." (Johansen cited by Sen 1977, p. 332.) This position is further illustrated by the following conclusion of Cloninger (1982, p. 33): "The possibility of reducing business risk by the acceptance of smaller amounts of moral risk could provide a rationale for the use of certain unorthodox business practices." If this were the case, the normative elements of the capsule of competition could be explainable by transactions among the actors; morality would be sustained by being good business, or curtailed until it was. One would not need to go outside the realm of competition to explain the normative forces that sustain it. As we see it, normative factors have their own foundations in people's values, personalities, and collectivities. While it is true that normative factors are affected by economic factors, causality also works the other way: normative factors affect economic ones; normative factors are not merely derivative.

Normative Factors and Other Policies

What holds for economic policies holds even more for those concerning other behaviors, from public choices to crime, to which neoclassical analysis has been applied in recent years. Janowitz (1983) shows, using historical data and public opinion polls, that since World War II Americans have become more aware of their rights and interests and less aware of their obligations to the community they share. For example, a 1979 survey shows that students hold very high among their rights the right to be tried by a jury, but very low among their obligations the duty to serve as a juror (Janowitz 1983, pp. 7–8). (For other data on "Me-ism" see Yankelovich 1981, and Verroff, Douvan, Kulka 1981.) Janowitz urges the introduction of a national service as a way to enhance "civic consciousness:" in the terms used here, to restore a balance between the I & the We. When this idea was the subject of a panel during the 1984 Annual Meeting of the American Political Science Association, a neoclassicist argued against the national service on the grounds that "we can get all the people we need by paying them." Such a position disregards, first, the economic value of a national service; volunteers to such a service may be paid minimum wages while those who serve in today's army are paid regular wages. Second, regularly paid employees make no contribution to right the imbalance that Janowitz and others have identified.

Neoclassical economists analyze crime in terms of costs and benefits. They argue that the probability of being arrested and convicted, the size of the penalty, and the size of the loot, i.e., costs and "benefits," correlate with the frequency of a large variety of crimes being committed, including murder and rape (Andreano and Siegfried 1980; Rottenberg 1979). The data are subject to considerable methodological controversies, but these need not concern us here. To the extent that these data have demonstrated self-interest plays an important role in situations hereto considered the domain of impulsive behavior, neoclassical economists provide an important correction to the over-socialized view of crime, a view that focuses almost exclusively on the role of education, subculture, peer pressure and other such factors. However, to the extent neoclassicists suggest that self-interest accounts for all or most of the variance, they vastly overstate their findings (Cook 1980), and their conclusions will tend to mislead policy makers. Thus, for instance, Rubin's statements (1980, p. 13) that "the decision to become a criminal is in principle no different from the decision to become a brick layer . . . the individual considers the net costs and benefits of each alternative and makes his decision on this basis," and "tastes are constant and a change in [criminal] behavior can be explained by changes in prices [such as penalty]," tend to mislead. They ignore the fact that despite whatever correlations are found between "prices" and level of criminality, much of the variance (in crime rates) remains unexplained, most likely because moral and other social factors are at work. Second, such statements overlook the fact that the "taste" for crime, like all others, is affected by normative and other social factors, e.g., by the extent to which the relevant subculture disapproves of the particular kinds of crime involved (Grasmick and Green 1981).

Similarly, statements such as Murray's (1984, p. 168) that "crime occurs when the prospective benefits sufficiently outweigh the prospective costs," are not only formulated in a way that makes falsification impossible (if no crime occurs under a given set of conditions, under which it is expected to occur, the benefits might be said to not "sufficiently" outweigh the costs), but also tend to mislead policy makers into disregarding the role of education, subculture, leadership, and role-models. Of special interest in this context is Wilson's (1985) discussion of the role of various "impulse control" movements and organizations in nineteenth century

America. Wilson points out that as industrialization advanced, young-sters who once left their homes only to work in homes under the supervision of other farmers or artisans, then started to reside in boarding houses in the cities, without any family bonds or authority. The result was widespread disorderly conduct. This was followed by numerous efforts to advance control of impulse and build up inner control, self-discipline, and "character." These included Sunday schools, YMCAs, temperance movements, and various religious and secular voluntary associations. Some had other goals, but impulse control was a by-product; others were aimed directly at instilling self-discipline.

The policy point is that one needs to work not merely on the cost-benefit, deterrence, incentive, and police side but also on the formation of preferences side, via moral education, peer culture, community values, and the mobilization of appropriate public opinion, factors that neoclas-sicists tend to ignore because they take preferences for granted, and their theories provide no analytical framework to conceptualize the ways in which preferences are formed and might be reformed. The trouble with theories that fit into a deontological paradigm is that they include nu-merous, complex, propositions that are difficult to quantify. They may have to be synthesized, made more parsimonious and more operational, before they can effectively play their role next to economic analysis.

This is not to suggest that one ought to or can form a public normative policy; much of morality is not subject to control by public officials. How-ever, once attention is paid to normative factors, policies can be fash-ioned that enhance, or at least do not undermine, these factors. The pro-vision of proper role-models, improvement of civic education in schools, and the formation of self-help groups, are cases in point. A major change in the moral climate between 1900 and 1917 promoted by a social move-ment (the Progressives) led to a considerable reduction in political cor-ruption and significantly improved the environment necessary for a modern economy, ranging from trust in financial institutions to curbing the ability of monopolistic firms to use the state to restrain competition (Hofstadter 1966).

The question has been raised as to whether there is a contradiction between the position advanced earlier, that moral commitments are "te-nacious," and the suggestions that one may draw on moral commitments as a resource to advance public policies. There is no contradiction once one recognizes that policy makers can appeal to existing commitments, can intensify them, or introduce new commitments where none exist. However, to change the direction of entrenched commitments signifi-cantly (say, change attitudes toward coworkers from a different race) is a rather more difficult undertaking (Stern and Aronson 1984, p. 72).

Interaction Effects

Beyond the effects that normative "inputs" have on various economic (and noneconomic) outcomes, such as saving and productivity, there are interaction effects between normative "inputs" and economic inputs that deserve attention. Most significant is the hypothesis that under certain conditions the addition of economic inputs results in *decline* in output because their introduction undermines the productive effect of normative "inputs"; i.e., the two inputs are said not to combine well.

Goodin (1980, p. 140) argues that "material incentives destroy rather than supplement moral incentives." Neoclassicists tend to design institutions for knaves, either assuming that all people are knaves or that those who wish to be "good" will do so anyhow, but the others need to be paid or punished. Goodin, however, suggests that such policies undercut the "good," normative, voluntary behavior, Thus, if volunteers read to blind patients in an institution, but its administrator, anxious to secure a more reliable service, will pay for some such reading, one would expect that under most circumstances volunteer reading will cease, exacting a sizable cost for whatever increase in reliability is attained. This is obviously not always or categorically the case. While blood is volunteered in the United Kingdom and sold in the United States, people *do* donate blood in the United States, although more might have volunteered if none were sold (Titmuss 1970).

The Morality of Cooperation

Much already has been written about another policy slant that neoclassical economics introduces: the emphasis on the merit of competition, of the market. The issue here is not the power of the market model as an economic theory, but the merits of using it to design policies when the conditions of perfect competition are absent. Neoclassical economists themselves have shown that under these conditions the perfect competition model may not apply (see Chapter 12, pp. 200–202). However, time and again, neoclassical economists argue for deregulation, the reduction of tariffs, and so on, as if steps in the *direction* of the free market will yield *some* of the benefits of a truly free market, which their own studies show cannot be predicted.

Beyond overselling the virtues of the market, neoclassicists underestimate the value of what is considered the opposite kind of behavior, that of cooperation. Reference was already made to the value of cooperation between employees and management. Its merit is evident elsewhere: in firms working together to deal with shared problems and to produce public goods (such as finding efficient anti-pollution devices or supporting basic research); in individuals willing to reduce their use of energy in peak hours to allow utilities to shut down polluting power plants (Stern and Aronson 1984, p. 72); in efforts to build consensus among various management groups in the same firm (Ofshe and Ofshe 1970); and in a national climate of collaboration between management and labor unions (Maital and Maital 1984, p. 281; Boulding 1962). Probably most damaging is the conceptual opposition between government and the free market, which tends to disregard the importance of a third realm, that of community, in which cooperation and values often find their support. Bentham's view that "community is a fiction" (cited by Bell 1980, p. 71) lingers well beyond his time.

The Lesson of Humility

Once one fully recognizes, absorbs, and deeply accepts the limitations of the human ability to know and the pivotal roles of affect and values, one's approach to the world, especially to decision-making, changes significantly. Instead of the hyperactive orientation of setting goals, marshalling the "most efficient" means, and "implementing"—which assumes that we are God-like creatures and the world (including our fellow human beings) is putty—one grows humble. Most times we lack the knowledge needed for sound decisions. Hence, we must proceed carefully, ready to reverse course, willing to experiment; in short, humbly.

Humility extends beyond the limits of the mind; it is fostered by the deontological assumption that others are to be treated also as ends and not merely as means. We hence become more willing to truly consult (not as a form of manipulation but as a way to form consensus), to take into account the need of others and of the community, both out of ethical and practical considerations.

Moreover, we do not treat emotions or values as merely hindrances to rational decision-making; we realize their legitimate role as a base for decision-making, and for curbing the choice of means by taking into consideration values other than the enhancing of efficiency.

The Significance of Membership and Structure

Once one fully takes into account that (1) individuals are not isolated, deciding and acting on their own, but are members of groups, deeply affected by their various We-nesses, and that (2) decisions are made to a significant extent by organs of collectivities (e.g., committees), the significance of structure comes into focus. The first step is to realize that the economic, social and political position of a person significantly affects one's ability to act, one's leverage, and scope of choice. Second, one realizes that the wisdom or inadequacy of a person's course is often and deeply affected by the structure of the collectivity in which that person is a member; for instance, how decentralized versus hierarchical the structure is. Most importantly, one understands that changes in the course of action often require not merely changing the "hearts and minds" of individuals but also changing economic, social, and political structures.

Under what conditions collective structures are subject to significant changes, is a significant and complex question the author addressed else-where (Etzioni 1968). Suffice it to note here that structural changes, espe-cially toward a more responsive community, require more than knowl-edge or even consensus; they often entail mobilization of power by those who are keen on change, to overcome the opposition of those committed to the status quo, as reflected in the civil rights, women's, environmental-ist, and the Progressive movements. This is not to suggest that those who favor change are automatically in the right and that those opposed are without merit; the point is that structural changes are rarely propelled merely by knowledge, emotion, and even values; the exercise of power (not necessarily force!) is often required. Hence, the need for a theory that treats both structure and power as pivotal elements.

NORMATIVE IMPLICATIONS

While the neoclassical paradigm and economics do not contain norma-tive factors in their schema, they themselves have clear, often previously noted, normative implications. Neoclassical economists distinguish be-tween positive ("scientific") and normative (prescriptive) economic the-ory, between factual, as-is statements and value judgments, ought-to-be statements. While many economists argue that they ought to stick to posi-tive work, others maintain that once the individuals (or clients or policy makers) are committed to a value, say equality, economists can address the question of how people ought to behave, on the assumption that people will wish to advance that value efficiently. It must be noted, how-ever, that many economists acknowledge that they are routinely involved in outright normative work, rendering value judgments (Alchian and Al-len 1977, p. 40; McKee 1982, pp. 7ff), especially when they provide policy advice, whether or not their "clients" have explicated their values and goals (Brandl 1985, pp. 2, 10–11). The question, what are the normative messages that economic theory emits? is thus a legitimate one.

A Preference for Efficiency

Economists who are concerned with efficiency (presumably, because it is morally neutral) often do not take into account that efficiency itself is a value among others (Ayres 1981, p. viii).

> ... Indeed, efficiency often conflicts with other highly valued social norms—goals such as equity, or fairness, and the desire to promote "al-truistic," or unselfish, behavior. The marketplace is the realm of in-equality and self-interest, where those with wealth can gratify their de-sires at the expense of those less well off. The latter may quite reasonably feel skeptical about the expansion of this realm.

He cites Kelman (1981):

> Part of the perceived value of things as varied as our national parks and our right to vote would appear to be their very character as part of a common treasure that we all share equally. . . . Such equal sharing would not occur if those things were placed in the market; it is possible only through non-market allocation. (Ibid.)

And Ayres concludes:

> . . . In line with hundreds of years of the Common Law, the [Clean Air] Act now says that every American has the right to an atmosphere that is healthful to breathe.

Not efficient, say many economists. An efficient society would apply to a kind of market test, cleaning the air only to the extent that the aggregate social "benefits" in improved health were as large as the aggregate costs of providing it. The equity issue lies hidden in this formula, because it disregards the very likely possibility that the health of some individuals would be diminished, say, to make cheaper products available for many others. (For additional discussion on the tendency of economists to assume that the market will produce justice—that efficiency and justice coincide—rather than to treat both as exogenous value judgments, see Schneider 1974, pp. 207–8.)

Discussing an economist's analysis of risk, Chelius (1979, p. 146) writes: "Viscusi implicitly views an efficient outcome as one that would have occurred if information were perfect. Harold Demsetz has characterized this perspective in another context as the Nirvana approach in economic analysis." He adds: ". . . why consider an equilibrium efficient only when the result is the same as when information is free? Why not assume hard-hats and machine guards are free and consider it inefficient if the market does not yield appropriate results based on this assumption?" (Reference is to W. Kip Viscusi, a major leader of risk analysis). But Viscusi himself states: "I think it's debatable whether, if a worker himself places a low value on his life, society as a whole should do the same." (Keller 1984.) In short, many a value judgment hides behind the reliance on the efficiency of the market.

The Moral Implications of Deference to Revealed Preferences

The neoclassical position that preferences are revealed in behavior and hence there is no need to study how they are formed or changed, introduces a major value judgment into neoclassical economic theory that has been often pointed out, and hence is mentioned here largely to complete the record. By arguing that the market best serves people's preferences, "what the individuals want," economists disregard the fact that preferences are to a significant extent socially formed and hence reflect the society's values, culture, and power structure (Boulding 1969; Tisdell 1983, p. 34; McPherson 1985, pp. 5–6). People in Western societies are after consumption and wealth; but is this because they are acquisitive in nature, or because they reflect the values of mature capitalism? True, studies of India and Nigeria by Inkeles and Smith (1974), studies of *Kibbutzim,* and recent experiences in the Soviet Union and Communist China, point to the ubiquitous power of consumer goods. But are they what people want when they have little, and soon move on to "higher" needs, as Maslow suggests, or is there no limit to their desire to use objects, using them also as a substitute for and expression of affection, self-esteem, and self-realization? Indeed, there is considerable evidence that what people consume largely reflects their culture and subcultures, their values and social definitions of the products (Douglas 1979; Thompson 1979). Within the United States, the rise of "voluntary simplicity," especially in the late 1960s and the 1970s, led people who had more money to consume less, not only proportionately but also absolutely (Elgin and Mitchell 1977; Leonard-Barton 1981).

In short, it seems quite clear that neoclassical economics, and its "consumer sovereignty" assumptions, in effect reflect a value system and a social, economic, and political structure—that of mature capitalism (Hirsch 1976)—rather than human nature. To maintain otherwise, leads those who internalize such a theory to assume that their buying preferences reveal normatively correct choices, because they made them, presumably on their own, while in effect they are largely culturally bound and conformist.

Beyond Pareto

In their discussion of general welfare neoclassical economists draw on the principle of Pareto optimality. On the face of it, it seems nobody could fault such an objective criterion as adjusting allocations only to benefit some if they do not harm others. In effect, the principle raises many moral questions, such as whether or not all preferences are to be judged of equal standing (drug addiction?), and whether the same status is to be accorded to choices by all individuals (including criminals?). Rhoads (1985, p. 185) provides a striking example of the neoclassicists' tendency to ignore rights and use people's preference "pure and simple": "Tullock, for example, makes no distinction between the views of those in this country who want to see commercial television portray blacks in a manner reducing white prejudice and the views of many South Africans who want to do the reverse: 'The fact that we approve of one and disapprove of the other indicates that we have a certain set of preferences. It does not indicate that there is a difference in kind between them or that both of them are not efforts to generate externalities.'" (Reference is to Tullock 1970. For additional criticism see Mishan 1981.)

Recently, a major new criticism has been raised by Whittington and MacRae (1986). They point to the fact that the results of Pareto-like analyses are highly dependent on who one includes in the concept of the society or community whose welfare one studies. At first the answer may seem obvious as implied in many a theoretical analysis: everyone. However, the value-judgment stands out once one asks, as the authors do: Whose preferences are included? Are future generations encompassed, and how far into the future? This is a major question for environmental policies, indeed for budget allotments to education, basic research, and infrastructure, all investments that pay off largely in the longer run. What about illegal immigrants of whom there are an estimated 20 million in the United States? What about starving people in other countries? There are numerous ways these questions can be answered; however, they all involve value-judgments that neoclassicists deny they are making, but which cannot be avoided.

A Distaste for Politics

Like many experts who strongly believe in their knowledge, neoclassicists tend to convey a dismay with political processes, especially the give-and-take involved. For example, Majone (1976, p. 610) states that many neoclassical economists "justify their preference for the effluent charge [on polluters] partly on the basis of its alleged ability to reduce bargaining and political compromise." Conversely, they reject the regulation and enforcement approach because of its political nature. Majone goes on to point out that from such a position it "is a short step to doubt the ability of a pluralistic political system to make wise choices." (Pp. 610–11.) Actually both procedures are subject to politics (for evidence that regulation *and* incentive schemes are both highly political, see Etzioni 1985c). One might add, if one accepts basic democratic tenets, that they ought to be so.

Political philosophers and political scientists, from Edmund Burke on, have recognized an essential prerequisite of democracy: elected representatives must have a mandate within which they are free to work out compromises. The same scholars have highlighted the danger to democratic processes when the electorate instructs its representatives specifically, or requires them to return to the electorate for endorsements for specific policies as distinct from general affirmation. In contrast, neoclassical economists, laboring under the pressure to find quantifiable inputs, have viewed the deviations of representatives from voters' specific "preferences" as "shirking" if not "opportunism" (Kalt and Zupan 1984, pp. 282–83). They seem unaware of the undesirable effects on democratic government of adhering closely to the specific wishes that voters expressed before the process of give-and-take started. (For additional documentation, see Rhoads 1985, Chapter 11.)

Dis-Educational Effects

More is at stake than a paradigm that drives some of its advocates to conceptual acrobatics in order to protect its we-need-no-normative-factors assumptions; there are educational effects on the youth and on the public at large. Neoclassicists each year expose millions of high school and college students to a paradigm that, as Solow (1981, p. 40) puts it, "underplays the significance of ethical judgments both in its approach to policy and [in] its account of individual and organizational behavior." Neoclassical economic textbooks are replete with statements such as ". . . the rational thing to do is to try to gain as much value as I can while giving up as little value as I can." (Dyke 1981, p. 29.) And, referring to worker-employer relations: "however, as in any transaction, each side will try to get the most while giving as little as it must." (Ehrenberg and Smith 1982, p. 32.)

An effort to protect the mono-utility assumption leads to a discussion that equates the Bible and dope as two consumer goods (Kamerschen and Valentine 1981, p. 82), while Walsh (1970, p. 24) treats as interchangeable relations to a bottle of booze (Jack Daniels) and to a person (Marina). Gifts are depicted by Alchian and Allen (1977, p. 96) as "equivalent to a sale at prices lower than the market-clearing price," and children are viewed (Becker 1976, p. 169) as "durable consumer goods."

After stating that it may seem immoral to classify children as akin to cars, houses, and machinery, Becker (ibid., p. 172), proceeds to do the same on page 173: "As consumer durables, children are assumed to provide 'utility.'" More expensive children are called "higher quality" infants, compared to Cadillacs, and so on. One wonders what is the effect on the attitude of potential parents to children, if they are systematically taught to think about their offspring as a trade-off to other "goods," such as cars?

"Economist's way of thinking . . . involves, in many cases . . . a sort-of cultivated hard-nosed crassness towards anything that smacks of 'higher things of life,'" write Brennan and Buchanan (1982, p. 6). This is illustrated by three studies still in progress but already capturing the media's attention and thus shaping the public's mind. A study by Schwartz suggests that dueling is an efficient way of settling disputes; Landes questions whether the costs of preventing hijacking are worth the expenditures; and Posner shows it is more efficient to buy and sell babies in an open market than it is to regulate adoption, which causes a black market (Wermeil 1984).

An empirical study of the educational effects of neoclassical teachings might well show that the students become somewhat more self-oriented and pleasure-seeking than they were before they were so exposed, just as they become more rational in their purchase and investment decisions. Such effects are evident in a series of free-ride experiments conducted by Marwell and Ames (1981). In eleven out of twelve experimental runs most participants did not free ride and contributed from 40 percent to 60 percent of their resources to a public good (the "group pot"). However, a group of economics graduate students contributed only an average of 20 percent. And while the other subjects were motivated by a strong sense of fairness, and a near unanimous definition of what it is (ibid., p. 308), economics students refused to define the term, or gave very complex answers, and those who did respond stated that making little or no contribution was fair (ibid., p. 309). (These findings could be caused by the way students of a given moral predilection choose their field of study and not merely by its teaching. However, courses do have consequences. A course in professional ethics given in a business school generated a rush of visits by students to the mental health service. Osiel 1984, p. 43.)

Beyond the effects on students there are effects on the public mentality. Here, too, the prevailing economic approach to moral values tends to debase them. Goodin, Walzer, and Kelman all point to the fact that society sets aside certain areas as "sacred," and that to make the public think about them in terms of costs and benefits "secularizes" them, stripping them from their special moral standing, and thus ultimately causes them to be treated the way neoclassicists say they are. For example, to create markets for rights (as part of an incentive scheme), say, selling pollution rights, undermines the taboos against such behavior; it normalizes it, and hence makes it less costly and more common.

A paradox arises to the extent that it is true that the market is dependent on normative underpinning (to provide the pre-contractual foundation such as trust, cooperation, and honesty) which all contractual relations require: *The more people accept the neoclassical paradigm as a guide for their behavior, the more the ability to sustain a market economy is undermined.* This holds for all those who engage in transactions without ever-present inspectors, auditors, lawyers, and police: if they do not limit themselves to legitimate (i.e., normative) means of competition out of internalized values, the system will collapse, because the transaction costs of a fully or even highly "policed" system are prohibitive. This holds even more so for the regulators that every market requires. If those whose duty it is to set and to enforce the rules of the game are out to maximize their own profits, a-la-Public Choice, there is no hope for the system. It is our position that they are not so inclined, but neoclassical education may push them in the amoral, anarchic direction.

In short, because the neoclassical paradigm is part of the modern mentality, and not merely an academic field, it affects the way people see their world and themselves, and the way they behave. Brennan and Buchanan face the question squarely. They ask "is Public Choice immoral?" because of its effects on the public's behavior. They answer that "dispelling illusions about the nature of the political order, may not be intrinsically 'immoral.'" (1982, p. 3.) The question, of course, is whether the notions the Public Choice school seeks to dispel are illusions. I do not suggest that neoclassicists (or anyone) should hide well-established truths from the public in order to keep them in ignorant innocence, mindlessly favorable to caring and sharing, to mutuality and civility. It does follow, however, that if it is true that people do seek to balance their pleasures with moral considerations, and if they are taught, to the contrary, that they are "really" only out to maximize their pleasure (and all that follows, that people behave morally only as long as it pays, and so on), there is likely to be a negative, anti-moral effect, one which a deontological paradigm and a socio-economics theory avoid.

At the same time, one should not deny that pleasure and self-interest constitute a major motivating force, and—in their place—a legitimate one. Socio-economics is hence to view pleasure and self-interest within the broader context of human nature, society, and ultimate values, rather than either ignore the self-oriented force, or build a paradigm, theory, and morality focused entirely on self.

Overview and Propositional Inventory

I. OVERVIEW

1. *Ethical Foundations:* Moderate deontological (consequences as a secondary criterion).

2. *Conception of Human Nature:*
   2.1. Divided self, in perpetual, but in part creative, conflict.
   2.2. Moral duties are a major source of intra self-divisions.
   2.3. Limited intellectual capabilities.

3. *Conception of the Social System:*
   3.1. Individual (I) and collectivity (We) are both essential elements and have the same basic conceptual and moral standing.
   3.2. The I&We is in a perpetual, but in part creative, conflict.
   3.3. While individuals shape collectivities, as collectivities shape individuals, the influence of collectivities is greater.

4. *Methodological Positions* (Inter-paradigmatic):
   4.1. Scientific Codetermination: Two kinds of forces affect the social realm as they affect one another. Specifically, deontological conceptions set the context within which utilitarian orientations—pleasure, self-interest, and rationality—are operative.
   4.2. Changes in behavior (such as amount saved, level of effort at work, extent to which taxes due are paid) reflect in part changes in preferences and in part changes in constraints. Value changes affect *both* preferences and constraints, but especially preferences. Changes in market forces affect both preferences and constraints, but especially constraints.
   4.3. Socio-economics (a deontological theory of social and economic

253

behavior) is to rely more on induction, less on deduction, than neoclassical economics (a utilitarian theory).

5. *Methodological Positions* (intra-paradigmatic):
   5.1. The purpose of theory is to predict *and* to explain.
   5.2. Parsimony is to be sacrificed to a limited extent in order to expand the scope of the variables covered (esp. social, psychic, and political) and to explain more of the variance of the behavior under study, while avoiding over-determination.
   5.3. Tautologies are to be avoided.

6. *I&We Paradigm, Core Assumptions:*
   6.1. Actors pursue two or more goals (utilities): seek pleasure (and hence self-interest), and seek to abide by their moral commitments.
   6.2. Actors' choices of means are largely based on values and emotions. To the extent that they draw on logic and evidence, their limited intellectual capabilities lead the actors to typically render sub-rational decisions.
   6.3. The actors are individuals acting within collectivities, not free-standing persons.

II. MAIN PROPOSITIONS AND SUB-PROPOSITIONS

A. Human Purposes (Utilities):

7. *It is productive to assume two (or more), but not large number, of utilities.*
   7.1. All items have at least two valuations: their ability to generate pleasure and their moral standing.
   7.2. Pleasure and moral commitments sometimes reinforce each other, but often are in conflict. I.e., the two valuations of any item are often of opposite signs.
   7.3. It is technically possible but unproductive to reduce the two kinds of valuations to one.
   7.4. The more individuals act under the influence of moral commitments, the more they are expected to persevere (when circumstances change). Conversely, the more individuals heed their pleasures or self-interest, the less likely they are to persevere.
      7.4.1. Moral commitments stretch out the learning curve.
   7.5. Moral commitments lower the transaction costs.
   7.6. When people violate their moral commitments to enhance their pleasures, such violations activate various defensive mechanisms before, during, and after the violation, and these have specific behavioral consequences.

7.6.1. Violations of moral commitments cause guilt that leads, among other consequences, to compensatory pro-social behavior.

7.6.2. Conflicts between pleasure motives and moral commitments are a major source of dissonance, leading to inaction and/or denial.

7.6.3. Conflicts between pleasure valuations and moral valuations result in inter-psychic stress, leading to the diminished capacity of the actor to render rational decisions.

7.7. Choices that are relatively heavily loaded with moral considerations, including many economic choices, are expected to be unusually difficult to reverse (are asymmetrical), to be very "lumpy" (or highly discontinuous), and to reveal a high "notch" effect.

7.8. When moral commitments are prominent they generate non-markets in some areas ("blocked exchanges"), e.g. in constitutional rights, and poor markets in others, e.g. in adoption.

B. Selection of Means

8. *Values and emotions are pivotal:*

8.1. Most choices are made without the processing of information, drawing of inferences, or deliberations. I.e., they are not decisions.

8.2. Most choices (whether deliberative or not) are made to a significant extent on the bases of values/emotions. (Not just the selection of goals but also of means.)

8.3. Values/emotions either fully form many choices, or set a context that limits the range of those options that are considered.

8.4. Values/emotions affect deliberations of those options that are considered by "loading" options with non-empirical, non-logical weights.

8.5. Values/emotions interrupt deliberations, preventing completion of reasoned decision-making sequences.

8.6. Values/emotions legitimate some subareas as those in which logical/empirical choices are mandated. I.e., the extent to which decision-making strives to be rational is deeply affected by values/emotions.

8.7. Choices made on the basis of values/emotions are not necessarily inefficient.

8.8. Knowledge plays a limited role in most decisions.

8.9. Even when knowledge is extensively used, such decisions are inefficient as compared to the results objective observers find could be reached.

9. *Collectivity processes are more important than individual ones in shaping both choices and decisions:*

    9.1. Many kinds of decisions are on average made more efficiently by organizational units of collectivities (such as executive boards of firms) than by individuals.

    9.2. The scope and level of innovation is in part collectively determined: the lower the culture ranks economic goals, productivity, efficiency, technology, science, the higher it ranks social cohesion, stability, and religion, the lower the scope and level of innovation.

C. Market as Sub-System; Society as System

10. *The scope of the transactions organized by the market is largely determined by the social capsule:*

    10.1. Competition is not *self*-sustaining. Its very existence, and the scope of transactions organized by it, depend to a significant extent on the attributes of the societal capsule within which it takes place; i.e., it is to a significant extent externally determined.

    10.2. The divergent interests and pursuits of actors in the market do not automatically mesh to form a harmonious whole; i.e., specific mechanisms are needed to keep competition (as contained conflict) from escalating into all-out conflict. Unregulated competition will self-destruct.

    10.3. The strength of the capsule is determined by the strength of the moral legitimacy it commands; by the intensity of the social bonds that competitors share; and by the relative power of the government compared to those in the market.

        10.3.1. Three mechanisms substitute for one another. Up to a point, each has its own role; at the same time, they affect one another and not just the capsule.

    10.4. The relationship between social bonds and competition is curvilinear; weak bonds are one factor that allows for all-out conflict; tight bonds will restrain, if not suppress, competition. Bonds of intermediate strength are most compatible with competition.

    10.5. Governments sustain competition to the extent they are the ultimate defender of rules and prevent violence; they undermine competition when they seek to determine the outcomes of competitions.

11. *There are no transactions among equals. Power is the source of Structure:*

    11.1. The price of an item reflects its costs, and the relative economic and political power of producers (providers, sellers, etc.) as compared to users (buyers etc.) and other parties (government regulators, consumer unions, farm lobbies, etc.). In short, cost + power = price.

11.2. The capsule is maintained to the extent that economic power is dispersed or prevented from concentrating, or economic power is being prevented from conversion into political power. The more economic power is segregated from political power, whatever its level of concentration, the higher the probability that the capsule will survive and be effective.

11.3. Structures able to limit the *political* power of economic competitors are as important to sustaining competition as is preventing a large concentration of economic power.

11.4. Manipulation of the government by powerful economic actors generates pseudo-concentration effect (comparable to that caused by the concentration of economic power, without there being any such concentration or collusion among economic actors).

12. *The more people accept the neoclassical paradigm as a guide for their behavior, the more their ability to sustain a market economy is undermined.*

Bibliography

Abelson, Robert P. 1976. "Social Psychology's Rational Man," In S. I. Benn and G. W. Mortimore, eds., *Rationality and the Social Sciences*. London: Routledge and Kegan Paul.

Abelson, Robert P., and Ariel Levi. 1985. "Decision Making and Decision Theory." In Gardner Lindzey and Elliot Aronson, eds., *Handbook of Social Psychology*. Vol. 1. 3rd ed. New York: Random House, pp. 231–310.

Abolafia, Mitchel Y. 1984. "Structured Anarchy: Formal Organization in the Commodity Futures Markets." In Patricia Adler and Peter Adler, eds., *The Social Dynamics of Financial Markets*. Greenwich, Conn.: JAI Press, pp. 129–50.

Abramowitz, Moses. 1979. "Economic Growth and Its Discontents." In Michael J. Boskin, ed., *Economics and Human Welfare*. New York: Academic Press, pp. 3–21.

Adler, Patricia A., and Peter Adler, eds. 1984. *The Social Dynamics of Financial Markets*. Grennwich, Conn.: JAI Press.

Ainslie, George. 1985. "Beyond Microeconomics. Conflict among interests in a multiple self as a determinant of value." In Jon Elster, ed., *The Multiple Self*. Cambridge: Cambridge University Press, pp. 133–75.

Aitken, Hugh G. J., ed. 1965. *Exploration in Enterprise*. Cambridge: Harvard University Press.

Ajzen, Icek, and Martin Fishbein. 1980. *Understanding Attitudes and Predicting Behavior*. Englewood Cliffs, N.J.: Prentice-Hall.

Akerlof, George A. 1970. "The Market for 'Lemons': Quality Uncertainty and the Market Mechanism." *Quarterly Journal of Economics*. Vol. 84 (August), pp. 488–500.

———. 1980. "A Theory of Social Custom, of Which Unemployment May Be One Consequence." *Quarterly Journal of Economics*. Vol. 94, pp. 749–75.

Akerlof, George A., and William T. Dickens. 1982. "The Economic Consequences of Cognitive Dissonance." *American Economic Review*. Vol. 72, pp. 307–19.

Alchian, Armen Albert, and William R. Allen. 1977, 1983. *Exchange and Production: Competition, Coordination and Control*. 2nd & 3rd eds. Belmont, Calif.: Wadsworth.

Alessi, L. 1983. "Property Rights, Transaction Costs, and X-Efficiency: An Essay in Economic Theory." *American Economic Review.* Vol. 73, no. 1 (March), pp. 64–81.

Alhadeff, David A. 1982. *Micro-economics and Human Behavior.* Berkeley: University of California.

Allvine, Fred C., and Fred A. Tarpley, Jr. 1977. *The New State of the Economy.* Cambridge, Mass: Winthrop.

Amemiya, Takeshi. 1981. "Qualitative Response Models: A Survey." *Journal of Economic Literature.* Vol. 19 (December), pp. 1483–1536.

Anderson, Carl A., and William J. Gribbin, eds. 1982. *The Wealth of Families.* Washington, D.C.: American Family Institute.

Anderson, Craig A., Mark R. Lepper, and Lee Ross. 1980. "Perseverance of Social Theories: The Role of Explanation in the Persistence of Discredited Information." *Journal of Personality and Social Psychology.* Vol. 39, no. 6, pp. 1037–49.

Andreano, Ralph, and John J. Siegfried eds. 1980. *The Economics of Crime.* New York: John Wiley.

Andress, F.J. 1954. "The Learning Curve as a Production Tool." *Harvard Business Review.* Vol. 32, pp. 87–97.

Argote, Linda. 1982. "Input Uncertainty and Organizational Coordination in Hospital Emergency Units." *Administrative Science Quarterly.* Vol. 27. no. 3 (September), pp. 420–34.

Argyris, Chris. 1985. *Strategy, Change and Defensive Routines.* Cambridge, Mass: Ballinger.

Arrow, Kenneth. 1951. *Social Choice and Individual Values.* New York: John Wiley.

———. 1974. *The Limits of Organization.* New York: W.W. Norton.

———.1975. "Gifts and Exchanges." In Edmund Phelps, ed. *Altruism, Morality, and Economic Theory.* New York: Russell Sage Foundation, pp. 13–28.

———. 1982. "Risk Perception in Psychology and Economics." *Economic Inquiry.* Vol. 20 (January), pp. 1–9.

Asch, Peter. 1983. *Industrial Organization and Anti-Trust Policy.* New York: John Wiley.

Asch, S.E. 1958. "Effects of Group Pressure Upon the Modification and Distortion of Judgements." In Eleanor E. Maccoby et al., eds., *Readings in Social Psychology.* 3rd ed. New York: Holt, Rinehart, and Winston, pp. 174–83.

Ashley, Richard K. 1984. "The Poverty of Neorealism." *Internal Organization.* Vol. 38, no. 2 (Spring), pp. 225–86.

Axelrod, Robert. 1984. *The Evolution of Cooperation.* New York: Basic Books.

Ayres, Richard E. 1981. "Forward." in Steven Kelman, *What Price Incentives?: Economics and the Environment.* Boston: Auburn House.

Azariadis, Costas. 1975. "Implicit Contracts and Underemployment Equilibria." *Journal of Political Economy.* Vol. 83. pp. 1183–1202.

Azzi, Corry, and Ronald Ehrenberg. 1975. "Household Allocation of Time and Church Attendance." *Journal of Political Economy.* Vol. 38, no. 1, pp. 27–56.

Bailey, Duncan, and Stanley E. Boyle. 1977. "Sales Revenue Maximization: An Empirical Investigation." *Industrial Organization Review.* Vol. 5, no. 1, pp. 46–55.

Baily, Martin Neal. 1974. "Wages and Employment Under Uncertain Demand." *Review of Economic Studies.* Vol. 41, pp. 37–50.

Baker, Wayne E. 1984a. "Floor Trading and Crowd Dynamics." In Patricia Adler and Peter Adler, eds., *The Social Dynamics of Financial Markets.* Greenwich, Conn.: JAI Press, pp. 107–28.

———. 1984b. "The Social Structure of a National Securities Market." *American Journal of Sociology.* Vol. 89. no. 4 (January), pp. 775–811.

Baldwin, James W. 1902. *Social Psychology.* 3rd ed. London: Macmillan.

Banfield, Edward. 1958. *The Moral Basis of a Backward Society.* Glencoe, Ill.: Free Press.

Baran, Arie, Joseph Lakonishok, and Aharon R. Ofer. 1980. "The Informational Content of General Price Level Adjusted Earnings: Some Empirical Evidence." *Accounting Review.* Vol. 55, no. 1. (January), pp. 22–35.

Barnard, Chester. 1947. *The Functions of the Executive.* Cambridge: Harvard University Press.

Barron's. November, 10, 1986, p. 16.

Barry, Brian. 1978. *Sociologists, Economists and Democracy.* Chicago: University of Chicago Press.

Barth, James R., and Joseph J. Cordes. 1981. "Nontraditional Criteria for Investing Pension Assets: An Economic Appraisal." *Journal of Labor Research.* Vol. 2 (Fall), pp. 219–46.

Barth, R. T., and I. Vertinsky. 1975. "The Effect of Goal Orientation and Information Environment on Research Performance: A Field Study." *Organizational Behavior and Human Performance.* Vol. 13, pp. 110–32.

Barzel, Yoram, and Eugene Silberberg. 1973. "Is the Act of Voting Rational?" *Public Choice.* Vol. 16 (Fall), pp. 51–58.

Baston, C.D., B.D. Duncan, P. Ackerman, T. Buckley, and K. Birch. 1981. "Is Empathic Emotion a Source of Altruistic Motivation?" *Journal of Personality and Social Psychology.* Vol. 40, pp. 290–302.

Baumgardner, Ann H., P. Paul Heppner, and Robert M. Arkin. 1986. "Role of Causal Attribution in Personal Problem Solving." *Journal of Personality and Social Psychology.* Vol. 50, no. 3, pp. 636–46.

Baumol, William J. 1967. *Business Behavior, Value and Growth.* Revised ed. New York: Harcourt, Brace and World.

Baumol, William J., and Richard E. Quandt. 1964. "Rules of Thumb and Optimally Imperfect Decisions." *American Economic Review.* Vol. 54 (March), pp. 23–46.

Baumol, William J., John C. Panzar, and Robert D. Willig. 1982. *Contestable Markets and the Theory of Industry Structure.* New York: Harcourt Brace Jovanovich.

Beauchamp, Tom L. 1982. *Philosophical Ethics: An Introduction to Moral Philosophy.* New York: McGraw-Hill.

Becker, Gary S. 1957. *The Economics of Discrimination.* Chicago: University of Chicago Press.

——. 1976. *The Economic Approach to Human Behavior.* Chicago: University of Chicago Press.

——. 1981. *A Treatise on the Family.* Cambridge: Harvard University Press.

Beckman, L. 1970. "Effects of Students' Performance on Teachers' and Observers' Attributions of Causality." *Journal of Educational Psychology.* Vol. 61, pp. 75–82.

Beer, Michael, Bert Spector, Paul R. Lawrence, D. Quinn Mills, and Richard E. Walton. 1985. *Human Resource Management A General Manager's Perspective.* New York: The Free Press.

Bell, Daniel. 1975. "The Revolution of Rising Entitlement." *Fortune,* April.

——. 1980. "Models and Reality in Economic Discourse." *Public Interest.* Special Issue, pp. 46–80.

Bellah, Robert N., Richard Madsen, William M. Sullivan, Ann Swidler, and Steven M. Tipton. 1985. *Habits of the Heart.* Berkeley: University of California Press.

Benedict, Ruth. 1934. *Patterns of Culture.* Boston: Houghton Mifflin Co.

Benn, S.I., and G.F. Gaus, eds. 1983. *Public and Private In Social Life.* New York: St. Martin's Press.

Benn, S.I., and G.W. Mortimore, eds. 1976. *Rationality and the Social Sciences.* London: Routledge and Kegan Paul.

Bentham, Jeremy. [1823] 1948. *An Introduction to the Principles of Morals and Legislation.* New York: Hafner.

——. 1960. *An Introduction to the Principles of Morals and Legislation: a Fragment on Government.* W. Harrison, ed. Oxford: Blackwell.

Berelson, Bernard, and Gary A. Steiner. 1964. *Human Behavior: An Inventory of Scientific Findings.* New York: Harcourt, Brace and World.

Berger, Peter L. 1986. *The Capitalist Revolution: Fifty Propositions about Prosperity, Equality, and Liberty.* New York: Basic Books.

Berkowitz, L., and L.R. Daniels. 1963. "Responsibility and Dependency." *Journal of Abnormal Social Psychology.* Vol. 66, pp. 429–36.

Berlin, Brent, and Paul Kay. 1969. *Basic Color Terms: Their Universality and Evolution.* Berkeley: University of California Press.

Berliner, Joseph S. 1972. *Economy, Society and Welfare: A Study in Social Economics.* New York: Praeger.

Beyleveld, D. 1982. "Ehrlich's Analysis of Deterrence." *British Journal of Criminology.* Vol. 22, p. 101.

Black, Fischer. 1982. "The Trouble With Econometric Models." *Financial Analyst Journal.* Vol. 35 (March/April), pp. 3–11.

Black, J.S. 1978. "Attitudinal, Normative, and Economic Factors in Early Response to an Energy-Use Field Experiment." Unpublished doctoral dissertation, Dept. of Sociology, University of Wisconsin.

Blau, Peter. 1964. *Exchange and Power in Social Life.* New York: John Wiley.

Blaug, Mark. 1976. "The Empirical Status of Human Capital Theory: A Slightly Jaundiced Survey." *Journal of Economic Literature*. Vol. 14 (September), pp. 837–55.

———. 1984, 1985. *The Methodology of Economics: or How Economists Explain*. 5th and 6th eds. New York: Cambridge University Press.

Blinder, Alan S. 1985. "Let's Hear It for Economists (No Kidding)" *Business Week*. March 18, p. 18.

Bliven, Naomi. 1985. ". . . But What Can You Do for Your Country?" Review of Morris Janowitz's *The Reconstruction of Patriotism: Education for Civic Consciousness*. *New Yorker*, February 11, pp. 12–26.

Blumenstiel, Alexander D. 1973. In George Psathas, ed., *Phenomenological Sociology: Issues and Applications*. New York: John Wiley, pp. 187–213.

Boffey, Phillip M. 1983. "Rational Decisions Prove Not to Be." *New York Times*. December 6.

Bohm, Peter. 1972. "Estimating Demands for a Public Good: An Experiment." *European Economic Review*. Vol. 3, pp. 111–130.

———.1973. "Necessary Conditions for Pareto Optimality." *Social Efficiency*. Appendix 1, pp. 128–42. New York: Macmillan.

Boland, Lawrence A. 1979. "A Critique of Friedman's Critics." *Journal of Economic Literature*. Vol. 17, no. 2 (June), pp. 503–22.

Borak, Jonathan, and Suzanne Veilleux. 1982. "Errors of Intuitive Logic Among Physicians." *Social Science and Medicine*. Vol. 16, pp. 1939–47.

Bosworth, Barry P. 1984. *Tax Incentives and Economic Growth*. Washington, D.C.: Brookings Institution.

Boulding, Kenneth E. 1962. *Conflict and Defense: A General Theory*. New York: Harper & Row.

———. 1964. Review of David Braybrooke and Charles E. Lindblom's *A Strategy of Decision: Policy Evaluation as a Social Process*. *American Sociological Review*. Vol. 29. pp. 930–31.

———. 1969. "Economics as a Moral Science." *American Economic Review*. Vol. 59, no. 1 (March), pp. 1–12.

———. 1979. Review of Collard, *Altruism and Economy: A Study in Non-Selfish Economics*. In *Journal of Political Economy*. Vol. 87, no. 6, pp. 1383–84.

———. 1981. *A Preface to Grant's Economics: The Economy of Love and Fear*. New York: Praeger.

Bower, Joseph L. 1983. *The Two Faces of Management: An American Approach to Leadership in Business and Politics*. Boston: Houghton Mifflin.

Bowers, W.J., and G. Pierce, 1975. "The Illusion of Deterrence in Isaac Ehrlich's Research on Capital Punishment." *Yale Law Journal*. Vol. 85. p. 187.

Bowie, Norman E., and Robert L. Simon. 1977. *The Individual and the Political Order*. Englewood Cliffs, N.J.: Prentice-Hall.

Brandl, John E. 1985. "Distilling Frenzy from Academic Scribbling: On Being a

Legislator." *Journal of Policy Analysis and Management,* Vol. 4, no. 3, pp. 344–53.

Brandt, Richard B. 1972. "Rationality, Egoism, and Morality." *Journal of Philosophy.* Vol. 69, no. 20 (November 9), pp. 681–97.

———. 1982. "Two Concepts of Utility." In Harlan B. Miller and William H. Williams, eds. *The Limits of Utilitarianism.* Minneapolis: University of Minnesota Press.

Brennan, Geoffrey, and James Buchanan. 1982. "Is Public Choice Immoral?" Paper presented at the 1982 Public Choice Society Meetings in San Antonio, Texas. March 5–9.

Britan, Gerald M. 1979. "Evaluating a Federal Experiment in Bureaucratic Reform." *Human Organization.* Vol. 38, no. 3 (Fall), pp. 319–24.

Brock, William A. 1983. "Contestable Markets and the Theory of Industry Structure: A Review Article." *Journal of Political Economy.* Vol. 91, no. 6, pp. 1055–56.

Brodeur, Paul. 1985. *Outrageous Misconduct: The Asbestos Industry on Trial.* New York: Pantheon.

Brown, Henry Phelps. 1977. *The Inequality of Pay.* Berkeley: University of California Press.

Brown, Paul. 1983. "Slipped DISC." *Forbes.* Vol. 132, October 10, p. 158.

Browning, Edgar K., and Jacqueline M. Browning. 1983. *Microeconomic Theory and Applications.* Boston: Little, Brown

Brubaker, E.R. 1975. "Free Ride, Free Revelation, or Golden Rule?" *Journal of Law and Economics.* Vol. 18, pp. 147–61.

Brunsson, Nils. 1982. "The Irrationality of Action and Action Rationality: Decisions, Ideologies and Organizational Actions." *Journal of Management Studies.* Vol. 19, no. 1, pp. 29–44.

Buchanan, James M. 1978. "Markets, States, and The Extent of Morals." *American Economic Review.* Vol. 68. no. 2 (May), pp. 364–68.

———. 1986. *Liberty, Market and State: Political Economy in the 1980s.* Brighton, Sussex: Wheatsheaf Books; distributed by Harvester Press.

Buchanan, James M., R. Tollison, and Gordon Tullock. 1980. *Toward A Theory of the Rent-Seeking Society.* College Station: Texas A&M University Press.

Buchanan, James M. and Gordon Tullock. 1965. *The Calculus of Consent.* Ann Arbor, Mich.: Ann Arbor Paperbacks.

———. 1975. "Polluters' Profits and Political Response: Direct Controls Versus Taxes." *American Economic Review.* Vol. 65. (March), pp. 139–47.

Buckley, J.J. 1984. "Compatibility of Multiple Goal Programming and the Maximize Utility Criterion." *Theory and Decision.* Vol. 16, no. 3 (May), pp. 209–16.

Bull, Clive. 1983. "Implicit Contrasts in the Absence of Enforcement and Risk Aversion." *American Economic Review.* Vol. 83 (September), pp. 658–71.

Burns, Tom R. 1986. "Actors, Transactions and Social Structure: Introduction to

Social Rule System Theory." In Ulf Himmelstrandt, ed., *Sociology: From Crisis to Science*. London: Sage.

Burt, Ronald S. 1983. *Corporate Profits and Cooptation: Networks of Market and Directorate Ties in the American Economy*. New York: Academic Press.

Burton, Roger V. 1963. "Generality of Honesty Reconsidered." *Psychological Review*. Vol. 70. no. 6 (November), pp. 481–99.

Business Week. "Japan U.S.A." (Special Report), July 14, 1986, pp. 44–55.

Business Week. August 25, 1986, p. 114.

Carlsmith, J.M., and A.E. Gross. 1969. "Some Effects of Guilt on Compliance." *Journal of Personality and Social Psychology*. Vol. 11, pp. 240–44.

Casson, Mark 1982. *The Entrepreneur: An Economic Theory*. Totowa, N.J.: Barnes and Noble.

Chaiken, Shelly, and Charles Stangor. 1987. "Attitudes and Attitudinal Change." *Annual Review of Psychology*. Vol. 38, pp. 575–630.

Chamberlin, E.H. 1948. *The Theory of Monopolistic Competition*. 6th ed. Cambridge: Harvard University Press.

Cheal, David J. 1984. "Wedding Gifts and the Making of Money." Paper presented at the 79th Annual Meeting of the American Sociological Association. San Antonio. August 27–31, 1984.

———. 1985. "Moral Economy: Gift Giving in an Urban Society." *Winnepeg Area Study Report no. 5*. University of Winnipeg. (January).

———. 1986. "Intergenerational and Life Course Management: Towards a Socio-economic Perspective." Prepared for the British Sociological Association Conference on the Sociology of the Life Cycle, March 24–27, Loughborough University.

Chelius, James R. 1979. Review of Viscusi (1979). "Employment Hazards: An Investigation of Market Performance." Cambridge: Harvard University Press.

Cheng, Joseph L.C. 1984. "Managing Coordination to Enhance Research Performance: An Organizational Approach." In Barry Bozeman, Michael Crow, and Albert Link, eds., *Strategic Management of Industrial R & D*. Lexington, Mass.: D.C. Heath.

Cheng, Joseph L.C., and William McKinley. 1983. "Towards an Integration of Organization Research and Practice: A Contingency Study of Bureaucratic Control and Performance in Scientific Settings." *Administrative Science Quarterly*. Vol. 28. pp. 85–100.

Chestnut, R.W. 1977. "Information Acquisition in Life Insurance Policy Selection: Monitoring the Impact of Product Beliefs, Affect Toward Agent, and External Memory." Unpublished doctoral dissertation, Psychology Dept., Purdue University.

Childress, James F. 1977. "The Identification of Ethical Principles." *Journal of Religious Ethics*. Vol. 5, no. 1, pp. 39–68.

Clark, Margaret, and Susan Fiske, eds. 1984. *Affect and Cognition*. Hillsdale, N.J.: Lawrence Erlbaum.

Cloninger, Dale O. 1982. "Moral and Systematic Risk: A Rationale for Unfair Business Practice." *Journal of Behavioral Economics.* Vol. 11, pp. 33–49.

Coase, Ronald. 1937. "The Nature of the Firm." *Economica.* Vol. 10, no. 16 (November), pp. 386–405.

Cohen, L. Jonathan. 1979. "On the Psychology of Prediction: Whose is the Fallacy?" *Cognition.* Vol. 7. pp. 385–407.

Cohen, Michael D., James G. March, and Johan P. Olsen. 1972. "A Garbage Can Model of Organizational Choice." *Administrative Science Quarterly.* Vol. 17, no. 1 (March), pp. 1–25.

Cohen, P.S. 1976. "Rational Conduct and Social Life." In Stanley Benn and G. W. Mortimore, eds. *Rationality and the Social Sciences.* London: Routledge and Kegan Paul, pp. 132–54.

Cohon, Jared. 1978. *Multiobjective Programming and Planning.* New York: Academic Press.

Colander, D.C., ed. 1984. *Neoclassical Political Economy: The Analysis of Rent Seeking and DUP Activities.* Cambridge, Mass.: Ballinger.

Coleman, Andrew. 1982. *Game Theory and Experimental Games.* New York: Pergamon Press.

Coleman, James S. 1984. "Introducing Social Structure into Economic Analysis." *American Economic Review.* Vol. 74, no. 2, pp. 84–88.

Coleman, James, Thomas Hoffer, and Sally Kilgore. 1981. *Public and Private Schools.* Chicago: National Opinion Research Center.

Coleman, J.S., T. Hoffer, and S. Kilgore. 1982. *High School Achievement—Public, Catholic, and Private Schools Compared.* New York: Basic Books.

Collard, David. 1978. *Altruism & Economy: A Study in Non-Selfish Economics.* New York: Oxford University Press.

Collesano, Stephen, with Matthew Greenwald, and John P. Katosh. 1984. "Consumer Information Seeking in Purchasing Life Insurance." In Seymour Sudman and Mary A. Spaeth, eds., *The Collection and Anlysis of Economic and Consumer Behavior Data.* Champaign, Ill.: Bureau of Economic and Business Research, University of Illinois.

Cook, Phillip J. 1980. "Punishment and Crime: A Critique of Current Findings Concerning the Preventative Effects of Punishment." In Ralph Andreano and John J. Siegfried eds., *The Economics of Crime.* New York: John Wiley pp. 127–36.

Cozzens, Susan E. 1985. "The Character of Science." Review of H.M. Collins' *Changing Order: Replication and Induction in Scientific Practice. Science.* Vol. 20, December 13, p. 1267.

Croce, Benedetto. 1953. "On the Economic Principle I." *International Economic Papers,* no. 3.

Crocker, K.J., and A. Snow. 1985. "The Efficiency of Competitive Equilibria in Insurance Markets with Asymmetric Information." *Journal of Public Economics.* Vol. 26, no. 2 (March), pp. 207–19.

Cross, John G. 1983. *A Theory of Adaptive Economic Behavior.* Cambridge: Cambridge University Press.

Crouch, Robert L. 1979. *Human Behavior: An Economic Approach:* North Scituate, Mass.: Duxbury Press.

Curtin, Richard T., and Thomas S. Neubig. 1979. "Outstanding Debt Among American Households." *Survey of Consumer Attitudes.* Ann Arbor: University of Michigan, April. pp. 1–2.

Cyert, Richard M., and James G. March. 1963. *Behavioral Theory of the Firm.* Englewood Cliffs, N.J.: Prentice-Hall.

Daft, Richard L., and Norman B. Macintosh. 1981. "A Tentative Exploration Into the Amount and Equivocality of Information Processing in Organizational Work Units." *Administrative Science Quarterly.* Vol. 26, pp. 207–24.

Dahl, Robert A. 1971. *Polyarchy: Participation and Opposition.* New Haven: Yale University Press.

Dailey, R.C. 1980. "A Path of R & D Team Coordination and Performance." *Decision Sciences.* Vol. 11, pp. 357–69.

Dalton, M. 1950. "Conflicts Between Staff and Line Managerial Officers." *American Sociological Review.* Vol. 15, pp. 342–51.

Davidson, Paul. 1982. *International Money and the Real World.* New York: John Wiley.

Davis, W.L., and D.E. Davis. 1972. "Internal-External Control and Attribution of Responsibility for Success and Failure." *Journal of Personality.* Vol. 40, pp. 123–36.

Dawes, Robyn M. 1976. "Shallow Psychology." In J.S. Carroll and J.W. Payne, eds., *Cognition and Social Behavior.* Hillside, N.J. Lawrence Erlbaum.

———. 1984. "The Road to Mundane Efficacy: Affirmative Action as an Example." Paper prepared for a day's discussion at Northwestern University, November 30.

Dawes, Robyn M., and B. Corrigan. 1974. "Linear Models in Decision Making." *Psychological Bulletin.* Vol. 81, pp. 95–106.

Dawes, Robyn M., John M. Orbell, and Alphons J.C. van de Kragt. 1983. "The Minimal Contributing Set as a Solution to Public Goods Problems." *American Political Science Review.* Vol. 77, pp. 112–22.

———. "Cooperation in the Absence of Egotistical Incentives." Unpublished.

Dawes, Robyn M., John M. Orbell, and Alphons J.C. van de Kragt, with S. Braver and L.A. Wilson II. 1986. "Doing Well and Doing Good as Ways of Resolving Social Dilemmas." In Henk A.M. Wilke, Dave M. Messick and Christel G. Rutte, eds., *Experimental Social Dilemmas,* Frankfurt am Main: New York: P. Lang.

Dawes, Robyn M., John M. Orbell, R.T. Simmons, and A.J.C. van de Kragt. 1986. "Organizing Groups for Collective Action." *American Political Science Review.* Vol. 80, no. 4, pp. 1171–85.

Day, R.H. 1967. "Profits, Learning and the Convergence of Satisficing to Marginalism." *Quarterly Journal of Economics.* Vol. 81, p. 302–11.

Deal, Terrence E., and Allen A. Kennedy. 1982. *Corporate Cultures: The Rites and Rituals of Corporate Life.* Reading, Mass.: Addison-Wesley.

Debreu, Gerard. 1959. *Theory of Value: An Axiomatic Analysis of Economic Equilibrium.* New York: John Wiley.

Demsetz, Harold. 1974. "Two Systems of Belief about Monopoly." In Harvey J. Goldschmid, et al., eds., *Industrial Concentration: The New Learning.* Boston: Little, Brown.

Denison, Edward F. 1979. *Accounting for Slower Economic Growth.* Washington, D.C.: Brookings Institution.

Derlega, Valerian J., and Janusz Grzelak, eds. 1982. *Cooperation and Helping Behavior: Theories and Research.* New York: Academic Press.

Deutsch, Karl W. 1963. *The Nerves of Government.* New York: Free Press.

Diaz-Alejandro, Carlos F. 1981. "Southern Cone Stability Plans." In W. Cline and S. Weintraub, eds., *Economic Stabilization in Developing Countries.* Washington, D.C.: Brookings Institution.

Dickens, William T. 1986. "Crime and Punishment Again: The Economic Approach with a Psychological Twist." *Journal of Public Economics.* Vol. 30, no. 1 (June), pp. 97–107.

Diesing, Paul. 1962. *Reason in Society.* Urbana: University of Illinois Press.

Domhoff, G.W. 1967. *Who Rules America?* Englewood Cliffs, N.J.: Prentice-Hall.

Donaldson, Gordon, and Jay W. Lorsch. 1983. *Decision Making at the Top.* New York: Basic Books.

Donnellon, Anne, Barbara Gray, and Michel G. Bougon. 1986. "Communication, Meaning, and Organized Action." *Administrative Science Quarterly.* Vol. 31 (March), pp. 43–55.

Douglas, Mary, ed. 1984. *Food in the Social Order: Studies of Food and Festivities in Three American Communities.* New York: Russell Sage Foundation.

Douglas, Mary, and Baron Isherwood. 1979. *The World of Goods.* New York: Basic Books.

Douglas, Mary, and Aaron Wildavsky. 1982. *Risk and Culture: An Essay on the Selection of Technological and Environmental Dangers.* Berkeley: University of California Press.

Douglas, Needham. 1969. *Economic Analysis and Industrial Structure.* New York: Holt, Reinhart, and Winston.

Downs, Anthony. 1957. *An Economic Theory of Democracy.* New York: Harper & Row.

———. 1967. *Inside Bureaucracy.* Boston: Little, Brown.

Dror, Yehezkel. 1964. "Muddling Through—'Science' or Inertia?" *Public Administrative Review.* Vol. 24. pp. 153–57.

Dumont, Louis. 1977. *From Mandeville to Marx, the Genesis and Triumph of Economic Ideology.* Chicago: University of Chicago Press.

Duncan, O.D. 1975. "Does Money Buy Satisfaction?" *Social Indicators Research.* Vol. 2, pp. 267–74.

Dunlop, John T. 1977. "Policy Decision and Research in Economics and Industrial Relations." *Industrial and Labor Relations in Review.* Vol. 30, no. 3, pp. 275–82.

Durkheim, Emile. 1947. *The Division of Labor in Society.* Glencoe, Ill.: Free Press.

——. 1954. *The Elementary Forms of Religious Life.* New York: Macmillan.

Dyer, Davis, Malcolm S. Salter, and Alan M. Webber. 1987. *Changing Alliances.* Boston: Harvard Business School Press.

Dyke, C. 1981. *Philosophy of Economics.* Englewood Cliffs, N.J.: Prentice-Hall.

Easterbrook, J.A. 1959. "The Effect of Emotion on Cue Utilization and the Organization of Behavior." *Psychological Review.* Vol. 66, no. 3, pp. 183–201.

Easterlin, R.A. 1974. "Does Economic Growth Improve the Human Lot? Some Empirical Evidence." In P.A. David and W.M. Reder, eds., *Nation's Households in Economic Growth. Essays in Honor of Moses Abramowitz.* New York: Academic Press.

Eccles, Robert G. 1985. *The Transfer Pricing Problem: A Theory for Practice.* Lexington, Mass.: D.C. Heath.

Edwards, Ward. 1954. "The Theory of Decision-Making." *Psychological Bulletin.* Vol. 51, no. 4, pp. 380–417.

Ehrenberg, Ronald G., and Robert S. Smith. 1982. *Modern Labor Economics: Theory and Public Policy.* Glenview, Ill.: Scott, Foresman.

Ehrlich, Isaac. 1973. "Participation in Illegitimate Activities: A Theoretical and Empirical Investigation." *Journal of Political Economy.* Vol. 81, p. 521.

——. 1975a. "The Deterrent Effect of Capital Punishment." *American Economic Review.* Vol. 65, pp. 397–417.

——. 1975b. "Deterrence: Evidence and Inference." *Yale Law Journal.* Vol. 85, p. 209.

——. 1977a. "Capital Punishment and Deterrence: Some Further Thoughts and Additional Evidence." *Journal of Political Economy.* Vol. 85, pp. 741–88.

——. 1977b. "The Deterrent Effect of Capital Punishment: Reply." *American Economic Review.* Vol. 67, p. 452.

Eichner, Alfred S., ed. 1983. *Why Economics is not yet a Science.* Armonk, N.Y.: M.E. Sharpe.

Einhorn, H.J. 1974. "Expert Judgment: Some Necessary Conditions and Examples." *Journal of Applied Psychology.* Vol. 59, pp. 562–71.

——. 1982. "Learning From Experience and Suboptimal Rules in Decision Making." In Daniel Kahneman, Amos Tversky, and Paul Slovic, eds., *Judgement Under Uncertainty: Heuristics and Biases.* Cambridge: Cambridge University Press, pp. 268–83.

Einhorn, H.J., and R.M. Hogarth. 1978. "Confidence in Judgement: Persistence of the Illusion of Validity." *Psychological Bulletin.* Vol. 85, pp. 395–416.

Elgin, D., and A. Mitchell. 1977. "Voluntary Simplicity." *CoEvolution Quarterly.* Summer, pp. 5–8.

Elster, Jon 1979. *Ulysses and the Sirens: Studies in Rationality.* New York: Cambridge University Press.

——. 1985a. "Sadder but Wiser? Rationality and Emotions." *Social Science Information.* London and Beverly Hills: Sage. Vol 24, pp. 375–406.

——. 1985b. *The Multiple Self.* Cambridge: Cambridge University Press.

Engel, James F., and Roger D. Blackwell, 1982. *Consumer Behavior.* 4th ed. Chicago: Dryden Press.

Engel, James F., David Kollat, and Roger Blackwell. 1968. *Consumer Behavior.* New York: Holt, Rinehart, and Winston.

England, G.W. 1967. "Personal Value Systems of American Managers." *American Management Journal.* Vol. 10, no. 1 (March), pp. 53–68.

England, G.W., and R. Lee. 1974. "The Relationship Between Managerial Values and Managerial Success in the United States, Japan, India, and Australia." *Journal of Applied Psychology.* Vol. 59, no. 4 (August), pp. 411–19.

Engler, Robert. 1961. *The Politics of Oil: A Study of Private Power and Democratic Directions.* New York: Macmillan.

Epstein, Edwin M. 1969. *The Corporation in American Politics.* Englewood Cliffs, N.J.: Prentice-Hall.

Epstein, T. Scarlett. 1975. "The Ideal Marriage Between the Economist's Macroapproach and the Social Anthropologist's Microapproach to Development Studies." *Economic Development and Social Change.* Vol. 24. no. 1 (October), pp. 29–45.

Ethics. 1978. Vol. 88, no. 2 (January), p. 185. Unsigned review of Becker.

Etzioni, Amitai. 1961. *A Comparative Analysis of Complex Organizations.* New York: Free Press.

——. 1965. *Political Unification: A Comparative Study of Leaders and Forces.* New York: Holt, Rinehart, and Winston.

——. 1967. "Mixed Scanning: A 'Third' Approach to Decision-Making." *Public Administration Review.* Vol. 27, no. 5. (December), pp. 385–92.

——. 1968. *The Active Society.* New York: Free Press.

——. 1975. *A Comparative Analysis of Complex Organizations,* rev. ed. New York: Free Press.

——. 1983. *An Immodest Agenda.* New York: McGraw-Hill.

——. 1984a. *Capital Corruption.* New York: Harcourt Brace Jovanovich.

——. 1984b. "Self-Discipline, Schools, and the Business Community." Prepared for the National Chamber Foundation.

——. 1985a. "Making Policy for Complex Systems: A Medical Model for Economics." *Journal of Policy Analysis and Management.* Vol. 4, no. 3, pp. 383–95.

——. 1985b. "Guidance Rules and Rational Decision Making." *Social Science Quarterly.* Vol. 66, no. 4 (December), pp. 755–69.

——. 1985c. "On Solving Social Problems—Inducements or Coercion." *Challenge.* (July/August), 35–40.

——. 1985d. "The Political Economy of Imperfect Competition." *Journal of Public Policy.* Vol. 5, no. 2, pp. 169–86.

——. 1986a. "The Case for a Multiple Utility Conception." *Economics and Philosophy*. Vol. 2, no. 2 (October), pp. 159–83.

——. 1986b. "Mixed Scanning Revisited." *Public Administration Review*. Vol. 46. no. 1 (January/February), pp. 8–14.

——. 1986c. "Founding a New Socioeconomics." *Challenge*. Vol. 29, no. 5 (November/December), pp. 475–82.

——. 1986d. "Rationality is Anti-Entropic." *Journal of Economic Psychology*, Vol. 7, pp. 17–36.

Farris, G.F. 1978. "Informal Organizations in Research and Development." Paper presented at the Joint National Meeting of the Institute of Management Sciences and Operations Research Society of America, New York.

Feather, N.T. 1969. "Attribution of Responsibility and Valence of Success and Failure in Relation to Initial Confidence and Task Performance." *Journal of Personality and Social Psychology*, Vol. 13. pp. 129–44.

Featherstone, Joseph. 1979. "John Dewey and David Riesman: From the Lost Individual to the Lonely Crowd." In Hebert Gans et al., eds., *On the Making of Americans: Essays in Honor of David Riesman*. Philadelphia: University of Pennsylvania Press, pp. 3–39.

Fellner, Carl H., and John R. Marshall. 1968. "Twelve Kidney Donors." *Journal of the American Medical Association*. Vol. 206. pp. 2703–7.

——. 1970. "Kidney Donors—The Myth of Informed Consent." *American Journal of Psychiatry*. Vol. 126. no. 9, pp. 1245–51.

Fenno, Richard F., 1966. *The Power of the Purse*. Boston: Little, Brown.

Festinger, Leon. 1957. *A Theory of Cognitive Dissonance*. Stanford, Cal.: Stanford University Press.

——. 1964. *Conflict, Decision, and Dissonance*. Stanford, Cal.: Stanford University Press.

Field, Alexander James. 1984. "Microeconomics, Norms and Rationality." *Economic Development and Cultural Change*. Vol. 32, no. 4 (July), pp. 683–711.

Fishbein, Martin, ed. 1980. *Progress in Social Psychology*. Hillsdale, N.J.: Lawrence Erlbaum.

Fishbein, Martin, and Icek Ajzen. 1975. *Belief, Attitude, Intention and Behavior: An Introduction to Theory and Research*. Reading, Mass.: Addison-Wesley.

Fishkin, James S. 1982. *The Limits of Obligation*. New Haven: Yale University Press.

Fiske, R.W., and R.A. Shweder. 1986. *Metatheory in the Social Sciences; Pluralisms and Subjectivities*. Chicago: University of Chicago Press.

Fitch, G. 1970. "Effects of Self-Esteem, Perceived Performance, and Change on Causal Attributions." *Journal of Personality and Social Psychology*. Vol. 16, pp. 311–15.

Folbre, Nancy, and Heide Hartman. 1986. "The Rhetoric of Self Interest and the Ideology of Gender." Prepared for presentation at the Conference on the Rhetoric of Economics, Wellesley College, April 17–19.

Foster, Carroll B. 1984. "The Performance of Rational Voter Models in Recent

Presidential Elections." *American Political Science Review.* Vol. 78, no. 3 (September), pp. 678–90.

Fox, Ronald J. 1982. *Managing Business-Government Relations.* Homewood, Ill.: Richard D. Irwin, Inc.

Frank, Robert H. 1985. *Choosing the Right Pond: Human Behavior and the Quest for Status.* Oxford: Oxford University Press.

——. 1987. "Shrewdly Irrational." *Sociological Forum.* Vol. 2, no. 1 (Winter), pp. 21–41.

Frankena, William K. 1973. *Ethics.* 2nd ed. Englewood Cliffs, N.J.: Prentice-Hall.

Frankfurt, Harry G. 1971. "Freedom of the Will and the Concept of the Person." *Journal of Philosophy.* Vol. 68 (January), pp. 5–20.

Frantz, Roger S. "X-Efficiency Theory: A Review of the Literature, 1966–83." Unpublished paper.

Freedman, Jonathan L. 1970. "Transgression, Compliance and Guilt. in *Altruism and Helping Behavior,* by J. Macaulay and L. Berkowitz. New York: Academic Press.

Freedman, J.L., S.A. Wallington, and E. Bless. 1967. "Compliance Without Pressure: The Effect of Guilt." *Journal of Personality and Social Psychology.* Vol. 7, pp. 117–24.

Freize, I. and B. Weiner. 1971. "Cue Utilization and Attributional Judgments for Success and Failure." *Journal of Personality.* Vol. 39, pp. 591–606.

Fried, Charles. 1964. "Moral Causation." *Harvard Law Review.* Vol. 77, no. 77 (May), pp. 1258–70.

Friedman, Milton, 1953. "The Methodology of Positive Economics." In *Essays in Positive Economics.* Chicago: University of Chicago Press.

——. 1962, 1982. *Capitalism and Freedom.* Chicago: University of Chicago Press.

Fromm, Erich. 1941 *Escape from Freedom.* New York: Farrar and Rinehart.

Furnham, Adrian, and Alan Lewis. 1986. *The Economic Mind: The Social Psychology of Economic Behavior.* New York: St. Martin's Press.

Galbraith, Jay R. 1973. *Designing Complex Organizations.* Reading, Mass.: Addison-Wesley.

Galbraith, John Kenneth. 1958 (and 1984 ed.). *The Affluent Society.* Boston: Houghton Mifflin.

——. 1967. *The New Industrial State.* Boston: Houghton Mifflin.

Gans, Herbert. 1962. *The Urban Villagers.* New York: The Free Press.

Gans, Herbert J., Nathan Glazer, Joseph R. Gusfield, and Christopher Jencks, eds. 1979. *On the Making of Americans: Essays in Honor of David Riesman.* Philadelphia: University of Pennsylvania Press.

Georgescu-Rogen, Nicholas. 1971. *The Entropy Law and the Economic Process.* Cambridge: Harvard University Press.

Glanzer M., and R. Glaser. 1961. "Techniques for the Study of Group Structure and Behavior: II. Empirical Studies of the Effects of Structure in Small Groups." *Psychology Bulletin.* Vol. 58, pp. 1–27.

Glassman, James K. 1984. Financial adviser, writing in *Wasingtonian*, April, p. 202.

Glazer, Amihai. 1985. "The Advantages of Being First." *American Economic Review.* Vol. 75, no. 3 (June), pp. 473–80.

Glazer, Nathan. 1985. "Interests and Passions." *The Public Interest.* No. 81, pp. 17–30.

Glueck, William F. 1974. "Decision Making: Organization Choice." *Personnel Psychology.* Vol. 27, pp. 77–99.

Goddard, C.T. 1982. "Debunking the Learning Curve." *IEEE Transactions on Components, Hybrids, and Manufacturing Technology.* Vol. 5–6, pp. 328–35.

Godwin, Kenneth, and Robert Cameron Mitchell. 1982. "Rational Models, Collective Goods and Nonelectoral Political Behavior." *Western Political Quarterly.* Vol. 35, no. 2, (June), pp. 161–81.

Goldberg, Victor P. 1974. "The Economics of Product Safety and Imperfect Information." *Bell Journal of Economics and Management Science.* Vol. 5 (Autumn) pp. 683–88.

Goldberger, Arthur S. 1974. "Unobservable Variables In Econometrics." In Paul Zarembka, ed., *Frontiers in Econometrics.* New York: Academic Press.

Goldsen, Rose K., Paul R. Gerhardt, and Vincent H. Handy. 1957. "Some Factors Related to Patient Delay in Seeking Diagnosis for Cancer Symptoms." *Cancer.* Vol. 10, no. 1 (January/February).

Goleman, Daniel. 1985. "Great Altruists: Science Ponders Soul of Goodness." *New York Times.* March 5.

Goodin, Robert E. 1980. "Making Moral Incentives Pay." *Policy Sciences.* Vol. 12 (August), pp. 131–45.

———. 1982. *Political Theory and Public Policy.* Chicago: University of Chicago Press.

———. 1985. "Two Kinds of Compensation." Paper presented to Conference on Ethical Approaches to Public Choice, University of York, September.

Goulden, Joseph C. 1984. *The Death Merchant.* New York: Simon and Schuster.

Gouldner, Alvin W. 1960. "The Norm of Reciprocity: A Preliminary Statement." *American Sociological Review.* Vol. 25, no. 2, pp. 161–78.

Granovetter, Mark. 1985. "Economic Action and Social Structure: A Theory of Embeddedness." *American Journal of Sociology.* Vol. 91, no. 3, pp. 481–510.

Grasmick, Harold G., and Donald E. Green. 1981. "Deterrence and the Morally Committed." *Sociological Quarterly.* Vol. 22, no. 1, pp. 1–14.

Greenberg, Paul D., and Edward M. Glaser. 1980. *Some Issues in Joint Union Management Quality of Work Life Improvement Efforts.* Kalamazoo, Mich.: W.E. Upjohn Institute for Employment Research.

Greer, Douglas F. 1980. *Industrial Organization and Public Policy.* New York: Macmillan.

Grether, David M. 1982. "Inference in Practice." Review of *Judgement Under Uncertainty* by Amos Tversky, Daniel Kahneman, and Paul Slovic, eds., In *Science.* Vol. 218, no. 4579 (December 24), pp. 1300–1.

Grether, David M., and Charles R. Plott. 1979. "Economic Theory of Choice and the Preference Reversal Phenomenon." *American Economic Review,* Vol. 69, no. 4 (September), pp. 623–38.

Grice, G.R. 1979. Review of *The Emergence of Norms* by Edna Ullmann-Margalit. *Philosophy.* Vol. 54, (July), pp. 420–21.

Grossman, Gregory. 1974. *Economic Systems.* Englewood Cliffs, N.J.: Prentice-Hall.

Guttridgte, G.H. 1942. *English Whiggism and the American Revolution.* Berkeley: University of California.

Hackman, J. Richard, and Charles G. Morris. 1975. "Group Tasks, Group Interaction Process, and Group Performance Effectiveness: A Review and Proposed Integration." In Leonard Berkowitz, ed., *Advances in Experimental Social Psychology.* Vol. 8. New York: Academic Press, pp. 45–99.

Hall, R.L., and G.J. Hitch. 1939. "Price Theory and Business Behavior." *Oxford Economic Papers.* Vol. 2 (May) pp. 12–45.

Hall, Richard G., Phillip E. Varca, and Terri D. Fisher. 1986. "The Effect of Reference Groups, Opinion Polls, and Attitude Polarization on Attitude Formation and Change." *Political Psychology.* Vol. 7, no. 2 (June), pp. 309–21.

Hall, Roger I. 1976. "A System Pathology of an Organization: The Rise and Fall of the Old *Saturday Evening Post.*" *Administrative Science Quarterly.* Vol. 21, no. 2 (June) pp. 185–211.

Hamermesh, Daniel S., and Neal M. Soss. 1974. "An Economic Theory of Suicide." *Journal of Political Economy,* Vol. 82, no. 1 (January/February), pp. 83–98.

Hammond, R., G.H. McClelland, and J. Mumpower. 1980. *Human Judgement and Decision Making: Theories, Methods, and Procedures.* New York: Praeger.

Hansen, F. 1972. *Consumer Choice Behavior: A Cognitive Theory.* New York: Free Press.

Hargreaves Heap, Shaun P. 1986–87. "Risk and Culture: A Missing Link in the Post Keynesian Tradition." *Journal of Post-Keynesian Economics.* Vol. 9, no. 2 (Winter), pp. 267–78.

Harsanyi, John C. 1955. "Cardinal Welfare, Individualistic Ethics, and International Comparisons of Utility." *Journal of Political Economy.* Vol. 63. pp. 309–21.

Hart, Oliver D. 1983. "Optimal Labour Contracts under Asymmetric Information: An Introduction." *Review of Economic Studies.* Vol. 50. pp. 3–36.

Hartshorne, H., and M.A. May, 1928. *Studies in the Nature of Character* Vol. 1: *Studies in Deceit.* New York: Macmillan.

Hartshorne, H., M.A. May, and F.K. Shutleworth. 1930. *Studies in the Nature of Character, Vol. 3. Studies in the Organization of Character.* New York: Macmillan.

Hayakawa, Hiroaki, and Yiannis Venieris. 1977. "Consumer Interdependence via Reference Groups." *Journal of Political Economy.* Vol. 85, no. 3 (June), pp. 599–615.

Hays, William. 1973. *Statistics for the Social Sciences.* New York: Holt, Rinehart, and Winston.

Heath, Anthony. 1976. *Rational Choice and Social Exchange: A Critique of Exchange Theory.* Cambridge: Cambridge University Press.

Heberlein, Thomas A. and G. Keith Warriner. 1983. "The Influence of Price and Attitude On Shifting Residential Electricity Consumption From On- To Off-Peak Periods." *Journal of Economic Psychology.* Vol. 4, pp. 107–30.

Heider, F. 1958. *The Psychology of Interpersonal Relations.* New York: John Wiley.

Heimer, Carol. 1985. *Reactive Risk and Rational Action: Managing Moral Hazard in Insurance Contracts.* Berkeley: University of California Press.

Heimer, Carol A., and Arthur L. Stinchcombe. 1980. "Love and Irrationality: It's got to be rational to love you because it makes me so happy." *Social Science Information.* Vol. 19, no. 415, pp. 697–754: London and Beverly Hills: Sage.

Hemenway, David. 1985. *Monitoring and Compliance: The Political Economy of Inspection.* Greenwich, Conn.: JAI Press.

Heiner, Ronald A. 1983. "The Origin of Predictable Behavior." *American Economic Review.* Vol. 73, no. 4 (September), pp. 560–95.

Hendry, David. 1980. "Econometrics—Alchemy or Science?" *Economica.* Vol. 47 (November), pp. 387–406.

Herendeen, James B., and Mark C. Schechter. 1977. "Alternative Models of the Corporate Enterprise: Growth Maximization, An Empirical Test." *Southern Economic Journal.* April, pp. 1505–14.

Hershey, Robert D. 1985. "Any Way You Figure, It's Political." *New York Times.* February 2.

Hill, Richard C. 1974. Review of *Economy, Society, and Welfare: A Study in Social Economics,* By Joseph S. Berliner. *Sociology and Social Research.* Vol. 58. p. 213.

Hirsch, Fred. 1976. *Social Limits to Growth.* Cambridge: Harvard University Press.

Hirshleifer, Jack. 1976; 1980, 2d ed. *Price Theory and Application.* Englewood Cliffs, N.J.: Prentice-Hall.

———. 1985. "The Expanding Domain of Economics." *American Economic Review.* Vol. 75. no. 6. pp. 53–68.

Hirshleifer, Jack, and John G. Riley. 1979. "The Analytics of Uncertainty and Information—An Expository Survey." *Journal of Economic Literature.* Vol. 17 (December), pp. 1375–1421.

Hirschman, Albert O. 1958. *The Strategy of Economic Development.* New Haven: Yale University Press.

———. 1970. *Exit, Voice, and Loyalty.* Cambridge: Harvard University Press.

———. 1982. "Rival Interpretations of Market Society: Civilizing, Destructive, or Feeble?" *Journal Economic Literature.* Vol. 20 (December), pp. 1463–84.

———. 1984. "Against Parsimony: Three Easy Ways of Complicating Some Categories of Economic Discourse." *Bulletin: The American Academy of Arts and Sciences.* Vol. 37, no. 8 (May), pp. 11–28.

Hirschmann, W.B. 1964. "Profit From the Learning Curve." *Harvard Business Review.* Vol. 42, pp. 125–39.

Hoch, Irving. 1985. "Retooling the Mainstream." *Resources*, No. 80 (Spring), pp. 1–4.

Hoffman, Elizabeth. 1985. "Entitlements, Rights, and Fairness: An Experimental Examination of Subjects' Concepts of Distributive Justice." *Journal of Legal Studies*. Vol. 14 (June), pp. 259–97.

Hoffman, Elizabeth, and Matthew L. Spitzer. 1982. "The Coase Theorem: Some Experimental Tests." *Journal of Law and Economics*. Vol. 25 (April), pp. 73–98.

Hoffman, Martin L. 1983. "Affective and Cognitive Processes in Moral Internalization." In E. Tory Higgins, Diane N. Ruble, and Willard W. Hartups, eds., *Social Cognition and Social Development*. Cambridge: Cambridge University Press.

Hofstadter, Richard. 1966. *The Age of Reform*. New York: Knopf.

Hogarth, Robin M. 1980. *Judgement and Choice*. New York: Wiley.

Holmstrom, Bengt. 1979. "Moral Hazards and Observability." *Bell Journal of Economics*. Vol. 10, no. 1 (Spring), pp. 74–91.

Holsti, Ole R. 1971. "Crisis, Stress, and Decision-Making." *International Social Science Journal*. Vol. 23, no. 1, pp. 53–67.

Holt, John. 1970. *What Do I Do Monday?* New York: Dutton.

———. 1972. *Freedom and Beyond*. New York: Dutton.

Holtz, J. and C. Wright. 1979. "Sociology of Mass Communications." *Annual Review of Sociology*. Vol. 5.

Holyoak, Keith J., and Peter C. Gordon. 1984. "Information Processing and Social Cognition," in Robert S. Wyer, Jr. and Thomas K. Srull, eds., *Handbook of Social Cognition, Vol. 1*. Hillsdale, N.J.: Lawrence Erlbaum.

Homans, George C. 1961. *Social Behavior: Its Elementary Forms*. New York: Harcourt, Brace & World.

Hornstein, Harvey A. 1976. *Cruelty and Kindness*. Englewood Cliffs, N.J.: Prentice-Hall.

Hornstein, Harvey A. Hugo N. Masor, and Kenneth Sole. 1971. "Effects of Sentiment and Completion of a Helping Act on Observer Helping: A Case for Socially Mediated Zeigarnik Effects." *Journal of Personality and Social Psychology*. Vol. 17, pp. 107–12.

Hornstein, Harvey A., E. Fisch, and M. Holmes, 1968. "Influence of a model's feelings about his behavior and his relevance as a comparison to other observers' helping behavior." *Journal of Personal and Social Psychology*. Vol. 10, pp. 222–26.

Houthakker, H.S., and I.D. Taylor. 1970. *Consumer Demand in the United States*. 2d ed. Cambridge: Harvard University Press.

Hyman, H.H. 1942. "The Psychology of Status." *Archives of Psychology*, No. 269. R.S. Woodworth, ed. New York.

Illich, I. 1971. *De-Schooling Society*. New York: Harper and Row.

Inglefinger, R., A. Erlman, and M. Findland. 1966. *Controversy in Internal Medicine*. Philadelphia: W.B. Saunder.

Inkeles, Alex, and David H. Smith. 1974. *Becoming Modern: Individual Change in Six Developing Countries.* Cambridge: Harvard University Press.

Isaac, R. Mark, Kenneth F. McCue, and Charles R. Plott. 1985. "Public Goods Provision in an Experimental Environment." *Journal of Public Economics.* Vol. 26, pp. 51–74.

Isen, Alice M. 1984. "Toward Understanding the Role of Affect in Cognition." In R. Wyer and T. Srull, eds., *Handbook of Social Cognition.* Hillsdale, N.J.: Lawrence Erlbaum.

Isen, Alice M., Thomas E. Shalker, Margaret Clark, and Lynn Karp. 1978. "Affect, Accessibility of Material in Memory and Behavior: A Cognitive Loop?" *Journal of Personality and Social Psychology.* Vol. 36, no. 1 (January), pp. 1–12.

Izard, C.E. 1977. *Human Emotions.* New York: Plenum.

Izard, C.E., J. Kagan, and R.B. Zajonc, eds. 1984. *Emotion, Cognition, and Behavior.* Cambridge: Cambridge University Press.

Jacobs, David. 1987. "Corporate Economic Power and the State: A Longitudinal Assessment of Explanations: Aggregate Concentration and Business Tax Rates." *American Journal of Sociology.* Vol. 93, no. 4, pp. 852–851.

Jacoby, J., and R.W. Chestnut. 1978. *Brand Loyalty Measurement and Management.* New York: John Wiley.

Janis, Irving. 1972. *Victims of Groupthink.* Boston: Houghton Mifflin.

———. 1983. "The Role of Social Support in Adherence to Stressful Decisions." *American Psychologist.* Vol. 38, no. 2 (February), pp. 143–60.

Janis, Irving, and Leon Mann, 1977. *Decision Making: A Psychological Analysis of Conflict, Choice and Commitment.* New York: Free Press.

Janowitz, Morris. 1983. *The Reconstruction of Patriotism: Education for Civic Consciousness.* Chicago: University of Chicago Press.

Jaques, Elliot. 1982. *The Form of Time.* New York: Crane, Russak.

Jencks, Christopher. 1979. "The Social Basis of Unselfishness." In Herbert Gans et al., eds., *On The Making of Americans: Essays in Honor of David Riesman.* Philadelphia: University of Pennsylvania Press, pp. 63–86.

Johnsen, Erik. 1968. *Studies in Multiobjective Decision Models.* Lund, Sweden: Studentlitteratur.

Johnson, D.L., and I.R. Andrews. 1971. "Risky-Shift Phenomenon Tested With Consumer Products As Stimuli" *Journal of Personality and Social Psychology.* Vol. 20, pp. 382–85.

Johnson, Harry G. 1965. "A Theoretical Model of Economic Nationalism in New and Developing States." *Political Science Quarterly.* Vol. 80 (June), pp. 169–85.

Johnson, T.J., R. Feigenbaum, and M. Weiby. 1964. "Some Determinants and Consequences of the Teacher's Perception of Causation." *Journal of Experimental Psychology.* Vol. 55, pp. 237–46.

Johnson-Laird, P.N. 1982. "Thinking as a Skill" (Ninth Bartlett Memorial Lecture). *Quarterly Journal of Experimental Psychology.* Vol. 34A, pp. 1–29.

Jones, E.E., and K.E. Davis. 1965. "From Acts to Dispositions: The Attribution

Process in Person Perception." In L. Berkowitz, ed., *Advances in Experimental Social Psychology*, Vol. 2. New York: Academic Press.

Jones, Russell. 1977. *Self Fulfilling Prophesies.* New York: John Wiley.

Juster, F. Thomas. 1985. *Preferences for Work and Leisure.* Institute for Social Research: University of Michigan.

——. 1985. "Empirical Observations on Socioeconomics." Paper presented to the 1985 Annual Meeting of the International Meeting of the International Society for Political Psychology, Washington, D.C.

——. 1986. "Rethinking Utility Theory." Unpublished.

Kagan, Robert A. 1986. "Warnings." Review of *Read The Label,* by Susan G. Hadden. In *Science.* Vol. 233. (September 5,), p. 1101.

Kagel, John H., et al. 1975. "Experimental Studies of Consumer Demands Behavior Using Laboratory Animals." *Economic Inquiry.* Vol. 13. (March), pp. 22–38.

Kagel, J.H., and D. Levin. 1985. *Individual Bidder Behavior in First-Price Private Value Auctions. Economic Letters,* Vol. 19, no. 2, pp. 125–28.

Kahn, Alfred. 1959. "Pricing Objectives in Large Companies: Comment." *American Economic Review.* Vol. 49, pp. 670–78.

Kahneman, Daniel, and Amos Tversky. 1973. "On The Psychology of Prediction." *Psychological Review.* Vol. 80, no. 4 (July), pp. 237–51.

——. 1979. "Prospect Theory: An Analysis of Decision Under Risk." *Econometrica.* Vol. 47, no. 2 (March), pp. 263–91.

——. 1982. "The Psychology of Preferences." *Scientific American.* Vol.246. pp. 160–73.

Kahneman, Daniel, Paul Slovic, and Amos Tversky. 1982. *Judgment Under Uncertainty: Heuristics and Biases.* Cambridge: Cambridge University Press.

Kahneman, Daniel, Jack L. Knetsch, and Richard Thaler. 1986. "Fairness as a Constraint on Profit Seeking: Entitlements in the Market." *American Economic Review.* Vol. 76. no. 4 (September), pp. 728–41.

Kalt, J.P. and M.A. Zupan. 1984. "Capture and Ideology in the Economic Theory of Politics." *American Economic Review.* Vol. 74, no. 3 (June), pp. 279–300.

Kamerschen, David R., and Lloyd M. Valentine. 1981. *Intermediate Microeconomic Theory.* 2nd ed. Cincinnati: Southwestern.

Kanter, Rosabeth Moss. 1983. *The Change Masters.* New York: Simon & Schuster.

Kaplan, Abraham. 1964. *The Conduct of Inquiry.* San Francisco: Chandler.

Kaptyn, Arie, and Tom Wansbeek. 1982. "Empirical Evidence on Preference Formation." *Journal of Economic Psychology.* Vol. 2, pp. 137–54.

Kariel, Henry. 1961. *The Decline of American Pluralism.* Stanford, Cal.: Stanford University Press.

Katona, George. 1975. *Psychological Economics.* New York: Elsevier.

Katona, George and E. Meuller. 1954. "A Study of Purchase Decisions." In L. Clark, ed., *Consumer Behavior.* New York: New York University Press.

Katz, D., and R.L. Kahn. 1966. *The Social Psychology of Organizations.* New York: John Wiley.

Katz, Elihu, and Paul F. Lazarsfeld. 1955. *Personal Influence: The Part Played by People in the Flow of Mass Communications.* Glencoe, Ill.: Free Press.

Katz, R., and M. Tushman. 1979. "Communication Patterns, Project Performance, and Task Characteristics: An Empirical Evaluation and Integration in an R&D Setting,: *Organizational Behavior and Human Performance.* Vol. 23, pp. 139–62.

Kearl, J.R., Clayne L. Pope, Gordon C. Whiting, and Larry T. Wimmer. 1979. "What Economists Think: A Confusion of Economists?" *American Economic Review.* Vol. 69. no. 2 (May), pp. 28–37.

Keeney, Ralph L. 1973. "A Decision Analysis with Multiple Objectives: The Mexico City Airport." *Bell Journal of Economics and Management Science.* Vol. 4 (Spring), pp. 110–17.

Keller, Bill. 1984. "What is the Audited Value of Life?" *New York Times.* October 26, pp. A24.

Kelley, Harold H. 1959. "Attribution Theory in Social Psychology." *Nebraska Symposium on Motivation.* Vol. 15. pp. 192–238.

———. 1967. "Attribution Theory in Social Psychology." In D. Levine, ed., *Nebraska Symposium on Motivation: 1967.* Lincoln: University of Nebraska Press, pp. 192–241.

Kelley, Harold H., and John W. Thibaut. 1978. *Interpersonal Relations: A Theory of Interdependence.* New York: John Wiley.

Kelman, Steven. 1981a. *What Price Incentives?: Economists and the Environment.* Boston: Auburn House.

———. 1981b. "Cost-Benefit Analysis: An Ethical Critique." *Regulation.* January/February, pp. 33–40.

———. 1987. "'Public Choice' and Public Spirit." *The Public Interest.* No. 87 (Spring), pp. 80–94.

Kenner, Hugh. 1985. "The Politics of Plain Style." *New York Times Book Review.* September 13, pp. 1, 39.

Kennett, David A. 1980. "Altruism and Economic Behavior II, Private Charity and Public Policy." *American Journal of Economics and Sociology.* Vol. 39, pp. 337–54.

Keohane, Robert O. 1984. *After Hegemony.* Princeton, N.J.: Princeton University Press.

Kerr, Clark, and Paul D. Staudohar, eds. 1986. *Industrial Relations in a New Age.* San Francisco: Jossey-Bass.

Kessel, Reuben A. 1980. *Essays in Applied Price Theory.* R.H. Coase and Merton H. Miller eds. Chicago: University of Chicago Press.

Key, V.O., Jr. 1958. *Politics, Parties, and Pressure Groups.* 4th ed. New York: Thomas Y. Crowell.

Kilmann, Ralph, Mary J. Saxton, and Roy Sepra and Associates, eds. 1985. *Gaining Control of the Corporate Culture.* San Francisco: Jossey-Bass.

Kim, Moshe. 1984. "The Beneficiaries of Trucking Regulation, and Producer

Gains in the Education Industry." *Journal of Law and Economics.* Vol. 27 (April), pp. 227–39.

Kindleberger, Charles P. "Social Responsibility of the Multinational Corporation." Remarks for a panel at the Bentley College Conference in Business Ethics, Waltham Mass. October 11, 1985.

Kinkead, Eugene. 1959. *In Every War But One.* New York: W.W. Norton.

Kirzner, Israel M. 1976. *The Economic Point of View.* Lawrence S. Moss, ed. Kansas City: Sheed and Ward.

Klausner, Michael. 1984. "Sociological Theory and the Behavior of Financial Markets." *The Social Dynamics of Financial Markets.* Patricia A. Adler and Peter Adler, eds. Greenwich, Conn.: JAI Press.

Koch, James V. 1980. *Industrial Organization and Prices.* Englewood Cliffs, N.J.: Prentice-Hall.

Kohlberg, Lawrence. 1968. "Moral Development." *International Encyclopedia of the Social Sciences.* Vol. 10. David L. Sills, ed. New York: Macmillian & Free Press.

———. 1981. *Essay on Moral Development.* San Francisco: Harper and Row.

———. 1983. *Moral Stages: A Current Formulation and Response to Critics.* New York: Karger.

Kolko, G. 1967. "Brahmins and Business, 1870–1914: A Hypothesis on the Social Basis of Success in American History." K.H. Wolff, B. Moore Jr., eds., *The Critical Spirit.* Boston: Beacon Press, pp. 343–63.

Kolm, Serge-Christophe. 1983. "Altruism and Efficiency." *Ethics.* No. 94. October, pp. 18–65.

Korchin, Sheldon J. 1964. "Anxiety and Cognition." In Constance Sheever, ed., *Cognition: Theory, Research, Promise.* New York: Harper and Row.

Kornhauser, William. 1959. *The Politics of Mass Society.* Glencoe, Ill.: Free Press.

Kozielecki, Jozef. 1975. *Psychological Decision Theory.* Dordrecht, Holland: D. Riedel.

Krebs, Dennis L., and Dale T. Miller. 1985. "Altruism and Aggression." In Gardner Lindzey and Elliot Aronson, eds., *Handbook of Social Psychology, Vol. 2.* New York: Random House, pp. 1–71.

Kreuger, Anne O. 1974. "The Political Economy of the Rent-Seeking Society." *American Economic Review.* Vol. 64 (June), pp. 291–303.

Kuhn, Thomas S. 1962. *The Structure of Scientific Revolutions.* Chicago: Phoenix Books, University of Chicago Press.

Kuhlman, John M., and Terry M. Davis. 1971. "The Automobile Rental Industry: An Economic Analysis of the Airport Concessionaire Agreements." *Antitrust Law and Economics Review.* Vol. 5 (Fall), pp. 59–70.

Kunkel, John H. 1970. *Society and Economic Growth, A Behavioral Perspective of Social Change.* New York: Oxford University Press.

Kunreuther, Howard. 1978. *Disaster Insurance Protection.* New York: Wiley.

Kuttner, Robert. 1984. *The Economic Illusion: False Choices Between Prosperity and Social Justice.* Boston: Houghton Mifflin.

———. 1985. "The Poverty of Economics." *The Atlantic Monthly*. February, pp. 74–84.

Kwitny, Jonathan. 1984. "Risky Havens: Tax Shelters Attract Attention of Masses—and Revenuers." *Wall Street Journal*. June 29, pp. 1, 26.

Kwoka, John E., Jr. 1984. "Magical Mystery Tour." *Society*. Vol. 22, no. 1 (November/December), pp. 10–12.

Laitner, John P. 1979. "Bequests, Golden-Age Capital Accumulation and Government Debt." *Economica*. Vol. 46, pp. 403–14.

Lancaster, Kelvin. 1966. "A New Approach to Consumer Theory." *Journal of Political Economy*. Vol. 74. no. 1 (February), pp. 132–57.

———. 1971. *Consumer Demand*. New York: Columbia University Press.

Landes, William. 1978. "An Economic Study of U.S. Aircraft Hijacking, 1961–76." *The Journal of Law and Economics*. Vol. 21, pp. 1–31.

Lang, Eugene M. 1977. "It's the Little Guys Who Need Export Aid." *Journal of Small Business Management*. Vol. 15, pp. 7–9.

Langer, Ellen J. 1982. "The Illusion of Control." In Daniel Kahneman, Paul Slovic, Amos Tversky, eds. *Judgement Under Uncertainty: Heuristics and Biases*. Cambridge: Cambridge University Press, pp. 231–38.

Lanzillotti, Robert F. 1958. "Pricing Objectives in Large Companies." *American Economic Review*. Vol. 48, pp. 921–40.

———. 1959. "Pricing Objectives in Large Companies: Reply." *American Economic Review*. Vol. 49, pp. 679–86.

Latané, B., and J.M. Darley. 1968. "Group Inhibition of Bystander Intervention in Emergencies." *Journal of Personality and Social Psychology*. Vol. 10, no. 3, pp. 215–21.

———. 1970. *The Unresponsive Bystander: Why Doesn't He Help?* New York: Appleton-Century-Crofts.

Latis, Spiro J., ed. 1976. *Method and Appraisal in Economics*. New York: Cambridge University Press.

Laughlin, P.R. 1980. "Social Combination Processes of Cooperative Problem-Solving Groups on Verbal Intellective Tasks." In Martin Fishbein, ed., *Progress in Social Psychology*. Hillsdale, N.J.: Lawrence Erlbaum.

Lave, Lester, 1962. "An Empirical Approach to the Prisoners' Dilemma Game." *Quarterly Journal of Economics*. Vol. 76. pp. 424–36.

Lawrence, Paul R., Harvey F. Kolodny, and Stanley M. Davis. 1977. "Human Side of Matrix." *Organizational Dynamics*. Vol. 6, Summer no. 1 (Summer), pp. 43–61.

Layard, P.R.G., and A.A. Walters. 1978. *Microeconomic Theory*. New York: McGraw-Hill.

Lea, S.E.G. 1978. "The Psychology and Economics of Demand," *Psychology and Economics*. Vol. 85 no. 3 (May), pp. 441–66.

Leamer, Edward E. 1983. "Let's Take The 'Con' Out of Econometrics." *American Economic Review*. Vol. 73, no. 1 (March/April), pp. 3–11.

Leckachman, Robert. 1976. *Economics at Bay: Why the Experts Will Never Solve Your Problems.* New York: McGraw-Hill.

Lee, Sang M. 1972. *Goal Programming for Decision Analysis.* New York: Oxford University Press.

Leff, Nathaniel H. 1985. "Optimum Investment Choices for Developing Nations: Rational Theory and Rational Decision Making." *Journal of Development Economies.* Vol. 18, no. 2/3, pp. 335–60.

————. 1986. "Trust, Envy, and the Political Economy of Industrial Development: Economic Groups in Developing Countries." Paper prepared for a conference on "The Role of Institutions in Economic Development," Cornell University, November.

Lefford, Arthur. 1946. "The Influence of Emotional Subject Matter on Logical Reasoning." *Journal of General Psychology.* Vol. 34, pp. 127–51.

Leibenstein, Harvey. 1966. "Allocative Efficiency vs. 'X-Efficiency.'" *American Economic Review.* Vol. 56 (June), pp. 392–415.

————. 1976. *Beyond Economic Man: A New Foundation for Microeconomics.* Cambridge: Harvard University Press.

Leijonhufuud, Axel. 1984. "Uncertainty, Behavior and Economic Theory: A Comment." American Economic Association Meetings, December 30.

Leonard-Barton, D. 1981. "Voluntary Simplicity, Lifestyles and Energy Conservation." *Journal of Comsumer Research.* Vol. 8, pp. 243–52.

Leontief, Wassily. 1985. "Interview: Why Economics Needs Input-Output Analysis." *Challenge.* March/April, pp. 27–35.

Leventhal, Howard. 1982. "The Integration of Emotion and Cognition: A View From the Perceptual-Motor Theory of Emotion." In Margaret Clark and Susan Fiske, eds. *Affect and Cognition.* Hillsdale, N.J.: Lawrence Erlbaum. pp. 121–56.

Levitan, Sar A., and Clifford M. Johnson. 1982. *Second Thoughts on Work.* Kalamazoo, Mich.: W.E. Upjohn Institute.

Lewis, Alan, 1982. *The Psychology of Taxation.* New York: St. Martin's Press.

Lewis, Michael, Margaret Wolan Sullivan, and Linda Michalson. 1984. "The Cognitive-Emotional Fugue." In Carroll E. Izard, Jerome Kagan, and Robert B. Zajonc, eds., *Emotions, Cognition, and Behavior.* Cambridge: Cambridge University Press, pp. 264–88.

Lichtenstein, Sarah, Baruch Fischoff, and Lawrence D. Phillips. 1982. "Calibration of Probabilities: The State of the Art to 1980." In Daniel Kahneman, Paul Slovic, and Amos Tversky, eds. *Judgement Under Uncertainty: Heuristics and Biases.* Cambridge: Cambridge University Press, 306–34.

Lincoln, James R., and Arne L. Kalleberg. 1985. "Work Organization and Workforce Commitment: A Study of Plants and Employees in the U.S. and Japan." *American Sociological Review.* Vol. 50 (December), pp. 738–60.

Lindberg, Leon N., and Charles S. Maier., eds. 1985. *The Politics of Inflation and Economic Stagnation.* Washington, D.C.: Brookings Institution.

Lindblom, D. 1965. *The Intelligence of Democracy.* New York: Free Press.

Lindenberg, Siegwart. 1983. "Utility and Morality." *Kyklos.* Vol. 36, Fasc. 3, pp. 450–68.

Lindsay, Cotton Mather. 1984. *Applied Price Theory.* Hindsdale, Ill.: Dryden Press.

Lipset, S.M., and William Schneider. 1983. *The Confidence Gap.* New York: Free Press.

Lipsey, Richard G., and Kelvin Lancaster. 1956. "The General Theory of Second Best." *Review of Economic Studies.* Vol. 24., pp. 11–32.

Lipsey, Richard G., and Peter Steiner. 1975. *Economics.* 4th ed. New York: Harper and Row.

Little, I.M.D. 1957. *A Critique of Welfare Economics.* Oxford: Clarendon Press.

Lodge, George C. 1976. *The New American Ideology.* New York: Knopf

Lodge, George C., and Ezra F. Vogel, eds. 1987. *Ideology and National Competitiveness.* Boston: Harvard Business School.

Loether, Herman, and Donald McTavish. 1980. *Descriptive and Inferential Statistics: An Introduction.* Boston: Allyn and Bacon.

Longley, Jeanne, and Dean G. Pruitt. 1980. "Groupthink; A Critique of Janis's Theory." In Ladd Wheeler, ed., *Review of Personality and Social Psychology.* Vol. 1. Beverly Hills, Cal.: Sage.

Longman, Phillip. 1985. "The Fall of The Idea of Thrift: How the Economists Came to Label Virtue a Vice." *Washington Monthly.* January.

Losco, Joseph. 1986. "Understanding Altruism: A Critique and Proposal for Integrating Various Approaches." *Political Psychology.* Vol. 7, no. 2, pp. 323–48.

Lovejoy, Arthur O. 1961. *Reflections on Human Nature.* Baltimore: Johns Hopkins Press.

Lowi, Theodore. 1969. *The End of Liberalism.* New York: W.W. Norton.

Luhmann, Niklas. 1979. *Trust and Power.* New York: John Wiley.

Lutz, Mark, and Kenneth Lux. 1988. *Humanistic Economics: The New Challenge.* Croton-on-Hudson, New York: Bootstrap Press.

Machlup, Fritz. 1952. *The Economics of Sellers' Competition.* Baltimore: Johns Hopkins Press.

———. 1967. "Theories of the Firm: Marginalist, Behavioral, Managerial." *American Economic Review.* Vol. 57, no. 1 (March), pp. 1–33.

MacIver, R.M. 1942. *Social Causation.* Boston: Ginn.

MacRae, D., Jr. 1978. "The Sociological Economics of Gary S. Becker." *American Journal of Sociology.* Vol. 83, no. 5, pp. 1244–58.

Magat, Wesley A., John W. Payne, and Peter Brucato, Jr. 1986. "How Important is Information Format? An Experimental Study of Home Energy Audit Programs." *Journal of Policy Analysis and Management.* Vol. 6, no. 1 (Fall), pp. 20–34.

Maital, Shlomo. 1982. *Minds, Markets, and Money.* New York: Basic Books.

Maital, Shlomo, and Sharone L. Maital. 1984. *Economic Games People Play.* New York: Basic Books.

Majone, Giandomenico. 1976. "Choice Among Policy Instruments for Pollution Control." *Policy Analysis.* Vol. 2, no. 4 (Fall), pp. 589–613.

Malinowki, Bronislaw. 1922. *Argonauts of the Western Pacific.* London: G. Routledge.

Malinvaud, E. 1972. *Lectures on Microeconomic Theory.* Amsterdam: North Holland.

Mandler, George. 1975. *Mind and Emotion.* New York: John Wiley.

Mannheim, Karl. 1949. *Man and Society.* New York: Harcourt, Brace.

Mansfield, Edward. 1982. *Microeconomics: Theory and Applications.* 4th ed. New York: W.W. Norton.

March, James G. 1978. "Bounded Rationality, Ambiguity, and the Engineering of Choice." *Bell Journal of Economics.* Autumn. p. 589.

———. "Decisions in Organizations and Theories of Choice." In Andrew H. Van De Ven and William F. Joyce, eds., *Perspectives On Organization Design and Behavior.* New York: John Wiley, pp. 205–44.

March, James G., and Johan P. Olson. 1984. "What Administrative Reorganization Tells Us About Governing." *American Political Science Review.* Vol. 77, no. 2 (June), pp. 281–96.

Margolis, Howard. 1982. *Selfishness, Altruism and Rationality: A Theory of Social Choice.* Cambridge: Cambridge University Press.

Marris, Robin, and Dennis C. Mueller. 1980. "The Corporation, Competition, and the Invisible Hand." *Journal of Economic Literature.* Vol. 18, no. 1 (March), pp. 32–63.

Marshall, G.D., and P.G. Zimbardo. 1979. "Affective Consequences of Inadequately Explained Physiological Arousal." *Journal of Personality and Social Psychology.* Vol. 37, pp. 970–85.

Marvel, H. 1976. "The Economics of Information and Retail Gasoline Price Behavior: An Empirical Analysis." *Journal of Political Economy.* Vol. 84, no. 5, pp. 1033–60.

Marwell, Gerald. 1982. "Altruism and the Problem of Collective Action." In V.J. Derlega and Januscz Grzelak, eds., *Cooperation and Helping Behavior: Theories and Research.* New York: Academic Press, pp. 207–26.

Marwell, Gerald, and Ruth E. Ames. 1981. "Economists Free Ride, Does Anyone Else?" *Journal of Public Economists.* Vol. 15, pp. 295–310.

Maslach, C. 1979. "Negative Emotional Biasing of Unexplained Arousal." *Journal of Personal Social Psychology.* Vol. 37, pp. 953–69.

Mason, Todd. 1987. "America vs. Its Unions: Double Trouble." *Business Week.* February 23, p. 45.

Matthews, John D., Kenneth E. Goodpaster, and Laura L. Nash. 1985. *Policies and Persons.* New York: McGraw-Hill.

May, Ernest R., ed. 1984. *Knowing One's Enemies: Intelligence Assessment Before the Two World Wars.* Princeton, N.J.: Princeton University Press.

Maynes, E. Scott, Robin A. Douthitt, Greg J. Duncan, and Loren V. Geistfeld. 1984. "Informationally Imperfect Markets: Implications for Consumers." In

Seymour Sudman and Mary A. Spaeth, eds., *The Collection and Analysis of Economic and Consumer Behavior Data.* Bureau of Economic and Business Research, University of Illinois.

Mayo, Elton. 1933. *The Human Problems of an Industrial Civilization.* New York: Macmillan.

McClelland, David C. 1986. "Some Reflections on the Two Psychologies of Love." *Journal of Personality.* Vol. 54, no. 2 (June), pp. 334–53.

McCloskey, Donald N. 1985. *The Rhetoric of Economics.* Madison, Wis.: University of Wisconsin Press.

———. 1986. "The Economic Consequences of Economists." Review of Herbert Stein's *Washington Bedtime Stories.* In *Washington Post Book World.* November 30, p. 1.

McConnell, Campbell R. 1975. *Economics.* 6th ed. New York: McGraw-Hill.

McConnell, Grant. 1966. *Private Power and American Democracy.* New York: Knopf.

McCraw, Thomas K. "Business Government." *California Managerial Review.* Vol. 26 (Winter), 1984. pp. 33–52.

———, ed. 1986. *America versus Japan.* Boston: Harvard Business School Press.

McGahey, R.M. 1980. "Dr. Ehrlich's Magic Bullet: Economic Theory, Econometrics, and the Death Penalty." *Crime and Delinquency.* Vol. 26, pp. 485–502.

McGrath, Joseph E. 1978. "Small Group Research." *American Behavioral Scientist.* Vol. 21. no. 5 (May/June), pp. 651–74.

McGrath, Joseph E., and David A. Kravitz. 1982. "Group Research." *Annual Review of Psychology.* Vol. 33, pp. 195–230.

McGregor, Douglas. 1960. *The Human Side of Enterprise.* New York: McGraw-Hill.

McKean, Roland. 1975. "Economics of Trust, Altruism, and Corporate Responsibility." In Edmund S. Phelps, ed., *Altruism, Morality and Economic Theory.* New York: Russell Sage Foundation.

McKean, John R., and Robert R. Keller. 1983. "The Shaping of Tastes, Pareto Efficiency and Economic Policy." *Journal of Behavioral Economics,* Vol. 12, no. 1 (Summer), pp. 23–41.

McKee, Arnold F. 1982. "Social Economics and Values." *International Journal of Social Economics,* Vol. 9, nos. 6–7, pp. 5–19.

McPherson, Michael S. 1984. "Limits on Self-Seeking: The Role of Morality in Economic Life." In David C. Colander, ed., *Neoclassical Political Economy.* Cambridge: Harvard University Press.

———. 1984b. "On Schelling, Hirschman and Sen: Revising the Conception of the Self." *Partisan Review.* pp. 236–47.

———. 1985. "Reuniting Economics and Philosophy." Paper presented in the Murphy Institute Lecture Series, *The Boundaries of Economics.* New Orleans, La.: Murphy Institute of Political Economy, Tulane University.

Meissner, W.W. 1981. *Internalization in the Psychoanalysis.* New York: International Universities Press.

Meltzer, Alan H. 1980. "Monetarism and the Crisis in Economics." *Public Interest.* Special Issue, pp. 35–45.

Milgram, Stanley. 1974. *Obedience to Authority.* New York: Harper and Row.

Miller, David M., and M.K. Starr. *Structure of Human Decision.* Englewood Cliffs, N.J.: Prentice-Hall.

Mintzberg, Henry, Duru Raisinghano, and Andre Theoret. 1976. "The Structure of 'Unstructured' Decision Processes." *Administrative Science Quarterly.* Vol. 21, no. 2 (June), pp. 246–75.

Mishan, E.J. 1979. "Evaluation of Life and Limb: A Theoretical Approach." *Journal of Political Economy.* Vol. 79 (July/August), pp. 687–705.

———. 1981. "The Nature of Economic Expertise Reconsidered." In *Economic Efficiency and Social Welfare: Selected Essays on Fundamental Aspects of the Economic Theory of Social Welfare.* London: George Allen and Unwin.

Moch, Michael K., and Edward V. Morse. 1977. "Size, Centralization and Organizational Adoption of Innovations." *American Sociological Review.* Vol. 42 (October), pp. 716–25.

Moe, Terry M. 1979. "On The Scientific Status of Rational Models." *American Journal of Political Science.* Vol. 23, no. 1 (February), pp. 215–43.

Moffit, R. 1983. "An Economic Model of Welfare Stigma." *American Economic Review.* Vol. 73, no. 5, pp. 1023–35.

Moment, David. 1967. "Career Development: A Future Oriented Historical Approach for Research and Action." *Personnel Administration.* Vol. 30, no. 4 (July/Aug), pp. 6–11.

Monsen, R. Joseph, John S. Chieu, and David E. Cooley, 1968. "The Effect of Separation of Ownership and Control on the Performance of the Large Firm." *Quarterly Journal of Economics.* Vol. 82, no. 3 (August), pp. 435–51.

Morgan, James N. 1978. "Multiple Motives, Group Decisions, Uncertainty, Ignorance, and Confusion: A Realistic Economics of the Consumer Requires Some Psychology." *American Economic Review.* Vol. 68. no. 2 (May), pp. 58–63.

Moriarty, Rowland T. 1983. *Industrial Buying Behavior.* Lexington, Mass.: Lexington Books.

Mowery, David C., Mark S. Kamlet, and John P. Crecine. 1980. "Presidential Management of Budgetary and Fiscal Policymaking." *Political Science Quarterly.* Vol. 95, no. 3 (Fall), pp. 395–425.

Mueller, Dennis C. 1979. *Public Choice.* New York: Cambridge University Press.

———. 1986. "Rational Egoism versus Adaptive Egoism as Fundamental Postulate for a Descriptive Theory of Human Behavior." (Presidential address.) *Public Choice.* Vol. 51, pp. 323.

Murray, Charles A. 1984. *Losing Ground: American Social Policy 1950–1980.* New York: Basic Books.

Musgrave, A. 1981. "Unreal Assumptions in Economic Theory: The F-Twist Untwisted." *Kyklos.* Vol. 34, pp. 377–87.

Myers, David G., and Helmut Lamm. 1976. "The Group Prolongation Phenomenum." *Psychological Bulletin.* Vol. 83, pp. 602–27.

National Academy of Sciences. 1986. "Research Briefings 1986; Report of the Research Briefing Panel on Decision Making and Problem Solving." Washington, D.C.: National Academy Press.

Navarro, Peter. 1982. "Public Utility Commission Regulation: Performance, Determinants, and Energy Policy Impacts." *Energy Journal.* March/April, pp. 119–39.

———. 1984. *The Policy Game: How Special Interests and Ideologues are Stealing America.* New York: John Wiley.

Needham, Douglas. 1969. *Economic Analysis and Industrial Structure.* New York: Holt, Rinehart and Winston.

Nelson, E.A., R.E. Grinder, and M.L. Mitterer. 1969. "Sources of Variance in Behavioral Measures of Honesty in Temptation Situations: Methodological Analyses." *Developing Psychology.* Vol. 1, pp. 265–79.

Nelson, Joan N. "The Political Economy of Stabilization in Small, Low Income, Trade-Dependent Nations." Unpublished.

Nelson, Richard R., and Sidney G. Winter. 1972. *Toward An Evolutionary Theory of Economic Capabilities.* Ann Arbor. University of Michigan Institute of Public Policy Studies.

———. 1982. *An Evolutionary Theory of Economic Change.* Cambridge: Belknap Press of Harvard University Press.

Neustadt, R.E., and H.V. Fineberg. 1978. "The Swine Flu Affair: Decision Making on a Slippery Disease." Washington, D.C.: U.S. Dept. of Health, Education, and Welfare.

New York Times. November 11, 1973. "Study Finds Patrol Cars Do Little to Reduce Crime." p. 1.

New York Times. January 14, 1979.

New York Times. March 31, 1983.

New York Times. October 26, 1984.

New York Times. March 10, 1985.

New York Times. March 18, 1985. "Japanese Companies in U.S. Seen Excelling."

New York Times. March 31, 1985.

Newbery, David M.G., and Joseph E. Stiglitz. 1984. "Pareto Inferior Trade." *Review of Economic Studies.* Vol 51.pp. 1–12.

Nicholson, Walter. 1978. *Microeconomic Theory.* 2nd ed. Hinsdale, Ill.: Dryden Press.

Nisbet, J.D., and W. Grant. 1965. "Vocational Intentions and Decisions of Aberdeen Arts Graduates." *Occupational Psychology.* Vol. 39, pp. 215–19.

Nisbet, Robert A. 1981. "Replies to Steven Kelman." *Regulation.* March/April, pp. 42–43.

Nisbett, Richard, and Lee Ross. 1980. *Human Inference: Strategies and Shortcomings of Social Judgment.* Englewood Cliffs, N.J.: Prentice-Hall.

Niskanen, William A., Jr. 1971. *Bureaucracy and Representative Government.* Chicago: Aldine, Atherton.

Nitsch, Thomas O. 1982. "Economic Man, Socio-Economic Man and Homo-economicus." *International Journal of Social Economics.* Vol. 9, nos. 6 and 7, pp. 20–49.

Nooteboom, Bart. 1986. "Plausibility in Economics." *Economics and Philosophy.* Vol. 2, no. 2, pp. 197–224.

Norman, D.A. 1980. "Twelve Issues for Cognitive Science." In D.A. Norman, ed., *Perspectives on Cognitive Science: Talks from the La Jolla Conference.* Hillsdale, N.J.: Lawrence Erlbaum.

North, Douglas C. 1981. *Structure and Change in Economic History.* New York: W. W. Norton.

Novak, Michael. 1982. *The Spirit of Democratic Capitalism.* New York: American Enterprise Institute/Simon and Schuster.

Nutt, Paul C. 1984. "Types of Organizational Decision Processes." *Administrative Science Quarterly.* Vol. 29, no. 3 (September), pp. 414–50.

Oi, Walter Y. 1973. "The Economics of Product Safety." *Bell Journal of Economics and Management Science.* Vol. 4 (Spring), pp. 3–28.

———. 1974. "The Economics of Product Safety: A Rejoinder." *Bell Journal of Economics and Management Science.* Vol. 5 (Autumn), pp. 689–95.

Ofshe, L., and R. Ofshe. 1970. *Utility and Choice in Social Interaction.* Englewood Cliffs, N.J.: Prentice-Hall.

Okun, Arthur. 1975. *Equality and Efficiency: The Big Tradeoff.* Washington, D.C.: Brookings Institution.

Olson, Mancur. 1965. *The Logic of Collective Action.* Cambridge: Harvard University Press.

———. 1982. *The Rise and Decline of Nations.* New Haven: Yale University Press.

———. 1984. "How Rational Are We?" Book review of Thomas C. Schelling's *Choice and Consequence. New York Times Book Review.* July 1, 1984, p. 10.

Ornstein, Norman J., and Shirley Elder. 1978. *Interest Groups. Lobbying and Policymaking.* Washington, D.C.: Congressional Quarterly Press.

Osiel, Mark J. 1984. "The Politics of Professional Ethics." *Social Policy.* Summer 1984, pp. 43–48.

Osterman, Paul. 1986. Review of *Career Mobility in a Corporate Hierarchy,* by James E. Rosenbaum. *Contemporary Sociology.* Vol. 15, no. 4 (July), pp. 587–88.

Ozga, S.A. 1955. "An Essay in the Theory of Tariffs." *Journal of Political Economy.* Vol. 63. no. 6 (December), pp. 489–99.

Papandreou, Andreas G. 1952. "Some Basic Problems in the Theory of the Firm." In B.F. Haley, ed. *A Survey of Contemporary Economics.* Vol. 2. Homewood, Ill.: Richard D. Irwin.

Parfit, Derek. 1984. *Reason and Persons.* Oxford: Clarendon Press.

Parker, Tom. 1983. *Rules of Thumb.* Boston: Hougton Mifflin.

Parsons, Talcott. 1937. *The Structure of Social Action.* Glencoe, Ill.: Free Press.

———. 1951. *The Social System.* Glencoe, Ill.: Free Press.

Parsons, Talcott, and Neal J. Smelser. 1956. *Economy and Society: A Study in the Integration of Economic and Social Theory.* Glencoe, Ill.: Free Press.

Pashigian, Peter B. 1984. "The Effect of Environmental Regulation on Optimal Plant Size and Factor Shares." *Journal of Law and Economics.* Vol. 27, no. 1 (April), pp. 1–28.

Passell, P., and J.B. Taylor. 1977. "The Deterrent Effect of Capital Punishment: Another View." *American Economic Review.* Vol. 67, p. 445.

Peck, J.K. 1976. "The Deterrent Effect of Capital Punishment: Ehrlich and his Critics." *Yale Law Journal.* Vol. 85. p. 359.

Peltzman, Sam. 1976. "Toward A More General Theory of Regulation." *Journal of Law and Economics.* Vol. 19, no. 2 (August), pp. 211–40.

Pelz, Donald C., and Frank M. Andrews. 1966. *Scientists in Organizations.* New York: John Wiley.

Perrow, Charles. 1981. "Normal Accident at Three Mile Island." *Society.* Vol. 18 (July/August), pp. 17–26.

———. 1986. *Complex Organizations.* 3rd ed. New York: Random House.

Peters, Thomas J. and Robert H. Waterman. 1983. *In Search of Excellence.* New York: John Wiley.

Pfeffer, Jeffrey. 1981. *Power in Organizations.* Boston: Pittman.

Phaup, Marvin. 1985. "Regulation and the Use of Knowledge." *Challenge.* January/ February, pp. 56–57.

Phelps, Edmund S. 1975. "Introduction." *Altruism, Morality, and Economic Theory.* New York: Russell Sage Foundation., pp. 1–9.

Pieters, Rik G.M., and W. Fred van Raaij. 1987. "The Role of Affect in Economic Behavior." In W. Fred van Raaij, Gery M. van Veldhoven, Theo M.M. Verhallen, and Karl-Erik Warneryd, eds., *Handbook of Economic Psychology.* Amsterdam: North Holland.

Piliavin, I.M., J. Rodin, and J.A. Piliavin. 1969. "Good Samaritanism: An Underground Phenomenon?" *Journal of Personality and Social Psychology.* Vol. 13, pp. 289–99.

Pittman, Russell. 1976. "The Effects of Industry Concentration and Regulation on Contributions in Three 1972 U.S. Senate Campaigns." *Public Choice.* Vol. 27 (Fall), pp. 71–80.

Polanyi, Karl, 1957 (1944). *The Great Transformation.* Boston: Beacon Press.

Polsby, Nelson W. 1964. *Congress and the Presidency.* Englewood Cliffs, N.J.: Prentice-Hall.

Popper, Karl. 1961. *Logic of Scientific Discovery.* New York: Basic Books.

Posner, Richard A. 1975. "The Social Costs of Monopoly and Regulation." *Journal of Political Economy.* Vol. 83 (August), pp. 807–27.

———. 1977. *Economic Analysis of Law.* 2nd ed. Boston: Little, Brown.

Powell, Walter W. 1985. "The Institutionalization of Rational Organization." Review of *Organizational Environments: Ritual and Rationality* by John W. Meyer and W. Richard Scott. *Contemporary Sociology.* Vol. 14, pp. 564–66.

Power, Christopher. 1984. "Investment Clubs Are Hanging in There." *Forbes*. Vol. 133 (June 4), pp. 188–92.

Pratt, John W., and Robert Schlaifer. 1979. "On the Nature and Discovery of Structure." (mimeo)

Psathas, George. 1973. *Phenomenological Sociology: Issues and Applications*. New York: John Wiley.

Public Citizen's Congress Watch. 1982. "An Ocean of Milk, a Mountain of Cheese, and a Ton of Money: Contributions from the Dairy PACs to Members of Congress." Washington, D.C.: Public Citizen's Congress Watch.

Public Opinion. June/July 1980, p. 33.

Quade, E.S. 1982. *Analysis for Public Decisions*. 2nd ed. New York: North Holland.

Radner, Roy. 1975. "Satisficing." *Journal of Mathematical Economics*. Vol. 2, pp. 253–62.

Rados, David L. 1972. "Selection and Evaluation of Alternatives in Repetitive Decision Making." *Administrative Science Quarterly*. Vol. 17, no. 2, pp. 196–206.

Rapping, Leonard A. 1979. "The Domestic and International Aspects of Structural Inflation." In James Gapinski, and Charles E. Rockwood, eds. *Essays in Post-Keynesian Inflation*. Cambridge, Mass.: Ballinger, pp. 31–54.

Rapoport, Amnon. 1985. "Provision of Public Goods and the MCS Experimental Paradigm." *American Political Science Review*. Vol. 79, no. 1 (March, pp. 148–55.

Reisman, David. 1950. *The Lonely Crowd*. New Haven, Conn.: Yale University Press.

Rhoads, Steven E. 1985. *The Economist's View of the World: Government, Markets, and Public Policy*. Cambridge: Cambridge University Press.

Riker, W.H., and P.C. Ordeshook. 1968. "A Theory of the Calculus of Voting." *American Political Science Review*. Vol. 62, pp. 25–42.

Riley, J.G. 1979. "Noncooperative Equilibrium and Market Signalling." *American Economic Review*. Vol. 69, pp. 303–7.

Roberts, Russell D. 1986. "Why Do We Feel Guilty Tipping Less Than 15%?" *Wall Street Journal*, November 25.

Robertson, James Oliver. 1985. *American's Business*. New York: Hill and Wang.

Roe, A. 1952. *The Making of a Scientist*. New York: Columbia University Press.

Rorty, Richard. 1979. *Philosophy and the Mirror of Nature*. Princeton, N.J.: Princeton University Press.

Rosaldo, Michelle Z. 1984. "Toward an Anthropology of Self and Feeling." In Richard A. Shweder and Robert A. LeVine eds., *Culture Theory: Essays on Mind, Self, and Emotion*. New York: Cambridge University Press, pp. 137–57.

Ross, H.L. 1973. "Law, Science, and Accidents: The British Road Safety Act of 1967." *Journal of Legal Studies*. Vol. 2, p. 1.

Roth, Alvin E. 1986. "Laboratory Experimentation in Economics." *Economics and Philosophy*. Vol. 2, no. 2 (October), pp. 245–73.

Roth, Alvin E., Michael Malouf, and J. Keith Murnighan. 1981. "Sociological versus Strategic Factors in Bargaining." *Journal of Economic Behavior and Organization*. Vol. 2 (June), pp. 153–77.

Rothenberg, Jerome. 1966. *The Economic Evaluation of Urban Renewal*. Washington, D.C.: Brookings Institution.

Rottenberg, Simon, ed. 1979. *The Economics of Crime and Punishment*. Washington, D.C.: American Enterprise Institute.

Rubin, Paul H. 1980. "The Economics of Crime." In Ralph Andreano and John J. Siegfried eds., *The Economics of Crime*. New York: John Wiley, pp. 13–25.

———. 1983. Review of Nelson and Winter, "Toward An Evolutionary Theory of Economic Capabilities." In *Journal of Political Economy*. Vol. 91, no. 4 (August), pp. 718–20.

Ruggie, John Gerard. 1983. "Continuity and Transformatioin in the World Polity: Toward a Neorealist Synthesis." *World Politics*. Vol. 35, no. 2 (January), pp. 261–85.

Rushton, J. Philippe. 1980. *Altruism, Socialization, and Society*. Englewood Cliffs, N.J.: Prentice-Hall.

Sadalla E., and J. Wallace. 1966. "Behavioral Consequences of Transgression." *Journal of Experimental Research in Personality*. Vol. 1, pp. 187–94.

Salamon, Lester M., and John J. Siegfried. 1977. "Economic Power and Political Influence: The Impact of Industry Structure on Public Policy." *American Political Science Review*. Vol. 71, pp. 1026–43.

Samuelson, Paul A. 1980. *Economics*. 11th ed. New York: McGraw-Hill.

———1983. *Foundations of Economic Analysis*. (Enlarged ed.) Cambridge, Harvard University Press.

Schachter, Stanley. 1966. "The Interaction of Cognitive and Psychological Determinants of Emotional State." In Charles D. Spielberger, ed., *Anxiety and Behavior*. New York: Academic Press, pp. 193–224.

———.1971. *Emotion, Obesity, and Crime*. New York: Academic Press.

Schachter, Stanley, and J.E. Singer. 1962. "Cognitive Social and Psychological Determinants of Emotional State." *Psychological Review*. Vol. 69. pp. 379–99.

Schattsneider, Elmer Eric. 1935. *Politics, Pressures, and Tariffs*. New York: Prentice-Hall.

Schelling, Thomas C. 1978. "Egonomics or the Art of Self Management." *American Economic Association Papers and Proceedings*. Vol. 68 (May), pp. 290–94.

———.1960. *The Strategy of Conflict*. Cambridge: Harvard University Press.

———.1984a. *Choice and Consequence*. Cambridge: Harvard University Press.

———.1984b. "Self-Command in Practice, in Policy, and in a Theory of Rational Choice." *American Economic Review*. Vol. 74, no. 2 (May), pp. 1–11.

———.1985. "The Mind as a Consuming Organ." In Jon Elster, ed., *The Multiple Self*. Cambridge: Cambridge University Press.

Scherer, F.M. 1980. *Industrial Market Structure and Economic Performance*. 2nd ed. Boston: Houghton Mifflin.

Schmedel, Scott R. "IRS Guidelines Give Some Insights into How Returns Are Scrutinized." *Wall Street Journal.* March 26, 1985, Sec. 2, p. 1.

Schmookler, Jacob. 1972. *Patents, Invention, and Economic Change.* Cambridge: Harvard University Press.

Schneider, F., and W.W. Pommerehne. 1979. "On the Rationality of Free-Riding: An Experiment." Unpublished Manuscript. University of Zurich, Switzerland.

Schneider, Harold K. 1974. *Economic Man: The Anthropology of Economics.* New York: Macmillan, and Free Press.

Schon, D. 1983. *The Reflective Practitioner.* New York: Basic Books.

Schott, Kerry. 1984. *Policy, Power and Order: The Persistence of Economic Problems in Capitalist States.* New Haven: Yale University Press.

Schultz, George. 1974. "Reflections on Political Economics." *Challenge.* March/April, pp. 6–11.

Schumpeter, Joseph A. 1934. *The Theory of Economic Development.* Cambridge: Harvard University Press.

Schutz, Alfred. *Phenomenology of the Social World.* Evanston, Ill.: Northwestern University Press.

Schwartz, Shalom H. 1970a. "Elicitation of Moral Obligation And Self-Sacrificing Behavior: An Experimental Study of Volunteering to be a Bone Marrow Donor." *Journal of Personality and Social Psychology.* Vol. 15, no. 4, pp. 283–93.

———. 1970b. "Moral Decision Making and Behavior." In J. Macaulay and L. Berkowitz, eds., *Altruism and Helping Behavior.* New York: Academic Press, pp. 127–41.

———. 1977. "Normative Influences on Altruism." In Leonard Berkowitz, ed., *Advances in Experimental Social Psychology.* Vol. 10. New York: Academic Press, pp. 221–70.

Schwartz, Warren, Keith Baxter, and David Ryan. 1984. "The Duel: Can These Gentlemen Be Acting Efficiently?" *Journal of Legal Studies.* Vol. 13. pp. 321–55.

Scitovsky, Tibor. 1976. *The Joyless Economy.* New York: Oxford University Press.

———. 1978. "Asymmetrics in Economics." *Scottish Journal of Political Economy.* Vol. 25, pp. 237–77.

Sears, David O., Richard R. Lau, Tom R. Tyler, and Harris M. Allen, Jr. 1980. "Self-Interest vs. Symbolic Politics in Policy Attitudes and Presidential Voting." *The American Political Science Review.* Vol. 74, pp. 670–84.

Selten, Reinhard. 1978. "The Equity Principle in Economic Behavior." In Hans W. Gottinger and Werner Leinfellner, eds., *Decision Theory and Social Ethics: Issues in Social Choice.* Dordrecht: D. Reidel, pp. 289–301.

Sen, Amartya K. 1977. "Rational Fools" *Philosophy and Public Affairs.* Vol. 6, no. 4, pp. 317–44.

Sexauer, B. 1977. "The Role of Habits and Stocks in Consumer Expenditure" *Quarterly Journal of Economics.* Vol. 91, no. 1 (February), pp. 127–42.

Shaw, Marvin E. 1964. "Communication Networks." In L. Berkowitz, ed. *Advances in Experimental Social Psychology*. New York: Academic Press.

Sheffrin, S. 1983. *Rational Expectations*. Cambridge: Cambridge University Press.

Shepherd, William G. 1982. "Causes of Increased Competition in the U.S." *The Review of Economics and Statistics*. Vol. 64 (November), pp. 613–26.

Sherif, Muzafer. 1952. "Group Influences Upon the Formation of Norms and Attitudes." In G.E. Swanson et al., eds., *Readings in Social Psychology*. Rev. ed. New York: Holt, Rinehart, and Winston, pp. 249–62.

Shiler, Robert J. 1984. "Stock Prices and Social Dynamics." In *Brookings Papers on Economic Activity*. Washington, D.C.: Brookings Institution, pp. 457–98.

Shorrocks, Anthony F. 1979. "On the Structure of Inter-Generational Transfers Between Families." *Economica*. Vol. 46, pp. 415–25.

Shweder, Richard A. 1986a. "Divergent Rationalities." In R.W. Fiske and R.A. Shweder, eds., *Metatheory in the Social Sciences: Pluralisms and Subjectivities*. Chicago: University of Chicago Press.

———. 1986b. "Storytelling Among the Anthropologists. *New York Times Book Review*, September 21, pp. 1, 38–39

Shweder, Richard A., and Robert A. Levine, eds. 1984. *Culture Theory: Essays on Mind, Self, and Emotion*. Cambridge: Cambridge University Press.

Siegel, Sidney. 1964. In collaboration with Albert Engvall Siegal and Julia McMichael Andrews. *Choice, Strategy and Utility*. New York: McGraw-Hill.

Sills, David S. 1957. *The Volunteers: Means and Ends in a National Organization*. Glencoe, Ill.: Free Press.

Simmons, Roberta G., Susan D. Klein, and Robert L. Simmons. 1977. *Gift of Life: The Social and Psychological Impact of Organ Transplantation*. New York: John Wiley.

Simon, Herbert A. 1957. *Models of Man*. New York: John Wiley.

———. 1959. "Theories of Decision Making in Economics and Behavioral Science." *American Economic Review*. Vol. 49, no. 3 (June), pp. 253–83.

———. 1976a. "From Substantive to Procedural Rationality." In S.J. Latis, ed., *Method and Appraisal in Economics*. Cambridge: Cambridge University Press, pp. 129–48.

———. 1976b. *Administrative Behavior: A Study of Decision Making Processes in Administrative Organization*. 3rd ed. New York: Free Press.

———. 1978. "Rationality as Process and as Product of Thought." *American Economic Review*. Vol. 68, May 2, p. 3.

———. 1979. "Rational Decision Making in Business Organizations." *American Economic Review*. Vol. 69. no. 4 (September), pp. 493–513.

———. 1981. *The Sciences of the Artificial*. 2nd ed. Rev. and enl. Cambridge: M.I.T. Press.

———. 1983. *Reason in Human Affairs*. Stanford, Cal.: Stanford University Press.

———. 1986. "The Failure of Arm Chair Economics." Interview in *Challenge*. November/December, pp. 18–25.

Sims, C.A. 1980. "Macroeconomics and Reality." *Econometrica.* Vol. 48, pp. 1-48.

Sims, Henry P., Jr., and Dennis A. Gioia and Associates. 1986. *The Thinking Organization.* San Francisco: Jossey-Bass.

Sjoberg, Lennart. 1980. "Volition Problems in Carrying Through A Difficult Decision." *Acta Psychologica.* Vol. 45, pp. 123-32.

Skinner, B.F. 1948. "Superstition in the Pigeon." *Journal of Experimental Psychology.* Vol. 38, 168-72.

Slovic, Paul, and Sarah Lichtenstein. 1982. "Facts versus Fears: Understanding Perceived Risk." In Daniel Kahneman, Paul Slovic, and Amos. Tversky, eds., *Judgement Under Uncertainty.* New York: Cambridge University Press, pp. 463-89.

———. 1983. "Preference Reversals: A Broader Perspective." *American Economic Review.* Vol. 73, no. 4, pp. 596-605.

Small, Maurice. 1900. "On Some Psychical Relations of Society and Solitude." *Pedagogical Seminary.* Vol. 7, no. 1, pp. 13-69.

Smiley, Robert, and S.A. Ravid. 1981. "The Importance of Being First: Learning, Price and Strategy." Working Paper, Cornell University, August.

Smith, Adam. [1759] 1969. *The Theory of Moral Sentiments.* New Rochelle, N.Y.: Arlington House.

———. [1759] 1976. *The Theory of Moral Sentiments.* Oxford: Clarendon Press.

———. [1776] 1937. *Wealth of Nations.* Modern Library Edition. New York: Random House.

Smith, Vernon L. 1980. "Relevance of Laboratory Experiments to Testing Resource Allocation Theory." In J. Kmenta and J. Ramsey, eds., *Evaluation of Econometric Models.* New York: Academic Press, p. 345-77.

Snortland, Neil E., and John E. Stanga. 1973. "Neutral Principles and Decision-Making Theory: An Alternative to Incrementalism." *George Washington Law Review.* Vol. 41 (July), pp. 1006-32.

Soelberg, P. 1967. "Unprogrammed Decision Making: Job Choice." *Industrial Management Review.* Vol. 9, pp. 1-12.

Solow, Robert M. 1980. "On Theories of Unemployment." *American Economic Review.* Vol. 70. no. 1 (March), pp. 1-11.

———. 1981. "Replies to Steven Kelman." *Regulation.* March/April.

Song, Young-dahl, and Tinsley E. Yarbrough. 1978. "Tax Ethics and Taxpayer Attitudes: A Survey." *Public Administration Review.* September/October, pp. 442-51.

Sorenson, Aage B., and Arne L. Kalleberg. 1981. "An Outline of a Theory of the Matching of Persons to Jobs." In Ivar Berg, ed., *Sociological Perspectives on Labor Markets.* New York: Academic Press, pp. 49-74.

Spangler, Miller B. 1983. "A Critique of Methods in the Quantification of Risks, Costs and Benefits in the Societal Choice of Energy Options." *Annals of Nuclear Energy.* Vol. 10, nos. 3/4, pp. 119-51.

Sproul, Lee S. 1981. "Managing Education Programs: A Microbehavioral Analysis." *Human Organization.* Vol. 40, no. 2 (Summer) pp. 113–22.

Srole, Leo. 1975. "Measurement and Classificatioin in Socio-Psychiatric Epidemiology: Midtown Manhattan Study (1954) and Midtown Manhattan Restudy (1974)." *Journal of Health and Social Behavior.* Vol. 16, pp. 347–63.

Starr, Martin K. 1985. *The Performance of Japanese-Owned Firms in America: Survey Report.* New York: Columbia University.

Stein, Herbert. 1984. *Presidential Economics: The Making of Ecnomic Policy from Roosevelt to Reagan and Beyond.* New York: Simon and Schuster.

———. 1986. *Washington Bedtime Stories: The Politics of Money and Jobs.* New York: Free Press.

Steinbruner, John D. 1974. *The Cybernetic Theory of Decision.* Princeton, N.J.: Princeton University Press.

Steiner, Ivan D. 1980. "Attribution of Choice." Martin Fishbein, ed. *Progress in Social Psychology.* Hillsdale, N.J.: Lawrence Erlbaum.

Stern, Paul C. 1984. *Improving Energy Demand Analysis.* Washington, D.C.: National Academy Press.

———. 1986. "Blind Spots in Policy Analysis: What Economics Doesn't Say About Energy Use." *Journal of Policy Analysis and Management.* Vol. 5, no. 2, pp. 200–27.

Stern, Paul C., and Elliot Aronson, eds. 1984. *Energy Use: The Human Dimension.* New York: W.H. Freeman.

Stewart, James B. 1983. *The Partners.* New York: Simon & Schuster.

Stigler, George J. 1961. "The Economics of Information." *Journal of Political Economy* (June), pp. 213–25.

———. 1962. "Information in the Labor Market." *Journal of Political Economy.* Labor Supplement. Vol. 70, pp. 94–104.

———. 1966. *The Theory of Price.* 3rd ed. New York: Macmillan.

———. 1968. "Competition." *International Encyclopedia of Social Science.* Vol. 3. New York: Macmillan, pp. 181–82.

———. 1971. "The Theory of Economic Regulation." *Bell Journal of Economics and Management Science.* (Spring), p. 321.

———. 1972. "Economic Competition and Political Competition." *Public Choice.* Vol. 13 (Fall), pp. 91–106.

Stigler, George J., and Gary S. Becker. 1977. "De Gustibus Non Est Disputandum," *American Economic Review.* Vol. 67, no. 2 (March), pp. 76–90.

Stigler, George J., and Claire Friedland. 1962. "What Can Regulators Regulate? The Case of Electricity." *Journal of Law and Economics.* Vol. 5 (October), pp. 1–16.

Stinchcombe, Arthur L. 1986. "Reason and Rationality." *Sociological Theory.* Vol. 4, no. 2 (Fall), pp. 151–66.

Stokey, Edith, and Richard Zeckhauser. 1978. *A Primer for Policy Analysis.* New York: W.W. Norton.

Strauss, Leo. 1953. *Natural Right and History*. Chicago: University of Chicago Press.

———. 1959. *What Is Political Philosophy?* Glencoe, Ill.: Free Press.

———. 1968. *Liberalism Ancient and Modern*. New York: Basic Books.

Stuart, Reginald. 1984. "To Regulate, to Deregulate or, Now, to Reregulate," *New York Times*. Monday, October 29, 1984.

Sunquist, James L. 1985. "Has America Lost Its Social Conscience?" The Brookings Institution. Paper presented at the Florence Heller Graduate School for Advanced Studies in Social Welfare, November 11, 1985.

Swedberg, Richard. 1987. "Economic Sociology." *Current Sociology*. Vol. 35 (Spring). pp. 1–221.

Swedberg, Richard, Ulf Himmelstrand, and Goran Brulin. 1985. "The Paradigm of Economic Sociology: Premises and Promises." *Research Reports from the Department of Sociology, Uppsala University*, Vol. 1985, no. 1, pp. 1–62.

Telser, Lester. 1973. "Searching for the Lowest Price." *American Economic Review*. Vol. 63 (May), pp. 40–49.

Thalberg, Irving. 1985. Review of David Pears's *Motivated Irrationality Ethics*. (July), pp. 943–45.

Thaler, Richard. 1980. "Toward a Positive Theory of Consumer Choice." *Journal of Economic Behavior and Organization*. Vol. 1, pp. 39–60.

Thaler, Richard, and H.M. Shefrin. 1981. "An Economic Theory of Self Control." *Journal of Political Economy*. Vol. 89. pp. 392–406.

Thomas, William I., and Dorothy S. Thomas. 1982. *The Child in America: Behavioral Problems and Programs*. New York: Knopf.

Thompson, Michael. 1979. *Rubbish Theory: The Creation and Destruction of Value*. New York: Oxford University Press.

Thurow, Lester C. 1980. *The Zero-Sum Society*. New York: Basic Books.

———. 1983. *Dangerous Currents*. New York: Random House.

Tisdell, C.S. 1983. "Dissent From Value, Preference and Choice Theory in Economics." *International Journal of Social Economy*. Vol. 10, no. 2, pp. 32–43.

Titmuss, R.M. 1970. *The Gift Relationship*. New York: Pantheon.

Tittle, Charles R. 1985. "Can Social Science Answer Questions about Deterrence for Policy Use?" In R. Lance Shotland and Melvin M. Mark, eds., *Social Science and Social Policy*. Beverly Hills: Sage, pp. 265–95.

Tobin, James. 1971. "Money, Wage Rates and Employment." *Essays in Economics. Vol. 1: Macroeconomics*. Chicago: Markham Publishing.

———. 1972. "Wealth, Liquidity and the Propensity to Consume." In B. Strumpel, J.N. Morgan, and E. Zahn, eds., *Human Behavior in Economic Affairs*. San Francisco: Jossey-Bass, pp. 37–56.

Toda, Masanao. 1980. "Emotion in Decision-Making," *Acta Psychologica*. Vol. 45, pp. 133–55.

Tolchin, Susan, and Martin Tolchin. 1983. *Dismantling America: The Rush to Deregulate*. Boston: Houghton Mifflin.

Toma, Eugenia Froedge. 1983. "Institutional Structures, Regulation, and Producer Gains in the Education Industry." *Journal of Law and Economics.* Vol. 26 (April), pp. 103–16.

de Tocqueville, Alexis. [1835–1840] 1945. *Democracy in America.* 2 vols. New York: Random House (Vintage Books).

Torrance, E. Paul. 1954. "The Behavior of Small Groups Under the Stress Conditions of 'Survival'." *American Sociological Review.* Vol. 19, pp. 751–55.

Tullock, Gordon. 1967. "The Welfare Costs of Tariffs, Monopolies, and Theft." *Western Economic Journal.* Vol. 5 (June), pp. 224–32.

——. 1970. *Private Wants, Public Means; an Economic Analysis of the Desirable Scope of Government.* New York: Basic Books.

——. 1974. *The Social Dilemma: The Economics of War and Revolution.* Blacksburg, Va: University Publications.

Turner, Barry A. 1976. "The Organizational and Interorganizational Development of Disasters." *Administrative Science Quarterly.* Vol. 21 (September), pp. 378–97.

Tversky, Amos, and Daniel Kahneman. 1974. "Judgement Under Uncertainty." *Science.* Vol. 185., no. 4157 (September 27), pp. 1124–31.

Uhlaner, Carole Jean. 1986. "Political Participation, Rational Actors, and Rationality: A New Approach." *Political Psychology.* Vol. 7, no. 3, pp. 551–73.

Ulen, Thomas S. 1983. Review of Nelson and Winter. In *Business History Review.* Vol 57, no. 4 (Winter), pp. 576–78.

Ullman-Margalit, Edna. 1977. *The Emergence of Norms.* Oxford: Clarendon Press.

Useem, Michael. 1979. "The Social Organization of the American Business Elite and Participation of Corporation Directors in the Governance of American Institutions." *American Sociological Review.* Vol. 44, (August), pp. 553–72.

——. 1984. *The Inner Circle: Large Corporations and the Rise of Business Political Activity in the U.S. and U.K..* New York: Oxford University Press.

Van de Kragt, Alphons J.C., John M. Orbell, and Robyn M. Dawes. 1983. "The Minimal Contributing Set As a Solution to Public Goods Problems." *American Political Science Review.* Vol. 77, pp. 112–22.

Varian, Hal R. 1984. *Microeconomic Analysis.* 2nd ed. New York: W.W. Norton.

Verhallen, Theo M.M., and W. Fred van Raaij. 1985. "A Behavioral Cost-Benefit Approach to the Explanation and Prediction of Behavior." Paper presented at 10th Annual Colloquium of the *International Association for Research in Economic Psychology.* Linz, Austria. July 1–5.

Veroff, Joseph, Elizabeth Douvan, and Richard A. Kulka. 1981. *The Inner American: A Self-Portrait from 1957 to 1976.* New York: Basic Books.

Viner, Jacob. 1950. *The Custom Union Issue.* New York: Carnegie Endowment for International Peace.

Viscusi, W. Kip. 1979. *Employment Hazards: An Investigation of Market Performance.* Cambridge: Harvard University Press.

Vogel, Ezra F. 1979. *Japan as Number One: Lessons for America.* Cambridge: Harvard University Press.

Volkart, Edmund H. 1951. *Social Behavior and Personality: Contributions of W.I. Thomas to Theory and Social Research.* New York: Social Science Research Council.

von Magnus, Eric. 1984. "Preference, Rationality, and Risk Taking." *Ethics.* Vol. 94 (July), pp. 637–48.

Wagner, Wolfgang, Erich Kirchler, and Herman Brandstatter. 1984. "Marital Relationships and Purchasing Decisions—To Buy Or Not To Buy, That Is The Question." *Journal of Economic Psychology.* Vol. 5, pp. 139–57.

Waldrop, M. Mitchell. 1984. "The Necessity of Knowledge." *Science.* Vol. 223 (March 23), pp. 1279–82.

The Wall Street Journal. June 25, 1985.

Wallach, Michael A., and Lise Wallach. 1983. *Psychology's Sanction for Selfishness.* San Francisco: W.H. Freeman.

Walras, Leon. [1874–77] 1954. *Elements of Pure Economics: Or the Theory of Social Wealth.* Translated by William Jaffe. Homewood, Ill.: Irwin.

Walsh, Vivian Charles. 1970. *Introduction To Contemporary Microeconomics.* New York: McGraw-Hill.

Walster, E., G.W. Walster, and E. Berscheid. 1978. *Equity: Theory and Research.* Rockleigh, N.J.: Allyn and Bacon.

Walton, Richard E., and Paul R. Lawrence, eds. 1985. *Human Resource Management HRM Trends & Challenges.* Boston: Harvard University Press.

Walzer, Michael. 1980. *Radical Principles.* New York: Basic Books.

———. 1982. "The Community." *New Republic.* March 31, pp. 11–17.

———. 1983. *Spheres of Justice.* New York: Basic Books.

Watson, J.G., and Sam Barone. 1976. "The Self Concept, Personal Values, and Motivational Orientations of Black and White Managers." *Academy of Management Journal.* Vol. 19, no. 1 (March), pp. 442–51.

Weber, Max. [1904–5] 1930. *The Protestant Ethic and the Spirit of Capitalism.* Trans. by Talcott Parsons; foreword by R.H. Tawney. New York: Scribner.

———. [1915] 1951. *The Religion of China: Confucianism and Taoism.* Trans. and ed. by Hans H. Gerth and Don Martindale. Glencoe, Ill.: Free Press.

———. [1916–17] 1958. *The Religion of India: The Sociology of Hinduism and Buddhism.* Trans. and ed. by Hans H. Gerth and Don Martindale. Glencoe, Ill.: Free Press.

———. [1921–22] 1968. *Economy and Society.* Gunther Roth and Claus Wittich, eds. New York: Bedminster Press.

———. 1947. *The Theory of Social and Economic Organization.* Trans. by A.R. Henderson and Talcott Parsons. London: William Hodge.

Weinberg, Meyer, and Oscar E. Shabat. 1956. *Society and Man.* Englewood Cliffs, N.J.: Prentice-Hall.

Weintraub, Sidney. 1978. *Capitalism's Inflation and Unemployment Crisis.* Reading, Mass.: Addison-Wesley.

Weitzman, Lenore J. 1985. *The Divorce Revolution.* New York: Free Press.

Weitzman, Martin. 1984. *The Share Economy: Conquering Stagflation.* Cambridge: Harvard University Press.

Wells, A. 1970. *Social Institutions.* London: Heinemann.

Wermeil, Stephen. 1984. "Is Analysis Out of Touch?: Scholars Blend Law, Economics." *Wall Street Journal,* December 18, p. 64.

West, Edwin G., and Michael McKee. 1983. "De Gustibus Est Disputandum: The Phenomenon of 'Merit Wants' Revisited." *American Economic Review.* Vol. 73, no. 5 (December), pp. 1110–21.

White, Alice Patricia. 1983. *The Dominant Firm: A Study of Market Power.* Ann Arbor, Mich.: UMI Research Press.

Whittington, D., and D. Macrae. 1986. "The Issue of Standing in Cost-Benefit Analysis." *Journal of Policy Analysis and Management.* Vol. 5, no. 4, pp. 665–82.

Wilber, Charles K., and Kenneth P. Jameson. 1983. *An Inquiry into the Poverty of Economics.* Notre Dame: University of Notre Dame Press.

Wildavsky, Aaron B. 1979. *The Politics of the Budgetary Process.* 3rd ed. Boston: Little, Brown.

Wildavsky, Aaron B., and Jeffrey L. Pressman. 1984. *Implementation: How Great Expectations in Washington are Dashed in Oakland: Or Why It's Amazing that Federal Programs Work at All.* Berkeley: University of California Press.

Wilde, Keith D., Allen D. Lebaron, and L. Dwight Israelsen. 1985. "Knowledge, Uncertainty, and Behavior." *AEA Papers and Proceedings.* Vol. 75 (May), pp. 403–8.

Williams, Edward E., and M. Chapman Findlay III. 1981. "A Reconsideraton of the Rationality Postulate." *American Journal of Economics and Sociology.* Vol. 40, no. 1 (January), pp. 18–19.

Williams, Robin M., Jr. 1968. "The Concept of Values." In David Sills, ed., *International Encyclopedia of Social Sciences.* Vol. 16, pp. 283–87.

Williamson, Oliver E. 1975. *Markets and Hierarchies: Analysis and Antitrust Implications.* New York: Free Press.

———. 1985. *Economic Institutions of Capitalism.* New York: Free Press.

Wilson, Bryan R. 1970. *Rationality.* Evanston and New York: Harper and Row.

Wilson, Graham K. 1981. *Interest Groups in the United States.* Oxford: Clarendon Press.

Wilson, James Q. 1973. *Political Organizations.* New York: John Wiley.

———. 1980. *The Politics of Regulation.* New York: Basic Books.

———. 1985. (Rev. ed.) *Thinking About Crime.* New York: Vintage Books.

———. 1985. "The Rediscovery of Character: Private Virtue and Public Policy." *The Public Interest.* No. 81, p. 316.

Wilson, James Q., Richard J. Herrnstein. 1985. *Crime and Human Nature.* New York: Simon and Schuster.

Winrich, J. Steven. 1984. "Self Reference and the Incomplete Structure of Neo-classical Economics." *Journal of Economic Issues.* Vol. 18, no. 4 (December), pp. 987–1005.

Winston, Gordon C. 1982. *The Timing of Economic Activity.* Cambridge: Cambridge University Press.

Winter, Sidney G. 1975. "Optimization and Evolution in the Theory of the Firm." In Richard H. Day and Theodore Groves eds., *Adaptive Economic Models.* New York: Academic Press, pp. 73–118.

von Winterfeldt, Detlof, and Ward Edwards. 1986. *Decision Analysis and Behavioral Research.* Cambridge University Press.

Wohlstetter, Roberta. 1962. *Pearl Harbor: Warning and Decision.* Stanford, Cal.: Stanford University Press.

Wolosin, R.J., S.J. Sherman, and A. Till. 1973. "Effects of Cooperation and Competition on Responsibility Attribution after Success and Failure." *Journal of Experimental Social Psychology.* Vol. 9, pp. 220–35.

Woodworth, R.S., and R.S. Schlosberg. 1954. *Experimental Psychology.* New York: Holt, Rinehart Winston.

Wright, W.F., and G.H. Bower. 1981. *Mood Effects on Subjective Probability Assessment.* Unpublished manuscript, Stanford University.

Wright, T.P. 1936. "Factors Affecting the Cost of Airplanes." *Journal of Aeronautical Science.* Vol. 3, no. 4.

Wrong, Dennis. 1961. "Oversocialized Concept of Man in Sociology." *American Sociological Review.* Vol. 26, no. 2, pp. 183–93.

Yankelovich, Daniel. 1981. *New Rules: Searching for Self-Fulfillment in a World Turned Upside Down.* New York: Random House.

Yatchew, Adonis J. 1985. "Labor Supply In The Presence of Taxes: An Alternative Specifications." *Review of Economics and Statistics.* Vol. 67, no. 1 (February), pp. 27–33.

Yerkes, R.M. and J.D. Dodson. 1908. "The Relation of Strength of Stimulus to Rapidity of Habit Formation." *Journal of Comparative Neurological Psychology.* Vol. 18, pp. 459–482.

Young, T. 1983. "The Demand for Cigarettes: Alternative Specifications of Fujii Model." *Applied Economics.* Vol. 15, pp. 203–11.

Zaid, Gabriel. 1979. *El progreso improductivo.* Mexico, D.F.: Siglio Veintiuno Editores.

Zajonc, R.B. 1980. "Feeling and Thinking: Preferences Need No Inferences." *American Psychologist.* Vol. 35, no. 2 (February), pp. 151–75.

Zeckhauser, Richard. 1982. Review of "Toward a Theory of the Rent-Seeking Society," ed. by James M. Buchanan, Robert D. Tollison, and Gordon Tullock. *Journal of Political Economy.* Vol. 90 (December), pp. 1303–6.

Zeleny, Milan. 1982. *Multiple Criteria Decision Making.* New York: McGraw-Hill.

Zelizer, Viviana. 1985. *Pricing the Priceless Child: The Changing Social Value of Children.* New York: Basic books.

Znaniecki, Florien. 1936. *Social Actions.* New York: Rinehart.

Name Index

Sims, C.A., 19, 294
Sims, Henry P., Jr., 294
Singer, J.E., 111, 291
Sjöberg, Lennart, 100, 103, 294
Skinner, B.F., 177, 294
Slovic, Paul, 109, 269, 273, 278, 281, 282, 294
Small, Maurice, 294
Smelser, Neal J., 142, 204, 289
Smiley, Robert, 225, 294
Smith, Adam, 22, 24, 28n, 29, 37, 199, 202, 210, 212, 294
Smith, David H., 247, 277
Smith, Mark Brian, *xvi*
Smith, Robert S., 239, 249, 260, 269
Smith, Vernon L., 294
Snortland, Neil E., 132, 294
Snow, A., 159, 266
Soelberg, P., 100, 147, 294
Sole, Kenneth, 52, 276
Solow, Robert M., 249, 294
Song, Young-dahl, 66, 294
Sorenson, Aage B., 294
Soss, Neal M., 28, 272
Spaeth, Mary, 266, 285
Spangler, Miller B., 294
Spector, Bert, 107, 262
Speilberger, Charles D., 291
Spitzer, Matthew L., 276
Sproul, Lee S., 173, 295
Srole, Leo, 9, 190, 295
Srull, Thomas K., 103, 276, 277
Stanga, John E., 132, 294
Stangor, Charles, 106, 176, 265
Starr, Martin K., 147n, 286, 295
Staudohar, Paul D., 78, 279
Streeten, Paul, *xv*
Stein, Herbert, 121, 194, 295
Steinbruner, John D., 117, 295
Steiner, Gary A., 100, 187, 190, 262
Steiner, Ivan D., 100, 103, 189, 295
Steiner, Peter, 24, 25, 283
Stern, Paul C., *xv*, 64, 163, 164, 188, 242, 243, 295
Stewart, James B., 295
Stigler, George J., 27, 40, 94, 158, 159, 200, 208, 217, 218, 221, 227, 228, 230, 295
Stiglitz, Joseph E., 202, 287
Stinchcombe, Arthur L., 82, 275, 295
Stokey, Edith, 85, 295
Strauss, Leo, 7, 296
Strumpel, B., 296
Stuart, Reginald, 296

Sudman, Seymour, 266, 285
Sullivan, Margaret Wolan, 282
Sullivan, William M., 9, 262
Sunquist, James L., 62, 296
Swanson, G.E., 293
Swedberg, Richard, 204, 218, 296
Swidler, Ann, 9, 262

Tarpley, Fred A., Jr., 2, 260
Tawney, R.H., 298
Taylor, I.D., 161, 276
Taylor, J.B., 289
Telser, Lester, 141, 296
Thalberg, Irving, 296
Thaler, Richard, 37, 38, 60, 83, 120, 278, 296
Theoret, Andre, 286
Thibault, John W., 100, 279
Thomas, Dorothy S., 296
Thomas, William I., 296
Thompson, Michael, 70, 247, 296
Thurow, Lester C., 2, 32, 54, 78, 141, 160, 163, 199, 222, 239, 296
Till, A., 110, 300
Tipton, Steven, 9, 262
Tisdell, C.S., 247, 296
Titmuss, R.M., 75, 80, 243, 296
Tittle, Charles R., 296
Tobin, James, 63, 140, 296
Tocqueville, Alexis de, 138, 297
Toda, Masanao, 103, 177, 296
Tolchin, Martin, 235, 296
Tolchin, Susan, 235, 296
Tollison, Robert D., 217, 264, 300
Toma, Eugenia Froedge, 207, 297
Torrance, E. Paul, 99, 297
Tuck, Steve, *xv*
Tullock, Gordon, 57, 217, 247, 248, 264, 297, 300
Turner, Barry A., 172, 297
Tushman, M., 197, 279
Tversky, Amos, 109, 119, 120, 142, 177, 269, 273, 278, 281, 282, 294, 297
Tyler, Tom R., 61, 292

Uhlaner, Carole Jean, 59, 297
Ulen, Thomas S., 3, 297
Ullman-Margalit, Edna, 179, 274, 297
Useem, Michael, 228, 297

Valentine, Lloyd M., 30, 158, 225, 249, 278
Van de Kragt, Alphons J.C., 60, 267, 297
Vanderbilt, Cornelius, 192
Van De Ven, Andrew H., 284

Subject Index